Atal Bihari Vajpayee

Atal Bihari Vajpayee's life in politics spanned the evolution of Hindutva politics from the days when the Jana Sangh was just a marginal player in Nehru's India to its rise to power as the Bharatiya Janata Party (BJP). His driving ambition from the day he entered Parliament was to make his party the national alternative to the Congress, and this book tells the gripping story of how he achieved this ambition, becoming the first non-Congress prime minister to serve a full five-year term, paving the way for the BJP's political dominance. In many ways Vajpayee represents a bridge between the Nehruvian age and the Narendra Modi years.

Spellbinding orator, coalition builder, wise statesman, benevolent father figure, Vajpayee was also a bundle of contradictions. He was both Hindutva loyalist and liberal centrist; eloquent poet and ruthless political tactician; faithful member of the puritanical Sangh Parivar who never hid his unconventional personal life. The political leader whom even his opponents dubbed 'the good man in the bad party', he became – with all his flaws and weaknesses – arguably India's most loved prime minister. Deeply researched, and with new insights and anecdotes from his closest confidants, this is the most revealing personal portrait there is of Atal Bihari Vajpayee.

Atal Bihari Vajpayee

Sagarika Ghose

juggernaut

JUGGERNAUT BOOKS
C-I-128, First Floor, Sangam Vihar, Near Holi Chowk,
New Delhi 110080, India

First published in hardback by Juggernaut Books 2021
Published in paperback by Juggernaut Books 2023

10 9 8 7 6 5 4 3 2 1

P-ISBN: 9788195996988
E-ISBN: 9789391165949

Typeset in Adobe Caslon Pro by R. Ajith Kumar, Noida

Printed at Thomson Press India Ltd

In the 75th year of Indian Independence, this book is dedicated to the spirit of India's Parliament

Contents

Contents

Introduction

Every year for the last twenty-five years, as the world celebrates Christmas Day, the Bharatiya Janata Party (BJP) leader Vijay Goel holds a birthday party for the 'maha-purush' he considers his ideal politician. The celebration is a 'bhajan sandhya', an evening of song and poetry, Goel's way of remembering former prime minister Atal Bihari Vajpayee on his birthday, 25 December. Goel once even arranged for the streets and homes of Old Delhi to be bedecked with flowers in Vajpayee's memory.

Goel, who cut his teeth in Delhi's combative student union politics and was a minister of state in the Vajpayee PMO (Prime Minister's Office), admits to being an unapologetic Vajpayee 'bhakt'. 'Yes, he is India's most loved prime minister,' he says, insisting that Vajpayee is even more loved than Jawaharlal Nehru, adding, 'Even when he was ill and couldn't leave his house, hundreds of people would ring me up asking to at least see him once.'

This is my second biography of an Indian prime minister, the first being of Indira Gandhi, *Indira: India's Most Powerful Prime Minister*, published four years ago. Why have I described Vajpayee as 'India's Most Loved Prime Minister'? The reason is that among India's prime ministers, while Indira Gandhi was the toughest wielder of power politics, Vajpayee was, by the end of his life, the recipient of a sympathetic love from wide cross-sections of the population who regarded him with near-universal goodwill. He was a politician of the Nehruvian 1950s, the democratic time when opponents were comrades and adversaries could become friends. The Congress leader Karan Singh, who ran against Vajpayee in Lucknow in the 1999 general elections, recalls the fight as the most cordial contest of his life. However bitter the battle, Vajpayee invariably brought a smile to the faces of his rivals. He radiated a sense of easy comfort, like a genial patriarch able to unite a disparate family. His foibles, failings, inconsistencies and inadequacies were unhidden, his (often weak and futile) struggles for the ideological centre an open dilemma for all to see. In his personal loves and likes there was no humbug or hypocrisy. He not only enjoyed his whisky and non-vegetarian food, he lived for most of his life with the woman he always called 'Mrs Kaul' and her husband, his friend 'Kaul Sahab', and once candidly admitted, '*Main kunwara hoon, brahmachari nahin* [I'm a bachelor, not a celibate].'

His sincere push for economic prosperity brought him gratitude, his self-deprecating humour revealed an all too frail human being. He was an ambitious and calculating politician, a jedi in the dark arts of political intrigue, but he still shied away from personal vindictiveness against opponents. Where Indira struck awe and fear and Nehru was the adored god-king placed on a pedestal, Vajpayee was loved as a family elder might be, sitting comfortably among all kinds of people, munching on his samosas and rasgullas, a familiar and reassuring paterfamilias. In 2007, in an opinion poll by *India Today* magazine, ORG Marg and AC Nielsen, Vajpayee was voted the people's favourite to be prime minister, ahead of Manmohan Singh and Sonia Gandhi.[1]

His was an epic journey of toil and painful progress, much longer and more harrowing than Indira Gandhi's shorter and more privileged life. Travelling across India year after year, by second-class train and tonga, bathing at railway stations, sleeping in public parks, fighting long and hard to establish his party as the Congress's 'national alternative' and ascending to the prime ministership only in his twilight years, by the end the old, weather-beaten man was so familiar and so fallible, so leavened by repeated failures and victories, so invincible at the polls – he won ten Lok Sabha terms and was a member of Parliament (MP) twelve times, with two terms in the Rajya Sabha – and seen as so valiantly trying to mainstream his party in India's political centre that he was regarded, even by his detractors, with indulgent approval.

No doubt, Vajpayee's image as the embattled liberal softie in a hard-line Hindu party was part cleverly crafted and only part genuine. He never broke with the religious majoritarianism that propelled him to power. He did not find the strength to quell forever the fires of extremism in his own party. Yet at key moments, by erring on the side of parliamentary constitutionalism, staunchly holding to the Nehruvian line in foreign policy and to the free-market line on the economy when in office, and by embodying, in his own ambiguous, poetry-reciting way, a resistance to bigotry and closed-mindedness, and by strategically publicizing his own disapproval of firebrand street-fighting Hindutva, Vajpayee not only wrestled with his own existential dilemma of trying to be the 'Hindustani Nehru' or the Bharatiya 'sanskritic' liberal, he also in the process created a template for Indian conservatism expressed in a democratic way.

This doctrine of 'Vajpayeeism' was by no means clearly articulated. Vajpayee didn't hesitate to show he was often plagued by self-doubt. He appeared as a bundle of contradictions, now challenging his ideological parent the Rashtriya Swayamsevak Sangh (RSS), now falling in line with it, one day an unapologetic champion of political Hindutva, the next day speaking the language of an inclusive society. The party he created in 1980 with L.K. Advani was, in its foundation and early years, positioned as 'Gandhian socialist' – a centrist, inclusive force that aimed, above all, to challenge the dominance of the Congress and become the 'national alternative'. Yet, just over a decade after the formation of the Bharatiya Janata Party, its cadres had willingly participated in the demolition of the Babri Masjid, an act that let loose a spiral of communal violence and religious polarization that still stalks

India. Through this critical period, Vajpayee chose to avoid confronting the Hindutva rabble-rousers. His decision to stay away from Ayodhya on the day the Babri Masjid was demolished reflected both his political limitations and his complicity with saffron nationalism.

For an earlier generation of the BJP (and for the Jana Sangh before it), he was the ultimate mascot, figurehead and trophy, infusing the party with his own harmonizing, all-embracing presence, in the process attracting the wrath of uber-Hindutva outfits like the Vishwa Hindu Parishad (VHP) and Swadeshi Jagran Manch (SJM). Advani provided the BJP its ideological direction and organizational vigour, raising the BJP from two seats in 1984 to a stunning 182 in 1998, an achievement Advani described as 'unparalleled in the history of parliamentary democracy'. Yet it was Vajpayee who provided the Ram movement's party its constitutional respectability. Advani wasn't the BJP's statesman, Vajpayee was. A perennial Pied Piper–like figure in Parliament and election rallies, Vajpayee rejoiced in his cult status and guarded it tenaciously. But he resisted the temptation to become a one-man show, adhering always to a collegiate style of decision-making and never, for better or for worse, imposing his will. Many saw this as weakness. But to him it was a matter of party discipline and a bid to stay relevant.

That collegiate BJP has completely changed today. In fact, the BJP's universe has transformed dizzyingly in the decade and a half since Vajpayee virtually bid farewell to public life in 2004. The shift from the Age of Atal to the Era of Narendra Modi has been swift and dramatic, to the point where the Vajpayee years have almost faded away into sepia-tinted photos from forgotten days. Goel and several others have, in a sense, become 'victims' of this transformation; those who were once in the former prime minister's charmed inner circle are now increasingly peripheral figures in the 'new' BJP. A dwindling number attends Goel's Vajpayee parties. Instead, the Modi-led BJP government organizes its own events marking 25 December as 'Good Governance Day'.

But the legacy of Atal Bihari Vajpayee – party builder, crafty politician, Hindu nationalist, poet and parliamentarian – can't be reduced to a single day merely commemorating governance. There are other, far more important reasons why Vajpayee the personality should be remembered, primarily because he strove, however imperfectly, to establish Hindu nationalism as a viewpoint located in India's parliamentary and democratic spectrum, as a set of ideas straining at the confining leash of the RSS. His was a belief system that did not baulk at an open reach-out to Pakistan, Kashmir, to Muslims and other religious minorities. Today the saffron top brass shuns iftar parties, but Vajpayee every year attended the Eid and Diwali parties hosted by the Congress's Ghulam Nabi Azad.

'Vajpayeeism' is the opposite of modern-day Moditva, the strident dogmatism hammering away at the Constitution itself, its high-pitched battle cry casting all opposition to itself as anti-national and seditious, while openly seeking a 'Congress-mukt Bharat'. For Vajpayee, an Opposition politician most of his life, such name-calling would have been unthinkable. He didn't constantly look for enemies; he was eager for new friends. In Vajpayee's time, a BJP government lost its majority by a single vote and resigned, revealing a commitment to the supremacy and integrity of Parliament. Today, such practices have become almost quaint. Using a political majority to bulldoze contentious legislation is the norm in the Modi era, as seen in the manner in which Jammu and Kashmir was suddenly downsized to a union territory by executive firman.

Two of Vajpayee's closest allies in his prime-ministerial years were Jaswant Singh, the ex-military man who did not come into politics through the RSS and maintained his distance from it, spoke pucca English, loved his Mozart and Tchaikovsky, and George Fernandes, the dishevelled socialist openly critical of the Sangh Parivar. Today such figures would be regarded as beyond the saffron pale and would be derided as the 'Khan Market Gang'. Today the rise of the populist nationalist Supreme Leader Modi has seen the BJP embark on a cultural 'war' against its ideological 'enemies', but the Vajpayee era was marked by bridge-building with diverse groups.

In that sense, Vajpayee was very much part of the post-Independence governing class and far more comfortable with a whisky-drinking son of a former Congress chief minister, Brajesh Mishra, than with RSS ideologues. Vajpayee had no truck with any cultural war against the Nehruvian social and political elite, as the Modi years have seen. This is another sharp contrast between Vajpayeeism and Moditva.

So, why does Vajpayee still matter in the age of Modi? In these times of relentless breaking news, public memories are shrinking into 24x7 news cycles. Gargantuan PR and media machines have built a larger-than-life personality cult around a single individual. In the process, the path-breaking ancestors under whose shadow the BJP organization was built are being rapidly pushed into obscurity, even irrelevance. After his 2014 victory, Narendra Modi removed all senior leaders, including past BJP presidents L.K. Advani and Murli Manohar Joshi, from the BJP's all-important parliamentary board and sidelined them into the 'margdarshak mandal' (think tank of party seniors). Vajpayee, incapacitated by ill health and retired from politics, was awarded the Bharat Ratna in 2015, and there are several government schemes named after him. His death in August 2018 led to an outpouring of grief. Yet there is an unmistakable sense that he, in some way, represents a bygone era in Indian politics, remembered with a touch of wistfulness by only some, and forgotten all too easily by most others. Some even dismiss his leadership: the BJP could never cross the 200-seat mark in an election under him, they say. This is deeply unfair to India's first non-Congress prime minister who completed a full term.

An exploration of the life of Atal Bihari Vajpayee is surely needed when the ideas he embodied are in danger of being forgotten, when there is so much we can learn from him. In this biography I have sought to re-establish Vajpayee as a living presence, without whom the rise of the BJP would not have been possible. I have attempted to present to readers his cerebral, clever, unconventional, ambitious, wily, droll, all-accepting, charismatic personality. As I researched the book, he reminded me of a slowly strengthening river, starting from a small, lonely spot, gradually gathering force, carrying within him layers of evolution – a river that when it finally reaches the ocean spreads into twisting tributaries of varied lived experiences.

The arc of Vajpayee's career spans virtually the entire length of post-Independence India. He contested elections in 1955 and was still fighting elections in 2004. In a public life of over five decades, he was witness to the many shifts and swings in Indian politics, mainly as a leading oppositional figure, but eventually as prime minister. As India completes seventy-five years since Independence, Vajpayee's life story mirrors the evolution of modern India, from the dreams of a young nation just freed from the yoke of colonialism to a country with superpower aspirations.

Another reason to decode the Vajpayee story is to understand the progress of BJP and Hindutva politics, from the days of the Jana Sangh, as a marginal player living in the shade of the towering Jawaharlal Nehru and Indira Gandhi–led Congress, to its twenty-first-century avatar as India's dominant party. It would perhaps be fair to say that there would be no Narendra Modi if there had not been an Atal Bihari Vajpayee to pave the way. Vajpayee was the political flagbearer of the Hindutva right for decades, playing a critical role in making the saffron parivar – ostracized for years as 'untouchable' after Mahatma Gandhi's assassination in 1948 – into an acceptable party for allies and governance. He shaped the debates on secularism, communalism, nationalism and Hindutva, which are so common today, and gave Hindu nationalism its intellectual parliamentary heft. While Advani was his staunch, lifelong comrade in this exercise, it was Vajpayee who became the most enduring symbol of a party whose rise from two seats in 1984 to consecutive majorities in 2014 and 2019 represents a voyage of struggle and hardship, and many defeats and failures, before the eventual triumph.

Hindutva politics has been alternately deified and demonized.

Majoritarian cultural nationalism and its stark, violent religious undertones are subjects of intense and fractious debate. The idea of a Hindu Rashtra, as espoused by the RSS, does strike at the foundational principles of India's Constitution, which derives its heart and soul from the concept of equal citizenship. As a long-serving and outstanding parliamentarian, Vajpayee was a steadfast constitutionalist. But as someone who emerged from the womb of the RSS – he joined as a swayamsevak or volunteer while still in school – Vajpayee's primary political attachment was always to the Sangh Parivar. He was a 'mukhauta' or mask to his critics, and indeed he masked Hindutva's darker side and enabled Hindu nationalism to gain the kind of democratic legitimacy and popularity that his ideological forebears Savarkar and Golwalkar could never achieve. Yet he was a talisman to his admirers. His balancing act between his constitutional commitments and Hindutva impulses was a lifelong tightrope walk, his doublespeak, humorous asides and long silences the devices he used to discover the tricky middle ground of reconciliation.

Vajpayee's unique ability to be the great reconciler of differences made him a politician tailor-made for the coalition era of the 1990s and early 2000s. It is this that makes him such an attractive figure for a 'new' hyper-polarized India to embrace, and should be considered his abiding legacy. Reconciler, bridge-builder, a pursuer of consensus, he possessed the quintessential virtue of the democrat: the ability to form friendships even with those who sharply disagreed with him.

Contemporary Indian politics is seeing a destructive schism of ideas and dialogue, to the point where conciliation and compromise seem almost impossible. Not only is this causing terrible institutional damage, the fractures are spilling on to the street, in conflicts and violence suggesting a nation at war with itself. In this context, the Vajpayee approach offers a template for a new generation of political leaders to understand. One of the reasons why I, as a professed liberal, embarked on this biography was to try to understand a viewpoint very different from my own. The Vajpayee playbook puts democracy – and its rules, norms, restraints and duties – first.

~

However, my attempt here isn't just about unravelling the political brand that Vajpayee represented, but also about uncovering the little-known facets of the complicated personality beneath the myths. Just who was the young Atal who grew up in a Hindu Brahmin household in Gwalior in Madhya Bharat, but whose remarkable life journey ended with his becoming a three-time prime minister? Who was this magician-orator who rose from being a journalist in RSS publications to the Sangh Parivar's national star and most loved public face? He was not born into privilege like Jawaharlal Nehru, yet he is considered by many as an equal of India's first prime minister in his parliamentary contributions. He wasn't a domineering dynast like Indira Gandhi, yet like her he was a masterful and ruthless practitioner of power politics. He could be as Machiavellian as P.V. Narasimha Rao – whose photo he proudly displayed in his home – but also as gentle as Manmohan Singh, with whom he bantered in Parliament. He was a public figure who loved solitude and appeared at times to be a solitary figure in his party; but at the same time, he had a close circle of friends and family to whom he was devoted. A maverick and untraditional Hindu nationalist who relished his drink and had eclectic tastes in food, Vajpayee, perhaps more than any other Indian prime minister, defies stereotypes. There are many instances when he delivered shrill communal speeches; he remained a self-confessed RSS swayamsevak to the last, he never broke with the RSS, however much he may have disapproved of overt religious mobilization. As he himself often said, he was not the so-called good man in the bad party, but part and parcel of the RSS–Jana Sangh–BJP. 'I'm like the branch of a tree,' he said, 'how can you say you like the fruit or branch of a tree, but not the tree?'

The uniqueness of Vajpayee lies in the fact that in his very persona he embodied a Hindu nationalism which was also striving to be a democratic force, its voice heard in Parliament, abiding more or less by the rules of democracy. The right-wing Hindu conservative viewpoint has a right to exist and to be heard, he argued, as long as it is argued within the boundaries of the Constitution. 'The route to democracy can never be via the temple [Ram Mandir],' he said, and although he rode the Hindutva tiger to power, his ambiguously voiced opposition to rath yatras as 'nautanki', and even his one-line remark to Gujarat Chief Minister Narendra Modi after the Gujarat riots, on 'rajdharma', still struck important notes. As prime minister he faced intense RSS and VHP ire as his government embarked on a liberalization drive and on a reach-out to Pakistan and in Kashmir. He defied the RSS, not only in government but also in his life by insisting on personal freedom in his relationships, perhaps the only BJP politician who had the gumption to mount such a rebuff to disapproving Sangh patriarchs, secure in his own indispensability.

I was fortunate to first meet Vajpayee in 1998, when he was prime minister of his thirteen-month government and I was a reporter with *Outlook* magazine. I, along with a colleague, reported and wrote an *Outlook* cover story on him, entitled 'The Swadeshi Nehru', in which we alluded to his 'Sanskritic liberalism', the tug of war he represented between the 'soft muslin' of the dhoti-wearing politician and the 'starched khaki' of the Sangh Parivar brotherhood, and how he, Nehruvian as he was, still embraced the politics of Hindutva. Vajpayee was not unpleased with the piece. But he was disappointed that we had not included any of his poetry in the article. When I met him subsequently he mentioned this, telling me I may not find English translations of his poetry. I discovered many facets to him in the course of writing that cover story: not just how much of a sharp contrast there was between some of his publicly professed stances and his own personal code, but also how well he cooked khichdi, kheer and puffy puris, how he loved the novels of John Grisham and Premchand,

and how he once confessed to a friend: '*Kaun desh sambhalega? Isse toh behtar hai ki Parliament mein ek bhashan thok do, aur ghar aake cinema dekho* [Who on earth can govern this nation? Better to make a rousing speech in Parliament and then come home and watch a movie].'

Vajpayee the person, now moderate, now hard-line, now droll, lovable foodie, now rabble-rousing demagogue, now the poetry-writing bon vivant, now the power-hungry politician, straddling the world of sanatani Hindu beliefs and progressive Nehruvianism, is rich material for a biographer. He was a Hindu pluralist and a democrat, who outgrew the narrow-mindedness of the RSS early on in his career yet shrewdly (and cynically) used the Hindutva movement to catapult himself and his party to power. In the vast and impressive range and depth of his Parliament speeches we can see how the statesman evolved slowly over time. His thoughtfulness on social change, his shifting stances on the economy, later pushing a reformist drive for liberalization, his sharp assertions of Indian self-interest in foreign policy, all were shaped by decades of public life, through well-researched argument and debate with brilliant parliamentary colleagues.

Vajpayee was, ultimately, the man of Parliament, who grew and developed in Parliament and who cut his teeth in the golden age of Parliament, namely, the 1950s and 1960s, a period which I describe as India's 'Nehruvian Enlightenment'. This was the time when, at least among the political elite, ideas of reason, rationality, tolerance and scientific inquiry held sway. Vajpayee was very much a part of this time.

The story of Vajpayee, the poet-politician who could disarm critics with his shy smile or a poetic line, is as much about a liberated personal philosophy as it is about no-holds-barred realpolitik. For me it has been a wonderfully nostalgic adventure to revisit the politician and prime minister I had covered many years ago as a reporter and to rediscover him in the light of today's times. As a tribute to the poet-politician, I have composed some rhymes of my own at the start of every chapter, which I hope readers will enjoy. Vajpayee's best epitaph should be in the poetry he so loved and to which he turned as balm. Among his favourites were these lines from Shivmangal Singh 'Suman', which suit him perfectly:

Kya haar mein, kya jeet mein
Kinchit nahin bhaybheet main
Sangharsh path par jo bhi mile
Yeh bhi sahi, woh bhi sahi.

Neither in victory nor in defeat
Am I ever afraid
Whatever comes my way in the path of struggle
All is fair, all is fine by me.[2]

1

Darkness at High Noon: 2004

A poem for Vajpayee:

Defeated yes, vanquished no
Remember: he existed, he governed, he even shone.
He was the precarious colossus
Most enigmatic of bosses,
To hold Hindu centrism in a crowd?
Other than him, they found none.

Ah, didn't he know that sixth sense moment,
When an election victory swells
But in this year's sunlit silence
He alone heard wavering warning bells.

~

13 May 2004. A white-hot summer day. Temperatures in Delhi spiked upwards and the sun blazed down with laser-like intensity. The heat in the NDTV studios began to rise too. News anchors and guests broke into a sweat despite the air conditioning. NDTV co-founder

Prannoy Roy and his fellow psephologist Dorab Sopariwala blinked and peered at the screens, unable to quite believe what was happening. The results of the general elections for India's fourteenth Lok Sabha were coming in thick and fast. The numbers were flashing on-screen. But could this really be happening? Was this real?

Opinion and exit polls, including NDTV's own projections, had been trumpeting an easy victory for Prime Minister Atal Bihari Vajpayee's BJP-led National Democratic Alliance (NDA). The highest opinion poll projections, the India Today-Aaj Tak poll had given the BJP and its allies as many as 335 seats in the 543-seat Lok Sabha. This would be Vajpayee's election, fought under the triumphant slogan 'India Shining', in the name of a well-loved, universally popular prime minister. Astrologers joined the chorus line. The zodiac, they said, was lined up for Vajpayee to rule uninterrupted until at least 2006.

Buoyed by recent state assembly wins, surging economic growth and the all-India Vajpayee aura, the government had advanced the poll dates by almost six months. It had cut short its own five-year term, convinced it would sail to victory.

But today, on this burning May day, it was Mayday for Vajpayee. The results were astonishing. It was turning out to be one of the biggest upsets in Indian politics. The BJP was crashing to a terrible defeat and – wonder of wonders – the Congress, that leaderless relic of the past, that supine group of ragtags barely held together by a tremulous Sonia Gandhi, had scripted an unexpected miracle.

In a stunning blow to all exit and opinion polls, the Congress won 145 seats, racing up from 114 in 1999, to emerge as the single largest party in the Lok Sabha, the Congress-led alliance sweeping up over 200 seats. Even the left put in a career-best performance of 59 seats. The BJP plunged to 138, crashing from its best-ever showing of 182 in 1999. The Vajpayee-led NDA alliance got just 186 seats. It was darkness at high noon.

How had every single opinion and exit poll got the results so badly wrong? Had people lied when they were being surveyed? 'Oh god, it was horrible, just horrible,' recalls Prannoy Roy. 'And our shock showed on our faces on air . . . The thing is, the results just did not show up in our data – that was the weird part.'[1] True, some polls, NDTV's among them, had changed considerably as the campaign wore on, from initial predictions of an NDA landslide to warnings of a cliffhanger by the last phase. But no one predicted the rout that now rushed in.

'The Congress didn't even have a leader,' says Sopariwala. 'Vajpayee was larger than life. The 2004 election will be remembered as the election every pollster got wrong.'[2]

As the spellbinding thriller unfolded on TV, Prime Minister Atal Bihari Vajpayee sat in a nimbus of still morning light in his home in New Delhi's 7 Race Course Road, the tree-shaded bungalow complex where India's prime ministers reside. By mid-morning the results were clear. The grizzled old general gazed at the empty battlefield. His armies were laid to waste, his colours trampled upon.

At seventy-nine, his once handsome, strong-jawed face had turned heavy with age. His neatly brushed hair was silver. His shoulders sagged. He sat enveloped in a deepening quiet. Perhaps his mind wandered to his favourite Kabir, the free-spirited fifteenth-century poet who sang '*Jheeni jheeni bini chadariya . . . so chadar sur nar muni ore, ore ke maili kini chadariya*.' The blanket covers both god and wise men. They wrap it round and the blanket gets dirty. Vajpayee's blanket is spoiled even if Kabir kept his blanket as good as new.

'I went to his house after the results,' recalls his aide Sudheendra Kulkarni. 'He was sitting with his head down and said very little. He looked shaken, completely shaken. He genuinely wanted to do more, he wanted to leave a big legacy behind.'[3]

Outside, a thicket of cameras and excited TV reporters jostled on the pavement. George Fernandes, defence minister and NDA convenor, came striding out of the prime minister's house, his face grim. 'We accept that we have been defeated and will sit in the Opposition,' he informed the press curtly. Cries went up, questions were hurled, but Fernandes walked away without a word.

Meanwhile, just over a kilometre away from the prime minister's residence, the Congress office at 24 Akbar Road burst into frenetic celebration. Fireworks were set off, dholaks began to rumble, handfuls of gulal were thrown around and whoops of joy rose up. So unexpected was the win that the Congress ran out of mithai, water and sharbat, as an avalanche of people descended on its doorstep. 'Oh my god! Kamal is winning! Kamal is winning!' shrieked Congress media-cell convenor Ambika Soni, referring to the Congress's Kamal Nath and not the BJP's shrivelled kamal (the lotus, the BJP's symbol). It slowly dawned on Sonia Gandhi's party that they were returning to power after almost a decade.[4] 'We were out-financed one-to-eight,' recalls Jairam Ramesh, a key Congress campaign manager in 2004. 'Vajpayee looked invincible, Pramod Mahajan had endless resources. But we crafted what became an iconic campaign, the aam aadmi campaign. It worked.'[5] Unable to compete with the BJP in the national media, the Congress consciously went local, putting out ads and messages in the local television channels, deliberately opting for the wider term 'aam aadmi' instead of 'garib'.

Sonia's low-key roadside campaign of nukkad sabhas and local rallies was a dramatic contrast to the BJP's high voltage, high-tech attack. The reassuring slogan '*Congress ka haath aam aadmi ke saath*' came up trumps, a triumph of old-style politics over the BJP's firehose of money and glamour. Vajpayee had referred to Sonia as the *matam ka masiha* (prophet of doom) during the campaign, but she had successfully jabbed sharp needles into the Shining India hot-air balloon. The grieving widow tugged at voters' heartstrings as she spoke of her husband's and mother-in-law's assassinations. In her heavily accented, laboured Hindi she declared: 'The BJP and allies talked about sushasan (able governance), but they gave us kushasan (bad administration).'[6] Now Sonia Shining rose on the debris of India Shining. Vajpayee, the Bharatiya legend-patriarch was defeated by a ponytailed 'foreigner'.

While the Congress celebrated, the BJP office at 11 Ashoka Road wore the silence of a morgue. Pramod Mahajan and Sushma Swaraj appeared for a morning briefing, then quickly disappeared, and the office was deserted by the afternoon. In a corner, saffron and green balloons slowly deflated and withered.

Raisina Hill, the slope in Central Delhi where the offices of the national government sit, was hushed. It was waiting to bear witness to a changing of the democratic guard. In the evening, Vajpayee and Deputy Prime Minister L.K. Advani came driving up Raisina Hill to offer the prime minister's resignation to the President. The grey-maned A.P.J. Abdul Kalam was waiting for his one-time boss.[7] As the sun began its downward journey, slanting its dissipating rays on the dome of Rashtrapati Bhavan, India's first non-Congress prime minister to rule for a full five years formally resigned. That evening he told the country: 'Victory and defeat are part of life which are to be viewed with equanimity. The voters have given their verdict. I accept the verdict. My party and alliance may have lost, but India and India's democracy have won.'

He revered the majesty of election results. However crushingly disappointed he was, however fervently he may have wanted to return to the prime minister's chair, he still saw himself as a pilgrim toiling under the mountain of the people's will. Defeat was intolerable, but the working of democracy was as immutable as fate.

~

A couple of days later, N.M. Ghatate came calling on his old friend. 'Appa' Ghatate, the genial, nattily dressed advocate, often spotted in a jacket and cravat, had been Vajpayee's closest friend since 1957. Appa's father, Babasaheb Ghatate, Hindu Mahasabha and RSS leader, was one of Vajpayee's early mentors. In the late 1950s, Appa, then a motorcycle-driving city slicker, often gave Vajpayee a ride to Parliament. That day, Ghatate found that his friend had by now somewhat recovered his spirits and was, as usual, joking with his staff. People milled around in his drawing room as Vajpayee directed wry asides at everyone. What is there, he said, *chunao mein kabhi haarte hain, kabhi jeette hain, isme kya hai* – you win some, you lose some. Advani looked more downcast than Vajpayee, remembered Ghatate.[8]

With his departure from Race Course Road imminent, he was informed that his personal team would be greatly reduced and he would have to decide who his personal secretary would be. Vajpayee pulled a face and joked, 'Maybe I'll keep Daulat Ram.' Daulat Ram was a lowly peon in the Lok Sabha library, someone whom Vajpayee never failed to hail and greet. 'Vajpayee was a simple person, he didn't care about trappings, the bungalow, flooring, curtains, carpets, decor or any of that,' said Ghatate. 'And he was quite useless with gadgets, often fumbling with the TV remote.' There was talk among his aides about the specific protocol for moving out. Vajpayee immediately shot back at them, '*Kya protocol? Bistar bandho aur chalo* [What protocol! Roll up the bedding and let's go].' Ghatate said, 'He just wanted to get out as fast as possible.'

A.S. Dulat, the tall, moustachioed former Research and Analysis Wing (RAW) chief, who had worked closely with Vajpayee on Kashmir called on him after the results. '*Sir, yeh kya ho gaya?*' Dulat asked. Vajpayee burst out laughing. '*Yeh unko bhi nahin maloom ki kya ho gaya* [Even they don't know what happened],' he said, referring to the Congress. He also mentioned the Gujarat riots. '*Woh* [failing to act against the state government after the riots] *humaare se galti hui* [We made a mistake].'[9]

Was he himself to blame for destiny slamming the door in his face, denying him a longer chapter in the history books? Against his own instincts, he had been led by his party to agree to an early election. In December 2003, the BJP had won big election victories in the heartland states of Madhya Pradesh, Rajasthan and Chhattisgarh. The victories had silenced the prime minister's antagonists in the Sangh Parivar and bolstered what was known as the 'Vajpayee Line' – economic liberalization, brakes on militant Hindutva and harmony with allies.

Two thousand three was a golden year. The monsoon had come gushing down leading to bumper harvests. The Sensex soared, confidence galloped, and a great leap forward in phone and road connectivity sent India's growth rate streaking upwards. Economists declared that India's economy was now booming.[10] Consumer durables, mobile phones, cars, two-wheelers and ready cash rained down, TV channels pumped out game shows that gave people a shot at becoming crorepatis, and the urban middle class, high on Feel Good and revelling in the new shopping malls and restaurants, kicked up its heels and shouted, yippee! Vajpayee was the amiable giant in politics, the father figure, even if only of the scrappiest of coalitions. He was lofty yet cosily familial, the Nice Guy Hindu Nationalist, the image seen to be a winner, especially since his nearest adversary was a thin-voiced, pretty woman from Italy who could barely speak Hindi and headed a weak, divided party.

Why even bother about rivals? Even internationally, Vajpayee was in full throttle. In April 2003 he made headline news worldwide when he offered warm-hearted peace to Pakistan at a rally in Srinagar. In May that year he stepped in style into Russia, where at the 300th Foundation Day of St Petersburg, he was seated at the head table with George Bush and Vladimir Putin. In June he led a dramatically successful visit to China, clinking glasses with Premier Wen Jiabao, almost solving the troublesome boundary question, conceding that the Tibetan Autonomous Region was an integral part of China and offering Indian mangoes and Bollywood movies aplenty as exports to the northern neighbour. And in July, pressured to join the US's 'shock and awe' war against Iraq, Vajpayee held out steadfastly, refusing to send troops or to join the Coalition of the Willing against Iraq, yet at the same time managing to stay such good friends with George Bush that Vajpayee was the only head of government the American president invited to lunch in September during the UN General Assembly meeting in New York. Earlier in September Ariel Sharon came visiting, the first visit by an Israeli prime minister to India, but

Vajpayee took care to visit Syria later in the year, signalling India's enduring ties with the Arab world. In October he went to Bali and was given a red-carpet welcome. The prime minister of modern but sagacious India was a welcome guest worldwide. Vajpayee was Nehru 2.0 abroad.

The time was ripe to advance the elections, said Vajpayee's closest advisers, L.K. Advani, BJP president Venkaiah Naidu and minister and political confidant-adviser Pramod Mahajan. Key ally fifty-four-year-old Andhra Pradesh Chief Minister Chandrababu Naidu added to the chorus. Why wait till October for the scheduled general elections? It was time for a snap poll for an even bigger mandate.

Chandrababu Naidu was an acclaimed global achiever, winning accolades from Davos to US business schools as the IT-enabled Indian administrator bringing smart new governance innovations to his state. Under his watch, Hyderabad had become Cyberabad, IT firms took off, and US President Bill Clinton made a special stop in Hyderabad during his India trip in 2000. 'CM Babu' held out dreams to computer-tapping fishermen and paddy farmers with home pages, to make quick fortunes. Chandrababu's halo blinded many to the ominous warnings his state was sending out. In the burning interiors of Andhra Pradesh, farmers complained that Naidu had only developed high-tech cities, that he and his supporters lived in big bungalows and had done nothing for the villages.[11] But Naidu, convinced of his own invincibility, wanted to race ahead to the hustings.

Naidu even claimed a martyr's halo. In 2003, on his way to the Tirupati temple, he had narrowly survived a Naxal attack. A landmine had exploded into his convoy, injuring him in the chest and face. Eager to capitalize on public sympathy, and confident of his dynamic go-getter high-tech image, Chandrababu Naidu wanted to press ahead for simultaneous state assembly polls in Andhra Pradesh and the general elections.

Deputy Prime Minister L.K. Advani had his own reasons for pushing for early polls. The lanky master strategist, the ambitious, calculating and efficient architect of the politics of the Ram Mandir was restless for the prime minister's post. As Vajpayee visibly aged and became increasingly unwell, he had already signalled that if the party won in 2004, he was inclined to pass on the baton and Advani was eager to seize the crown.

Advani revealed his impatience when he suddenly announced that he would embark on another rath yatra. In an election fought under Vajpayee's leadership, with the Vajpayee Line of the sober centre or moderate pluralism as the guiding principle, the rath yatra, synonymous with militant Hindutva mobilization, was jarring. But declaring, 'This is not a rath yatra, it's a yatra,'[12] Advani took off on what he called his Bharat Uday Yatra. This was a long road journey from south to north, intended to establish that he was possible prime minister-in-waiting, intended not only to launch himself but also to take the spotlight away from pushy, younger dynamos particularly the fifty-five-year-old Pramod Mahajan, seen by many as a future BJP leader.

Three years younger than Vajpayee, Advani was slim and fighting fit where the former was overweight and beset with ill health. Advani had been home minister, and was elevated to deputy prime minister in 2002 at the insistence of the RSS. It was he who had devised and led the 1990 Ram Rath Yatra, hacking a 10,000-kilometre-long jagged wound into India's fragile flesh and plunging the BJP into the Ram Mandir movement, which devoured the Babri Masjid and India's secular values. It was Advani's bloodstained path through India that had, ultimately, brought the prime minister's crown to Vajpayee. As the parent of the BJP's exponential growth, Advani saw himself as the natural helmsman to take over from his tiring senior.

The prime minister's men were walking on air. They were oozing with self-belief. They were arrogant and certain of victory, qualities epitomized by the fashionably dressed Mahajan. The Vajpayee government's controversial sharpie, formidably well connected and expert in the electoral dark arts, he had held several portfolios in

Vajpayee's government and functioned as his political adviser. Although reared in the RSS, Mahajan was the antithesis of the invisible, self-effacing swayamsevak. He was a flashy, cell phone–brandishing Mr Fixit who, when not schmoozing with tycoons in five-star hotels, was confabulating in backrooms on smart election deals.

'I want Vajpayee to become India's first prime minister to be sworn in four times,' enthused Mahajan to TV journalist Rajdeep Sardesai while being interviewed at the Taj Mahal Hotel in Delhi in early 2004. 'No prime minister has been sworn in four times after elections since 1952. I want Vajpayee to be a record breaker.'[13] Mahajan symbolized the 'new' BJP, a party which was no longer shaped by the moral absolutism of the RSS or the asceticism of its pracharak culture. Mahajan would easily switch from kurta-pyjama to designer shirts and well-tailored suits and could often be spotted at the capital's luxury nightspots. Fiercely ambitious and well networked with Mumbai's business elites, he was Vajpayee's trusted aide but also his potential Achilles heel, always on the lookout for short-term fixes rather than choosing to abide by ideological rigour or party discipline. Vajpayee's close and trusted friend, the Rajasthan BJP's Bhairon Singh Shekhawat never liked Mahajan. Once when Vajpayee decided to send Mahajan to contest elections from Jaipur, Shekhawat met Vajpayee to dissuade him and said: 'Today my party workers are happy to work hard on puris and sabzi. If Mahajan comes here, they will all demand fancy cars and five-star hotels.' Vajpayee gave in to his old friend, yet continued to believe in Mahajan's political nous. Mahajan was the main planner of the BJP's 2004 media blitz, the progenitor of the slogan the BJP went into the battle with: 'India Shining'.

The Delhi businessman Sudhanshu Mittal was Mahajan's close friend and worked with him. 'India Shining was Pramod Mahajan's brainchild,' says Mittal. 'The idea was to showcase the government's achievements, India was on the move . . . you can't say victory or defeat of any government depends on an advertising campaign. But think about its sheer recall value.'[14] A high-pitched TV campaign centred on Vajpayee's personality cult was mounted. For the first time in Indian elections, a social media campaign was begun; recorded voice messages from Vajpayee, saying, '*Main Atal Bihari Vajpayee bol raha hoon*', were sent out on individual residential landline phones. 'It's not just an election with the There Is No Alternative (TINA) factor, it's an election with the TITA (There Is The Atal) factor,' proclaimed Mahajan.[15]

Mahajan's residence on Delhi's 7 Safdarjung Road became the site of the BJP's cutting-edge digital war room, buzzing with volunteers, ad agency professionals and computer geeks. Sitting in marble-floored, air-conditioned rooms, well supplied with coffee dispensers, the BJP keyboard warriors worked on a Mission 2004 website. Party cadres were put to work to daily monitor fourteen hours of news channels and produce detailed reports, listing 'negative' stories or comments.[16] Emails and SMSs were sent out to a database of 25 lakh email addresses and 15,000 phones. Call centres were set up, T-shirts and caps were printed, and ads flashed out on youth channels like Channel V and MTV. Spokespersons were provided with up-to-date information and encouraged to take part in as many TV shows as possible.

On 12 March 2004, the magazine *Frontline* published a cover story, 'The Feel Good Factory', revealing the brutal inequalities of so-called Shining India. 'The Sensex might be on a dream run and the markets booming and investors thrilled. But it is still worth recalling that this happens in a country where 65% households do not have a bank account and tens of millions of farmers live and die in debt,' the magazine wrote.[17] Kulkarni showed the magazine to Vajpayee, who read it in detail and turned his face away.

'Shining India' discomfited the veteran. Something was off. The sunlight this summer was bright but vacant. It did not make him optimistic. Former minister Yashwant Sinha records Vajpayee telling him: '*Pagal hue hain ki chunav pehle karayenge?* [Are they crazy to call an early election?]' Advani too admits that Vajpayee gave his consent to advancing the Lok Sabha polls 'rather reluctantly'.[18]

Vajpayee had learnt – over decade after long decade of travel, criss-crossing India, toiling through crowds, trudging on dusty, smoke-swirled tracks – to listen for the voice of his instincts. Call it his experienced grasp of electioneering, or a sixth sense born of decades of campaigning and trying to sense the disposition of a crowd. With an unerring and formidable grip on the political pulse, the ten-time Lok Sabha winner tailored his speeches and pitched the right kind of folk tales, the most germane political taunts – for maximum audience impact. In almost half a century of contesting polls, when it came to predicting his prospects, he was rarely wrong.

One set of events in particular troubled him: the Gujarat riots of 2002. The careful centrism of his government, his own well-projected middle-of-the-road persona, Vajpayee the peacemaker with Pakistan, the elder statesman at the UN, had come under serious attack two years earlier when savage communal riots tore through Gujarat in February–March 2002, the news splashed across newspaper front pages around the world. Later the US would even refuse a visa to then Gujarat chief minister Narendra Modi for failing to protect religious harmony in the state. For Vajpayee, the riots had become a cause of deep worry: he feared that Muslims would turn against the BJP and his studied efforts at reaching out to the community would come to naught. Says a senior BJP leader, 'The Gujarat riots hung heavy on him. He worried that they could cost him the election.' The riots had cast a pall of gloom over the well-marketed feel-good factor. Over 1000 had died in the riots, and Vajpayee had made it plain in his own way that he wanted Narendra Modi to step down as chief minister. But against the overwhelming opinion favouring Modi within the party, he did not push for his way.

On 12 April 2004, in the thick of the campaigning, the Supreme Court delivered a scathing judgement. Referring to the Gujarat state government as 'modern-day Neros', the court held:

> Those who were responsible for protecting life and properties and ensuring that investigation is fair and proper seem to have shown no real anxiety . . . were looking elsewhere when Best Bakery [a small bakery in Vadodara where fourteen people were killed during the riots] and innocent children and helpless women were burning, and were probably deliberating how the perpetrators of the crime can be saved or protected.

. . . were probably deliberating how the perpetrators of the crime can be saved or protected.

Thunderstruck at the court's fury, Vajpayee retreated into a shell. He suddenly fell quiet, watching warily as Sonia Gandhi and the Congress sharpened their attacks on him and screamed out loud about the Best Bakery judgement at rallies. 'The Muslims turned against us en masse and the Hindus got divided,' says Yashwant Sinha. Vajpayee realized that the riots were both a moral and a psephological hazard, that his failure to act against Modi had not just damaged his pluralist credentials, but had imperceptibly changed his image. From the reassuring 'Stable Atal', he had looked like a dithering and weak leader, a pushover unable to assert his prime ministerial authority. As if to castigate himself for the Gujarat failure, Vajpayee told the press after the 2004 results: 'I am the most responsible for the defeat since the elections were fought in my name. I am ready for prayaschit [penance].'[19]

In the 2004 campaign he was let down by his own all-accepting, collegiate nature. He believed that Modi's resignation was imperative for the BJP's journey towards the moderate right-wing, but gave way before the party, professing commitment to the party's *sarv sammati* (consensus). He had misgivings about the Shining India campaign, but gave way before the thrusting enthusiasm of younger colleagues. His instincts told him that early polls may be a mistake, that he should not cut short his own tenure – but again he gave way before his party and fell in line with Advani. He was a serious politician, serious about elections. Polls were about dialogue with the people, emotional exchanges, drollery with substance, speeches delivered with skill and brio, and kavi sammelan–style wordplay and panache. He didn't understand elections that were about big money, pomp and image-building. The claptrap of gadgetry confounded him. But he went along with his party's young guns in a new high-tech campaign.

This pattern of disagreeing but falling in line was not just instinct on Vajpayee's part, it was also strategic and pragmatic. By making his objections known and yet accepting his party's line, he trod the nuanced grey zone of political ambiguity that enabled manoeuvre and compromise, and boosted his own popularity. Neither was he ever too convinced about his own way either. 'Vajpayee had, above all, a democratic mind,' says Mittal. 'There was nothing feudal or autocratic about him, no "my way or the highway". Collective decisions of the organization were uppermost.'[20] No decisions were to be slammed down from on high; instead, the way forward emerged from the chaos of voices and the untidiness of compromise.

And so Vajpayee didn't resist the party's drive for early elections, putting at rest public speculations about early polls and declaring at the grand BJP national executive meeting in Hyderabad on 11 and 12 January 2004: 'The party has recommended unambiguously that we should seek the people's mandate at the earliest for completing the unaccomplished part of our mission. We should have a fresh mandate so that we can march more confidently towards our goal of making India a developed nation by 2020 . . . The NDA is ready. The BJP is ready.'

Here in Hyderabad, with the Hussain Sagar Lake shimmering in the winter sun, he perhaps reminded himself of his own infallibility. Hadn't he been a people's representative for ten terms,[21] a parliamentarian for over forty years? Wasn't he the magician orator who cast a spell over multitudes, the evergreen Dev Anand of Indian elections contesting polls since 1955? Hadn't he been the prime-minister-in-waiting since 1996 and sworn in as prime minister three times? He had been tested enough by the people, and surely, in the end, the people would stand by him.

His heart and head pulled in opposite directions. Often, he found it difficult to align his heart to his head which strategized about the politics around him. This internal conflict resulted in indecisiveness, long spells of silence, his spoken words getting fewer and fewer. Others picked up the baton and ran with it, while he sank deeper into the listening mode.

In two year-end 'musings' – messages to the country published in newspapers in 2001 and 2003 – Vajpayee had tried to cast off the formality of high office and directly confide in voters. In his article 'Musings from Kumarakom', written at the end of 2000 and published in 2001, he dwelt at length on India's diversity and the strength the country gained from 'our syncretic national culture', yet stating that the Ram Mandir at Ayodhya was a national (not religious) sentiment. He also called for a recommencement of talks with Pakistan. In his 'Musings from Goa' at the end of 2002 (after Modi's big majoritarian win in the Gujarat assembly polls) he was at pains to insist that Hindutva was a liberal idea and should not be pitted against secularism and acceptance of diversity. In this context, he had tough words to say about those who propagate a 'narrow-minded Hindutva' in a 'rigid and extremist manner'. The ideas of 'Vajpayeeism' – liberalization, rejection of swadeshi economics, peace with Pakistan and ideological moderation – were under way. Yet, all the while he remained acutely aware of the fragility of the tiny boat he was attempting to sail, a boat on which his own power depended. 'The people know that we have not had sufficient time to accomplish our mission,' he said hopefully in January 2004, 'they know our record is good. The people are in a mood to give us five more years.'[22] The boat was waiting to catch the winds in its sails. But it didn't get the time it needed.

~

Days after Vajpayee announced 'the BJP is ready' in Hyderabad, the thirteenth Lok Sabha was dissolved on 6 February 2004. The ruling party had hoped for a quick election and a new Parliament by late March 2004, but the Election Commission announced a three-month long, four-phase election. The long, gruelling summer saw a first-of-its-kind campaign: a media and advertising blitz, film stars and playback singers roped in to address rallies. 'There aren't any real issues in elections anymore,' grumbled former chief election commissioner (CEC) J.M. Lyngdoh. 'It's all being dictated by market forces. The election system has been reduced to a farce where political parties are asking you to choose between Coke and Pepsi.'[23]

The BJP's campaign pitch was Vajpayee, Vajpayee and Vajpayee. Every party poster was plastered with technicolour images of him as a larger-than-life superman. So what if he was now seventy-nine. It would be a long, luminous twilight, the rich velvety glow of age lighting up India's youthful dreams. He was indispensable to the BJP. Without him the party could not complete its dash to political centrism, to a right-wing version of Nehruvian constitutional democracy mixed with an embrace of the free market. Six years earlier, he had been pitched as 'The Man India Awaits', the strong, trusted patriarch-leader and Hindu karta-dharta who would provide a break from the chronic instability of the coalition politics of the 1990s. At that time he had been uncertain about his NDA experiment. But now, in 2004, both the BJP and Vajpayee were confident that, in the final analysis, they had hit upon the right formula for success. While Vajpayeeism dominated the campaign, there was barely any mention of the Ram Mandir or of swadeshi economics. The Sangh Parivar was consigned to the margins. The Vajpayee BJP actively wooed the Muslim vote.

The BJP's Vision Document of 2004 was a cheerful declaration of glossy Vajpayeeism. There were photos of Vajpayee on every page, fifty-four in over forty-eight pages, including a 1950s photo showing Vajpayee seated and Advani standing behind him – the picture of a harmonious duopoly. The Vision Document blared out grand promises of a galloping GDP and digital economy, and highlighted the 'historic' foreign policy success of the India–Pakistan joint declaration of January

2004. There was almost no mention of the Sangh's pet obsessions, no mention of the demand to axe Article 370 and no strident demand for a Uniform Civil Code (UCC), instead only a pledge to support the UCC as an 'instrument of gender justice'. And there was only one reference to the Ram Mandir – about the need to achieve it by negotiation and judicial process. Bye-bye Sangh Parivar. Hail Vajpayee.

Since over half a dozen allies had abandoned the NDA, most notably the Dravida Munnetra Kazhagam (DMK) in Tamil Nadu, the notion of 'coalition dharma' – attracting as many new allies as possible – was reignited and Vajpayee took an active role in sending friendly signals to Sharad Pawar's Nationalist Congress Party and Ram Vilas Paswan's Lok Janshakti Party.

Two thousand four was Vajpayee's election. In the past, the airily detached star performer would wait to be handed a campaign schedule by his party and obediently amble off to his public meetings. He was not the sweating, perspiring, hard-campaigning worker-ant, he was always the on-stage talent who didn't work too hard. But in 2004 he travelled furiously, zig-zagging from Jawahar in Maharashtra to Santiniketan in West Bengal, from Chennai to Nellore in Andhra Pradesh and to Guwahati, wearing an Assamese japi hat in Guwahati, sporting a red safa in Amritsar and a Peshwa topi in Maharashtra, covering thousands of kilometres between January and May.

Confident that he would be rewarded for his peacemaking efforts with Pakistan, Vajpayee took two calculated risks. The first was another determined bid for peace with Pakistan at the South Asian Association for Regional Cooperation (SAARC) summit in Islamabad in January 2004. After two failed attempts – his Lahore bus journey in 1999 and the Agra summit with General Pervez Musharraf in 2001 – once again Vajpayee set off for Islamabad, to shake hands with the mercurial general. This time the meeting achieved a striking joint press statement in which Pakistan committed that it would not 'permit any territory under its control to be used to support terrorism'.

A major peace move with Pakistan before general elections could have backfired badly. It could have led to terror strikes and dented Vajpayee ahead of the polls. But he took the risk, telling the SAARC summit: 'History can remind us, guide us, teach us or warn us. It should not shackle us.'[24]

Weeks ahead of the polls, Vajpayee took another, even bigger risk. The Indian cricket team went to play a Test and one-day international series against Pakistan in March–April, the first Test series in Pakistan in more than a decade and the first visit to Pakistan by an Indian cricket team after the Kargil war. What?! expostulated his critics. An India–Pakistan cricket series before a general election? What if the team was hit by terrorists? What if India lost and Pakistan triumphed? It could bring disaster at the polls.

But the Vajpayee of 2004 was not the uncertain Vajpayee of 1999 looking to Advani for direction. Now he was leader-in-chief, the Olympian, sculpted into India's own political Mount Rushmore. He laid down his will and had his way, and off went captain Sourav Ganguly and his merry men to Karachi, Rawalpindi, Peshawar and Lahore.

And India won. Fireworks flashed into the Lahore sky as Ganguly lifted the Samsung Cup. India's men in blue captured Pakistani hearts. Adoring, tumultuous crowds cheered them from Peshawar to Lahore. In India, street-side fireworks, clouds of Holi colours, kites and blasting loudspeakers marked a surging nationalism from Vadodara to Vizag. '*Jeet mubarak, sapna sach ho gaya, Kashmir toh apna tha, Karachi aur Lahore bhi apna ho gaya* [The dream has come true. Kashmir was always ours, now Karachi and Lahore are ours too],' ran a widely circulating SMS. When the victorious young cricket team in smart blue blazers posed for photos with the prime minister at his residence, Vajpayee's gamble seemed to have paid off: in the photo the prime minister and the cricket team both stood at the head of high-achieving India.

~

The BJP's 'Young Turks' exuded confidence. Hindutva was shelved, sadhus and sants consigned to the margins; flamboyantly right-wing men like Jaitley and Mahajan took centre stage, pushing for bold global futures, technological innovations and aggressive tactics to outsmart the Opposition.

At the start of the campaign, Vajpayee stood forth as the proud liberalizer. In March he arrived at the India Today Conclave, beaming and invigorated, smartly dressed in a black bandgala. He called for a renewed mandate for a government determined to press for the bold new Indian century, and onward and upward towards peace in the neighbourhood, globalization, liberalization and 'sensible economics over the temptation of short-term political gains'.[25] Ahead of the conclave he said in an interview: 'Making economic reforms work for the benefit of the people is one of our achievements. People were worried about disinvestment but now they understand its virtues . . . we take credit for having broadened, deepened and accelerated the reforms process.'[26]

He was an unapologetic believer in pragmatic, free-market economics, preferring to dismiss the swadeshi fanatics in the RSS who had made his life so difficult for the past five years. By 2004, Vajpayee had taken his place with the continuum of India's prime ministers from Nehru to Indira to P.V. Narasimha Rao; he had much more in common with centrist, conservative Congressmen than with the extremities of Hindutva. Not quite a 'half-Congressman', as Hindutva hotheads called him, but someone sitting at the same table as democratic right-wingers and conservative Congressmen like Madan Mohan Malaviya, C. Rajagopalachari and Morarji Desai.

From January to April 2004, over a fifty-five-day-long election schedule, Vajpayee addressed over a hundred rallies in his characteristic style: droll, mildly threatening, bitingly mocking, often hilarious and sending his audience into peals of laughter.

But Sudheendra Kulkarni, who travelled with Vajpayee through the entire election tour, sensed that Vajpayee was simply not happy with the campaign. 'He made a big effort, but he could see what others couldn't,' says Kulkarni, 'that the Opposition had got united. He told me, "*Agar humein koi hara sakte hain, toh humaare log hara sakte hain.* [If there's anyone who can defeat us, it's our own people – referring to the VHP, SJM and the extremist Hindutva lobby.]"' He saw that Sonia Gandhi had suddenly become very active, and after a rally in Punjab he told Kulkarni, '*Yeh devi waapas aa rahi hai* [The lady (Sonia) is coming back].' As Sonia and her children, Rahul and Priyanka, entered the arena – Rahul as the first-time candidate from Amethi – the BJP's attacks on the Gandhis became shriller and more personal, even vicious. 'A jersey cow and a hybrid calf have come to contest elections,' shouted then Gujarat chief minister Narendra Modi.[27] The EC censured Modi for his remarks. The BJP's descent into attacks on the Gandhis, when the 2004 campaign was designed as a positive pitch around Vajpayee, revealed a growing insecurity. Vajpayee insisted that party men should not hurl personal insults at anyone, but delivered sarcastic asides at the Gandhis in his own way: 'In our party, leaders are not born, they have to prove themselves.'[28] In Chennai he cried that Sonia's 'foreign origins' are still a 'major factor' and 'must be debated'.[29] Tellingly, Vajpayee made no mention of 'India Shining' or 'Bharat Uday' in his speeches. His belief in the slogan was draining out fast. By now opinion polls were scaling down the BJP's numbers.

Murli Manohar Joshi, former human resource development minister and former BJP president, had been Vajpayee's comrade since their early years in the RSS. Joshi had been one of the swadeshi hawks in the Vajpayee cabinet, bitterly opposed to the liberalization drive. 'Vajpayee was uncomfortable about the India Shining slogan from the start,' insists Joshi.[30]

Others in the party were bounding forward, aglow with the expectation of victory. Seventy-six-year-old Advani had started his Bharat Uday Yatra from Kanyakumari. It was to be an 8000-kilometre journey, first to Amritsar, then from Porbandar to Puri. The yatra was flagged off in grand style by the BJP top brass, with Christian priests, the diwan of the Ajmer Sharif dargah and even cricketer K. Srikkanth in attendance. 'We have here a microcosm of new India and all that we stand for,' announced Advani on a burningly hot Kanyakumari morning. 'We have Muslim stalwarts, Christian priests, artistes and sportsmen. All of them are joining BJP and setting aside differences.'[31] This was no crazy Hindutva yatra with saffron madmen dancing in its wake; instead, this was designed as a victory march of the BJP founders, cast as constitutional nationalists, championing India, not Bharat. Advani was making a grab for his slice of the glory, but his campaign too revolved around 'Image Vajpayee'. There was no question of the BJP not winning; it only remained to be seen by what margin they'd win.

Then, midway through the campaign, an incident occurred. It became the point from which the BJP campaign hurtled into confusion and growing panic.

From the morning of Monday, 12 April 2004, lines of women – almost 15,000 – many with infants in their arms, began to gather in Lucknow's dusty Chandrashekhar Azad Park.

Vajpayee's campaign manager here was his long-term associate, the BJP leader Lalji Tandon. It was Tandon's seventieth birthday, and by the time he arrived thousands had already gathered under a vast white shamiana erected in the park. After the customary round of speeches, and after Tandon had left, at around 2 p.m., the organizers made an announcement: free saris would be distributed at a counter that had been set up a few metres from the dais. Within seconds, hundreds of frenzied women began to rush towards the distribution point, running and jostling for their free sari. An infant fell down and was instantly crushed to death. As his mother began to wail, more women surged forward. A stampede ensued. Women fell face down in the dirt, others fell over them, some fainted, trapped under the press of bodies. Nine women and two children were killed on the spot, and by the end of the day twenty-one lay dead. Within an hour of the announcement, the park was littered with the chappals, shoes and bags of dead and injured women, and weeping adolescents wandered in the chaos. TV images showed a stack of dead bodies in a van and a young girl wailing next to a woman lying prone: '*Kyon gayi thhi sari lene, kyon gayi thhi?* [Why, why did you go to get that sari?]'

Vajpayee was campaigning in Jharkhand at this time. Shocked and flabbergasted at the news of the stampede, he cut short his rallies and rushed to Lucknow, the constituency he had represented four times since 1991. Payment of Rs 1 lakh each to the families of the dead was immediately announced, and Lalji Tandon was sacked as campaign manager. When Vajpayee went to file his nomination papers three days later, on 15 April, the mood was sombre, and all celebrations were cancelled. 'It is a great tragedy, we are mourning,' he whispered to reporters. 'It is most tragic, unfortunate and painful.'[32] The incident sent shock waves across the country. Could India really be shining if an offer of saris costing only Rs 40 each provoked so much desperation among women that a resulting stampede led to the loss of twenty-one lives? Now the message from the spirit of elections was unmistakable. Returning from Lucknow, Vajpayee told his long-time aide Shiv Kumar, '*Sarkar toh gayi. Hum haar rahen hain* [This government is gone, we are going to lose].' When Shiv Kumar countered him to say that a defeat is just not possible, Vajpayee replied, 'Which world are you living in? I know. I campaign among people. I can feel it. We are losing.'[33]

The sari stampede became a turning point in the campaign. Vajpayee's manner changed. He began to look disgruntled, worried and irritated. In a TV interview he appeared downcast, his face lined with worry. He was visibly tiring before the elections too. 'I don't want to do it any more,' he told a senior BJP leader. 'Let somebody else do it. Let *saien* ["brother" in Sindhi – a mocking reference to Advani] take a shot at it.' He began to sound off colour in interviews. In one interview he said he was becoming tired of running a coalition; in another he said the party had agreed that there should be a successor to him. 'This is my last election,' he told NDTV. 'I am worried about the role money power is playing in democracy. Jantantra is becoming dhantantra. In the future this money power can become an abhishaap [curse] for India.'[34] The NDA seems poised for a return, journalists informed him a month before the results. 'Says who?' shot back Vajpayee, presciently, as if he knew something others did not. 'It's only you in the media who say so. What does the BJP have? Only small states like Gujarat and Rajasthan. What if we lose in UP and Bihar? Where does that leave us?'[35]

The Lucknow tragedy became a metaphor for the hollowness of the India Shining slogan: the promised world of a digital economy and showy double-digit GDP growth and globalizing businesses sat in cruel contrast to the skinny, sunburnt dead bodies lying in the hot dust of a ramshackle park, where bedraggled women and children had died in pursuit of a single cheap sari.

As Vajpayee had anticipated, reports began to come in that the Gujarat riots had taken their toll on the BJP's prospects. Muslims across Uttar Pradesh mobilized against the BJP and in cosmopolitan urban areas, there was growing revulsion over the riots. Vajpayee had never hidden his dislike of the Narendra Modi brand of aggressive Hindutva, even though he had never acted against it. The 2002 Gujarat riots had shaken him and after visiting riot victims' camps in Ahmedabad, he had pointedly remarked about the need for Chief Minister Modi's government to live up to its 'rajdharma', or ideal of impartiality. He had wanted to dismiss Modi after the riots but the majority in the party stood firmly with the Gujarat strongman. Rather than confront his party colleagues, Vajpayee chose to stay silent. It was a crucial failure, one that haunted him through the campaign. 'If Vajpayee had been able to dismiss Modi as Gujarat chief minister in 2002, his leadership would have been unassailable and we would have won . . .' says Yashwant Sinha. 'Shining India collapsed not because of the fault of the Central government but the particular fault of Vajpayee that he did not assert himself and get rid of Modi.'[36]

When the results came out, it was clear that the BJP lost most urban seats, places where voters would have seen images of the Gujarat pogroms, India's first televised riots. The middle and upper classes in urban areas turned away from the BJP, put off by the communal face of Vajpayee's party.[37] Modi had campaigned robustly, but his presence yielded little result. The BJP's seats declined sharply in Modi-led Gujarat, where there was a perceptible anti-BJP mood, and voters delivered a firm rebuff to Modi's strident pitch. In 2004, the Congress won as many as 12 seats in Gujarat – its highest since 1991.

Even in Andhra Pradesh, where Chandrababu Naidu had been certain of victory, things began to go awry. After having pushed for early polls, Naidu began to fall behind. Instead, the Congress leader Y.S. Rajashekhar Reddy's padayatra surged through the state, gathering huge crowds. When the election results were declared, Naidu's Telugu Desam Party (TDP) – the Vajpayee alliance's crucial ally – slumped to just five seats out of 42. The Congress alliance dominated Andhra Pradesh with 34 seats, the Congress itself winning 29. The BJP drew a blank.

Tamil Nadu was a disaster too. On the advice of sangh ideologues like S. Gurumurthy who insisted that an alliance with the All India Anna Dravida Munnetra Kazhagam (AIADMK) would mop up at least 20 seats in the state, Advani and Venkaiah Naidu had persuaded the BJP to break its alliance with the DMK and move closer to Jayalalithaa's AIADMK. While the AIADMK was wooing the BJP, the DMK withdrew its support to Vajpayee. 'I still hold Vajpayee in high esteem,' said DMK supremo M. Karunanidhi, Vajpayee's old friend, emphasizing the good-man-in-the-bad-party line, 'we have no difference of opinion with him.'[38] Rich in overconfidence, the BJP failed to read the signs. Weak, badly attended rallies across the state forced the BJP to scale down its expectations, but nothing prepared Vajpayee for the final result: DMK chief Karunanidhi delivered Tamil Nadu to the Congress. The BJP alliance got nothing. Again, zero. If Naidu had delivered in Andhra Pradesh and if the BJP had not ditched the DMK, it is possible Vajpayee may have returned as prime minister.

Yet it wasn't just Andhra Pradesh and Tamil Nadu, even in Uttar Pradesh, the karmabhoomi of the leader himself, astoundingly enough, the BJP failed. The party's vote bank split. 'Brand Atal' flopped. And India Shining bit the dust. Factional fights and a four-cornered contest brought the BJP down. The four-way fight between the BJP, Congress, Samajwadi Party (SP) and Bahujan Samaj Party (BSP) fractured the vote and did not benefit the ruling party. Vajpayee's party got a devastatingly low tally of 10 seats, plummeting from 29 in 1999, its worst performance in recent years. Embarrassingly, BJP state stalwarts were dumped. BJP state chief Vinay Katiyar was flung out of Lakhimpur Kheri. Murli Manohar Joshi was tossed out from the high-prestige seat of Allahabad, which he had won three times since 1996. The BJP vote bank could not withstand a rising BSP, which, increasingly cultivating a 'savarna' image, snatched away Brahmin votes. The saffron party's efforts to win over Muslims resoundingly failed. The SP, led by Mulayam Singh Yadav, came in first in Uttar Pradesh, Mayawati came second and the BJP was a distant third, with the Congress one seat behind, at 9. Vajpayee won his own seat – Lucknow – handsomely but it was of little consequence given the drastic losses in the state.

Overall, it was like a massacre. Vajpayee's top ministers were vanquished. In fact, as many as twenty-five ministers were defeated. The veteran petroleum minister Ram Naik, winner of five successive Lok Sabha elections, was ignominiously worsted in the Mumbai North seat by a raw newbie, the film actor with the 'Virar ka chhokra' image, Govinda. 'I'm shocked, it was totally unexpected,' seventy-year-old Naik gasped to journalists.[39] Foreign minister Yashwant Sinha was thrown out of his seat, Hazaribagh. 'It was humiliating,' recalls Sinha, 'a shock from which I have never recovered.'[40] In Delhi the Congress felled the BJP in 6 out of 7 seats.

~

A few days after the results, Vajpayee and his entourage travelled to his holiday home, the place he called his 'second home' in Manali, where they went almost every year. This was a red-roofed brick-and-stone bungalow set amid lawns and trees, its walkways lined with rows of flowering plants. It was situated in a village called Prini, next to the Holiday Inn there.

Sitting in the lawns of his Prini bungalow, as birds chirruped around him, the former prime minister, clad in brown kurta and pyjama, delivered a bouncer. He told an interviewer: 'We did not imagine the Opposition would use the Gujarat tragedy in the way it did, the way films and cassettes were circulated. *Modi ko nahin hatane se humein nuksan hua, Gujarat dango se humein nuksan hua*. I wanted to remove Modi, *agar mukhya mantri badle jaate toh zyada achcha hota*.'[41] If he had been able to force the resignation of Modi after the riots, the BJP would have won the election, concluded Vajpayee, going on to add that at the party's executive meeting later in Mumbai there would be a debate on Modi's future. It was the mascot's last growl. With his remaining strength he spoke plainly.

But the sangh was in no mood to listen, infuriated as it was by the results and feverish for vengeance against the heretic Vajpayee, the 'half Congressman' who had driven them to a terrible loss through his secular, liberal line, forsaking ideological Hindutva. Many in the sangh were coming around to the view that Modi, not Vajpayee, was the future. 'Our cadres and core voters developed a disinterest in this election,' complained RSS spokesperson Ram Madhav. 'There was a perception of dilution of ideology.'[42] 'The BJP betrayed the Hindus. The Hindus have punished them,' blustered VHP leader Pravin Togadia.[43] Sangh wrath was also directed at Advani, who was seen as someone who did not stand up for Hindutva ideology, but the main target was Vajpayee. 'We had a vyakti [personality] in Vajpayee,' was the common refrain among influential members of the sangh, 'but he strayed from our vichardhaara [ideology]. This cost us the election.'[44]

In this gathering storm over his leadership, Vajpayee's Manali interview hit the BJP hard. Here was Vajpayee openly declaring that the party's failure to act against the Gujarat riots and inability to force the resignation of Gujarat Chief Minister Narendra Modi had cost it the general election. Advani stayed silent, but RSS chief K.S. Sudarshan, Vajpayee's long-time bête noire, stormed into the fray to take up for his favourite, Modi. There is no link between the 2002 Gujarat riots and the election results, fulminated Sudarshan. If there was such a link, why would the BJP have won the assembly elections in Madhya Pradesh, Rajasthan and Chhattisgarh in 2003, he demanded.

After Vajpayee's bombshell interview, party leaders hurriedly assembled in Delhi. Emerging from the meeting, BJP president Venkaiah Naidu hurled a public snub at Vajpayee, declaring to the press, 'There is no proposal to change the BJP government in Gujarat nor will this issue be on the agenda in the national executive in Mumbai.'[45] Once again, far away in his mountain fastness, the weakening patriarch hit back. Reacting to Naidu's snub, he again joined issue with his party: 'We are a party of debate. We have never been afraid of debate, we debate, whether we win or lose.'[46]

By the time he returned to Delhi, however, a somewhat chastened Vajpayee said, '*Modi ko hataane ka sawaal purana ho chuka hai, khatam ho chuka hai* [The issue of Modi's removal is now a thing of the past].' There was no debate on Modi at the party executive meeting in June 2004, held in Mumbai. And in a clear signal to a by now marginalized Vajpayee, Naidu asserted three times that the BJP was not a party based on a single personality. When journalists asked Vajpayee for a response, he simply put a finger to his lips, signalling 'no comment'. At a public meeting in the city, Vajpayee was greeted with that familiar but now weak cheer, '*Abki bari Atal Bihari*'. He responded instantly in Marathi: '*Ata nako bari, pushakal jhale* [Not again, I have had enough].'[47] A year later, also in Mumbai, Vajpayee announced that he was leaving active politics and the era of Vajpayee came to an abrupt and sudden end. If the 1962 war was a body blow to Nehru, the 2004 election broke Vajpayee and destroyed Vajpayeeism.

~

In the summer of 2005, Ghatate went to have a quiet lunch with Vajpayee in his new home in 6A Krishna Menon Marg. He found his old friend in a reflective, pensive mood. By now Narendra Modi was the rising star of the BJP, the unquestioned leader in Gujarat, and Advani was a pale shadow of himself. Modi's Gujarat success was the talk of the party. A few weeks ago, RSS chief K.S. Sudarshan had lambasted the BJP's seniors. Vajpayee was not among India's best prime ministers, said Sudarshan, and Vajpayee and Advani should now step aside and make way for newer, younger leaders.[48]

'Many new people are coming up. The party is different, perhaps I am also different,' Vajpayee said. He mentioned that a BJP leader was coming to see him. When Ghatate asked why he was coming, Vajpayee smiled and said, 'He must be coming because of *kuch kaam* [some work]. Not everyone is like you who comes to see me without any reasons.' On the recent sudden death of former foreign secretary and adviser to Manmohan Singh, J.N. Dixit, Vajpayee said, 'He was a very nice man. But the problem with him was that he was very hard-working and also used to worry about the consequences.' He then said with a mischievous smile, 'Brajesh [Mishra, who was Vajpayee's principal secretary and National Security Adviser] also used to work very hard. But I used to worry about the consequences.' Later that year, Vajpayee announced his retirement from public life.[49]

In December 2005, the BJP celebrated its silver jubilee, the twenty-fifth year of existence, at a function in Mumbai. Organized by Pramod Mahajan, it was a gigantic gathering, complete with live webcasts, film shows and a play which featured horses and elephants. Giant speakers pumped out thumping music. Lotus flowers and Bollywood-style pillars decorated the grounds. On-stage, a giant lotus-shaped structure was created, out of which stepped senior BJP leaders, among them Vajpayee. He looked wan, his shoulders stooped and his walk faltering. The curtain was poised to fall.

He began his short speech. He said he was like the sage Parashuram. Parashuram had become angry at the breaking of the Shiv Dhanush and wanted to have his revenge. But when he realized that it was broken by none other than Lord Ram who was about to be king, the once angry sage happily participated in the coronation of the god-king. I am retiring from active politics, bowing out, Vajpayee hinted, with the telling last line that henceforth Advani and Pramod Mahajan would be the 'Ram and Lakshman of the BJP'. The master of talking in riddles took his curtain call, leaving an unspoken question hanging before his audience: I leave, but which way will you, my party, turn? Down my smooth tarmac road towards the twenty-first century, or back down that jagged track lined with mobs and mandirs?

On-stage, the gathered BJP leaders looked shell-shocked. Pramod Mahajan beamed in glee at being publicly named and ranked alongside Advani by Vajpayee, and stuck out his tongue. Sushma Swaraj stood stony-faced, while Arun Jaitley looked dumbstruck. Advani, at this time facing RSS rage over his recent praising of Pakistan founder Muhammad Ali Jinnah, remained impassive, his face betraying no emotion at being ranked alongside the younger Mahajan. Party workers shook their heads, asking each other exactly what had just been said. The meeting was suddenly plunged into disarray, everyone so confused that the party even forgot to sing the customary national anthem. By the time the crowd had gathered its wits and looked towards the dais again, Vajpayee had gone. 'Only Vajpayee could think of announcing his retirement in this dramatic way,' chuckled Ghatate. 'He was a maestro who knew how to run politics.' Yet, as Vajpayee quit, the BJP floundered in a leadership and ideological crisis. Those who blamed the loss of 2004 on Vajpayee's deviation from ideological Hindutva were forced to admit that by the end of 2005 it was their 'secular' alliance partner, Nitish Kumar and his Janata Dal (United) (JD(U)), who had brought a thumping victory to the NDA in Bihar. The question therefore was still open: to embrace or abandon the secular Vajpayee line?

'A chapter of politics has closed,' Vajpayee had said in his Manali interview, 'we will have to see what the next chapter will be.' In the months after his dramatic resignation, he would occasionally be spotted in Parliament, walking in with a stick and quietly taking a seat behind the first row. In December 2005, at a function in Parliament to commemorate the fourth anniversary of the 2001 attack on Parliament, Pranab Mukherjee, Karan Singh and Shivraj Patil lined up to help him as he stumbled slowly forward with his stick. In 2006 Vajpayee was invited as chief guest to Advani's residence to a showing of two videos of two 'Bharat Suraksha Yatras' undertaken by Advani and Rajnath Singh that year. But after watching the first video of Advani's yatra, Vajpayee pleaded ill health and left, later apologizing to Rajnath Singh. By 2006 he was seen in Parliament only rarely.

~

On 22 July 2008, the Manmohan Singh–led UPA faced a trust vote. That morning an ambulance rolled slowly up to Parliament. It stopped at the porch. Attendants emerged, and lifted an MP on to a wheelchair. Atal Bihari Vajpayee was being brought to the House to vote. He was wheeled into the inner lobby of Parliament, no longer able to walk. The lion of the Lok Sabha sat hunched alone and apart from the others in his wheelchair, as the House proceeded noisily.

Lobby clerks clustered around. They brought him a sheet of paper. A security official held up his hand as he tick-marked his vote. In the House, the votes were counted. The UPA survived. The Lok Sabha erupted in high-pitched pandemonium. Outside, Vajpayee was wheeled out and helped back into the ambulance.

'It was a shock to see him in the condition he was in that day,' recalls former Lok Sabha Secretary General P.D.T. Achary. 'What a Parliamentarian he was. What speeches. Everyone would troop into the House just to listen to him. Every word hit like a thunderbolt.'[50] Speaking in poetic Hindi, tossing his head from side to side, pausing, gesticulating, suddenly attacking, suddenly comical, Vajpayee cast a spell over his listeners.

That day in July 2008, Vajpayee left Parliament forever, his home for over four decades. He left the chamber where his political career had taken off, where Vajpayee the politician was born, where he had so often risen to his feet and enthralled the House with his oratorical wizardry. He left Central Hall where he had plotted and gossiped.

Moderate-pluralist? Hindu nationalist? Poet-intellectual? Compromiser with extremists? All of those, but above all he was an ambitious politician to whom politics was everything. Politics was poetry, politics was an exhilarating joust, politics was life itself; without politics, his mind and body both gave way. Shadows fell across the sunlit road. Atal Bihari Vajpayee drove away from Parliament for the last time, from the House where it all began.

2

The Boy from Gwalior: 1924–1957

A poem for Vajpayee:

> He was his father's son, powered by word and rhyme
> Thinking: there must be a bigger world than this.
> Arya Samaj, RSS, socialism, Hinduism:
> Fitting platforms for a star biding his time.

~

Gwalior in Madhya Pradesh nestles in the shadow of the Gwalior fort, which looms majestically over the city from its hilltop perch. The fort dominates the skyline, just as the presence of the city's princely family – the Scindias of Gwalior – hovers over the clamorous urban centre. Gwalior was once a wealthy, important state and an administrative, religious and cultural centre, one of just five princely states granted a twenty-one-gun salute by the British Raj.

The Scindia princes who ruled Gwalior from the early eighteenth century were loyalists of the Raj. A poem from the 1940s describes how '*angrezon ke mitra Scindia ney, chhodi rajdhani thi . . . khoob ladi mardani woh toh Jhansi wali Rani thi*',[1] or how the Scindias sided with the Raj and betrayed the Rani of Jhansi, the warrior queen who died fighting the British during the 1857 uprising. Yet the Scindias were enlightened kings, promoting industry, endowing educational institutions and building roads and irrigation canals. The last maharaja of Gwalior was the racehorse-owning, polo-patronizing anglophile 'George' Jiwajirao Rao, calling himself George after Britain's King George V. Jiwajirao acceded to the Indian Union at Independence. In the decades after Independence, the royal privileges of the House of Scindia transmutated into power through electoral politics. Jiwajirao's wife Rajmata Vijaya Raje Scindia and three of their children went on to contest and win elections and the Scindia influence over the politics of the entire Gwalior region soon became formidable.

On 25 December 1924,[2] a boy was born in Gwalior, very far away from the maharajas' world of polo-playing aristocratic privilege. But rising from the crowded by-lanes under the great fort, he would journey to much greater heights of power than the maharajas who once ruled over him.

Destiny handed him a piquant birthdate. He grew up to embrace Hindu nationalist politics, but on his birthday every year – 25 December or Christmas Day – the sounds of carols, hymns and church bells would ring out everywhere, as if fate was sending him an annual reminder of the many religions that made up his world, and of India's long traditions of spiritual coexistence.

In the crowded Shinde ki Chhawani area near the Kamal Singh ka Bagh locality, down a narrow gali, was a small double-storeyed house. Here lived a Kanyakubj Brahmin family, the family of schoolmaster Krishna Bihari Vajpayee, and it was here that his youngest son, Atal Bihari Vajpayee, was born. It was a bookish, scholarly household which cherished learning and was suffused with quiet sanatani Hindu beliefs. Pandit Krishna Bihari was a poet and schoolteacher, and his father, Shyam Lal Vajpayee, was a Sanskrit scholar and a fount of Sanskrit and Hindi couplets, which he would recite regularly, drawing out their contemporary relevance. Pandit Shyam Lal set strict tests for his grandchildren on Tulsidas's *Ramcharitamanas* and quizzed them intensively on its details. Poetry came to me as an inheritance, the poet-prime minister would often say, I write poetry to make sense of the world and to find strength.

The family's ancestral home was in Bateshwar, in the Agra district of Uttar Pradesh, popularly called 'Braj ki Kashi', wafted by cool breezes off the Yamuna. Bateshwar gets its name from Bateshwar Nath, or Shiva. Legend has it that Shiva, whenever he was not in the mountains, came to sit under the great banyan or 'bat' tree in Bateshwar to meditate. One hundred and one mandirs once lined the river here, and every evening after the aarti, flag-festooned lanes still ring with the sounds of temple bells, chants and conch shells, as if in perpetual welcome to the wandering divine. On his birthday in 1994, Vajpayee wrote a poem on Bateshwar:

The Yamuna's bank, mounds of sand,
On stilts a home of grass and thatch,
A courtyard swept with cow dung.
Sounds of bells, the tulsi patch,
On mother's tongue, the nectar of the Ramayana's lines.[3]

Bateshwar was scenic and transcendental, yet held little future prospects for a growing family. Already as a young man Krishna Bihari, very keen to study English, had journeyed out of Bateshwar to Agra and Etawah. With the promise of a job in Gwalior state he was advised by his father to settle in Gwalior, where his family might find brighter futures. Krishna Bihari moved with his wife, Krishna Devi, to Gwalior – in keeping with the family's pious heritage, taking with them a family idol of Shiva – where he soon got a job as a teacher in a local school, and quickly became known for his poetic compositions. Krishna Bihari was later promoted as district inspector of schools in the Gwalior Department of Education. Krishna Devi shared her husband's passion for educating their children, and was keen that her brood study as hard as they could. She often despaired of her naughty youngest son, whom she called 'Atalla', for he was forever running off to play marbles (kanche) or to help himself to laddoos from sweet shops in Naya Bazar – laddoos from the famous Bahadura Sweets here would remain a lifelong favourite – or snack on Gwalior chivda and jalebi or hang out with friends at the Gwalior mela.

Atal Bihari had three older brothers, Avadh Bihari, Sada Bihari and Prem Bihari; two older sisters, Vimla and Kamla; and a younger sister, Urmila. In a black-and-white group photo with his siblings, taken in later years, Vajpayee stands out as the tallest, most striking and self-confident. He played kabaddi and hockey, raced his bicycle, took part in poetry recitals, competitions and cultural shows and competed fiercely in students' union elections. And he was his father's favourite. 'I will make sure my Atal shines like a star one day,' Krishna Bihari told a friend.[4] He was an attractive boy, both grave and funny – with a fleshy, good-natured face, expressive eyes and a disarming manner. 'As a child we never saw him studying,' recalled his sister Vimla, 'but our father was very fond of him.'[5]

Krishna Bihari, a scholar of Sanskrit and Hindi, gained renown as one of Gwalior's best poets, writing in both Khadiboli and Brajbhasha. One of his compositions, '*Eeshwar Prarthna*', was sung at school assemblies across the state. Vajpayee barely in his teens, eagerly rushed to join his pitaji in the whirl of kavi sammelans across the region. He hero-worshipped his father and learnt techniques of poetry from him. 'Poetry was on a high beat in those days, it was not about cheap humour and cracking jokes . . . poets were bound by style and form,' he wrote.[6] He later recalled how, when his father walked with him to school, 'I would clutch my father's finger reciting poetry as we walked. My father would often stop me and correct my language and rhythm, making sure I chose the right words.'[7] The son knew he had inherited his father's talent, he knew he had the gift of the word – both spoken and written – and he was anxious to explore the heights of his poetic abilities. 'Given the literary atmosphere at home . . . I began frequenting kavi sammelans, first as a member of the audience and then as a promising young poet.'[8] One of his first compositions was on the Taj Mahal. Instead of writing yet another eulogy to the beauty of the Taj, he wrote on the exploitation of the labourers who built the monument.

Yeh Taj Mahal, Yeh Taj Mahal,
Yamuna ki roti dhar vikal,
kal kal, chal chal,
Jab roya Hindustan sakal;
Tab ban paya Taj Mahal.
Yeh Taj Mahal, Yeh Taj Mahal.

This Taj Mahal, this Taj Mahal,
Uneasy flows the Yamuna,
Murmuring, burbling,
When all of Hindustan wept,
that is when the Taj Mahal could be built.[9]

He schooled in Saraswati Shishu Mandir in Gwalior, in the Anglo Vernacular Middle [AVM] School in Barnagar, Ujjain, and in Gorkhi Mahavidyalaya in Gwalior, where school records still show his name and his roll number, 101. As an educationist himself, Krishna Bihari had high expectations of his youngest son and asked his teachers to mark Vajpayee more strictly.[10] In fact, Krishna Bihari served as headmaster for a while in the AVM School when Vajpayee was a student there. In school in 1934, Vajpayee experienced a 'life-changing moment' when at a baal sabha he stood up to speak in a debate on the 'Development of railway lines laid down in India by the British', which he had memorized: he suddenly found himself tongue-tied. He could not finish his speech, he began to stammer and his classmates booed him mercilessly. 'I was afraid, I had not prepared properly, I was stammering and the speech was discontinued midway. That was when I learnt a lesson that changed my life,' he recalled at a Lok Sabha election rally in 1996. 'I took a pledge: never rote-learn a speech.'[11] It was a lesson learnt to superb effect. All his life he would prepare his speeches meticulously and organize them in his head, but never memorize them. He would keep his rich bank of folklore, mythological tales, jokes and political barbs at hand, to deploy whenever the audience mood was right. This expert mix of the prepared and the impromptu would captivate his listeners from Parliament to public rally grounds, his oratorical sorcery bringing him unforeseen rewards.

He was an adventurous adolescent, keen on new experiences beyond the cramped little lane in Shinde ki Chhawani. He sought out the company of like-minded people, gravitating towards platforms where he would get a chance at public speaking. At thirteen he joined the Arya Kumar Sabha or the youth wing of the Arya Samaj, regularly attending its weekly satsangs, and went on to become its general secretary in 1944. The Arya Samaj, with its message of reform and its interrogation of Hinduism's orthodoxies, aiming for a return to Vedic purity, appealed to his rebellious and irreverent spirit. Should traditions remain stagnant? Should rituals not be questioned? He would ask these questions all his life.

After school Vajpayee went on to Victoria College (now Maharani Laxmi Bai College) in Gwalior, where he graduated with a BA in English, Hindi and Sanskrit. It was here in Victoria College that he met and became deeply attracted to a fellow student, Rajkumari Haksar. He was a friend of her brother's and a frequent visitor to the Haksar Haveli – the family home of the Haksars, a Kashmiri Pandit clan settled in Gwalior. In his provincial, overwhelmingly male world, he had never met such an articulate young woman, unafraid to voice her views. A quiet romance blossomed between the handsome Atal and the vivacious Rajkumari, but their paths diverged as he was swept up in an all-consuming involvement with political activism and she moved to Delhi with her parents.

Through the adrenalin-charged 1940s, the young and exuberant

Vajpayee threw himself into political as well as poetic and literary activity. A regular at RSS shakhas since school, he completed three years of the RSS's OTC or Officer Training Camp course in Gwalior, Lucknow and Nagpur between 1941 and 1944, becoming an RSS preacher (vistarak) by 1946. In these years he also headed the Arya Kumar Sabha, joined and led the Gwalior Students Federation and participated in scores of poetry recitals and competitions. In all this hectic activity, he drifted away from the girl he loved.

Vajpayee and Rajkumari would not meet again until Rajkumari was already married and living in Delhi with her husband, when she re-entered his life, their love story continuing until the end of their days, as the later chapters in this book narrate.

In college in the roiling tumult of the pre-Independence years, he became drawn to the early brahmachari pracharaks (celibate preachers) of the RSS, seeing them as selfless, family-less, asset-less, penurious strivers for the Hindu cause. His personal choices were unconventional and he refused all offers of marriage placed before him by his parents. 'However hard she tried, Ma [Vajpayee's mother] could not persuade Atal to get married,' Vimla would recall.[12]

'Poetry and politics rarely go together,' wrote Vajpayee,[13] but in his own life and career they intermingled with ease, and he revelled in both. The tone was set in college, when he eagerly participated in poetry competitions and stood for student elections. In Victoria College, contesting in student union elections against a wealthy rival, he used wordplay to win support and outwit his opponent. The adversary's name was Chandrasen, so playing on his name, Vajpayee cried, '*Chandi ke chand tukdo ke liye apna amulya vote mat becho* [Don't waste your priceless vote hoping for scraps from a rich man].'

'I won and was elected to the post of president,' he said proudly, six decades later. Political competition and poetic sparring became intertwined in his persona. Visiting another college for a poetry competition, he dragged a friend into a college bathroom for a rehearsal and began to declaim so captivatingly that a crowd gathered outside and began to clap.[14]

After he had graduated from Victoria College, he was uncertain about his future and worried about how he would finance his post-graduate studies. 'I became worried about my future at this time,' he recalled in an article.[15] 'It was 1945–46. My father had retired from government service. My sisters were of marriageable age. Dowry had assumed the shape of a curse. From where would I find the resources for a post-graduate degree?' A decade later, the memory of his family's torments over dowry would echo in one of his Parliament speeches when he lashed out against 'this vicious custom which has distorted our culture down the ages'.[16]

Luckily, help was at hand from the Gwalior 'mahal'. Maharaja Jiwajirao, who knew Vajpayee's poet-father and his talented son and had heard of the family's straitened circumstances, offered him a scholarship of Rs 75 a month. The scholarship was enormously welcome, and 'the wrinkles of tension on father's face gradually started to disappear and the family heaved a sigh of relief, and I, too, took a plunge in happy dreams of the future'.[17] For Vajpayee, the Gwalior princely family would remain an object of lifelong protective respect; he would often reverentially touch Vijaya Raje Scindia's feet even when she later became his party colleague in the BJP. When they journeyed together by train, he would remain standing until Vijaya Raje had taken her seat.

In the 1940s, college graduates from Gwalior aspiring for a post-graduate degree mostly sought admission in the Dayanand Anglo-Vedic [DAV] College in Kanpur as there were no postgraduate institutions in Gwalior. Vajpayee's brother Prem Bihari was already a law student at DAV College, and off went Vajpayee too to Kanpur. To his great surprise he found he had an unlikely batchmate.

After Vajpayee got his scholarship, the retired Krishna Bihari suddenly announced that he too would be joining the same college, to pursue his long-standing interest in law. He enrolled in the LLB course. 'It was an unusual incident. Father's decision put all of us in a wonder,' recalled Vajpayee.[18]

He wrote on the incredulity of the situation and the manner in which professors and students would laugh and question them about each other, with some self-mockery. 'Have you ever seen or heard of a college where both father and son studied together, and that too even in the same class?' he would later write.[19] 'My father was above 50. With his white hair and walking stick, the principal virtually jumped out of his chair when he came to know the elderly gentleman had come to enrol . . . [but] The situation was posing a problem for both of us, and it was decided that my father will remain in one section while I will move to another . . . In the hostel where the father and son lived together, crowds of students would turn up just to see us,' Vajpayee wrote. The intriguing arrangement reveals the closeness that the father and son shared. Both equally erudite, their cerebral relationship born during shared poetic adventures was layered with shades of an intimate competitiveness. Father and son graduated in the same year, 1947, Vajpayee passing his MA with a third division and Krishna Bihari clearing the LLB examination with a second division.[20]

The Vajpayees of Gwalior, like thousands of middle-class families across India, prized a good education above all; sons were pushed to higher studies in the hope of social, personal and material advancement. The father would not only push his son, but would also thirstily participate in the pursuit of education himself, old man and youth together rowing into wider waters that one day would bear the son far away, with the father as travelling companion for at least some part of the journey. An early photo shows the child Atal seated at the feet of Krishna Bihari, the father's powerful personality looming over the boy.

There were paternal high expectations on one side and there was some filial rebelliousness on the other. Vajpayee idolized Krishna Bihari, and his self-image was that of his father's epigone, yet he made life choices of which his father didn't approve. In 1997 when he established a trust for a free library and a computer training centre for children in Krishna Bihari's name, he said, I am only a pocket edition of my father. 'Pitaji was a parakrami purush [a courageous man],' he recalled in an interview in later years.[21] He described his father's death as the saddest day of his life and often spoke rather wistfully that, entranced as he was by politics, he grew distant from his father's world of books and the pursuit of knowledge. 'In poetry one communicates primarily with oneself,' he wrote, 'in politics there is always the subtle danger of ignoring the self in the process of communicating regularly with some mass gathering.'[22] After his MA, Vajpayee embarked on an LLB course, but partly because he had not achieved spectacular academic distinction, and mostly because he was by now completely caught up in the political storm around him, he dropped out and became a full-time RSS worker.

This was the time of azadi, of struggles for freedom and liberty. Universities and colleges had become pulsating battlegrounds of political debate – in his words, they had become 'akharas' (wrestling arenas). An electrifying tension was in the air. Krishna Bihari had hoped his 'shining star' and favourite son would embark on a career in law or government service. But Vajpayee would choose to go down a road very different from what his father wished for him. 'Politics has its own honoured place in a nation's life, I have no regrets that it became the main calling in my life,' he wrote.[23]

~

The 1930s and 1940s were a period of intense nationalist ferment and social upheaval. The freedom struggle, led by Mahatma Gandhi, engulfed India. The Congress was increasingly poised in confrontation with the steadily growing power of the All-India Muslim League, led by Muhammad Ali Jinnah. Communal divisions were building up, and the seeds of Partition were being sowed. The Hindu Mahasabha began to grow more influential, its president Vinayak Damodar Savarkar declaring in 1938: 'We Hindus are a nation by ourselves . . . Hindu nationalists should not at all be apologetic to being called

Hindu communalists.' Paramilitary outfits sprang to life on both sides of the religious divide: the Khaksars were founded in 1931 as a group of Punjabi Muslims and before that, in 1925, a Nagpur doctor, Keshav Baliram Hedgewar, founded the organization that would be Vajpayee's cocoon and platform, and the wind beneath his wings: the Hindu nationalist Rashtriya Swayamsevak Sangh.

By 1940 the RSS had grown to almost 1,00,000 well-trained, extremely disciplined volunteers. Spreading out from its Nagpur base to Punjab, the United Provinces and to other states, it was committed to right-wing Hindu nationalism, standing in uncompromising opposition to the Muslim League and Muslim political mobilization. The outbreak of World War II plunged India into further turmoil. The Muslim League at its Lahore session, in its Lahore resolution of 23 March 1940, adopted the 'Pakistan' slogan and demanded that 'areas in which the Muslims are numerically in a majority as in the north-western and eastern zones of India should be grouped to constitute "Independent States" in which the constituent units shall be autonomous and sovereign'.[24] This was the first formal demand for 'autonomous and sovereign' Muslim territorial areas, a (possibly deliberately) ambiguous formulation without any clear mention of either Pakistan or partition. In August 1942, Gandhi gave the call for the British to quit India, calling on every Indian to 'do or die'. In the Quit India movement that followed, Congress leaders were rounded up and jailed across India, leading to a massive and spontaneous people's upsurge that coursed through India like wildfire, the movement's later stages marked by armed militancy, even as the Raj brutally cracked down.

The Quit India movement veered into Vajpayee's life in an unexpected manner, and became embarrassingly embedded in his political career. In 1942, Quit India protests began in Gwalior, some of which turned violent. Worried and disapproving that his two younger sons were a little too enthused by the anti-government agitation, Krishna Bihari sent Vajpayee, already at eighteen a member of the

RSS, and his brother Prem Bihari away from Gwalior to Bateshwar, hoping to keep them isolated from the raging civil disobedience.

In the afternoon of 27 August 1942, Vajpayee and his brother Prem Bihari were strolling in the Bateshwar market listening to folk songs or 'ala'. Suddenly, at around 2 p.m., two youths, Liladhar Bajpai (Kakua) and Shiv Kumar (Mahuan), burst upon the scene, shouting that Gandhiji and hundreds of freedom fighters had been arrested and 'here you all are listening to songs'. The music stopped. Shouts of 'Quit India' and '*Angrez, Bharat chhoro*' rang out. Galvanized, a hysterical crowd followed Liladhar to a nearby government office, the Bateshwar Forest Office, where they set upon and destroyed the building. In the crowd jostled the two Vajpayee brothers.

Days later Vajpayee signed a confessional statement dated 1 September 1942 before a magistrate, written in Urdu: 'Kakua alias Liladhar and Mahuan . . . persuaded the people to break the forest laws. Two hundred people went to the Forest Office . . . I along with my brother followed . . . I and my brother stayed below and all other people went up . . . I do not know the name of any other person, except Kakua and Mahuan, who was there.'[25] When the crowd then pushed towards the neighbouring town of Bichkoli, where another building was ransacked, Vajpayee stayed back. 'I did not render any assistance in demolishing the government building,' Vajpayee said in his statement. Within hours the police swooped down and arrested several protesters. Liladhar was convicted and sentenced to three years of rigorous imprisonment.

This rather craven confessional statement and alleged informing on Liladhar Bajpai shadowed Vajpayee all his political life. Accusations were regularly made that Vajpayee turned approver against Liladhar and helped the British colonial government send a freedom fighter to jail. Vajpayee was accused of playing a 'nefarious' and unsavoury role in betraying a nationalist to save his own cowardly skin. However, the charge of Vajpayee turning government approver is not true. His confessional statement was not used in Liladhar's trial; instead it was evidence provided by others that led to Liladhar's conviction. In 1998, when *Frontline* magazine published its investigation into Vajpayee's role in the Quit India movement, Ghatate, then Vajpayee's lawyer, initially sent a legal notice to *Frontline* and attacked the authenticity of the confessional statement (saying it wrongly records Vajpayee's father's name as 'Gauri Shankar'), but in an interview to the editor N. Ram, Vajpayee admitted that, yes, he had signed the confessional statement saying he had not played an active part in the crowd and was only a bystander.[26]

Vajpayee was not an approver, but the fact remains that Liladhar went to jail. Vajpayee got off lightly with only 23 days in custody; he did not play any role in the 1942 uprising and thus was never a freedom fighter. This was not surprising. The Golwalkar-led RSS and the Savarkar-led Hindu Mahasabha kept away from the 1942 movement. The future founder of the Jana Sangh and Hindu Mahasabha member Syama Prasad Mookerji, soon to become Vajpayee's boss, remained in his post as a Bengal minister during 1942, even as the Raj ruthlessly hunted down thousands of Indian patriots. Vajpayee remained tainted by the allegations about his role in 1942, and said in an interview six decades later, 'Ever since I've been contesting elections, 1942 has remained stuck to me, when the whole world knows that I had nothing to be ashamed of in that episode.'[27]

Though uninvolved in the freedom struggle, Vajpayee nursed a passion for political activism. The volatility of the 1940s – the decade that hurtled headlong towards India's independence as well as the biggest man-made catastrophe ever to hit the subcontinent, Partition – pushed him to a restless longing to be involved in the seismic events of the time. The RSS believed in Hindu dominance over Indian nationalism, remained anchored in the attempt to regain notions of 'ancient Hindu glory', rejected Gandhi's multi-denominational identity for India, rejected the Muslim as an equal partner, and instead placed Islam and the Muslim as the putative enemies of Bharat. This was the ideological choice that Vajpayee made early in life.

By the last years of World War II, the Muslim League had made major gains, taking advantage of the Congress absence from the scene (tens of thousands of Congress leaders and workers were jailed after 1942, and kept in prison until 1945) to form ministries in Assam, Sindh and Bengal by 1943. The Pakistan slogan began to catch on among sections of Muslims, and the Hindu Mahasabha too stepped up its mobilization campaigns. Religious enmities were fanned and boiled over, and India teetered on the edge of a volcano. Interestingly, as we have noted, Syama Prasad Mookerji had formed an alliance with the Muslim's League's Fazlul Huq in Bengal in 1941 and Mookerji served as a minister in Fazlul Huq's government in Bengal in 1941–42, showing how many intense ambitions were at play. In 1944, talks between Gandhi and Jinnah failed, the sharply bitter competition between the Congress and the League intensifying after the 1945–46 elections in which both the Congress (in general seats) and the League (in Muslim seats) did very well. Jinnah remained insistent on his demand for Pakistan, and on 16 August 1946 the Muslim League gave the call for 'Direct Action' to be undertaken by the 'Muslim nation' to achieve a separate Muslim homeland. Almost immediately, massive, unprecedented and unstoppable riots erupted from Bengal to the United Provinces to Punjab and across North India, continuing into 1947 – culminating in a communal cataclysm that tore India apart. 'A madness has seized the people,' cried Nehru agitatedly.

The 'high-level bargain'[28] by which the Congress quickly gained power and agreed to a division of India on religious lines was unacceptable to an anguished Gandhi. With a small group of companions, the seventy-seven-year-old moral titan, the lifelong disdainer of conventional political power, trudged, with inspiring courage, through the riot-torn villages of Noakhali and then through the slums of Calcutta and Delhi, awakening brotherhood and humanity between mobs bent on slaughtering each other, going on fasts for peace, declaring, 'I want to fight it out with my life. I would never allow the Muslims to crawl on the streets of India. They must walk with self-respect.'[29] January 1947 in Noakhali was called Gandhi's finest hour but the Mahatma's heroic appeals fell on deaf years. A year later he would be shot dead by the Hindu fanatic Nathuram Godse. By 1947, India was independent, but it was partitioned, with Pakistan born amid a religious holocaust in which over a million died.

These were the agitated times, filled with the mayhem of communal hatred, in which Atal Bihari Vajpayee grew to manhood, the religious infernos of the 1940s propelling him towards his own particular brand of trenchant nationalism. Colossal transformations had juddered through India since his birth. A colonized country had wrested independence, in the process opening raw religious wounds. At Independence in 1947, Vajpayee was twenty-three years old and a full-time RSS pracharak. 'I still remember the celebration of Independence Day,' he wrote. 'It was a strange coincidence of agony and ecstasy for me. We were ecstatic that 1000 years of foreign rule had ended, and agonized due to the division of the motherland.'[30]

The religious wars of his youth pushed him towards fiery communal Hindu politics. Joining the RSS was almost an act of rebellion against the gentler Gandhian dialogic politics of satyagraha and non-violence. His oft-repeated line in later years 'India cannot be secular by encouraging Muslim communalism . . . we can't light the fires of communalism on one side and expect communal calm on the other' was a lifelong conviction born of the uproar of Partition years.[31] The provincial hotbloods of Vajpayee's generation, steeped in the little traditions of the Hindus in the Hindi belt, the devotional poetry, the family shrines and community temples, were intensely conscious of their social distance from Oxbridge-educated Congress leaders like Nehru and the Presidency-town English-speaking elites. Hindu nationalists were enraged by Partition and the Mahatma's repeated magnanimity towards Jinnah. To Hindu radical youth, the fire-and-brimstone slogans of the militant nationalist Bal Gangadhar Tilak ('Swaraj is my birthright and I shall have it') or of Subhas Chandra Bose ('Give me blood, and I shall give you freedom') held out more seductive hopes of revolution and, if necessary, mortal combat for the motherland. Bose was a committed opponent of Hindu nationalism and a believer in inter-community ties, yet his version of forceful, manly nationalism appealed to ardent RSS youths. The rigid Hindu communalism of the RSS variety was spreading fast, not just as a reaction to the Muslim League and Partition, but as a way of expressing militant worship of the fledgling nation against its enemies, the Raj, the League and westernized elites.

'Those were days of heady nationalism,' recalls Murli Manohar Joshi, who, although a decade younger than Vajpayee, first met him when they were both new recruits in the RSS. 'We gravitated towards the RSS because of its promise of strength, its camaraderie, its character-building.' Did the anti-Muslim aspects of the organization influence them? 'It was a different time. We cannot judge everything from the position of today. We believed in the concept of the Indic civilization, that all those who lived in India were Hindus, as a civilizational term.'[32]

Vajpayee was a third-generation poet and a first-generation Hindu nationalist. There is no evidence to show that either Krishna Bihari or Shyam Lal Bihari was involved in Hindu politics. Krishna Bihari was in government service in a loyalist princely state; he disliked the RSS and disapproved of Vajpayee's involvement in it. 'My father was not attached to the RSS,' Vajpayee notes.[33] He, on the other hand, was attracted to the Hindutva cause from adolescence and was in high school when he composed and delivered one of his first poems at an RSS shakha in Gwalior, belting out in loud emotional tones: '*Hindu tan man, Hindu jeevan, rag rag Hindu mera parichay . . . Hindu tan man, Hindu jeevan* [My body and soul are Hindu, my life is Hindu, my entire being is Hindu, Hindu is my identity].' 'I wrote this poem when I was in the tenth class,' he recalled in his article 'The Sangh Is My Soul'. 'And I still stand by my words.'

He was a passionate Hindu nationalist, but there was little about him that was austere or orthodox or dogmatic. His poems and speeches struck forceful notes, yet at the same time they are qualitatively different from Savarkar's fierce drive for a Hindu Rashtra. Savarkar wrote:

> The qualities of god permeate into his worshipper. Whilst considering the cow to be divine and worshipping her, the entire Hindu nation became docile like a cow. It started eating grass. If we are now to found a nation on the basis of an animal, let that animal be a lion. Using its sharp claws in one leap, the lion fatally knocks and wounds the heads of wild mammoths. We need to worship such a Narsinha.[34]

The atheist Savarkar's image of Hindutva as a fearsome lion with sharp claws, ready to strike its enemies, doesn't quite echo in any of Vajpayee's early writings or speeches. In his '*Hindu Rag Rag*' poem, he writes: '*maine dikhlaya Hindu marg, maine sikhlaya brahmagyan, mere vedo ka gyan amar, mere vedo ki jyoti prakhar* [I showed the Hindu path, I learnt the knowledge of the universe, the eternal knowledge of the Vedas, the strong light of the Vedas].' Savarkar popularized the ideology that Vajpayee would uphold all his life, and Vajpayee would often stand forth as a Hindu hardliner. His admiration for Savarkar was flamboyantly displayed in a famous Pune speech when he gushed emotionally: '*Savarkar mane tej . . . tyaag . . . tap . . . tatva . . . tark . . . tarunya . . . teer . . . talwar* [Savarkar means energy . . . sacrifice . . . fire . . . essence . . . argument . . . empathy . . . arrow . . . sword].'[35]

He even attempted to translate some of Savarkar's poems into Hindi, yet his own expressions of Hinduism in poetry and writings are cultural and traditionalist rather than livid or fiery. Savarkar was a fervent revolutionary and militant Hindu supremacist; Vajpayee was a literary and carefully ambiguous Hindu nationalist with a morally ambivalent approach. 'Hinduism to me is the highest manifestation of humanism, there is no single holy book. Instead Hindu society creates the Hindu religion, which is why Hindu philosophies have endured down the ages.'[36] He regarded Hinduism as unchallengeably dominant, as the repository of Indianness, and to him, the 'Hindu was the child of Bharat'.[37] Like all RSS men he had a deep-seated notion that India was not the Muslim's first love, the way it was for the Hindu. Yet Vajpayee's Hindutva was located in an Arya Samaji Hindu purism and social reformism, and over the years would be further tempered by parliamentary politics. What drew him to the RSS at the outset was the camaraderie of young men, the promise of opportunities galore and the encouragement of soft-spoken, intense-eyed pracharaks like U.K. 'Babasaheb' Apte, one of Hedgewar's key aides, to whom he was drawn to from the start. He loved the attention the RSS gave him. 'Poetry drew him to his involvement in the RSS,' recalls Joshi, 'and in the RSS he was noticed because of his ability to speak and recite.'[38]

~

Back in 1939, when Vajpayee was a fifteen-year-old regular at the Sunday morning satsangs of the Arya Kumar Sabha, a visitor arrived in town. He came from Nagpur. He was the spartan and unassuming Narayanrao Vishwanath Tarte, one of the first pracharaks of the RSS, who would introduce Vajpayee to the RSS.[39] The local boys called him 'mamu' (uncle). 'What I am today is the making of Shri Tarte,' Vajpayee wrote in 1995. 'Next to him, I was inspired by Deendayal Upadhyaya and Bhaurao Deoras [brother of the future sarsanghchalak Balasaheb Deoras].'[40]

In 1940, when the RSS founder K.B. Hedgewar died, leadership of the RSS passed to Madhav Sadashiv Golwalkar. Golwalkar remained the RSS sarsanghchalak (chief organizer) for thirty-three years and was called 'Sri Guruji' by the RSS, his written work becoming like an RSS charter. A Maharashtrian Brahmin and Hindu supremacist, Golwalkar was a lifelong brahmachari, who looked like a wandering prophet with his flowing beard, wind-blown long hair and piercing gaze, his charisma winning him many young devotees in search of a hero, among them the young Vajpayee (and Advani), who regularly touched his feet. Golwalkar's arguments[41] – that the Indian nation was defined by the Hindu race, by the Hindu culture and by Hindu symbols, and that swayamsevaks were to be trained like missionaries to toil and sacrifice to create the Hindu Rashtra – remain the basis of RSS doctrine. Hindus were the only true nationalists; Muslims, Christians and communists were not. And those enslaved by Islam or Christianity had to be liberated and brought back into the Hindu fold. In later years, Golwalkar, struck by Vajpayee's oratory and spark, would become one of his chief mentors, and always remained indulgently fond of the poetic Atal.

Tarte started RSS shakhas in Gwalior, causing some excitement in the Arya Kumar Sabha. 'What do you boys do in the evenings?' a senior in the Arya Kumar Sabha, Bhoodev Shastri, asked Vajpayee and his friends. 'Nothing,' they replied. Beyond a game of marbles and a walk to the Gwalior mela, what was there to do in those quiet mofussil evenings that gave way to the enveloping silent dark of small-town India? 'Why don't you go to the shakha, you may like it,' said Shastri. The boys rushed to see. They were eager to join this new club where members wore short pants, played sports and exercised and learnt about a heart-thudding nationalism. Vajpayee began to regularly attend a shakha in Gwalior's Laxmiganj. 'It was my first association with the RSS. It had only Maharashtrian boys, and naturally all the swayamsevaks used to speak only Marathi. I liked the games played in the shakha as well as the weekly bauddhiks [lectures],' he would later write.[42] There was lively competition between the Maharashtrian boys and the Hindi speakers. The Maharashtrians in the shakha were called 'kadikhau' (people who eat kadi – Maharashtrians) and Vajpayee was dubbed 'rangde' (untrained); and, in Maharashtrian company every evening, Vajpayee learnt a modicum of Marathi – what he called 'Gwalior ki apni Marathi' – that would bring him applauding audiences in Mumbai and Pune.

The early RSS shakhas were small-town Hindu nationalist clubs, the Hindi heartland equivalent of a men's gymkhana where swayamsevaks met daily for an hour, morning or evening, to play games, march, sing patriotic songs and listen to stirring orations. There was much heated discussion on national problems. Above all, there was a strong sense of mission to regenerate and revitalize Hindu society. Explaining why he chose to be an RSS pracharak, Deendayal Upadhyaya, later to become Vajpayee's backer and close colleague, would write: 'Muslim goondas may besmirch the honour of the highest citizens . . . this is so because the samaj [Hindu society] they belong to is weak and degenerate . . . do you believe the samaj will stand by you in case of an emergency? No it will not, for the simple reason it is disorganised . . . our sisters and daughters are carried away by Muslims and we . . . are obliged to look on in utter helplessness.'[43] This ideological call to arms, the call to transform Hindus into a macho citizen-army – the need for Hindu virility is often emphasized by Golwalkar, who exhorts swayamsevaks to 'Be Men with a capital M' – coupled with the freely socializing caste-less, class-less, one-big-family atmosphere, was in stark contrast to the Gwalior boys' humdrum lower-middle-class lives frozen in hierarchy, ritual and reverence. Vajpayee fell rapidly under its spell.

Home was formal, stultifying, ordinary. The shakha was egalitarian, liberating, new, where he could immerse himself in the male bonding he loved. He started to drift away from his own family, many of them more socialist than Hindu nationalist, and drew closer to the RSS family, thrilling to the attention he received. So enamoured of the RSS did he become that he would even attend shakhas in secret; it was a clandestine rebellion against Krishna Bihari. 'Our father worked in government service, this was British India, he could have got into trouble if anybody came to know that his son was in the RSS,' recalls sister Vimla, who used to secretly throw Vajpayee's khaki shorts over the wall so he could sneak off unnoticed to the shakha.[44] Vajpayee's involvement with the RSS not only worried his father but also caused disagreements between Vajpayee and his brothers. Interestingly, after he joined politics, every time Vajpayee campaigned in Gwalior he stayed at the home of an RSS–Jana Sangh colleague, Narain Krishna Rao Shejwalkar, and almost never in his family home.

While Krishna Bihari disapproved of the RSS, another son of his too was drawn to the RSS: the stocky, studious Prem Bihari, who had also been a law student in DAV College in Kanpur. Vajpayee writes admiringly of the changes he saw in his sibling as a result of his membership of the shakha. He noticed how Prem Bihari, fussily Brahmanical about who cooked his food, was encouraged by the RSS to change his mind, shed caste taboos and eat with the rest of the community. 'How deftly the RSS handled the situation with my brother,' he notes in 'The Sangh Is My Soul'.

'The RSS does not only change individuals, it changes the collective mind . . . in our civilisation an individual can attain great height. But what about society? Now for the first time the RSS concluded that by changing individuals we could change society . . . I like the sangh. I like its ideology and above all I like the RSS attitude towards people . . . "man making" is the prime job of the RSS.' When he first joined the shakhas, he would always wear his janeu. But in times when India was awakened by the Gandhian campaigns against untouchability, he became painfully aware that this totem of high-caste status was distancing him from others and took his janeu off. It was liberating to be rid of the sacred thread that marked and froze his individuality. However, in a later interview, he insisted that it would be a mistake to think that just because he had cast off the janeu or because some others cut off their 'choti' that they had in any way abandoned Hindutva. Through his school and college years his relationship with the RSS only grew deeper, and although he was a pracharak, he always referred to himself only as a 'swayamsevak', adopting the wandering, threadbare life of RSS full-timers and living out of a single suitcase for years.

Interestingly, in spite of his involvement in the RSS, Vajpayee briefly became a communist. In the 1940s, while in college, he joined the All India Students Federation (AISF) for a short while and also became president of the Gwalior Students Federation in 1944. (The same year he was general secretary of the Arya Kumar Sabha.) The AISF was perceived as linked to communist parties. Socialism was the dominant ideology of the time, and Vajpayee was drawn to exhortations of an equal society, an inclination he would repeatedly voice in the RSS as well as when he would later found the BJP on the plank of 'Gandhian socialism'.

The influence of the left stayed with him all his life. As a member of Parliament, he repeatedly directed high praise at socialists like Ram Manohar Lohia and communists like Indrajit Gupta and revelled in his friendships with communists like Bhupesh Gupta, whom he called 'dada', and Hiren Mukherjee, whom he called Hiren-da, and who in turn addressed Vajpayee as 'my dear Atal' in his letters to him. Capitalism, he argued, was to be critiqued, because it exploits the common man, but socialism wasn't the answer because it crushes individual freedoms. 'The way forward, is to keep political power and economic power separate because if they combine, we get a dictatorship.'

The RSS offered extreme Hindu nationalism; the AISF spoke of a worldwide revolution for equality; and the Arya Samaj held out the promise of social reform and a purist return to the superiority of the Vedas. All these appealed to Vajpayee in varying degrees, but however adrift he may have been ideologically at times, there was one organization he, an RSS member since boyhood, would never join or be attracted by, no matter how drawn he may have been to Gandhi or impressed by Nehru. And that was the Indian National Congress. When Ghatate once asked him why he had joined the communists, he said simply, 'I was looking for an opportunity to speak and they gave me a platform.'[45] He resigned from the AISF once Russia became an ally of imperialist Britain and stayed with Golwalkar's flock. As mentioned earlier, by 1947 Vajpayee had quit his LLB studies, left DAV College, Kanpur, and become a full-time worker of the RSS. A long, complex and changeable relationship between Vajpayee and the RSS began, starting with the young man being actively promoted as the prized journalistic and political talent, in many ways a '*laadla beta*' (treasured son).

~

In 1947, at Independence, the RSS had launched the monthly magazine *Rashtradharma* from Lucknow, and Vajpayee was appointed joint editor of the magazine in Lucknow in 1948–49. He was a fluent and communicative writer and a meticulous editor, and plunged into writing, editing and proofreading with enthusiasm. He had already made a powerful impression on RSS leaders with his poem '*Hindu Tan Man, Hindu Jeevan, Rag Rag Hindu Mera Parichay*'. Now the poem was reprinted in the magazine. Vajpayee's lyrical and bold writings began to be widely talked about in RSS circles, and also began to be noticed by the leading lights in Hindi literary circles. On 14 January 1948, the RSS launched a weekly magazine, *Panchjanya* (the name of Lord Krishna's conch in the Bhagavad Gita), with fanfare in Lucknow, and Vajpayee was appointed its first editor.

The magazine was launched by someone who would play a defining role in Vajpayee's career, who had already noticed Vajpayee's speaking and writing skills, which he would use to build the political arm of Hindu nationalism. This was Deendayal Upadhyaya, who was the RSS secretary in Uttar Pradesh and ran *Rashtradharma*. Eight years older than Vajpayee, Upadhyaya was slight, bespectacled and nondescript-looking, yet he was a tireless and self-effacing grassroots organizer and RSS pracharak, often called 'the ideal swayamsevak'. His organizational abilities were impressive, and he had risen quickly up the RSS ranks as organizing secretary in Uttar Pradesh, as one of Golwalkar's most trusted deputies. In Lucknow, he now kept a supervisory eye on Vajpayee, working closely with him in his editorial work.

Deendayal Upadhyaya dedicated every fibre of his being to the Hindu nationalist cause, motivated by the mission of a Hindu revival and by ideas he later described as 'integral humanism'. These were ideas that set out to reject all westernized influences and create an Indian 'humanism', not a western one. It rejected both capitalism and communism as doctrines that centralized power and instead saw the ideal society as one where all sections of society pursue a unity of interests, and where enlightened, awakened humans lead an integrated life. The four castes are complementary to each other and function as 'different limbs of the Virat Purusha'.[46] Upadhyaya's aim was to unite and reawaken Hindus and fire them up – spiritually and actively – with the overall aim of revitalizing Hindu society, drawing on Gandhian ideas of decentralized community life rather than a top-down centralized state. 'Integral humanism' was a mesh of Hindutva and Gandhianism, the idea rather utopian and opaque.

In early 1948, just as Vajpayee was getting ready for his new responsibility as editor of *Panchjanya*, an existential crisis struck the RSS. On 30 January 1948, a gathering at Birla House was preparing for Mahatma Gandhi's multi-faith evening prayer meeting. As Gandhi walked slowly towards the raised lawn, supported by his nieces Abha and Manu, a one-time RSS and Hindu Mahasabha member, thirty-nine-year-old Nathuram Godse, lunged forward. Placing himself squarely in front of Gandhi, he whipped out his Beretta pistol and pumped three bullets into the Mahatma at point-blank range. Gandhi died instantly.

Shocked, revolted and grief-stricken, India recoiled from Hindu nationalists of all stripes. An enraged Nehru and Home Minister Sardar Vallabhbhai Patel clamped a ban on the RSS – now boasting an army of 6 lakh members with over 500 shakhas in central India[47] – and declared it unlawful. Thousands of swayamsevaks and leaders were arrested. Golwalkar was arrested on 3 February. So far, the rising tide of anti-Muslim and anti-partition sentiment had been strengthening the appeal of the RSS and the Mahasabha. Now public opinion turned violently against the Hindu nationalists. Prominent Hindu activists and Brahmins were lynched in Maharashtra, the RSS headquarters in Nagpur was attacked and Golwalkar's house was pelted with stones. Godse's subsequent trial did not find evidence of any direct participation of the RSS or the Mahasabha in Gandhi's murder, but public opinion held them responsible, and their status plummeted.

Unlike Patel, who may have thought of the RSS as 'patriots . . . [whose] trend of thought is diverted'[48] and even harboured hopes that the RSS could be persuaded to join the Congress, Nehru regarded the RSS with implacable hostility. 'We have a great deal of evidence to show that the RSS is an organisation which is in the nature of a private army and is proceeding on strictest Nazi lines, even following the techniques of organisation . . . it attracted . . . considerable numbers of lower middle class young men and women who are normally not too intelligent and for whom life appears to offer little . . .' wrote Nehru to his chief ministers.[49] For the RSS and for pracharak Vajpayee, these were dangerous times. *Panchjanya* and *Rashtradharma* ceased publication. Their offices were sealed and many staffers arrested. A terrified Vajpayee managed to avoid arrest and fled to Allahabad, where he began work on another newspaper, *Dainik Swadesh*. But this too was banned and its offices sealed. Vajpayee again managed to avoid arrest by moving to Varanasi, where he started another RSS periodical, *Chetna*, while underground.

Like many RSS leaders at this time, he steadfastly refused to accept that Godse had anything to do with the RSS and insisted that Gandhi and the RSS had a mutually respectful relationship. In 1995, he argued in Parliament: 'I object to the mention of the name Godse . . . Godse was opposed to the RSS, he used to criticise the RSS in his newspaper. Inquiry was held into Mahatma Gandhi's murder, not once, but twice. The conclusion drawn was that the RSS had no hand in it . . . We pay our respects to Gandhiji.'[50] Golwalkar showers high praise on Gandhi and his 'unimpeachable character, utter selflessness and fearlessness',[51] and describes how, in 1934, Gandhi was impressed by the RSS camp in Wardha. Yet Golwalkar vociferously rejected the cardinal Gandhian teaching of Hindu–Muslim unity, which he refers to as 'that blasted slogan'.[52] 'Those who declared, "no swaraj without Hindu-Muslim unity" have thus perpetrated the greatest treason on our society.'[53] For Nehru's secular government, such sentiments – blatant violations of Gandhianism – were totally unacceptable.

With the cadres jailed and RSS banned, Golwalkar sprang to the rescue of his beleaguered organization. In letters to Nehru and Patel written after he was released in August 1948, he promised RSS cooperation in return for a lifting of the ban on the organization. The Congress and the RSS must cooperate, indeed are destined to cooperate, he wrote, as the Congress 'is capable of doing good in the political field' and the RSS has 'achieved success in the cultural field by creating in the populace a spirit of patriotism'.[54] Patel, for his part, suggested that the RSS merge with the Congress and 'carry on their patriotic endeavour only by joining the Congress and not keeping separate and by opposing'.[55] As a precondition for lifting the ban, Patel demanded the RSS adopt a written constitution and pledge loyalty to the Indian flag and Constitution. Golwalkar was again imprisoned. In December 1948 the RSS launched a massive 'show of strength' satyagraha, in which over 60,000 activists participated, the scale of which startled Nehru and Patel. Thousands were arrested and slammed into jail. Patel kept insisting on the RSS adopting a written constitution, which was, after some wrangling, drafted by three RSS leaders, Patel satisfied that the RSS had committed to 'make loyalty to the Indian Constitution and respect for the National flag more explicit . . . and to provide clearly that violent and secret methods will have no place in the sangh'.[56] On 11 July 1949, the ban on the RSS was lifted and Golwalkar was released.

Vajpayee remained aloof from these agitations even as thousands of his fellow RSS workers were hauled off to jail. In 1950, he was appointed editor of the RSS-inclined Hindi daily newspaper *Veer Arjun* and arrived in Delhi.

He had nowhere to stay. He would simply put his head down and sleep wherever he could find a place, mostly living in the *Veer Arjun* office in Old Delhi and sleeping on a charpoy.[57] Exhilarated to be in the capital, he plunged into the life of the city. His good-humoured and attractive temperament soon drew many to him. Food was his great love: he would often walk to Parathewali Gali in Old Delhi to devour ghee-laden parathas and spicy vegetable curry, and he was both excellent cook and gourmet, treating buddies to his delicious preparations of kheer and khichdi.

He would soon find himself in the company of someone quite different from himself. The path of the chivda-loving Hindi poet from small-town Bharat now crossed with that of a highly educated London-returned Bengali barrister and intellectual from Calcutta, and his life changed forever.

Syama Prasad Mookerji hailed from an elite Bengali bhadralok family. The son of Sir Ashutosh Mookerji, a high court judge and vice chancellor of Calcutta University, Syama Prasad had been called to the bar in England and, like his father, had also become vice chancellor of Calcutta University, at the age of only thirty-three. He started his political career in the Congress, grew disillusioned with the party, furious at the rise of the Muslim League, and joined the V.D. Savarkar–led Hindu Mahasabha in 1939. He was later elected as its president. He joined Prime Minister Jawaharlal Nehru's first cabinet as industries minister, but became enraged by what he perceived was Nehru's pro-Pakistan tilt and 'appeasement' of Pakistan. On 8 April 1950, the day Nehru signed the Nehru–Liaquat Pact with then Pakistan prime minister Liaquat Ali Khan, pledging that neither India nor Pakistan had any 'extraterritorial' claim on the minorities in each other's countries, Mookerji resigned from the Nehru cabinet, declaring India had 'deserted' the Hindus of East Pakistan.

Searching for a new political platform and cadres, Mookerji's gaze fell on the RSS, massive and highly organized as it was. The RSS for its part, bruised by the 1948 ban and jail terms, having assured Patel that it would function as a 'cultural' and 'democratic' (and not political) organization, allowed individual members to join

Mookerji to establish a political party to advance its views. Aiming to create a national alternative and a 'well organised Opposition to the dictatorship of Congress rule',[58] Mookerji needed a volunteer force. 'Congress policies are disintegrating the country,' Mookerji announced in a public address in April 1951. 'The need of the hour is a new All Bharat political party.'[59]

With the help of the RSS, Mookerji now founded this new party, its initial core group consisting of RSS swayamsevaks, Hindu traditionalists and Arya Samaj members. On 21 October 1951 in Delhi, the Bharatiya Jana Sangh was officially born. RSS men like Balraj Madhok and Deendayal Upadhyaya were included in its working committee. For his personal secretary – to translate his speeches into Hindi, take dictation, even help with chores, to be part stenographer, part personal helper – Mookerji chose Upadhyaya's young colleague, by now widely recognized for his Hindi writing skills: Atal Bihari Vajpayee.

Golwalkar himself shunned politics, preferring to keep the RSS focused on the larger goal of establishing the pure, virile, Hindu society and Hindu identity across India. But many in the RSS, Golwalkar notes, had 'developed a liking for political work to a degree uncommon and undesirable for a swayamsevak'.[60] With the risk of a ban ever present, and acutely conscious that there was no one to speak for the RSS in politics, politically ambitious RSS men yearned for a public platform.

The leader of the RSS group sent to the Jana Sangh was the dedicated organization man Deendayal Upadhyaya, about whom an impressed Mookerji said that if he had two or three more people like Deendayal he would 'change the entire political map of India'.[61] With his induction into the Jana Sangh alongside Upadhyaya, Vajpayee plunged into political work and took up his duties assisting Mookerji.

As he began to travel ceaselessly with Mookerji, twenty-six-year-old Vajpayee learnt valuable lessons from the burly, sophisticated fifty-year-old barrister. He absorbed from Mookerji a conviction about the primacy of politics and electoral contests, as distinct from the social, religious and cultural activism of the RSS. He learnt about the need to mount a political challenge to the suffocating dominance – or what Mookerji called 'dictatorship' – of the Congress. Mookerji was an outstanding parliamentary speaker and polemicist whom Vajpayee observed and emulated. He imbibed from Mookerji the political symbolism of challenging the Nehruvian approach to Kashmir. Mookerji was a proponent of the Hindu nationalist cause, but primarily a politician trying to establish his party as an alternative to the Nehru-led Congress. During his apprenticeship with Mookerji, Vajpayee began to understand how to become a candidate in elections, rather than just remain a soldier in a cultural war. At the inauguration of the Jana Sangh, Mookerji said: 'We have thrown our party open to all citizens of India, irrespective of caste, creed or community.'[62]

Between narrow religious activism and democratic political contests, Mookerji had opted for the latter, and so would Vajpayee, always insisting that those who fought and won elections must call the shots in government over those who only pursued religio-social programmes. 'Dr Mookerjee [sic] was no wild-eyed fanatic,' wrote British historian Hugh Tinker, 'he was a constitutionalist and a parliamentarian; a conservative in the best sense.'[63] This description also fits Vajpayee.

In fact, the nub of Vajpayee's future conflict with the RSS was this: Vajpayee strained for his own supremacy over the khaki brotherhood as the elected politician, while the RSS, as the religio-social-cultural parent body, sought to perpetually establish its control over him.

There was another result of his apprenticeship with Mookerji: his intellectual horizons irreversibly broadened. All his life Vajpayee would remain an admirer of India's westernized, English-speaking, educated elite – from Nehru to Syama Prasad to the communist Hiren Mukherjee to Indira Gandhi and, much later, the Mayo College–educated, shoulder-flapped-shirt-wearing military man Jaswant Singh and the United Nations–returned jazz aficionado and Scotch-drinking, chain-smoking Indian Foreign Service officer Brajesh Mishra. The RSS was drawn overwhelmingly from the provincial lower middle class (though high-caste groups), from the families of local stationmasters, priests and office clerks. As such it always viewed the westernized metropolitan upper class with hostility and resentment. But Vajpayee was different, more impressed by rather than adversarial with India's anglophiles. In 'I Recollect', Vajpayee writes with generous appreciation about Nehru, Indira Gandhi and Rajiv Gandhi, even about Lal Bahadur Shastri and Morarji Desai, but intriguingly, in the extended twenty-six-page essay, there are no similarly lengthy references to any of his own ideological or party colleagues, except two lines on Deendayal Upadhyaya.[64] However hard he defended authentic Bharatiya traditions, or Advani ranted against 'Macaulayputras', Vajpayee was no angry cultural warrior against India's westernized class.

~

In 1951–52, independent India held its first general elections. As the world watched the largest democracy with bated breath, excitement filled the air in the country. Bullock carts, cycles and tongas were pressed into service. Freedom-fighters-turned-politicians hit the campaign trail, and lorries with posters of Nehru and the slogan 'Congress ko vote' trundled along. Accusations flew: 'Nehru eats beef' and 'Jana Sangh murdered Gandhiji'.

These elections, in anticipation of which Mookerji had established his party, were a blow for the Jana Sangh. All over India its candidates lost their deposits. Any hopes of challenging the Congress as a national party were dashed as the Nehru-led Congress swept to a landslide win with 364 of 489 seats. To its bitter disappointment, only three Jana Sanghis won, among them Mookerji from Calcutta South East. Vajpayee, however, recalled later that Mookerji drew comfort from the fact that the Jana Sangh – with a 3.06 per cent vote share – had narrowly qualified as a national party, the Election Commission having stipulated a 3 per cent vote share for such a qualification. For the youngest Opposition party in the age of Nehru, this was, Vajpayee thought, remarkable.[65]

With only three seats, the Jana Sangh was badly mauled and needed new energy. The party's hopes were now pinned on the 'pure' RSS man, the indefatigable Upadhyaya who had become Jana Sangh general secretary. Upadhyaya would remain in this post for fifteen years until 1967, diligently building the party from three seats in 1952 to thirty-five in 1967. At its first annual session in Kanpur, in December 1952, the Jana Sangh planned two future agitations to attack the Nehru-led Congress: first, on the issue of Hindu refugees from East Pakistan, and second, starting countrywide protests against Nehru's policies on Kashmir. Two young men met again at Kanpur and spent time together exchanging ideas, Vajpayee, and the slim, bespectacled RSS pracharak who had been working in Rajasthan and whom Upadhyaya had now brought into the Jana Sangh, L.K. Advani.

Anxious to rebuild his party after a crushing defeat, Mookerji began what the Jana Sangh called its Kashmir satyagraha, or agitation for the 'full integration of Kashmir', demanding the Indian Constitution be applied in Kashmir in full, that Kashmir have no special privileges as granted by Nehru, like its own Constitution and flag. Mookerji began to travel hectically, trying to popularize his ideas on Kashmir. The slogan the Jana Sangh raised at this time was '*Ek desh mein do vidhan, do nishan, do pradhan nahin chalenge*' (You cannot have two constitutions, two flags and two prime ministers in one country). Vajpayee went everywhere with Mookerji, assisting with his speeches as well as delivering his own, his oratorical talents growing every day. 'Mr Nehru has repeatedly declared that the accession of the state is hundred per cent complete. Yet it is strange to find that one cannot enter the state without a previous permit from the government,'[66] Mookerji raged, as he began a campaign to enter Jammu and Kashmir without the required permit.

On 11 May 1953, Mookerji was arrested at the Madhopur checkpost at the Punjab–Jammu and Kashmir border for trying to enter Kashmir without the required permit. Vajpayee, along with crowds of supporters, had accompanied him as far as Pathankot. Mookerji was taken to Srinagar and placed under arrest in a cottage near Nishat Gardens. He fell ill shortly afterwards and was shifted to the Srinagar government hospital, where the very next month, on 23 June, he died of a sudden heart attack while still in custody. Vajpayee was distraught at the death of his boss, and years later lashed out at the Nehru government for arresting Mookerji in Kashmir. Why was Mookerji not preventively arrested before he entered Jammu and Kashmir, Vajpayee asked. Decades later he said it appeared the Nehru government had 'entered into a conspiracy and it would be decided that Mookerji would be allowed to enter but not allowed to leave'.[67] Vajpayee had lost the leader with whom his political journey began. Yet Mookerji's death opened up new political opportunities for Vajpayee and became a turning point for him. He now became a full-time politician.

The passing of Mookerji so soon after the party was founded was a blow to the Jana Sangh, suddenly bereft of any real leaders and robbed of the respectable sheen which the RSS lacked and which the highly distinguished Mookerji had provided. The RSS now moved for greater control, not wanting the party to fall into the hands of someone who did not share its views, and the de facto leadership of the party passed to Upadhyaya, who with his RSS group came to dominate the party and its subsequent presidents. As Upadhyaya set about rebuilding the Jana Sangh in the RSS mould, Vajpayee – now recognized as the party's best speaker in Hindi and a hit with the crowds – became one of Upadhyaya's most valued public faces, a promising politician both he and Golwalkar would groom to take over from where Mookerji left off.

It was an uncertain start, though. A year and a half after Mookerji's death Vajpayee got a chance to step into electoral politics for the first time. Lucknow MP Vijayalakshmi Pandit, Nehru's sister, resigned from her seat in 1954 to take up diplomatic assignments overseas, and the seat fell vacant. For the by-polls in March 1955, Upadhyaya immediately announced that the thirty-year-old Vajpayee would be the Jana Sangh candidate for Lucknow. Vajpayee worked like a trojan, rushing headlong into the campaign, holding public meetings day and night, bounding around by cycle and tonga.

But the Jana Sangh was no match for the mighty Congress, its candidate Sheorajvati Nehru, a stern-faced Gandhian and a relative of Jawaharlal Nehru's, sweeping the polls. Vajpayee finished third, but polled 28 per cent of the vote, making what was expected to be a two-party contest into a three-cornered race. A 28 per cent vote share was an early glimpse not only of the potential of the 'Hindu vote' but also of his ability to score at the ballot box.

He did not win, but it was clear he was made for electoral politics, with his gift of communication, his warm and engaging style, and his capacity for endless bonhomie with the cadres – qualities that would stand him in good stead in his five-decade-long electoral odyssey. There are several accounts of Vajpayee's first campaigns for the Jana Sangh. In 1952, in a bid to deploy his public-speaking skills for the party, he was sent to Jhansi to help the Jana Sangh candidate's campaign there. A small group of karyakartas came to receive him at the train station as he stepped off the carriage in a threadbare dhoti and kurta, carrying only a small jhola. One of the karyakartas suggested that they hire a tonga to get to the campaign venue. 'A tonga?' Vajpayee asked. 'But how did you all come here?' 'We came by cycle,' they replied. 'Our bikes are parked in the stand.' 'Then why tonga, let's just go on your cycle.' Off they sped to the meeting, Vajpayee perched on a bicycle's front horizontal bar.

In these early years, Vajpayee's dishevelled appearance often led party workers to underestimate him, until they heard him address a gathering. In 1953, the Jana Sangh organized a public meeting in Mumbai and requested the Delhi leadership to send good speakers. On the appointed day, a youthful Vajpayee in his rumpled clothes stepped off the Dehradun Express at Bombay Central station. 'Is your name Atal Bihari Vajpayee?' asked the local Jana Sangh representative. 'Yes, it is! I'm the one sent by Jana Sangh general secretary Deendayal Upadhyaya for the public meeting.'[68] The Jana Sanghi looked him up and down. Was this scruffily dressed youngster to be the main public speaker? As they drove to the meeting, Vajpayee gazed bedazzled at Mumbai's high-speed hustle and bustle. The Jana Sanghi became even more sceptical, and also noticed that Vajpayee's kurta was not only crumpled but torn. 'Are you going to deliver a speech from a Jana Sangh platform in a torn kurta?' he asked. 'Not a problem,' replied Vajpayee brightly. 'I'll wear a jacket on top of it.' The local representative was discomfited. Why had Deendayal sent this inexperienced bumpkin all the way from Delhi?

But when the dishevelled yokel in his torn kurta took the stage, his presence seemed to grow larger. As he began to speak the audience gasped in astonishment. Vajpayee's words caught his audience in a vice-like grip. He drew the audience in so completely that when he closed his speech they sighed in disappointment then burst into admiring applause. Upadhyaya's frontman had delivered.

Slowly the swayamsevak discovered his true metier. He was no cultural revolutionary for Hindutva, he was a politician who thrilled to electoral competition. The pursuit of political power, jostling with other talented men in the national ring, matching wits with them, playing the game of thrones – how much more exciting this was than any long-drawn-out, dour crusade for the 'pure' Hindu Rashtra. He was not a founder member of the Jana Sangh. But he would soon prove to be its unparalleled vote catcher.

Despite his defeat in the 1955 by-election, his star began to rise in the Jana Sangh. He and his poetry were very popular and many of his poems were recited in shakhas. Revelling in the attention and in the wholehearted support of Golwalkar and Upadhyaya, Vajpayee settled into his groove.

His public-speaking style was homegrown, earthy and non-confrontational, with a winning quality that disarmed opponents. In public, this ready charm flowed. Once he started electioneering, his competitive instincts with other politicians were always to the fore and he deployed his quick wit as a weapon. In those days, Baghpat in western Uttar Pradesh was the unchallenged stamping ground of the Jat chieftain Chaudhary Charan Singh, the influential farm leader, popular for his land reforms. The Jana Sangh decided to hold a public meeting in Baghpat, although some within the party protested, saying nobody would come to hear the Jana Sangh in Charan Singh's domain. Immediately, Vajpayee dug in his heels and cried, of course we must hold a rally in Baghpat, that's exactly where we should! Easier said than done, as no one in the area was willing to give out their premises for the rally. So the Jana Sanghis had to make do by setting up ramshackle benches from a local school. As Vajpayee started speaking, some people in the crowd started waving black flags and shouting, 'Atal Bihari murdabad.' Vajpayee pitched his voice higher than their yells and declared, 'When a beautiful child is born, mothers put a black mark on him, to ward off the evil eye. This mark is called a tikala. Those people,' he said, gesturing at them, 'are not showing me the black flag, they're just putting the tikala on me.' On hearing this, the demonstrators sheepishly put their flags down and joined the rally.

In one of his poems, '*Man ka Santosh*', written in later years, Vajpayee wrote:

On earth, among the living,
Only a human being
Feels alone in a crowd . . .,
If the mind be pure, Ganga will be found even in a bowl.'[69]

Ganga in a bowl. A pool of purity. Over the years he would produce speech after mesmerizing speech which would create 'Ganga in a bowl', a spotlight of pure eloquence. As enormous success with crowds began to come his way, he kept improving on his style, adding poetry here, a joke there.

~

Over the next five years the Jana Sangh came increasingly under the RSS umbrella as Upadhyaya got down to extending its network and revving up the organization, appointing RSS men as 'sangathan mantris' to build the party in the states. Cow protection was a key ideological plank. In 1955, the Jana Sangh founded the Bharatiya Mazdoor Sangh with Dattopant Thengadi, another Maharashtrian Brahmin like Golwalkar and RSS man from Nagpur, as general secretary to combat the communist influence among workers, the communists seen as grave threats to the Hindu Rashtra. Many older Jana Sanghis quit the party at this time, alleging too much domination and interference by the RSS as the party increasingly became an RSS front organization. In later years, this tug of war would repeat: the politician Vajpayee, who started out as a key RSS transplant in the Jana Sangh, would eventually become a political counterweight to RSS dominance.

Two speaking stars of the Jana Sangh emerged: Vajpayee and Balraj Madhok, Vajpayee in Hindi and Madhok in English. Four years older than Vajpayee, the rangy, dynamic Madhok was a prolific writer of books – he was Mookerji's biographer – and articles, a well-travelled regular on the social circuit and an excellent speaker in English. He was politically far more experienced than Vajpayee, having worked to set up the right-wing Praja Parishad party in Jammu. Madhok was a diehard right-wing radical, both on nationalism and on the economy, a trenchant opponent of socialism and an avid believer in the free market.

With Mookerji dead, and the Jana Sangh hit by a string of desertions, in a leadership vacuum, these two young men stepped up. They were to become bitter rivals. From 1953 onward, twenty-eight-year-old amiable and charming Vajpayee and thirty-two-year-old articulate and well-read Madhok became the party's most visible faces. Vajpayee began to help Upadhyaya in party work and drew closer to him. Vajpayee's popularity with the public and cadres as well as the encouragement showered on him by Upadhyaya and Golwalkar made Madhok resentful of him. Madhok, the free-marketeer, was always suspicious of Vajpayee's then fuzzy populist left-of-centre orientation as well as Upadhyaya's ideas on decentralized society and integral humanism.

When general elections rolled around in 1957, Upadhyaya pulled out all the stops for Vajpayee, determined to send him to the Lok Sabha. Elections took place in a fraught atmosphere. There had been major public protests in several places as a result of many of India's states being reorganized along linguistic lines a year earlier. Elections, however, were held on schedule, and not wanting to risk another loss like Lucknow, this time Upadhyaya made Vajpayee contest from as many as three seats – Lucknow, where Vajpayee had scored a good vote percentage in the 1955 by-polls; Mathura, where a suitable candidate could not be found as people were scared of losing their deposits and only wanted to contest assembly seats; and the Brahmin-dominated Balrampur, from where it was calculated that Vajpayee, being a Brahmin, might win.

Balrampur, a small princely state close to Ayodhya which merged with Uttar Pradesh in 1947, is located in the Awadh region of Uttar Pradesh. The Urdu poet Ali Sardar Jafri was born in Balrampur. With Hindu and Muslim communities living in close proximity, Balrampur was no stranger to Hindutva politics. Swami Karpatri, a radical Hindu leader, started his hard-line party Ram Rajya Parishad here in 1948. In 'I Recollect' Vajpayee recalls Balrampur's religious conflicts, revealing that the election was fought on the plank of Hindu consolidation. Several landlords in the constituency were Muslim, and during his campaign, he writes, they had prohibited the striking of gongs and blowing of conch shells in many places. Small and medium farmers who 'lived under the perpetual terror' of these Muslim landlords were drawn to the Jana Sangh, he claims.[70] Vajpayee's election agent in Balrampur was Chandikadas Amritrao Deshmukh, better known as 'Nanaji' Deshmukh, a highly ideologically committed pracharak, who would work as Vajpayee's close colleague but would later become a detractor, decades later falling out with Golwalkar's golden boy and finding himself walking out of the exit door of politics even as Vajpayee continued his glittering upward journey.

Projected as a public face from the start, actively encouraged and mentored by both Golwalkar and Upadhyaya, Vajpayee stood out and gained almost instant recognition in the small new party, in a way he would never have been able to had he, for example, been an anonymous struggler in a crowded Congress. Hindu nationalism may not quite have been his own ideological obsession, yet it was the ideal springboard for his stardom. He was the boy from Gwalior with the gilded tongue, the cheerful figure who struck an instant rapport with the crowds. Any difficult task might be accomplished, any uncomfortable question dealt with, when the words were so effortless and the poetry so good.

In Balrampur, the election was fought along religious lines – an early example of Hindutva polarization – but Vajpayee managed only a narrow win, defeating his Muslim Congress rival Haidar Hussain by a small margin of just 10,000 votes, although he got a 52 per cent vote share and polled 1,18,380 votes.[71] As he candidly admitted, 'Had the Congress fielded a Hindu candidate perhaps I would not have won the election.'[72] He flopped in the other two seats he contested, losing in Lucknow and losing his security deposit in Mathura. He had very few resources and only a handful of workers. 'All I had was two jeeps, one given to me by the party and one which I had hired. When the voting was on, the jeep I was travelling in got stuck in a jungle and I was unable to reach the designated place in the constituency.'[73]

The Jana Sangh won three other seats (two from Maharashtra and a second one in Uttar Pradesh), thus upping its seat tally by one and its vote share to 5.93 per cent). After his Balrampur win, Vajpayee pulled ahead of Madhok, who contested from Delhi and lost. Madhok was able to enter Parliament only three years later, through a by-election, by which time Vajpayee had already become well noticed in the House and the leader of the Jana Sangh's parliamentary party (the combined Lok Sabha–Rajya Sabha group of the Jana Sangh), a position he would hold until 1977.

On a note of pride, Vajpayee recalled the Jana Sangh's success, comparing the Sangh with other 'Hindu' parties: 'Bharatiya Jana Sangh succeeded in retaining its all-India recognition while several other parties, namely, the Hindu Maha Sabha and Ram Rajya Parishad failed to retain their recognition.'[74] His 1957 victory from Balrampur was the first of an epic electoral record. He would win ten Lok Sabha elections and lose only three (including his loss in the 1955 Lucknow by-election). After two of his Lok Sabha defeats, he entered the Rajya Sabha both times: in 1962, after his defeat in Balrampur; and in 1984, after losing from Gwalior, after which he entered the Rajya Sabha in 1986. Always operating in national and not state politics, winning from almost anywhere he contested, Atal Bihari Vajpayee was thus the permanent parliamentarian, occupying the benches for almost half a century, from 1957 to 2004–06. Once he set foot in the great house of the people, the boy from Shinde ki Chhawani never looked back.

3

The Rise of the Saffron Nehru: 1957–1971

A poem for Vajpayee:

Ah the joys of this great House of the People,
Where Nehru thundered and strode,
Debate, argument, comradeship among equals,
Grandeur future generations would behold.

~

15 May 1957. In the packed chamber of the Lok Sabha, members turned their eyes towards a thirty-three-year-old first-time parliamentarian who rose to speak. He wore a dhoti, kurta and waistcoat, and his voice was full of energy. First congratulating President Rajendra Prasad on his re-election and declaring that the President is above all parties, he launched into a spirited attack on the Nehru government:

> I stand in opposition but opposition for the sake of opposition is not my purpose . . . The government's Kashmir policy is weak and

> indecisive . . . In the Vedas God has been described as 'neti, neti' – 'not this, not that'. God is not this, God is not that. These words, '*neti neti*' (No, No) very well describe the government's policy in respect of the problem of the Hindus in Kashmir and Goa and East Bengal. Will one third of the territory of Kashmir be liberated on the strength of arms? No, no. Shall we gift it to Pakistan? No, no. Then what shall we do? . . . What is our policy? It can only be defined as '*Neti Neti*.'[1]

The members looked up. *Neti neti?* Who was this new member using Sanskrit phrases and speaking in Hindi, at a time when most speeches in Parliament were made in English? He was a Lok Sabha debutant and his parliamentary career was poised for a dazzling take-off, with Parliament as his window to India.

Vajpayee pressed on in refined, Sanskritized Hindi.

> Not an inch of land [in Kashmir] must be surrendered to the aggressor [Pakistan] . . . There are danger signals. Pakistan is preparing for war . . . In just ten years since India's independence and partition we are faced with the twin dangers of external aggression and internal break up . . . Why was [the reorganization of states] not done properly? The legitimate demands of the people of Maharashtra and Gujarat have not been accepted. I hail from Uttar Pradesh and live in Madhya Pradesh . . . I know about the intense feelings of the people there about a state of their own. These sentiments can neither be ignored nor suppressed . . . the language problem has not been properly solved, and the seeds of separation have been sown.[2]

The members listened, some impressed, others erupting into objections. Massive agitations had been flaring up in Tamil Nadu since the 1930s on the perceived imposition of Hindi and moves to introduce compulsory Hindi in schools, and the Constituent Assembly had fiercely debated the status of Hindi and its designation as a 'national language'. Now, in protest at Vajpayee's unapologetic use of Hindi, some members walked out of the House. But one member listened intently, recognizing at once another to-the-manner-born parliamentarian. Prime Minister Jawaharlal Nehru was impressed from the start by the strong-voiced, Hindi-speaking Opposition MP. The Cambridge-educated Fabian socialist and the Jana Sanghi from Gwalior were separated by both thirty-five years and sharply antagonistic political views. Yet they were united in allegiance to this House, which protected the frail plant that was Indian democracy – both were determined that this plant must grow to be as mighty and as sheltering as the great Indian banyan. Vajpayee's deep admiration for Nehru, whom he idolized and emulated, began early in his parliamentary years and never flagged throughout his life; it was a reverence that repeatedly revealed itself in his speeches and writings.

The years from 1950 until Nehru died in 1964 can be described as the Age of Nehru. The first prime minister ruled supreme: freedom hero, handsome prince, an upholder of the European Enlightenment's values of reason, rationality, religious tolerance and free inquiry, he was unchallenged in government and party. Nehru had suffered and struggled for India's independence; he was Mahatma Gandhi's anointed heir, and his moral stature at home and abroad towered over his peers. Nehru's Congress, wedded to his determined secularism and welfare state, won landslide victories in the elections of 1952, 1957 and 1962. Challenging the Congress – with its national lustre and its internationally feted and domestically adored prime minister – was a fearsomely daunting task at this time, but the small group of Jana Sanghis was fired by the rightness of its cause, both inspired and provoked to action by the Nehru cult.

Vajpayee's self-image was set in these years: the perennial Opposition politician fighting in the shadow of the Nehru–Gandhis and tilting at a crushingly dominant Congress. This identity fundamentally shaped the politics he played all his life. He entered Parliament for the first time, awed by the surroundings and eager to participate. 'My very first speech on foreign policy [delivered on 19 August 1958] attracted attention of the House,' he recalls with pride. 'My Hindi was chaste. The members liked my fluent style. On 20th August 1958, Prime Minister Nehru . . . sought the permission of the Speaker to speak something in Hindi [sic]. The members welcomed this gesture by clapping their hands. When Shri Nehru after referring to me by name started speaking in Hindi, the members once again expressed their happiness over it.'[3] Nehru had gone into an extended explanation about the need for a non-interfering stance in India's foreign policy, but then, as a considered response to Vajpayee's statement that 'in order to keep silent both speech and discretion are required', had also argued on the benefits of registering India's voice and speaking out at international forums. Nehru's public reply, that too in Hindi, to the newcomer MP was like a bow from India's uncrowned king.

Vajpayee shared the prime minister's passion for world affairs. 'Foreign policy has been my favourite subject,' he wrote.[4] Nehru, while struck by the young Opposition MP's interventions, answered his taunts with mocking retorts too. In an exchange in 1959, when Vajpayee blustered that India must never allow the Chinese into an area called Bara Hoti (in the middle sector of the India–China border), 'which belongs to us from time immemorial', Nehru retorted sarcastically, 'I am sorry I am not [as] personally acquainted as the Honourable member appears to be with "time immemorial".'[5]

The atmosphere in the House was heady, exemplifying democracy's greatest practice: debate and contestation, without enmity. Nehru distrusted the RSS and heartily disliked the Jana Sangh, seeing it as a symbol of reactionary communalism. 'If there is any organization in India which is really communal, it is the Jana Sangh,' Nehru once said in response to Syama Prasad Mookerji. 'It is a wholly reactionary organization. All the reactionary minded people in India – I say this deliberately, the princes and jagirdars who are to my mind the real backward classes, are behind the Jana Sangh. They are financing it.'[6] On one occasion Vajpayee sat listening while the prime minister launched another of his scathing attacks on the Jana Sangh. As he ended, Vajpayee leapt to his feet and shouted out: 'I know that the prime minister does a shirshasana [headstand] every morning, but this doesn't mean he should see my party upside down!' After a moment's pause, Nehru laughed out loud and the House guffawed.

Vajpayee's impish wit was a welcome addition to the Lok Sabha. On a speech on deaths in railway accidents, he cried: 'Our Railway minister [Jagjivan Ram] has both "*Jag*" and "*Jivan*" in his name, but travellers lose both "*Jag*" [the world] and "*Jivan*" [life]. They are left only with Ram, the last portion of the Railway Minister's name.'[7] Again, the House roared. In 1959 when Nehru dismissed the communist-ruled Kerala government, he was assailed in Parliament, including by his own MP son-in-law, Feroze Gandhi. Teased Vajpayee: 'Panditji's rath (like Dharmaraj of the Mahabharat) used to float a few inches above the ground, but has now come down to the ground. But the Communists who were overground will now go underground.'[8] For India's early democrats of the 1940s and 1950s, argument and counter-argument strengthened – not weakened – the painstakingly erected scaffolding of democracy. Whatever the disagreements, that vital structure must hold, be kept upright, be reinforced. The right to dissent and to oppose were crucial: they were the rivets that fastened democracy's frame.

Vajpayee kept up a robust assault on Nehru's peaceful coexistence approach to China and on the 1954 India–China Panchsheel treaty. On 8 May 1959, he delivered a roaring intervention on Tibet and Chinese aggression. 'The first blow to India–China friendship was struck on the day Chinese armies "liberated" Tibet . . . we committed a great blunder by accepting Chinese suzerainty over Tibet . . . We require China's friendship even today but the palace of that friendship cannot be built on the corpse of the independence of Tibet.'[9] On 21 August Vajpayee moved a resolution demanding that the Government of India should take Tibet to the United Nations. 'How can India remain silent,' he demanded, 'when before our eyes a nation . . . is being destroyed?'[10]

However vigorously he opposed him, Vajpayee's admiration for Nehru didn't falter.

'With his complete commitment to democracy he [Nehru] considered the institution of Parliament a sacred temple,' Vajpayee writes. 'His very presence charged the atmosphere in the House, lending it greater prestige, greater seriousness.'[11] He recalls an incident when MPs protested at derogatory remarks made against them by Nehru's personal assistant M.O. Mathai. Members insisted that the matter be raised in the Privileges Committee[12] and Mathai be censured for insulting MPs. Nehru first attempted to defend his personal aide but then agreed to send the issue to the Privileges Committee saying nothing should be done that leads the public to believe that anything is being covered up. 'This small incident throws ample light on Pandit Nehru's personality,' writes Vajpayee.[13] In the 1990s, he suggested that a recently installed 16-foot statue of Nehru be placed on a stand, at a height, so it looked as if the first prime minister was always watching over the House. His suggestion was turned down, but it revealed his mind. Whenever he sat in Parliament, he felt himself being watched over by Nehru's spirit.

For Nehru, Hinduism's ancient genius lay in its philosophical richness. But he was repulsed by its present-day dogmas and rigidities and convinced of the need to bring modernity and reform to Hindu practices that had become oppressive and cruel. The Nehruvian secular state saw religious identities as entirely private and not enforceable by law. The Hindu Code Bill – or a set of laws creating a civil code in place of Hindu personal law – was Nehru's attempt at modernizing Hindu society. The Hindu Code Bill, or three separate bills which were introduced in the First Lok Sabha (1952–57), outlawed polygamy among Hindus, provided for adoption of girls and gave daughters equal rights of inheritance. Conservatives like Syama Prasad Mookerji and militant traditionalists like the Hindu Mahasabha were outraged from the outset. 'The government did not dare to touch the Muslim community,' Mookerji had raged.[14] Already, religious leaders like Swami Karpatri had founded organizations like the Ram Rajya Parishad to agitate against Nehru. Vajpayee's own RSS brethren had marched on the streets shouting 'may Pandit Nehru perish'.[15] India's first President, Rajendra Prasad, was also a critic of Hindu reforms, and in the end the bills that were passed were less far-reaching than Nehru had wanted. Nevertheless, Nehru's government succeeded in driving a modern coach and horses through the tangled web of Hindu practices. One of the most contentious of Nehru's attempts to reform Hindu practices was the introduction of the law banning dowry. The legislation was debated in Parliament in 1961, after almost a decade of Hindu traditionalist outrage.

The Jana Sangh at this time was positioned as nationalist-conservative rather than a radical Hindu party. In its first manifesto it called itself a party of 'Bharatiya sanskriti and maryada' (Indian culture and dignity) which also wanted a 'progressive, modern and enlightened' nation.[16] This orientation did not substantially change after the death of Mookerji and the takeover of the party by the RSS, and the Jana Sangh continued to distance itself somewhat from the obscurantist Hindu politics of the Ram Rajya Parishad. With Nehruvian secularism as the governing norm, the Jana Sangh was aspiring for legitimacy as a 'normal' Opposition, and in the dowry debates, Vajpayee took a middle-of-the-road moderate-conservative line.

In the blistering heat of May 1961 was held the first joint sitting of both Houses of Parliament. The atmosphere in the House was as scorching as it was on Delhi's streets outside. Both Houses met to pass the Dowry Prohibition Bill, over which there was a complete deadlock.

In the debate, the thehrauni (agreement money) – a part of the dowry as a precondition for marriage – caused furious disagreement. Some argued that this was like assigning a 'cost' to the bridegroom. The government maintained that wedding gifts, jewellery, cash and clothes would be excluded from the term 'dowry', as these could be well-intentioned presents. In his speech, Vajpayee put forward a middle path between traditional Hindu practices and state-driven social change. He suggested an amendment: wedding gifts not be abolished completely but that there should be a limit of Rs 2000 on the total value of appliances to be given at the time of marriage. Although his amendment failed, the fact that the Dowry Prohibition Act was passed in the 1961 joint sitting and became a law was a matter of deep personal satisfaction for him.

With three sisters in his family, seven siblings altogether, the large family having to get by on the father's schoolmaster salary, worries about resources were a constant of his growing-up years. He remembered well his parents' anguish about dowry and recognized dowry as an evil of 'demoniac proportions'. So painful were his memories that he maintained that in addition to a strictly implemented law, dowry could only be eradicated by 'awakening the conscience of the people'.[17]

'What was needed,' he said in his speech, 'is that the country should make economic progress, education should be spread, the caste barriers should be broken and boys and girls allowed to marry each other without any inhibition. Marriages should no longer be arranged in heaven but should be fixed by mutual consent. This alone can end the system of dowry.'[18] In modernizing Hindu practices, in bringing liberal values to ancient 'evils', Vajpayee, once an active Arya Samaji, was closer to the progressive Nehru than to traditionalists who rejected the reforms in their entirety, seeing them as threats to Hindu family life.

He drank to the full of Nehruvian modernism, initiated in his early thirties into Nehru's world of parliamentary norms and processes. These would remain sacred for Vajpayee. Throughout his parliamentary career, he was never unruly in the House, and in later years counselled younger party colleagues to learn to debate and argue and not hastily jump into the well of the House. 'In Parliament there is less discussion but more noise,' he wrote in 1996, 'democracy is not a game of simple majority of numbers, a majority of 51 versus a minority of 49.'[19]

Nehru's inordinate influence on Vajpayee in these years was noticed in the Jana Sangh and the RSS. Vajpayee's outspoken detractor in his own party, Balraj Madhok, whom Vajpayee on one occasion in Parliament sternly rebuked for criticizing Nehru, accused Vajpayee of being Nehru's 'planted man' in the Opposition. Vajpayee once admitted in Parliament that he was well aware of what was being said about him: 'I know when I mention the name of Pandit Jawaharlal Nehru some members of my own party make comments on it.'[20] Whatever the comments, Nehru would be Vajpayee's parliamentary lodestar, his lifelong 'rajkumar'.

It wasn't just Nehru who spotted Vajpayee's talents. During this time, when Lok Sabha Speaker M. Ananthasayanam Ayyangar was asked by Delhi University students who the best speaker in the House was, Ayyangar replied without hesitation: 'Actually there are two, Hiren Mukherjee in English and Atal Bihari Vajpayee in Hindi.' When friends informed Vajpayee of this compliment from Ayyangar, Vajpayee let loose one of his colourful gags. 'Outside he praises me, in the House he ignores me. *Ananthasayanamji ko uthane ke liye mujhe dhol bajana padta hai* [I have to beat a drum to wake him up – Ananthasayanam also being the name of the god Vishnu in a reclining pose].'

~

Let us now turn to a friendship – or lifelong association – which began in these years. It would become Vajpayee's most important political relationship. This was the half-century-long partnership that took the Hindu nationalist movement to its electoral heights: the Atal Bihari Vajpayee–L.K. Advani collaboration.

They first met in their twenties in 1952 in Kota, Rajasthan, where Advani was a pracharak and Vajpayee was visiting, accompanying Syama Prasad Mookerji on his travels. They met again later in the same year at the Kanpur session of the Jana Sangh, both newly inducted into the party as part of Deendayal Upadhyaya's RSS troupe. In Kanpur they spent a great deal of time together, exchanging ideas and marvelling at Mookerji's oratory and impressive command over English. Advani remembers Vajpayee as 'an extraordinary young man' who was 'lean and intense looking with something smouldering within him, the fire in the belly producing an unmistakable glow on his face'.[21]

Parliament was an ultra-serious place and speeches and arguments needed to be painstakingly prepared. The Jana Sangh realized that in this demanding arena Vajpayee and their three other first-time MPs needed help. Upadhyaya as Jana Sangh general secretary now called upon a diligent, English-speaking RSS pracharak who had been working in Rajasthan for a decade and managing the Jana Sangh in the state since 1952. Lal Krishna Advani, thirty years old but with a gravity and all-knowingness much beyond his years, arrived in Delhi. He began to work closely with Vajpayee, researching social and economic issues, poring over law books and constitutional history, drafting statements and formulating questions to prepare the parliamentary interventions that Vajpayee would unleash with his verbal splendour.

From now, 1957, emerged the two-man alliance that became the bedrock of Hindu nationalist politics in India and provided it not just political but also intellectual leadership. At first glance, beyond party ideology and their Hindu nationalist mission, they had little in common. Vajpayee was the older, the poet-journalist-swayamsevak, the Hindi heartland Brahmin, the mighty orator and suave exponent of classical Hindi, adored by party men and darling of crowds, already a leader by 1957 and now being carefully groomed by Golwalkar and Upadhyaya to become the Jana Sangh's political star. Advani was the younger, an anglicized Sindhi born and educated in Karachi, someone who studied Latin in school and whose family migrated to India after Partition.

Where Vajpayee was poetic and broad-brush, Advani was the meticulous, micro-detailing organization man; where Vajpayee was the glamorous public performer, Advani was (for most of his life) the behind-the-scenes planner; where Vajpayee was the quintessential wily and ambitious politician taking care to keep his image intact, Advani was the more what-you-see-is-what-you-get party activist who didn't baulk at playing the fire-breathing ideologue; Vajpayee was on stage, Advani was the man of the sangathan (organization). But the artful speechmaker and the efficient party organizer would soon enter into a marriage made at the ballot box. They played off each other's strengths, made up for each other's weaknesses and crafted an alliance both intimately respectful and stealthily competitive, both mutually deferring and tensely territorial, which gave the Hindu nationalist movement its centre of gravity. Were they close friends? Were they diehard rivals? Suffice it to say they needed each other for their political goals, Advani more often than not the hero-worshipping acolyte to Vajpayee's self-confident celebrity.

The 'moderate' vs 'hard-line' stereotypes ascribed in later years to Vajpayee and Advani respectively are quite erroneous: both were equally hard-line at times and equally liberal at times. 'Atalji was seen as a liberal and I was projected as a hardliner,' writes Advani. 'This hurt me initially as I knew that the reality was entirely contrary to the image I had come to acquire.'[22] But Advani admits that even though he was hurt, party men convinced him that it helped the party if one leader was seen as liberal and another as hard-line, as each could then mobilize different constituencies. Vajpayee too was acutely aware of this image crisis and often played along. 'Advaniji has, at times, been misunderstood and as a result become a victim of the dichotomy between image and reality,' he wrote in 2008.[23]

The differences were tactical, and over the years hidden jealousies and resentments would surface about each other in the public domain, even though Advani would be at pains to emphasize that he had always unquestioningly accepted Vajpayee as his senior and leader.[24] It can even be said that Advani was more forthright and honest about his chosen methods to challenge the Congress, while Vajpayee remained more crafty and political, assiduously cultivating the good-man-in-the-bad-party image. Both were highly ambitious politicians and used the Hindutva movement to seize power, yet both were firm devotees of India's parliamentary traditions.

They started working together in earnest in 1957, as together they prepared to make place for Hindu nationalism under the blindingly radiant Nehruvian sun. Shared memories of this long, herculean battle for political oxygen would become the foundation of their relationship.

Long associations inevitably tend to be multilayered, a chiaroscuro of warmth and bitterness. Initially there was no competition, Vajpayee being a nationally recognized mass leader by the 1970s, the election sure-shot, the handsome Opposition star and universal favourite in the party. Advani was still the bespectacled office helpmate, the drafter of parliamentary speeches and bills. Being so close to Vajpayee and listening to his 'magical' speeches, Advani admitted to developing a complex about his own public-speaking abilities.[25] Yet, in later years, as Vajpayee's leadership faltered at the altar of election results and as Advani in the 1990s emerged from the shadows as a crowd-rousing hardliner and expert organizational mobilizer in addition to the political strategist he already was, the shift in balance of power would make Vajpayee silently furious. Advani would always acknowledge Vajpayee as his senior and mukhiya of the Jana Sangh–BJP family, yet he yearned for his own place in the political limelight, and his pleading about his lack of oratorical skills was only a thin cover for his desire to claim what he thought was rightfully his, namely, the top job in government.

It was a bond that could, at times, be described as unrequited love. Advani was openly gushing about Vajpayee, showering him with praise in public, while Vajpayee never quite returned the compliments and often treated his partner with wariness and even some envy. 'Advani hero-worshipped Vajpayee to the extent that he seemed resentful of anyone who came close to Vajpayee,' says the journalist Vir Sanghvi, who is a close friend of Vajpayee's adoptive daughter Namita and her husband, Ranjan Bhattacharyya.[26] In later years, Advani's resentment even extended to Rajkumari Kaul's family and also to Vajpayee's PMO aide Brajesh Mishra. Always cherishing the memories of the time they had spent together as young bachelors in the house they had once shared in Rajendra Prasad Road when they were both new to Delhi and to Parliament, Advani took an open, even possessive, delight in Vajpayee's friendship and often showed a reluctance to share Vajpayee's company with others. Vajpayee did not count Advani among his inner circle of intimate friends, even though Advani invariably described Vajpayee as his closest friend, guide and mentor. In 1995, at the peak of his influence in the party as party president, Advani, in a canny move, stepped aside and declared the universally liked Vajpayee as the prime ministerial candidate. He was not only in awe of Vajpayee's oratory and national stature but also strategically aware that it was Vajpayee alone who could make the BJP acceptable in a coalition era and haul in a centrist constituency for the 1996 general elections, the first general election in which a vulnerable Congress was not led by a Nehru–Gandhi. Advani, unlike Vajpayee, didn't hesitate to get his hands dirty with his party's hard-line cadres, throwing in his lot with the bloodstained mandir agitation for his coldly ambitious strategy to build his party. Yet he placed that formidable machinery entirely at the disposal of Vajpayee. Politically, Vajpayee ran circles around Advani, while the latter lumbered on with the Hindutva ideologue tag, even though Vajpayee himself often turned up the Hindutva pitch when he felt he needed to.

Vajpayee was cleverly absent in Ayodhya when the Babri Masjid fell. He made it clear that he disapproved of rath yatras, although he benefited from the political fortunes they netted, and at the same time he also subtly publicized his genuine disagreements with the RSS, which Advani, on the other hand, played down. Whether in the mandir agitation or later, in supporting Narendra Modi, Advani remained fixated on building the party and keeping the cadres galvanized, allowing Vajpayee the liberal 'secular' hand-wringing space, while he trudged in the mucky trenches of bigotry and hatred. Vajpayee delivered the gold-starred speeches and softened hearts and minds in Parliament, but when it came to negating the self entirely for the party, Advani scored over him. There are instances of Vajpayee's anger against Advani: such as his outburst at then BJP president Venkaiah Naidu describing the duo as equally ranked lauhpurush-vikaspurush (Iron Man and Development Man), and his open scorn of Advani's rath yatras as 'drama' and 'nautanki'. But there are no instances of Advani ever directing open anger against Vajpayee. Yet in government Vajpayee deferred to Advani, trusting his views and acuity and, more often than not, took his advice. 'Advaniji has been my friend and comrade in arms over fifty years . . . my able deputy in steering the nation,' Vajpayee writes. 'We have had our differences in the course of our long association . . . but unity of purpose has marked our relationship.' The words are cordial if not effusive, quietly appreciative about someone he obviously respected greatly.[27]

In later years, particularly after 1991 when the RSS chose Advani instead of Vajpayee as leader of the Opposition in Parliament, tensions developed between the Vajpayee and Advani households, and the Advani and Vajpayee 'camps' began to become hostile to each other. Both families, each possessively adoring of their respective patriarchs, would become suspicious that the other was trying to upstage them. When Vajpayee's star was sinking, Vajpayee's family remained stubborn on his sole stalwart status and believed that Advani's strident hard-line image was harming the BJP, while Advani's household was impatient with him being the perennial No. 2.

There was another significant reason for bouts of chill. Many in the RSS disapproved of Vajpayee's relationship with Rajkumari Kaul née Haksar and unsavoury, uncharitable remarks were often made about Rajkumari by some in the Sangh Parivar. This put the Kaul family's – particularly Rajkumari's daughter Namita's – backs up. They felt hunted, misunderstood, and fell prey to an 'us' versus 'them' mentality, sometimes clubbing Advani with their baiters in the sangh.

'Advani was very straight,' says A.S. Dulat. 'He would build the party through the ideology he fiercely believed in. Vajpayee was much, much more of a politician.'[28] The journalist Vidya Subrahmaniam writes that while Advani's 'definitive articulations left nothing to the imagination' Vajpayee had a 'chameleon like ability to change with the mood'.[29]

Liberal, illiberal, conservative, progressive – rigid definitions did not suit Vajpayee and his politics of poetic ambiguity. If there is any definition that suits him it is that of a natural-born pragmatic politician who took care to keep himself ideologically agile and flexible and clung tenaciously to his leader image. Vajpayee was far better than Advani at shelving ideology when it suited him, and for sheer cunning and political nous, he was light years ahead of Advani.

~

Let us now turn back to 1957 and the start of Vajpayee's first decade in Parliament. It was a time of hectic transformation for him, when the RSS activist and journalist grew slowly but steadily into Vajpayee the parliamentarian. Parliament opened broad new vistas. Nehru electrified and stimulated him. His ideas of India changed forever, and India's incorrigible heterogeneity, its 'vividhita', or diversity, became entrenched in his mind. He encountered colleagues like C.N. Annadurai (founder of the DMK) from Tamil Nadu, Minoo Masani from Mumbai and Hirendranath Mukherjee from Calcutta. His own constellation of qualities – sense of humour and ready wit – won him many new friends. However, not everyone was charitable towards him. Zareer Masani, the son of Minoo, writes his father considered Vajpayee a 'drunkard demagogue not to be trusted', while he thought of Madhok as 'very gentlemanly'.[30]

Parliament was the mother of all kavi sammelans, the nation's highest stage for performances of oratory. So elated was he at his first Lok Sabha win that when he received his first MPs' salary he was eager to celebrate. Grabbing the arm of his friend Jagdish Prasad Mathur, the organizing secretary of the Jana Sangh, he took him to the Indian Coffee House for coffee and masala dosas, went shopping at Khadi Gramodyog for two kurta-pyjama sets for Mathur and dhoti-kurta for himself, and then bought a paan each for them.

He valued the camaraderie and brotherhood of the party. In his first days in the Jana Sangh he lived at the party's rundown central office in Ajmeri Gate in Old Delhi, as did many others like Upadhyaya and Advani. One day his party comrades waited in vain for Vajpayee's scheduled arrival in the evening, and kept his dinner ready and waiting. But he failed to turn up and they went to bed. Early next morning, a rumpled Vajpayee arrived, with suitcase and bedding roll in hand. 'We waited for you last night,' they said. 'My train arrived late so I thought rather than disturb you I would just go and spend the night in the Ramlila Maidan,' he replied sheepishly. He was described as a fakir and a mastmaula (carefree and lively soul), accustomed to living rough, sleeping little and travelling light.

In 1957, however, that style of living changed. From small party premises, he now found himself in a spacious Delhi home. As an MP he was allotted a bungalow on the broad, tree-lined Rajendra Prasad Road, which he shared with another Jana Sangh MP, Premjibhai Assar, who had won from Ratnagiri in Maharashtra, and with Advani. Resources were meagre and, inside, the house was bare and plain. They would all share the household chores, and Assar's wife would cook for all of them, though occasionally Vajpayee would take over the kitchen and produce 'delicious' fare.[31] In the bone-chilling Delhi winter, Vajpayee shared an overcoat with another newly elected Jana Sangh MP, the short-statured but articulate Uttamrao Patil, MP from Dhulia, on whom the overcoat hung oversized over his arms. Parliament hung, in a similarly extra-large size, over the tiny frame of the Jana Sangh.

Establishing the Jana Sangh's voice and identity in Parliament with just four MPs was not going to be easy, and the party's dwarf shoots had to struggle for air amid a forest of towering trees. 'We four members . . . had never been a member of any legislature . . . were quite new to legislative work,' recalled Vajpayee. 'We neither had any previous experience nor was any experienced member there to whom we could turn to for help.'[32] Since they were few in number they were allotted the backbenches, from where it was difficult to catch the Speaker's eye; and once, irritated at not getting a chance to speak, Vajpayee even staged a walkout. 'Walkouts,' he said in 1994, 'are democratic procedure. It is better to remain outside rather than get into the House and disturb its proceedings.'[33] When Ghatate asked Vajpayee at this time, 'Why doesn't your name appear in the newspapers?' Vajpayee replied, 'At present, I am only observing.'[34]

There was a lot to observe. A brilliant array of speaking talents raged and thundered in Parliament in these years: the Communist Party of India (CPI) stalwart Hiren Mukherjee, quoting from Shakespeare to Tagore in his Oxford-accented speeches that held the House spellbound; the sophisticated Minoo Masani, who was to co-found the Swatantra Party in 1959; the socialist barrister Nath Pai, who could quote from English, Marathi and Sanskrit texts with equal fluency; and the effervescent Feroze Gandhi, a rising parliamentary phenomenon who unleashed bumper doses of mocking attacks at his own father-in-law's government. The razor-sharp Bhupesh Gupta, CPI member in the Rajya Sabha, lashed out with great effect, every intervention meticulously researched. Bhupesh Gupta didn't have an Oxford accent, neither was he airily intellectual, but his dogged, pugnacious style, backed by an enormous marshalling of facts, made him a parliamentary gladiator. Vajpayee told his friends that he would like his own speeches to be compared with Gupta's hard-hitting interventions. 'Debates were diverse, purposeful and substantive . . . stalwarts sitting in Opposition, fully matched the stature and competence of those sitting in the Treasury benches . . . Vice Chairman of the House presided with sage like dignity . . . Speaker was the custodian of the rights of the Opposition,' noted Advani admiringly.[35] What a time to be in Parliament!

As he soaked in the art of argument and counter-argument, the humour and fellowship of the House, as he listened carefully to the virtuoso performances of his colleagues, Vajpayee began to develop his own speaking skills and grow in wisdom and understanding about legislative work. 'He learnt a great deal from Parliament,' recalls

Murli Manohar Joshi. 'He learnt about the diversity of India, the art of taking people along, Parliament made him part of a bigger and wider world.'[36]

~

If he sparred and jousted in Parliament, in his party too he jostled for supremacy manoeuvring rivals out of the way in his own quietly hard-nosed style. After the death of Mookerji, Vajpayee and Balraj Madhok emerged as the Jana Sangh's two most prominent faces. The 1957 elections brought only tiny gains, and Upadhyaya increasingly harnessed RSS cadres for the Jana Sangh cause. Along with building the party's base, the pursuit of political power depended on nationally recognized and popular faces. Syama Prasad Mookerji had been a brilliant speaker in English, both in Parliament and in the field, and the party desperately needed speaking talents. Vajpayee was on course to fill Mookerjee's shoes, but because he spoke exclusively in Hindi he was cut off from the South, leaving a gap in the party for an English-speaking orator. This role was increasingly taken by the competent and outgoing Balraj Madhok, who spoke English fluently and, as co-founder of the Jana Sangh, always regarded Vajpayee as an upstart. Madhok was in the founding team of the Jana Sangh and had worked to establish the Praja Parishad party in Jammu as early as 1947 when Vajpayee was still only a *Rashtradharma* journalist. Madhok always considered himself far senior to both Vajpayee and Advani in the party hierarchy. Vajpayee privately called Madhok an 'egoist'.[37]

In these years, the RSS and Jana Sangh were continually accused of communalism and of fomenting communal riots, particularly riots in Raipur in 1957 and Jabalpur in 1961. 'The murderers of Gandhi' and 'communal' tags hung around the party's neck. Worried about again being banned or restricted by Nehru, the Jana Sangh made serious efforts to move towards a more pragmatic moderate-conservative position, with Vajpayee and Madhok espousing the cause of alliances with other parties to take on the Congress, although they differed in their choice of alliance partners. Madhok firmly rejected any alliance with left-leaning parties, whereas Vajpayee was open to tie-ups with socialists and communists. As they both grew in stature, Vajpayee and Madhok, friends in earlier days, stood poised in intense competition.

Although they both came to the RSS from the Arya Samaj, Madhok was a very different character from Vajpayee. He was a Punjabi Khatri, not a Hindi-belt Brahmin. Unlike Vajpayee, who wrote lyrical, ardent poetry in Hindi, Madhok was a history lecturer and an analytical and prolific writer of political commentary and several books. Madhok – more gregarious and sociable than the reserved Vajpayee – was often spotted at foreign embassy functions in Delhi. Unlike Vajpayee, who at this stage was socialist-minded and ready to seize the populist line, Madhok was an open right-winger, espousing a combination of Hindu nationalist politics and free-market economics, openly supportive of a pro-America stance. Unlike Vajpayee and Upadhyaya, Madhok was a trenchant enemy of socialism, particularly the Hindu socialism of some in the Sangh Parivar.

Vajpayee, by contrast, played the politics of careful strategic ambiguity, not articulating his ideas as vociferously as Madhok but adhering to a pro-common-man, vaguely socialist-populist line. Later, Madhok would push for a Jana Sangh alliance with the newly formed centrist liberal Swatantra Party. Madhok's anti-socialist ideas, and push for an alliance with the Swatantra, found little favour with Upadhyaya or with party cadres, who were more inclined towards Vajpayee's populist stance. The Sangh Parivar rank and file stood with Vajpayee rather than with Madhok, which eventually led to Madhok's isolation.

In 1968 Vajpayee spoke in favour of worker strikes and their demand for minimum wages and criticized Madhok's attack on Indira's 1969 bank nationalization, saying the Jana Sangh must always be on the side of the 'common man' and never be seen as 'pro-rich' or the defender of business.[38] In 1969 Vajpayee declared: 'No one can have any quarrel with socialism's concern for the underdog or its insistence on social justice.'[39] In 1970 he said: 'People are interested not by ideologies but by fundamental bread and butter needs.'[40] In another telling speech that shows how he always placed politics over any rigid ideology, Vajpayee said in 1972: 'We are going neither right or left. We are certainly going forward, adjusting ourselves to the time and the demands of the time.'[41] Thoroughly irritated and put off by Vajpayee's leftist utterances, Madhok stormed out of a party meeting in Patna in 1969. He made no secret of his dislike for Vajpayee, speaking against him openly and constantly, and calling him a 'communist'. Madhok was also impatient with what he saw as the leftist drift of Upadhyaya's integral humanism, which to Madhok was a borrowing from the communist M.N. Roy.

In an ironical twist of history, as prime minister, it would be Vajpayee who would uphold free-market economics, only to be assailed by the socialistic-swadeshi elements within the Sangh Parivar. As prime minister, Vajpayee in fact upheld Madhok's line on the economy, even though in the 1950s and 1960s they were angry opponents on the issue of the free market and state control.

Madhok lost the 1957 elections but entered the Lok Sabha in 1961 through a by-election in Delhi and soon made an impact as a speaker. He was elected president of the Jana Sangh in April 1966. During his presidency the Jana Sangh participated in a massive demonstration against cow slaughter in Delhi in November 1966, which attracted large numbers of protesters (across North India the numbers were estimated between 1,25,000 and 7,00,000), among them trishul-waving Naga sadhus. The protests suddenly turned uncontrollable and some sadhus attempted to storm Parliament. Vajpayee and others who were also part of the demonstrations rushed to try to calm the unruly mob and prevent them from attacking the Lok Sabha. For Vajpayee it was particularly important that the Sangh Parivar not be seen attacking Parliament, the place where he was building his profile, and where the Jana Sangh was seeking to become part of the 'normal' parliamentary Opposition. Arguing the Jana Sangh's positions on foreign policy, economy and social issues, Vajpayee did not want to be seen as overwhelmed by the trishul-brandishing, cow-obsessed Hindutva army.

The cow agitation turned bloody. Indira Gandhi, sworn in as prime minister only that year, allowed the protests to get out of hand. Police opened fire, leading to deaths and mass arrests. Shops and buildings were torched and government buildings vandalized. By nightfall the army was out in the streets of Delhi for the first time since 1947, and Madhok himself, along with over a thousand others, was arrested. The cow-protection agitation did not achieve much, but bolstered the visibility of the Jana Sangh and made headlines.

Sangh Parivar cadres were galvanized by the police action on sadhus and sants, and carried an emotionally surcharged mood into the elections of 1967, in which, under Madhok's presidency, the Jana Sangh streaked upwards to its best so far performance of thirty-five seats, with Madhok himself winning from New Delhi with a huge margin. Vajpayee too won handsomely from Balrampur. After the 1967 polls there was a tussle between Madhok and Vajpayee on who would be leader of the parliamentary party, but Vajpayee was elected unanimously.

After 1967, Madhok and Vajpayee clashed again over Vajpayee's enthusiastic push for alliances with leftist parties in forming the Samyukta Vidhayak Dal (SVD) governments. Both stepped up hostilities towards the other, Vajpayee planting unfavourable stories about Madhok in *Panchjanya* through his friend, the RSS ideologue and then editor Devendra Swarup. An incensed Madhok dubbed Swarup a Vajpayee 'chamcha' and even distributed leaflets against Vajpayee at the party's all-India session in Patna in 1969. In later years, Madhok accused Vajpayee and Advani of being lightweights who had no role in the founding of the Jana Sangh and who had diluted the party's identity by making it a watery version of the Congress as a result of Vajpayee's misguided 'secular' pretensions and leftward lurch.[42]

With Madhok, in his tenure as Jana Sangh president, often directing open criticism at Vajpayee and also resisting RSS influence in the party, then RSS sarkaryavah (general secretary) Balasaheb Deoras, who was close to Vajpayee, became set on removing the high-profile free-marketeer. Madhok's presidency 'created serious destabilizing problems for the party', wrote Vajpayee's ally, Advani,[43] glossing over the fact that it was during Madhok's presidency in 1966–67 that the Jana Sangh had hauled in a record thirty-five seats. After Deendayal Upadhyaya's death in 1968, Vajpayee assumed the presidency and further marginalized Madhok. Advani became Jana Sangh party president at the end of 1972, and after the party's Kanpur session in 1973, Madhok was expelled from the party on grounds of 'indiscipline'. With Madhok neutralized, the Vajpayee–Advani era began for India's Hindu nationalist politics.

'If it were done when 'tis done, then 'twere well / It were done quickly,' said Shakespeare's Macbeth. Whether Madhok now or decades later another firebrand, Govindacharya, or the independent-minded Uttar Pradesh OBC (other backward caste) leader Kalyan Singh, once Vajpayee decided to act against his detractors, he did it quickly, and with a manipulativeness that was as pointed as it was invisible. Another example is relevant here. The BJP's high-profile Arun Jaitley joined the Jana Sangh in 1977, but it was only after almost two decades on the margins that in 1999 Jaitley first became a minister and then an MP in 2000. Jaitley, firmly in the 'Advani camp' from the start, confessed to a friend that he always suspected someone in the BJP did not quite want him and that person was Vajpayee.

The fall of Madhok was a testament to Vajpayee's formidably shrewd power play and his ability to win the RSS over to his side when he wanted to. The poet-politician and Uttar Pradesh Brahmin knew how indispensable he was to both Golwalkar and Upadhyaya, and he encircled, overwhelmed and finally cast out Madhok. Nor did he brook any other rivals. Apart from Madhok, there were other party colleagues too who would grumble in later years that Vajpayee never did allow others to rise to the limelight or gain prominence in Parliament. Dattopant Thengadi and Sundar Singh Bhandari, his colleagues in the Rajya Sabha, fell by the wayside. His politics was like his poetry, pleasant and gently delivered, but with a powerful impact. To his rivals or to those he was suspicious of, or didn't quite like, Vajpayee could be a subtle Machiavelli.

~

His first parliamentary term a great success, Vajpayee was recognized as a forceful and intelligent Opposition face. 'As a spokesman for the Bharatiya Jana Sangh, I had succeeded in establishing its separate identity,' he wrote proudly.[44] He was noticed in the press and by foreign observers, and given a Leader Grant by the US Education Exchange Program to observe the 1960 US elections, which brought John F. Kennedy to power. Visiting America for the first time, Vajpayee stayed with Ghatate, then a student in Washington. He wore his dhoti on the trip, and once when Ghatate and Vajpayee strolled into a store, a sudden gust of wind blew up Vajpayee's dhoti. 'Hey, what sexy trousers!' exclaimed the shop girl behind the counter. Vajpayee blushed in embarrassment but continued to wear his preferred Bharatiya attire throughout this trip.

As the campaign for the 1962 general elections began, Upadhyaya, again determined not to lose Vajpayee's voice in Parliament, had him contest from two seats – Balrampur and Lucknow. In Balrampur Vajpayee campaigned hard, walking, cycling and travelling by jeep across dirt tracks. His rallies were crowded, and riding high on his successful debut in Parliament he basked in the certainty of another win.

But the spirited Opposition parliamentarian who put him on the mat so regularly had awakened Nehru's competitive instincts and the Congress put up a no-holds-barred fight against Vajpayee in Balrampur. It fielded Subhadra Joshi, who was as untiring a campaigner as she was beautiful and articulate, and who regularly attacked Vajpayee as communal and the Sangh as a fascist organization, organized along the lines of the Nazi party.[45] Nehru also prevailed on the reigning movie heart-throb at the time, Balraj Sahni, to campaign for Joshi. Nehru visited the constituency once during the campaign and, as a mark of respect for his well-liked adversary, made a speech in which, in an apparent gesture to Vajpayee, he said, 'There are some good people in the Jana Sangh.' Vajpayee would later write that most voters took Nehru's remark as referring specifically to him, and this helped him win votes, although he couldn't hold the seat.[46]

The results were deeply disappointing. Vajpayee lost Balrampur narrowly by 2000 votes. He was defeated in Lucknow by the Congress by a substantial margin. He was shocked, writing that he had worked hard to nurture his constituency well, and his defeat by only 2000 votes was 'unanticipated'. What was particularly galling is that almost all the Jana Sangh candidates in the assembly segments in his constituency won: 'they [the victorious Jana Sangh MLAs] were able to cross the river but I was drowned midstream'. There appear to be some niggling suspicions in his mind about the role played by his own party in his openly expressed surprise at the Jana Sangh's MLA candidates in the same constituency winning while he, the sitting MP, flopped. Writing about his earlier 1957 rout in Mathura, he said, 'I regret that the local unit of the Party . . . should have remained firm in its resolve to get the majority of votes cast in my favour.'[47] He was bitterly disappointed that his parliamentary success story was so abruptly interrupted just as he was getting started and writes at length on how his constituents all came to meet him to tell him that they had voted for him en masse. 'After I lost the election I resolved henceforth not to maintain more than necessary contact [with Balrampur] . . . I wanted to give a chance to the Congress candidate to work . . . but I was firmly determined to seek re-election . . . and avenge my defeat.'[48]

However, the ever-supportive Upadhyaya, refusing to let Vajpayee bow out of Parliament, sent him to the Rajya Sabha from Uttar Pradesh, and Vajpayee was back on the House benches. The Jana Sangh had only two members in the Rajya Sabha, but despite this the then chairman of the Rajya Sabha, Dr Radhakrishnan, allotted him a seat in the first row, giving him ample opportunity to speak. He hit the ground running, hammering away daily at the government. Nehruvian democracy made it possible for Nehru's opponent to flourish unimpeded.

The Congress again swept the 1962 polls, winning 361 seats, but challengers were beginning to rear their heads. Although Vajpayee lost, the Jana Sangh bettered its tally considerably, going from four to fourteen. Wrote the *New Age*: 'It is the Jana Sangh that promises, because of its militant and disciplined character, far greater opposition to the Congress in the years to come. One might or might not like this particular expression of the Hindi electorate . . . but it is undoubtedly a force of great importance.'[49] The Swatantra Party, more aristocratically liberal than the Hindu conservative Jana Sangh, won eighteen seats. Jawaharlal Nehru was still dominant, but the Opposition was stirring. Small new waves were rising and beating at the feet of the titan.

The years 1962–67 would be tumultuous: it would be five years of invasions, deaths and political and social upheaval, with protests breaking out in different parts of India: student protests, agitations over language and statehood, and Hindu campaigns on cow protection. There would be upheavals in the life of the Jana Sangh too, with Vajpayee increasingly catapulted to even higher rungs of leadership. Later, in 1962, the Jana Sangh would get a huge opportunity to skewer Nehru, and this it would do with all its might.

In October 1962, the Chinese army came swarming down from the Himalayas, crossed the McMahon lLine – the effective border between India and China – pushed back the poorly prepared Indian lines of defence and overran Indian territory. Within days, in massive assault, the Chinese were in Ladakh and Arunachal Pradesh. The government was woefully unprepared. Nehru, who had extended a warm hand of friendship to the Chinese in 1954 when the spirit of 'Hindi–Chini bhai-bhai' filled the air, was stunned. Over a thousand Indian soldiers were killed, the Chinese captured Indian territory and India was humiliated. The war ended when the Chinese themselves announced a ceasefire. The Chinese invasion left Nehru 'a shattered man' recalled Vajpayee – their 'betrayal' had broken his heart. 'Thereafter he never again looked his old lively self.'[50]

The Jana Sangh scented blood. Always a hawk on China, Vajpayee demanded an immediate summoning of Parliament in a special session. Such were the democratic freedoms available in Nehru's India that even at the height of an armed conflict an Opposition leader could demand a special session of Parliament. In late October, Vajpayee and a Jana Sangh parliamentary party delegation drove to Nehru's office to demand that Parliament be called. Both Houses were summoned on 8 November 1962, and Vajpayee launched a no-holds-barred attack on the government without any fear that he would be labelled a 'traitor'.

'In this time of agni pariksha . . . we must openly accept that we have gone gravely wrong, committed a sin,' Vajpayee said in a high-decibel speech. It was a 'matter of shame' that the army was so terribly unprepared; India, he bellowed, was engaged in a life-and-death struggle against an imperialist power which was more dangerous than those in the past because it had attacked India in the name of Hindi–Chini bhai-bhai.[51] The repeated use of the words 'sin' and 'shame' reveals how Vajpayee played to public rage over the invasion of the motherland and abject failures of her protectors.

Hoping to capitalize on the anti-Congress mood after 1962, the Jana Sangh went on the political offensive. In four by-elections in May 1963, the Jana Sangh, Swatantra Party and Socialist Party united to put up single candidates, the Jana Sangh's first stab at being part of a mainstream anti-Congress Opposition alliance. In sensational results, three candidates – Minoo Masani, Ram Manohar Lohia and J.B. Kripalani – swept the Congress out. 'There was a wave of anti-

Congressism in the country,' wrote Vajpayee.[52] But the Jana Sangh's moving spirit, Deendayal Upadhyaya, fielded from Jaunpur, lost in the only election he ever contested, refusing to play for votes on his caste identity, and adhering to a strict code of conduct.

At the party's 1963 annual session in Bhopal, Vajpayee's popularity in the party was on display. Party men applauded him when he delivered a denunciation of China, calling for India to draw closer to the West and to Southeast Asia, which also feel the 'threat from China'. He tore apart Nehru's Kashmir policy and loudly disapproved of any talks with Pakistan on Kashmir. Speaking offstage to party men in Bhopal on Article 370, he said, 'Don't worry, 370 *dheere dheere ghis jayega* [slowly Article 370 will erode away].' When reminded of this statement in later years, he joked, '*Hum ghis gaye,* but not 370.'[53]

The Jana Sangh member's outstanding speeches were now being frequently reported in the press. In December 1963, the disappearance of a relic of the Prophet from a mosque in Srinagar sparked riots in Kashmir and Bengal, and blame was directed at the RSS. 'The Central government should conduct an inquiry [on the Calcutta riots],' demanded Vajpayee in another 'nationalist' speech. 'It would be against the truth to allow the impression that whatever was done was by the Hindus and nothing was done by elements in league with Pakistan.'[54]

On 27 May 1964, Jawaharlal Nehru died. Vajpayee's tribute to Nehru was deeply emotional, his eulogy in the Rajya Sabha on 29 May sounding like the lament of a devoted fan:

> A dream has been shattered, a song silenced, a flame has vanished in the infinite. It was a dream of a world without fear, without hunger, it was the song of an epic that had the echo of the Gita, and the fragrance of the rose . . . Bharat Mata is stricken with grief today – she has lost her favourite prince, her rajkumar. Humanity is sad today – it has lost its devotee. Peace is restless today – its protector is no more. The leading actor of the world's stage has completed his

> final act and gone . . . the freedom of which he was the protector and general is today in danger. We have to protect it with all our might . . . the leader has gone, the followers remain. The sun has set, now we have to find our way in the light of the stars . . . that vibrant personality, that attitude of taking even the opposition along, that refined gentlemanliness, that greatness we may not see again in the near future . . . we have nothing but respect for his great ideals.[55]

~

After Nehru's death, the mild-mannered, diminutive and stout-hearted Gandhian from Uttar Pradesh, Lal Bahadur Shastri, was sworn in as prime minister. Vajpayee warmed to him from the start, noting the contrast between Nehru's regal upbringing and Shastri's rise from abject poverty as a sign of the maturity of Indian democracy and declaring him a 'worthy successor' to Nehru.[56]

With the passing of Nehru, the Jana Sangh's dream of becoming a national alternative to the Congress began to grow bigger. The political arena bristled with competition and ambitions about new opportunities. Vajpayee was now well into his second parliamentary term, leader of the Jana Sangh's parliamentary party, the party now the official Opposition in Madhya Pradesh and Uttar Pradesh. The elected politicians in the Jana Sangh, Vajpayee and Madhok, sought to establish their independent authority, away from the faceless unelected RSS men who dominated the party workers' ranks, and away from control of Nagpur. Vajpayee, harbouring his own ambitions to be party leader and finding himself in the newspaper headlines more than anyone else in his party, was chafing at the RSS's constant attempts to call the shots despite his closeness to Upadhyaya. A fault line now opened between him and his ever-supportive mentor.

In 1963, the Jana Sangh president Raghu Vira, a scholarly and moderate-conservative former Congressman, died in a car crash and, after an immediate short-term replacement, in 1965 the party selected Bachhraj Vyas as Jana Sangh president. Vyas was a faceless, unknown secretary of the Nagpur RSS. It was a move designed to re-establish RSS dominance in the party and install a president who would function as a Golwalkar mouthpiece. As Jana Sangh president, Vyas presided over the Vijayawada session of the party held in January 1965. The move to foist an unknown RSS man as head of the party when there were big talents waiting in queue infuriated Vajpayee and he made his displeasure known. What?! Would the high-profile interlocutor of Nehru now have to work under a nobody from Nagpur, when Jana Sangh presidents in the past, Mookerji onward, had been well-known public figures? Madhok was furious too. Both boycotted the Vijayawada session.

Vajpayee's 1965 boycott of the Jana Sangh's Vijayawada session was the first public show of a rising young parliamentarian's increasing unease with the closed-minded RSS leadership attempting to run the Jana Sangh in its way. This was his first confrontation with the RSS, which over the years would intensify, not necessarily as an ideological clash but as a struggle for power within the 'Hindu' fold. After the Vijayawada friction, Upadhyaya moved quickly to mend fences with his protégé. When the session ended he made straight for Vajpayee's home, at that time 1 Feroz Shah Road, and remained with him for a few days, never mentioning Vijayawada, his silence eloquent of his disapproval. Vajpayee was perplexed by Upadhyaya's silence and surprisedly told friends that his party boss had not asked him even once why he did not go to Vijayawada.[57] Vajpayee's absence at Vijayawada became another canker in his relationship with the sangh.

There would be other inflection points between Vajpayee and the RSS. In all his speeches in Parliament through the 1960s, Vajpayee was at pains to insist that the Jana Sangh was a 'secular' party which did not discriminate between religions, although it was against any form of special privileges to Muslims. 'The Bharatiya Jana Sangh is an advocate of the secular state,' he declared in 1961. 'We advocate a state in which there will be no discrimination on religious grounds.

The doors of the Jana Sangh are open to every citizen of the country . . . but this does not mean separate powers should be demanded in the name of the minorities'.[58] For the Golwalkar-led RSS, however, there could be no compromise when it came to the Hindutva ideological mission. The Jana Sangh's attempts to combine Hindu traditions with modern democracy would lead to tussles between the party's parliamentary politicians and its ideologues and cadres. Ideological 'purity' versus the drive for political success would remain a source of strain between Vajpayee and his organizational parent body.

There was another important reason why relations between Vajpayee and the RSS cooled at this time. In 1966, a year after the Vijayawada face-off, Golwalkar suddenly stripped Vajpayee of his 'pracharak' rank. He remained only a swayamsevak, which is why he would often smilingly say, 'I have always been a swayamsevak.' His breeziness hid the gnawing insecurity and rebelliousness he increasingly began to feel towards the RSS from this time. There's a reason why Golwalkar acted as he did.

As we have seen in the previous chapter, when Vajpayee was a student in Gwalior's Victoria College, he had met and fallen in love with Rajkumari Haksar and hoped one day to marry her. But she was a Kashmiri Pandit, and although he himself was a Kanyakubj Brahmin, he didn't win the approval of her clannish patrician family. Life took them separate ways, but he cherished always the memories of the beautiful and spirited girl with whom he had fallen deeply in love.

By the time Vajpayee established himself in politics, Rajkumari was married to Brij Narain Kaul, lecturer and warden at Ramjas College in Delhi University, and had settled in Delhi. According to Vajpayee's biographer Vijai Trivedi, around 1964, Rajkumari even decided to divorce her husband and marry Vajpayee.[59] But at this time Vajpayee was a rising young parliamentarian who was seeking to ascend the party ladder and he was advised by a senior RSS pracharak that marriage to a divorcee would harm his political career. Subsequently, Rajkumari and her family moved in with Vajpayee on the understanding that she would never be seen in public with him. Talk of their relationship outraged and discomfited the sangh, there was ugly gossip which led to a distancing on both sides. A family friend recalls that the vulnerable and modest Kaul family felt unfairly targeted by those in the sangh who whispered and gossiped about them, the daughters particularly protective of their mother. Vajpayee's closeness to the Kauls is revealing of him: he wanted the sophisticated and educated companionship (Rajkumari was related to Indira Gandhi) of his old Gwalior friend, and he would have it, and to hell with saffron wrath. But the RSS simply could not stomach the fact that not only was their main politician living openly with a married woman and her family, but seemed to care two hoots for their opinion on the matter.

There were also rumours about Vajpayee's taste for high living. An apocryphal joke about Vajpayee in sangh circles ran thus: 'Netaji watched a blue film in Daryaganj, then ate some murg mussalam at kake di hatti, then jumped into a car to go to a rally to lecture people so movingly on poverty that the audience all burst into tears.'[60] There were even whisperings of Vajpayee in America sitting through a meal in which beef was served and telling a companion, 'This is American cow, not Indian.'[61] Madhok (who had ample reason to be bitter about Vajpayee) writes in his autobiography that Jagdish Prasad Mathur once complained to him that Vajpayee had turned his residence on Rajendra Prasad Road into a 'den of immoral activities', with a succession of girls visiting. 'Every day new girls were coming there,' writes Madhok, and goes on to say that he suggested to Vajpayee that he get married; otherwise both his and the party's reputation would suffer.[62] According to Madhok, Golwalkar, hearing these stories, told him: 'I have to run an organization so like Shiva I drink poison every day.'[63]

Whether these accounts were true or not, there was indeed nothing puritanical or piously moralistic about Vajpayee, who was ever keen to experience life's pleasures and express his fun-loving side. At a friend's birthday party in Delhi he once turned up in a Pathani suit, saying,

'*Main desh ka ghulam hoon, vesh ka nahin* [I am a slave of the country, not of any dress].'[64] There was little the sangh could do about his rumoured wayward behaviour. After all, he was their prized trophy, the Jana Sangh's lead performer and its best electoral bet. However much the RSS may have shuddered in puritanical horror at stories of his romancing, whisky-drinking, meat-eating ways, they were helpless against his political stardom.

~

In 1965 armed conflict between India and Pakistan broke out in the Rann of Kutch and Kashmir. India's little big man, Prime Minister Shastri, did not flinch. Showing grit and will, India launched a full-scale military retaliation, the 1965 war ending with the Tashkent Declaration, or the Soviet-moderated peace agreement between India's Shastri and Pakistan's Ayub Khan. The Jana Sangh opposed the peace talks at Tashkent and a party delegation led by Vajpayee called on Shastri asking him not to go to Tashkent. Vajpayee inveighed against the Tashkent Declaration in Parliament: India's withdrawal from areas which were 'legally Indian' would betray the sacrifice of Indian troops. On 11 January 1966, a day after signing the peace agreement, Lal Bahadur Shastri, prime minister for only eighteen months, died in Tashkent.

Vajpayee's attack on Shastri during the 1965 war and the Tashkent agreement had been so ferocious that he feared it may have led to Shastri's ill health. He candidly admitted that he got the 'guilty feeling' that Shastri's death may have been triggered by his harsh criticism of him. He later found to his relief that it was a heart ailment and not shock that had taken Shastri's life.

After Shastri's death, on 24 January 1966, forty-nine-year-old Indira Gandhi was sworn in as India's prime minister. Everyone, including her own party, grossly underestimated the 'pretty lady'. Over the next decade, not only did she vanquish her party rivals but she would also become the Jana Sangh's nemesis, Vajpayee's formidable arch-rival, who would goad him to take up the Opposition torch with even greater vengeance.

Initially though, Indira was the tremulous, inexperienced '*goongi gudiya*', and with Nehru and Shastri gone and the Congress seemingly leaderless, the Jana Sangh readied for battle. The polls of 1967 were a year away. Vajpayee was again named as the candidate from Balrampur. The Jana Sangh was now a much more established, better-funded party than before, with its organizational strength spread across states. Once again, Vajpayee came up against his old adversary Subhadra Joshi, who again accused him of being a communalist and whom he accused of being a communist. He was determined to win this time: 'Some Congress leaders had suggested to me that I should leave Balrampur and seek election from elsewhere. Their logic was that I could win from any constituency. But I turned down their suggestion,' he writes.[65]

The results of the 1967 elections hit India like a crash of thunder. They were the most startling results so far in post-Independence India. The Congress – giant of Indian politics – fell to its knees, managing to cross the majority mark with only ten seats, at 283, falling below 300 for the first time since 1952. The Opposition surged ahead. The Swatantra Party scooped up forty-four seats and the Jana Sangh won thirty-five. Vajpayee and Madhok both pulled off spectacular victories in Balrampur and New Delhi, respectively, Vajpayee defeating Subhadra Joshi.

In this election powerful Congressmen like K. Kamaraj, S.K. Patil and Atulya Ghosh all lost, even though the debutante Indira Gandhi won from Rae Bareli. Noted a business weekly: 'If the electorate has shown any general bias, it is perhaps towards the right.'[66] In assembly elections the same year, the Congress slumped in North India, and Samyukta Vidhayak Dal governments took charge across the Hindi belt and kept the Congress out. The SVD, as mentioned earlier, was a coalition of the Jana Sangh, the socialists and the communists drawing on the alliance experience they had established in the 1963 by-polls.

Vajpayee, always extremely keen on coalitions, even with ideological adversaries, and always yearning to be part of the political mainstream, avidly pushed their cause in the party, saying that the very reason the Jana Sangh was in politics was to gain power. He was a strong votary for the Jana Sangh's participation in coalitions, even if it meant a masking of ideology. The main aim, after all, was to topple the Congress.

The 1967 elections were described as a 'watershed in Indian politics'[67] when the era of Congress dominance came to an end. The Jana Sangh was now second to the Congress in terms of vote share and third in the Lok Sabha, behind the Swatantra Party. Its long apprenticeship for some day seizing power at the Centre had begun. Vajpayee's own thinking would transform too: now, dethroning the Congress and making a bid to be the national alternative would be uppermost in his mind, the Hindu cultural revolution being only the utilitarian vehicle to get there. For the next three general elections until 1984, Vajpayee would win his seat every time.

He was forty-three in 1967 and in his prime. Now, when he began to speak in Parliament, some MPs would fall silent, others would troop into the Lok Sabha to hear him, a Hindi-speaking parliamentarian still a novelty in the House. His speeches were carefully crafted, and argued and delivered in style; they spanned a vast and impressive range of subjects, from Chinese aggression, secularism, the Hindi language, even 'Indianization' of the army, and were peppered with Sanskrit shlokas, Urdu couplets and folkloric parables. He had kept up vociferous attacks on Nehruvian secularism throughout Nehru's tenure: 'The government has set up a commission to stop the misuse of properties of Hindu maths and temples. I welcome it. But are the properties of mosques and churches not misused? Should a secular state not have a law applicable to all?'[68] He lashed out at the use of the Preventive Detention Act against the Jana Sangh: 'Why is he [Ram Prasad Das, organizing secretary of the Jana Sangh] alone arrested? You could have arrested the whole Working Committee. I suggest you ban the Bharatiya Jana Sangh.'[69]

He was in excellent health. None of the ailments that would dog him in later years had made an appearance, and he ate lustily, recited poetry in the evenings and barrelled around with a diverse group of friends in the evenings, sometimes heading to Kake da Dhaba in Delhi for chaat, or to the Indian Coffee House in Delhi's Connaught Place or wolfing down chicken in Lucknow. He was called 'pandit' by many, and it was expected that he would be a strict vegetarian. When a local newspaper in Lucknow once carried a photograph of him biting into a chicken leg, and outraged party men asked if he was indeed eating chicken, Vajpayee exclaimed, 'Chicken? Arre, that was a baingan [brinjal].' In the evenings, he was a regular at Ghatate's dinner parties. At one of these dinners, the phone rang and another guest, Balasaheb Deoras (Vajpayee's friend, later to become sarsanghchalak), answered and called out to Vajpayee, 'Your Rajmata is on the phone.' To which Vajpayee responded quick as a flash: 'Yes, of course, Rajmata, Bharat Mata, Gau Mata, all are mine [sic].'[70]

His earthy Hindi–Hindu identity was to the fore when, in November 1967, the Indira Gandhi government brought in an amended Official Languages Act guaranteeing the indefinite use of Hindi and English as India's official languages – or the 'virtually indefinite policy of bilingualism'. Vajpayee spoke up strongly for Hindi, the English language for long the Jana Sangh's bugbear, seen as part of the imperialist Macaulay's weapon to colonize the 'Bharatiya' mind. Advani notes, however, that Vajpayee, because of his friendship with Annadurai, contributed to a 'balanced language policy of the Jana Sangh',[71] acutely aware that an insistence on Hindi would stall the party's southward journey. 'I would like to assure my non-Hindi friends with all force at my command that we do not want to force Hindi on them, but they should not force English on us . . . we want equal status for Hindi and English.'[72]

Parliament was smoothening his hard edges, opening his eyes to new possibilities. That Annadurai, leader of Tamil Nadu's anti-Hindi agitation, someone who had once argued for a separate Dravidian state, could become close personal friends with a Hindi-upholding 'nationalist' Vajpayee showed the binding power of a shared parliamentary spirit.

As his party's leader in Parliament, and growing in stature and experience as an MP, Vajpayee was now keener than ever to establish the Jana Sangh as a national alternative to the Congress and, as Madhok's presidency drew to a close, was hopeful of assuming the post of party president himself. Particularly so because his line of thinking – of a populist, socialist-leaning, alliance-friendly approach – had now become dominant within the Jana Sangh, and Madhok's line, of rejecting any alliance with the left, had been spurned.

But Vajpayee's hopes were dashed. It was Deendayal Upadhyaya, the publicity-shunning party organizer, the person who 'wielded moral authority over tens and thousands of his followers'[73] and who preferred an alliance-less 'go it alone' stand for the Jana Sangh, who succeeded Madhok. He was elected as the Jana Sangh president at its important Calicut session in December 1967. It was at this session that Upadhyaya gave a new call in his presidential speech – the Jana Sangh must go along with people's agitations, which he said were 'natural and necessary', provide leadership to them, and not cooperate with those who want to 'perpetuate the status quo'.[74]

The emphasis on people's movements and their potential to overturn the social status quo had similarities with socialist ideas and is part of a school of thought we are describing as the 'Hindu left', to which both Vajpayee and Upadhyaya at this time subscribed. Advani would later use Upadhyaya's injunction of joining with 'people's agitations' to justify the BJP's decision to join the 'people's movement' to 'liberate' the Ram Mandir.

Upadhyaya was a completely different personality from Vajpayee – unassuming, meticulous, doctrinaire and deeply wedded to the Hindutva cause. His election as Jana Sangh president marked a return of RSS control over the party, after Madhok's energetic presidency had attempted to position the Jana Sangh as a pro-capitalist, free-market,

Swatantra Party–type entity. In 1967 Madhok too was hopeful of re-election as president, but both he and Vajpayee lost out to Upadhyaya.

Vajpayee was passed over as a choice for the Jana Sangh presidency after the big win of 1967. But history invariably parts the waters for those who have been marked to play a leading role in it. If Lal Bahadur Shastri had not passed away in Tashkent in January 1966, Indira Gandhi would not have been sworn in as prime minister a few weeks later. Nehru may not have ruled unchallenged if Sardar Patel had not passed away as early as in 1950. Just a month after his appointment as Jana Sangh president, Deendayal Upadhyaya was killed during a train journey, on 11 February 1968, at the age of fifty-one. He was found dead on the tracks near Mughalsarai station, with a currency note crumpled in his hand. Investigations later revealed he had been murdered in a robbery attempt, although Vajpayee continued to insist that robbery could not have been the motive and there was a larger conspiracy.[75] Madhok in his autobiography makes the sensational allegation that not only was Upadhyaya's death a 'pre-planned murder' and a 'conspiracy', but also that Vajpayee and Nanaji Deshmukh and even Balasaheb Deoras – who he alleged covered up for them – were all involved in it. Those who conspired to kill Upadhyaya, wrote Madhok, were 'jealous self-seekers' in the RSS and the Jana Sangh.[76] After Upadhyaya became Jana Sangh president, he had not given any important party posts to either Vajpayee or Nanaji Deshmukh, and Madhok writes, the two persons who benefited directly from Upadhyaya's death 'were those he had been keeping away from important posts'.[77] According to Madhok, Vajpayee treated Upadhyaya's death as an accident, not a murder, and told him that Upadhyaya was a hot-headed man who must have got into a quarrel with someone, and died when he got pushed out of the train.[78]

Madhok's allegations are, however, outlandish. Vajpayee was too admiring and too indebted to Upadhyaya to wish him harm however intensely he may have wanted to be party president at the time. Whatever the tensions in his relationship with the RSS, he had a tender bond with his mentor who had been a manav-shilpi (personality builder) for him. A day after Upadhyaya's death he paid a ringing tribute to him in Parliament.

'He was not a member of Parliament,' Vajpayee said in open recognition of Upadhyaya's crucial role in his own career, 'but if any one individual could be given the credit for those Bharatiya Jana Sangh members of Parliament who are sitting in this and the other House, if anyone could be given the credit for fashioning the Jana Sangh, fostering it and leading it to success, it is Upadhyayaji.'[79] Decades later, when the BJP was founded, Vajpayee recalled that with Syama Prasad Mookerji having died in jail and Upadhyaya slain on a train, the party's hardships during its political journey could be summed up as *ek pair rail mein, ek pair jail mein* (one foot in the rail, one foot in jail).[80] In 1996, three decades after Upadhyaya's death, Vajpayee confessed to still missing his soft-spoken backer. 'The void created by Shri Deendayal Upadhyaya's death continues to be felt,' he wrote.[81]

With Upadhyaya gone, the RSS turned to its irreverent, high-achieving son, who first professed reluctance and burst into showy tears but was finally cajoled to take on the post.[82] In 1968, Vajpayee, at the age of forty-three, became president of the Jana Sangh, remaining in the post until 1972. He was the Jana Sangh supremo but his party was heading into turbulent weather. If the death of Syama Prasad Mookerji had been a calamity for the Jana Sangh, the death of Upadhyaya was a body blow from which it never recovered.

Vajpayee tried to galvanize his party as best he could, reassuring them, '*Deendayalji ne ek jyoti lagayee, hum uski jwala kar denge* [Deendayal lit a lamp, which we will transform into a blaze].' He travelled incessantly, meeting party men, trying to soothe ruffled feathers and shore up the morale of the cadres grieving over the loss of their leader. The slogan '*Andhere mein ek chingari, Atal Bihari, Atal Bihari*' was raised. But party morale soon took another beating. After SVD governments in Bihar, Uttar Pradesh and Punjab collapsed – alliance partners Jana Sangh and socialists simply unable to forge working relationships – mid-term assembly elections were held in 1969 in which the Jana Sangh was badly defeated in all three states, while the Congress triumphed. Vajpayee's line as Jana Sangh president had been politically pragmatic, steering away from ideological extremes, focused on the Jana Sangh gaining power – and never mind ideology. But this politically strategic, accommodating Vajpayee-led Jana Sangh would soon find itself blown out of the water within two years of him assuming the party presidency.

A new force was rising. This was a force that would choke the Jana Sangh of its lifeblood, a force that it would be unable to combat and would lead to its ultimate demise. This new force was Indira Gandhi. In July 1969, in a sensational move, Indira Gandhi had nationalized fourteen private commercial banks, using the takeover of the banks to stand forth as a messiah of the poor; it was a shrewd strike at her rivals within the party, enabling Indira to project herself as a pro-poor revolutionary against the conservative old guard. Vajpayee, immediately realizing what a potent rallying cry this was, sprang to attack Indira in Parliament.[83] 'What is the emergency about the nationalization of banks?' he bellowed. 'Was the country facing an economic crisis? If there was a crisis at all it was a crisis of the Congress Party . . . a crisis of the Prime Minister.'[84]

In October the same year, the Congress split. Reduced to a minority government over the next year, Indira Gandhi called mid-term polls in March 1971. Yoking a massive tide of pro-poor populism to her persona she went to the people with the powerful slogan '*Garibi hatao*' (remove poverty). The Indira phenomenon spread across India at lightning speed.

In 1971, the Jana Sangh joined a pre-poll coalition of opposition parties including Swatantra and socialists – the Grand Alliance – to fight the hegemonic Indira. Vajpayee stood for elections from the home town he never forgot and often visited: Gwalior. The Jana Sangh had now netted a big fish: it had succeeded in getting Rajmata Vijaya Raje Scindia to join the party after her stints in the Congress and the

Swatantra. For the Jana Sangh, the Scindias provided big opportunities for expansion, given the popularity of the 'mahal' (royal palace) across the Gwalior–Guna belt. For the 1971 polls, the boy from Gwalior's Shinde ki Chhawani thus made a strategic shift from Balrampur to Gwalior.

Gwalior always stayed close to his heart. As an MP in Delhi, he would often jump on to a train to Gwalior to walk around its streets, snack on a laddoo or two from Bahadura Sweets, breathe Gwalior's familiar woodsmoke-scented air and listen to its temple bells. One day Rajmata Vijaya Raje Scindia, then not in the Jana Sangh, noticed Vajpayee holding an open umbrella, walking unescorted in the city's crowded Patankar Bazaar. She telephoned the local Jana Sangh leader to say, 'What kind of party are you? One of your biggest MPs is walking around alone, can't you organize a car for him?' The party official immediately dispatched a car, which Vajpayee returned, saying he didn't need a car when he was in Gwalior.

'Whenever he came back here, he would simply take my son's cycle and ride off to meet his old friends,' recalls his niece Kanti Mishra.[85] His family later recalled his trips to see them. He would come to the family house and take everyone out for a film, once taking as many as sixty-two family members to see the film *Pakeezah* when it was released. He would cook them delicious snacks and himself gorge on dahi vadas and besan, til and mungare laddoos. His niece Vinita remembers he would round up all the youngsters to take them to the Gwalior mela, give them all kharchi (pocket money) and then take them to his favourite chaatwallah. Family reunions in Gwalior were fleeting. Beyond these visits, Vajpayee's real family were the pedigreed Haksar–Kauls in Delhi.[86]

In 1971, Vijaya Raje Scindia spearheaded the Jana Sangh campaign in the Gwalior–Guna–Bhind region. The Jana Sangh pulled out all the stops for the election there, the Scindia family name dominating the Jana Sangh effort. Vajpayee had a packed schedule, addressing scores of meetings, and being welcomed as a prodigal son. In one of the meetings he learnt that a local MLA who was working in his campaign had a small son who was stricken with cancer. 'What are you doing here when you have a sick child at home?' demanded Vajpayee. 'Go home at once. *Agar haar jayenge toh haar jayenge, isme kya hai?* [What does it matter if we lose?]' As it turned out the Jana Sangh swept through this region, Vajpayee winning Gwalior, and the mother–son duo, Vijaya Raje Scindia and Madhavrao Scindia, winning from Bhind and Guna, respectively.

But the 1971 results were no cause for rejoicing for the Jana Sangh. The Congress, led by Indira Gandhi, won a gargantuan victory with 352 seats. The Jana Sangh, led by Vajpayee, had scored in the Gwalior region because of the Scindias, but failed elsewhere, plummeting to just twenty-two seats, its tally drastically reduced from the thirty-five it had won in 1967. In the 1967 elections, observers of the Jana Sangh had noted that the party was taking further steps towards moderation and shunning Hindu rigidities. But the Jana Sangh's evolution towards moderation was now rudely interrupted. Instead, the party seemed to be teetering on the brink of extinction as the Indira revolution galloped forward. Armed with a massive two-thirds majority won in her name, Indira Gandhi wiped out the Opposition and was sworn in as prime minister for the third time on 16 March 1971.

The poor showing of the Jana Sangh in 1971 persuaded Vajpayee to step down as party president at the end of 1972. He was succeeded by L.K. Advani. Advani who had entered the Rajya Sabha in 1970 from Delhi was a first-class party organizer and was seen by many as the second Upadhyaya, similarly self-effacing and indefatigable. With Advani as party president, Upadhyaya gone and Madhok expelled, the Vajpayee–Advani era began for India's Hindu nationalist politics, at a time when Nehru's daughter unleashed a political storm.

The dominance of the Indira-led Congress was even more bludgeoning than that of the Congress in the Nehru years. Once again his all-too-familiar adversary – the mighty Congress – sat on Delhi's throne and once again Vajpayee took up the burdens of the Opposition man against a charismatic Nehru–Gandhi. Leading the small twenty-two-member band of the Jana Sangh in Parliament, he stepped into the era of Indira Gandhi.

4

Battling Indira Gandhi: 1971–1980

A poem for Vajpayee:

Man of the opposition versus woman of state,
The lamp must blaze at any cost.
Let her hector, let her imprison, let her attempt to dominate,
We'll fight until her crown is tossed.

~

At the end of 1971, Vajpayee was a worried man. He had been Jana Sangh president for almost four years, its tallest leader and the fire-and-brimstone parliamentarian. As a four-time MP, his own personal standing was high, but his party was lurching from defeat to defeat. Upadhyaya's death had left a gaping void. Party workers were listless and dejected; leaders were glum. The strength of the Jana Sangh had dropped from thirty-five seats to twenty-two. In fact, the entire Opposition was in the doldrums. In the 1971 polls, the Congress rebels, or Congress (O), got only sixteen seats, the Communist Party of India (Marxist) (CPI(M)) got twenty-five, the Swatantra Party slumped to eight and the Socialist Party managed only three.

In the assembly elections of 1968–69, the Jana Sangh had been trounced by the Indira Gandhi–led Congress. In assembly elections in March 1972, the Jana Sangh was pummelled again. Riding on the victory in the Bangladesh war, Indira Gandhi blew her rivals into the wilderness. The Jana Sangh was routed, winning a measly five seats each in Himachal Pradesh and Maharashtra, and losing as many as thirty in Madhya Pradesh. Indira Gandhi monopolized both uber-patriotism and pro-poor populism – hers was a nationwide personality cult never before seen in India. As messiah of the poor, war heroine and Nehru's daughter, she was almost invincible. The Jana Sangh faced a crisis of survival.

Vajpayee was alarmed by the scale of his party's losses. Far from becoming a blaze that he had hoped to ignite after Upadhyaya's death, the Jana Sangh lamp was struggling to stay alight in the Indira gale. In November 1971 he said in an interview, 'The defeat in the elections had deeply disappointed the party workers . . . they were asking themselves whether the party would have been in a better position if it had not entered into an alliance [the Grand Alliance against Indira].'[1] Cadres blamed the leaders and became restless to throw themselves into rebellious activism against the dominant Indira.

Taking responsibility for the defeats, Vajpayee faced up to a home truth: he was not up to the organizational challenges of rebuilding the Jana Sangh. Always the on-stage speaking talent, more the show horse than the workhorse, he was no hands-on party organizer, he had little talent or inclination to toil at repairing the nuts and bolts of the party machinery. He was no Upadhyaya.

He deployed a tactic which he would often use in the years ahead to maintain his moral pedestal in the face of setbacks: he would resign. He made up his mind to quit as Jana Sangh president and hand the baton to someone else. During the 1971 campaign, he had delivered one of his wry witticisms about his future as party president. When party workers had burst into the usual slogan, '*Humaara neta kaisa ho, Atal Bihari jaisa ho* [We want a leader like Atal Bihari]', he had remarked, 'See how clever they are. They're saying they want a leader *like* me, not me.'

He first turned to his trusted companion L.K. Advani to be his replacement. But the Jana Sangh's former parliamentary secretary, unused to the limelight, refused, uncertain about his public-speaking skills or his ability to helm the party. But Vajpayee was set on stepping aside and at the Jana Sangh meeting in Bhagalpur in May 1972, he asked Bhai Mahavir, the scholarly, Upadhyaya-era veteran Jana Sanghi, to preside, declaring, '. . . there should be frank discussion and delegates should be free to criticize the leadership.'[2] He then offered the presidentship to Bhai Mahavir and to Vijaya Raje Scindia, who both said no. Vajpayee turned again to Advani, saying, 'No more of this fruitless search now. You have no option but to say yes to what I say.'[3] Advani, strongly backed by the RSS, agreed, and became Jana Sangh president in December 1972, remaining in the post until 1977.

In his fourth parliamentary term, Vajpayee was still the leader of the Jana Sangh parliamentary party, the twenty-two-member dwarf entity standing in the shadow of a giant Indira. His own luminosity in the House was undimmed. Where once he had attacked her father, Nehru, now his oratorical firepower was directed at the daughter. Speeches and interventions slammed into the House, intended as flaming arrows at the target. 'The Prime Minister wants to be . . . *Ekoham dwitiyo nasti* – I am the only one, there is no other. Such a feeling leads to dictatorship, the Prime Minister should beware of it," he roared.[4] When friends asked how Indira Gandhi was reacting to the Jana Sangh's fall from thirty-five to twenty-two seats, Vajpayee grinned. '*Ab toh humaari taraf bahut pyar se dekhti hai* [Now she looks at us with great affection].' His one-line gags entertained his friends no end. In a public speech in Gujarat around this time he announced he was ready to take sanyas, or renounce the world. Hearing this, Ghatate presented him with the dress of a sanyasi: a kafni (loose saffron kurta) and kamandal (water vessel). Vajpayee joked, 'Appa, why do you take my statements so seriously?' At a function once while Vajpayee was walking on the approach carpet towards the dais, another MP attempted to step across him and tripped. 'Don't try floor-crossing,' Vajpayee told him.

Immersed in parliamentary and party work, the personal life of the forty-seven-year-old bachelor revolved around his college friend and love, Rajkumari Kaul, and her family. Rajkumari's husband, Professor Brij Narain Kaul, was the warden of Ramjas College in the late 1960s. Vajpayee was a fixture in their home in these years. Often students of Ramjas College, sneaking a few drinks in their hostel rooms, would find warden Kaul looking in on them. Some of them took to complaining to the friendly-looking warden's wife, Mrs Rajkumari Kaul née Haksar, who would smile brightly and tell them, 'Why don't you come to my house when the warden goes to the hostel?' Delighted to find this unlikely ally, the students took to visiting the warden's home, but instead of just Rajkumari they would often find the Jana Sangh leader Atal Bihari Vajpayee in his dhoti and kurta also there. He seemed quite at ease and very much part of the furniture, usually sitting at the dining table with a cup of tea. While the hospitable Rajkumari rustled up home-made delicacies, Vajpayee would chat with the students, give them advice and even offer to help them get jobs as the Jana Sangh was fairly influential in Delhi University in those days.[5] Some of the 'Ramjas boys', a group later dubbed the 'Ramjas Club', became close to the maternally caring Rajkumari, and one of them, Ashok Saikia, would go on to become an officer of the Indian Administrative Service (IAS) and, in later years, Vajpayee's trusted joint secretary. Saikia, a low-profile and unassuming officer, was like a brother to Rajkumari's daughter Namita, and also Rajkumari's eyes and ears in Vajpayee's office. Always strongly attracted to the academic life, Vajpayee said in a 1995 speech, 'I once planned to get a PhD from Lucknow University . . . I always wanted to be a professor. If the country had not been partitioned, I would never have entered politics.'[6] The genteel Kashmiri Pandit Kauls and the academic atmosphere of their home was a haven away from the ups and downs of political life.

Rajkumari had not only been the object of his affections in college, but they were also strongly bonded by their shared history of growing up in Gwalior. They were two home-town buddies in the big city of Delhi, intimately connected by the memories of their time as students at Victoria College. A close friendship between a male and female college student may have been a modernist novelty at this time but they revelled in their attachment. Vajpayee the RSS bachelor gained a readymade family in the Kauls. For her part, the feisty Rajkumari got to participate in Vajpayee's exciting and high-profile political ascent, worlds away from a college professor's modest, anonymous life. Vajpayee was so often at the Kauls' home that it seemed perfectly natural that when he was allotted a large Lutyens' bungalow of his own that they should all move in with him.

Apart from the Kauls', the Jana Sangh chief would regularly be at his friend Appa Ghatate's home for dinner, in the early days enjoying a glass or two of wine or champagne, or sitting around in an adda sharing pegs of whisky with friends. Vinod Mehta, editor of *Outlook*, who got to know Vajpayee well when he was prime minister, recalled, 'In his early days Vajpayee used to be a heavy drinker and had quite a glad eye too. But his drinking became much less as the years wore on.'[7] On the campaign trail, in fact, Vajpayee was partial to downing bottles of ice-cold Coca-Cola. When party men once asked if the chilled Coke ever affected his throat, he replied, '*Mera gala toh khul jaata hai isse* [My voice opens up with this].'[8]

He was always up for a laugh with friends. He once went to watch the World War II film *Night of the Generals* at Delhi's Golcha cinema hall. A few rows ahead sat his parliamentary colleague the fiery CPI MP Bhupesh Gupta, who turned his head and spotted Vajpayee. 'Arre Vajpayee,' called Gupta, 'I see you've come to watch this film, but do you understand English?' Instantly Vajpayee shot back: 'Better than you understand Russian.' He was a Hindi cinema buff, often dragging party colleagues to movie theatres in Delhi to watch Raj Kapoor films. He wore his post of party boss lightly, once even napping with party men on a cement bench at a railway station in Shimoga. His personal identity was unorthodox, even bohemian, drawn to people irrespective of ideology and marked by a love of good food and drink, the company of friends, poetry and literature, a zinda dil (marked by love of life), khush mizaj (good-humoured) personality. In 1969, he wrote in *Rashtradharma*, 'We must rid Hinduism of its andhavishwas [superstition], rudhivadh [conservatism] and sankirnata [narrow-mindedness].'[9] His political identity was that of the Hindu nationalist interrogator of the Congress. Yet he was no Hindu traditionalist. He saw no contradiction in this mesh of avant garde personal choices and a traditionalist cause, both part of his evolving persona and shifting views. 'It is not enough for a tradition to just remain frozen,' he wrote. 'It should take us forward, make us better. Stagnant water in a lake becomes rotten. Indian culture is both ancient and new, which is why its impact is constantly changing yet is everlasting.'[10] The excitement of change, of moving forward, had bubbled in him since the time he was an attention-loving boy, delighting in occupying centre stage at kavi sammelans.

In his late forties his thick hair had begun to grey and his hearty eating and drinking had led to significant weight gain. He was no longer the eager, wide-eyed debutant from Gwalior, instead he was the man about town in Delhi, an insider in the circle of power. In Parliament by turn both grave and hilarious, regularly voicing demands for democracy and liberty against the Indira wall, he stridently and repeatedly pointed to Congress failures and corruption. He ranged over vast ground, his razor-sharp intellect and satirical wit tailor-made for Parliament. His speeches in these years show impressive research, and mastery of facts, suggesting a new Constituent Assembly,[11] arguing for Hindi to be designated as the 'national language', advocating the right to recall elected representatives,[12] arguing on the need to abrogate Article 370,[13] and demanding to know if governors had become 'puppets dancing to New Delhi's tunes'.[14] He regularly interrogated Indira's secularism: 'You cannot fight the communalism of other classes by encouraging Muslim communalism.'[15] He raged against Nehru's and Indira's socialism: 'Nationalisation is considered synonymous with socialism and it is felt that if the government takes over an industry or trade or commerce, socialism would arrive and the people would become happy. In our country, nationalisation has come to mean governmentalisation . . . governmentalisation has not been able to make people happy.'[16]

Unchallenged in his tiny party, the veritable big fish in a small pond, the glittering hard-working parliamentarian had a great sense of devotion and accountability to Parliament. 'Governments will come and go but Parliament will stay forever,' he would say in 1994. 'We must keep Parliament alive by upholding traditions, norms, rules, *maryada mein rehkar, seemayon ke bheetar* [upholding the dignity of the House and staying within limits].'[17] Over his five decades in Parliament he introduced as many as twenty-two bills, twenty of them while in the Opposition. In his 1971 constitutional amendment bill, he sought to restrict the power of the government over the judiciary and argued that the seniormost judge of the Supreme Court should be appointed Chief Justice of India, without any interference from the government of the day. The bill – submitted in 1971 – came up for discussion in August 1973, a few months after Indira Gandhi had infamously superseded three senior judges to install her own nominee as chief justice. 'Dark shadows can be seen on the horizon . . . the government may not hesitate to strike at the independence and impartiality of the judiciary,' warned Vajpayee.[18] He quoted an Urdu couplet to attack Indira's assaults on the judiciary: '*Kapda sada gala ho to mumkin nahin rafoo, seetey thhe astin gareban phat gaya, / Barey gunah barh gaye ujre gunah se, dhone se aur damaney eema chikat gaya* [If a cloth is worn out, it cannot be mended. If you sew a sleeve, the whole garment gets torn. If you hide an offence it comes to light all the more. If you wash a blot, it sticks more firmly].'[19]

His love for parliamentary debate in full flow, his self-image entrenched as the anti-Congress battleaxe, his attacks on the government were trenchant and constant. But he had too many friends on both sides of the aisle to ever be nasty or personal and there was always some fun to be had in the fight. He was a denizen of Delhi's Lutyens' zone – the enclave of colonial villas set amid tree-lined avenues built in the style of British architect Edwin Lutyens – where political VIPs live. He may have grown up in Shinde ki Chhawani but he lived in Lutyens' bungalows all his political life and however much he liked to deride the 'Durbar of Delhi',[20] he was a regular at the capital's book launches, official functions and overseas tours, a popular figure in Delhi's battle-hardened political clique. 'I was on a visit to a European country,' he told Parliament in April 1972, 'the weather was very cold, but inside the Embassy nimbu pani [lime water] was being served to guests . . . [Why] should lime water be served to guests even during snowfall? It was at my instance . . . that some wine was served . . . Our efficiency lies in having a good synthesis of ancient traditions and modernism.'[21]

By the early 1980s, he had moved to the house which is most associated with him, 6 Raisina Road. Here the security was as easy-going as himself and the chai and samosas came in a never-ending stream. While living on Raisina Road, in the 1980s, he would occasionally walk home from Parliament with communist MPs Geeta Mukherjee, Hanan Mollah and Saifuddin Chowdhury, who would be going back to their rooms in Vithalbhai Patel House. Communists and Hindu nationalist strolled along together, in the comradeship that Parliament should always exemplify for the nation to see.

On 21 October 1972, the Jana Sangh completed twenty-one years of existence. Vajpayee's comments in a foreword he wrote for a party publication reveal his mind about his party: ideology was on the back burner, politics was uppermost; Hindu culture and so on were only the accompanying orchestra; displacing the Congress and seizing power were the main anthem and priorities. He was at pains to assert: 'On economic policy, the Jana Sangh's approach is based on pragmatic considerations and not on dogma . . . the Jana Sangh is a centrist party . . . not a splinter group of malcontents . . . it offers a powerful alternative to the Ruling Congress.'[22]

As the Indira Gandhi cult gripped the country, Vajpayee observed Nehru's daughter with grudging admiration, even though he believed she lacked her father's grand qualities. 'She was in the grip of some unknown fear,' he writes, 'she had a deep sense of insecurity in some corner of her mind. Watching everybody, not saying anything openly, thinking that the whole world was conspiring against her.'[23] But Indira was cleverer than her father, he notes, and knew how to turn the levers of power. She certainly came charging at the Jana Sangh: 'I am used to Shri Vajpayee and his party attacking me,' she snapped in 1970. 'They demean me by levelling baseless allegations . . . his party has two main aspects, the first is the communal aspect and the second is still more dangerous of distorting history . . . we want to fight it [the Jana Sangh's communalism] with all the strength at our command.'[24]

The 'Indira revolution' was on the rampage, drastically shrinking the ideological space for right-wing politics. Sensing the change in the national mood, Vajpayee too seized the platform of pro-poor left-leaning populism and – with the ever-present possibility of another ban on the RSS – attempted to distance the party from any Hindu militancy. With Advani as party president, the two Hindu nationalists stood guard at the Jana Sangh in the high noon of Indira's secular-socialist reign, determined to keep the party's lamp burning.

They were helped by a new politics–inclined RSS chief. On 5 June 1973, M.S. Golwalkar, RSS sarsanghchalak for over three decades, died. He was succeeded by a man he had carefully chosen: the law graduate Madhukar Dattatreya Deoras, or 'Balasaheb' Deoras. Like Golwalkar, Deoras was a Maharashtrian Brahmin, but unlike his predecessor, who was politically aloof, Deoras was a dynamic organization man, keen to push the RSS into politically activist roles. In fact, Golwalkar had chosen Deoras as he believed Deoras would be best suited as sarsanghchalak were the RSS to be banned again.[25]

For Vajpayee, Golwalkar had been a source of constant support.

Golwalkar had spotted the talents of the young swayamsevak from Gwalior from the outset, encouraged him in politics and made sure it was only his photos that were plastered on election posters, much to the chagrin of his rivals. '*Politician aadmi hai, raaste mein dhakel dega* [Be careful, he's a politician, he'll push you off on the journey],' Golwalkar once teased Ghatate about Vajpayee, when the two were planning a train trip together from Nagpur to Delhi, revealing a fond indulgence of the young Vajpayee.[26] Golwalkar was gone, but with the politically ambitious Deoras in charge at the RSS, Vajpayee found another ally in pushing forward an activism-oriented, alliance-focused approach to take on the Congress. Like Golwalkar and Upadhyaya, Deoras too was acutely aware of Vajpayee's value as the universally liked frontman, crucial for the Hindu nationalists to gain wider acceptability.

~

Indira Gandhi's aggressive nationalism aroused RSS and Jana Sangh admiration, even as they resented her triumphs. On 16 December 1971, when the House rose in standing ovation after Indira Gandhi announced Pakistan's surrender, Vajpayee too jumped to his feet and delivered an ardent speech: '. . . today the blood of the fighters for their freedom in Bangladesh and of Indian jawans is flowing together . . . our prime minister really deserves congratulations on this occasion'.[27]

Smarting from the poll defeats dealt them by Indira, the Jana Sangh pushed hard for electoral reforms. In 1970, the Indira Gandhi government set up a joint parliamentary committee (JPC) to examine the case for such reforms. Vajpayee consistently raised red flags about how defections were making a mockery of the party system, and how the use of big money was destroying free elections. In fact, through his political career Vajpayee would regularly voice apprehensions about the destructive role of money power in elections, in 1962 moving a private members bill seeking amendments to the 1956 Companies Act and 'forbidding the use of corporate funds for political parties and campaigns'.[28] In 1972 the Jana Sangh passed a resolution that election expenses of parties should be borne by the state and kept protesting that the election system, reliant on money power and personality cults, was unfairly weighted against their party. In 1974 Vajpayee argued his case for state funding of elections: 'Is democracy a cheap process? Will we hesitate to spend some money for the good health of democracy? . . . if politics is to be saved from moneybags and if elections are to be cleansed Rs 16 crore [his suggestion for government expenditure in assembly elections] is not a big expense.'[29]

He kept up his attacks on Indira's dictatorial rule. Warning the House of the government's inclination to bring in constitutional amendments, he argued: 'Certain things cannot be changed with a two-thirds majority. For example, can a two-thirds majority declare the Indian republic to be a monarchy? It cannot. Can a two-thirds majority in parliament declare Prime Minister Indira Gandhi as Maharani Indira Gandhi? It cannot.'[30] Comparing Indira unfavourably with her father, he said, '. . . when Nehruji was angry, he made a good speech. So at times we used to tease him. But we cannot make the mistake of teasing the prime minister. She gets angry on her own. In a public meeting she said she could deal with the Bharatiya Jana Sangh in five minutes. Can any democratic prime minister speak like this?'[31]

Many of his exchanges with the government though, true to his style, were lightened by jocularity and wit. Yashwantrao Balwantrao Chavan, the Maharashtra Congressman, was one of his favourite quarries. 'The Finance Minister's embarrassment is clear . . . yesterday our friend Shri Piloo Mody praised him . . . but the difficulty for the Finance Minister is that the more Piloo Mody praises him, the more our friend Indrajit Gupta will condemn him.' This brought on laughter from the benches.[32] When Chavan, as finance minister, kept promising, 'We will arrest the price rise, we will arrest the price rise', Vajpayee came up with a mocking one-liner: 'Mr Chavan is not the home minister, he can't arrest anything.' He quipped to his friends, 'Chavan used to wear a dhoti when he was chief minister of Maharashtra, but when he became defence minister in Nehru's cabinet he started wearing a churidar pyjama like Pandit Nehru. On Lal Bahadur Shastri becoming Prime Minister he again started wearing the dhoti. Now that Indira Gandhi [famous for her elegant saris] is Prime Minister, I wonder what Chavanji will wear.'[33] When Tamil Nadu was hit by a cyclone and Chief Minister M. Karunanidhi appealed for Central help, Vajpayee told his circle: 'I hope Indiraji gives him financial assistance, he has only karuna [sympathy] and no nidhi [money].'[34]

In March 1972, he lashed out derisively:

> The election results have placed exceptional power and authority in the prime minister's hands . . . all power is concentrated in New Delhi . . . Central ministers have been reduced to courtiers at the Delhi Durbar . . . the prime minister's secretariat has become a parallel cabinet . . . the Prime Minister is standing at the pinnacle and her colleagues lying at her feet . . . Is this situation not fraught with the dangerous possibility of one individual getting established as a dictator? . . . These days the atmosphere in New Delhi makes one choke. It is not easy to breathe freely. Raising a voice of dissent is looked upon as a revolt . . . the chanting of the Prime Minister's name on All India Radio from morning to night, saturated propaganda on Cinema screens . . . how can those sitting in the Opposition fight all this?[35]

A year before the Emergency was imposed in 1975, he would be on his feet in the House almost continuously, bellowing about the looming dangers to democracy.

> It is not impossible to come to power by raising attractive slogans, spending money like water and by openly misusing government machinery. But power for what? Is power for power's sake or is it for the transformation of society? Is power only for enjoyment? Is

power for writing your name in history or in the time capsule or for cutting out other people's name? Is power for satisfying your ego?[36]

~

For all her political dominance, by late 1972, the Indira revolution began to unravel with astounding speed. After the Bangladesh war, millions of refugees streamed into India. In 1972, 1973 and 1974, the monsoon failed and food prices skyrocketed. In 1973 the OPEC countries pushed a fourfold rise in oil prices – the 'oil shocks' – and prices rose even further. Sensing the public anger, Vajpayee rolled into Parliament on a bullock cart, with accompanying supporters yelling, '*Desh ka neta Atal Bihari*,' and brandishing placards saying 'Taxation on petrol is criminal loot'. Interestingly, just a day earlier Indira Gandhi had driven down Delhi's streets in a horse-drawn carriage to raise awareness on fuel conservation, so Vajpayee's bullock-cart ride could have been a flamboyantly 'Bharatiya' riposte to her.

As inflation soared and factories closed, strikes and food riots erupted in almost every part of the country. Deoras, Vajpayee and Advani scented opportunity and struck out determinedly to find alliances and strategies in this time when, according to Deoras, the 'masses had risen in revolt'.[37] The Jana Sangh and RSS, which were thirsting to mobilize against Indira, plunged into playing leadership roles in the agitation.

In January 1974, students in Gujarat led the Nav Nirman movement in which the RSS's student affiliate, the Akhil Bharatiya Vidyarthi Parishad (ABVP), played a leading role. The Jana Sangh also joined in, leading campaigns against price rise. Protests tore through Gujarat and Chief Minister Chimanbhai Patel was forced out of office.

From Gujarat the protests spread to Bihar, here too the ABVP taking the lead and combining with left groups to form the Chhatra Sangharsh Samiti to mount street protests and gheraos. The RSS was deeply involved with the Bihar student agitation and an RSS pracharak based in Patna, with a master's in mathematics from Banaras Hindu University (BHU), played an important part. He was K.N. Govindacharya, then thirty-one, who would go on in later years to be a powerful figure in the BJP, an Advani camp follower and Vajpayee bête noir.

In Bihar, rebellious students turned to a veteran Gandhian and invited him to lead them. Seventy-two-year-old Jayaprakash Narayan, or 'JP', now stepped into the fray and assumed leadership of the Bihar movement. Waves of protests and demonstrations began in the state. In Parliament Vajpayee struck a melodramatic tone, fully supportive of the Bihar students. 'It's not the failure of a party, it's the failure of the whole system. People are losing faith in democracy . . . Bihar is burning, the streets of Bihar are red with blood. The government is bent on tyranny.'[38] On 5 June 1974, in Patna's Gandhi Maidan, JP gave the echoing call: '*Sampurna kranti.*' Total revolution.

'Total revolution', with its anarchist overtones, was in many ways an assault on democracy and a rejection of law and order. But, however extra-constitutional and lawless the JP movement was, it presented a unique opportunity to the Jana Sangh to regroup and stage a comeback after numbing defeats. In a do-or-die moment, the RSS and Jana Sangh also adopted 'Sampurna kranti'.

In 1974, Indira Gandhi cracked down harshly on the railway workers' strike and George Fernandes, at this time head of the National Railway Union, was arrested. In a debate on a no-confidence motion moved against the Indira government, Vajpayee delivered a biting speech:

> Is it not true that never before in the last 26 years was there so much unemployment as at present? Is it also wrong to say that garibi hatao has raised people's expectations? If they now demand that these expectations be fulfilled what is anti-national about it? . . . It was immoral to arrest George Fernandes and his colleagues. You are outdoing the British in evil deeds.[39]

In September 1974 in Hyderabad, the Jana Sangh held a camp to train party cadres in 'agitation work'. Justifying the Jana Sangh's support to the JP movement, Vajpayee made a telling comment: 'It is becoming increasingly difficult to dislodge the Congress by the ballot box since elections proved to be an unequal battle, since the Congress has money power. The war has to be fought in the streets, in the chambers, in the legislatures, in the corridors of power, in all sensitive power centres of the establishment.'[40] In another statement, Vajpayee said, 'The fight inside the legislature has to be supplemented by the fight *inter alia* for bringing about necessary electoral reform.'[41] The fight inside Parliament was no longer enough. Given the party's obsession with the lopsided electoral system, the battle must take place on the streets.

Vajpayee, seemingly the high-minded democrat, was prepared to abandon parliamentary norms and practices in the fight for power, his words the opposite of his actions. He would reveal the same split personality in the 1990s during the Ram Mandir agitation when he privately complained against rath yatras but publicly supported them. Since the Congress was undefeatable in elections, radical nihilist street protests were not just needed, they were the only way.

At this time, JP, according to Advani, told him and Vajpayee, 'I need your co-operation. You should join me and my movement.'[42] In Hyderabad, Advani announced that the dominance of the Congress could only be ended if the Jana Sangh accepted JP's proposal.[43] With Deoras's blessings, Advani and Vajpayee met JP in Patna in November 1974 and resolved that the RSS–Jana Sangh would take the vanguard in the JP-led anti-Indira movement.

JP now set about creating a broad coalition – from Jana Sangh to the left – to take on Indira. 'How can you invite a communal party like the Jana Sangh to join your movement?' CPI(M) leader E.M.S. Namboodiripad asked JP. 'Didn't you lead anti-RSS protests after the assassination of Mahatma Gandhi?'[44] But so strong was JP's opposition to Indira Gandhi, so determined was he to make common cause even with those he had once scorned, that he formed his improbable rainbow coalition, which carried within it the seeds of its own destruction.

With the Gujarat assembly dissolved and fresh elections in the state ahead, Vajpayee the enthusiastic votary of Opposition alliances made strenuous efforts to argue the cause of a single, united political bloc against Indira. The Jana Sangh–Morarji Desai alliance emerged as an anchor for these formations and finally led to the birth of the Janata Party. The Opposition put up combined 'Janata' candidates (the first time the word 'Janata' was used in elections) in two by-elections, an assembly by-poll in Bhopal and a Lok Sabha by-poll in Jabalpur. Both candidates – the Jana Sangh's Babulal Gaur in Bhopal and the pugnacious twenty-nine-year-old socialist Sharad Yadav in Jabalpur – pulled off wins. These by-elections at the end of 1974 and beginning of 1975 were spectacular gains for the Opposition and hit the ruling party like a tornado. They showed how effective a united Opposition was proving to be now, even though the Opposition Grand Alliance had failed against Indira Gandhi in 1971. To fight the Congress in Gujarat, JP and Congress (O) leader Morarji Desai formed a four-party coalition of the left and right – Congress (O), Bharatiya Lok Dal, Jana Sangh and Socialist Party – named the Janata Front, a precursor to the Janata Party.

Sharad Yadav recalls how, after his Jabalpur victory, he arrived in Delhi to stay at Vithalbhai Patel House but found that no arrangements had been made for his meals. On hearing this, Vajpayee not only sent him food but also regularly invited the young socialist, who was highly critical of the RSS, to his home for meals. For Yadav, Vajpayee became 'my beloved person'.[45] A little over two decades after his Jabalpur win, Sharad Yadav would take his place as a minister in Vajpayee's government.

In early 1975, things began to move fast. Opposition parties met in Delhi in February 1975, JP at this time exhorting the police and army not to 'obey orders that are illegal and unjust', a call he would repeat in June at his famous Ramlila Maidan rally. On 6 March, JP led a gigantic Opposition march – the 'great march' – to Parliament. It consisted of massive processions of almost half a million people winding through Old and New Delhi. At a joint rally afterwards, JP called for Indira Gandhi's resignation and for more agitations and protests across India.

On 7 March, the Jana Sangh cleverly held a huge meeting of thousands of its party delegates from different states to coincide with JP's march, as if to emphasize the Jana Sangh's integral role in the JP movement. Vajpayee and Advani invited JP to the meeting as chief guest. At this meeting JP gave the Jana Sangh what it was thirsting for – a certificate of legitimacy and a path to joining conventional politics. This thrilled the ambitious Vajpayee the most, chary as he always was at being marooned on an ideologically isolated island. At the meeting JP struck a note of solidarity with the Jana Sangh and declared, 'If you are a fascist, then I too am a fascist.'

In mid-June results of the Gujarat assembly were declared. The Congress was vanquished by the Janata Front. On 12 June 1975 a court verdict struck with lightning force. Justice Jagmohan Lal Sinha of the Allahabad High Court declared that Indira Gandhi's 1971 election was invalid and barred her from holding office or contesting elections for six years. It was a deadly blow to the prime minister.

On the evening of 25 June 1975, an enormous crowd gathered at the Ramlila Maidan to hear JP quote the poet Ramdhari Singh Dinkar, '*Singhasan khali karo ki janta aati hai*' (Vacate the throne, the people are coming), asking the army and police to mutiny, to not obey 'unconstitutional orders'. That night, just a few minutes before midnight, the President of India signed the Emergency order proclamation. The lights went off in Delhi's newspaper offices. Printing presses ground to a halt. Through the intervening night of 25–26 June all the main Opposition leaders were arrested. Indira Gandhi slammed down the Emergency.

On 30 June, Deoras was jailed. On 4 July the RSS was banned.

Vajpayee would later recall that if Indira had resigned in 1975 after her election was declared invalid by the court she could have become the unchallenged leader of the Congress party, but she chose to 'throttle democracy' to stay in power, for which 'history would never forgive her'.[46] Indira Gandhi for her part always maintained the Hindu nationalists were a greater evil than the Emergency. Later that year she said defiantly: 'If the Jana Sangh comes to power it will not need an Emergency. It will chop off heads.'[47]

~

Delhi in June is blazing hot. A merciless sun drives the city into a heat-crazed stupor. Dust devils rise, pursued by burning winds. Keen to flee the oven, Vajpayee and Advani were rather pleased that a meeting of the JPC on a proposed law on defections was being held in cool, breezy Bangalore on 26 June. Vajpayee arrived in the garden city on 24 June, and Advani, accompanied by a Congress (O) politician, Shyam Nandan Mishra, on the morning of 25 June. They were all staying at the Legislators Home located next to the assembly building. At around 7.30 a.m. on 26 June, the phone rang in Advani's room. A Jana Sangh party secretary informed him that Jayaprakash Narayan, Morarji Desai and other Opposition leaders had been arrested the night before. 'The arrests are continuing. The police may shortly be coming to arrest Atalji and you,' he warned Advani.[48]

Advani and Mishra hurried to Vajpayee's room. They decided they would not resist arrest, and got down to preparing a statement condemning Jayaprakash Narayan's incarceration. They switched on the radio. Indira Gandhi's voice floated out in an unscheduled broadcast, saying the Emergency had been imposed to save the country from a massive conspiracy by the Opposition and to meet the threat of internal disturbances. Around 10 a.m. the Karnataka police arrived and knocked on their doors. Shyam Nandan Mishra was doing his morning yoga at the time and was in the shirshasana posture. He asked the police if they had a warrant. The police went away and returned with the warrant, but this time Mishra pointed out that they had got his father's name wrong. As the arguments stretched on, Vajpayee interrupted: 'Come on, Shyam babu, don't delay, let's go to our sasural.'[49] Along with Vajpayee, Advani and Mishra and the socialist politician Madhu Dandavate were also arrested. They were taken straight to Bangalore Central Jail. As they were led away, Mishra remarked, 'This madness cannot last long, we'll all be out in two or three weeks.'[50] He was wrong. Most of the arrested Opposition leaders would be in jail for over a year, Advani for nineteen months. According to Amnesty International, more than 1,10,000 were arrested and detained without trial in the first year of the Emergency. Twenty-two Emergency prisoners died in prison.

The four Opposition politicians arrested that day in Bangalore – Vajpayee, Advani, Madhu Dandavate and Shyam Nandan Mishra – were housed in two rooms facing each other, one shared by Mishra and Dandavate, the other by Vajpayee and Advani. They were handed utensils, crockery, vegetables and cereals and asked to cook their own food. Vajpayee volunteered to take charge of the cooking.

The next few days passed relatively quietly. Advani and Vajpayee began to learn Kannada. Advani would read or write in his diary and Vajpayee would compose angry, bitter poetry which would later be included in a collection called *Kaidi Kavirai ki Kundalian* (The Prisoner Poet's Verse). In one of these poems, 'Vedna', Vajpayee wrote:

Kothri sooni,
vedna dooni,
jhinguron ka svar,
vedhta antar.
Bandh hai akash
ghut raha hai nishvas.

This desolate cell,
The heart's anguish swells,

The chirping of crickets,
Slices through me.
The sky shut out,
I cannot breathe.[51]

In another poem on the banning of the RSS, *'Anushasan ke Naam par Anushasan ka Khoon'* (In the Name of Discipline, Discipline Is Slain), he wrote:

Anushasan ke naam par,
anushasan ka khoon.
Bhang kar diya sangh ko,
kaisa chadha junoon!
Matri puja pratibandhit?
. . . Kah kaidi kavirai,
tod kanooni kara
goonjega Bharat Mata ki,
jai ka naara.

In the name of discipline,
Discipline is slain.
The Sangh is banned,
What madness arises?
What madness!
Restraining mother worship?
. . . Says the poet enchained,
breaking legal restraints,
the slogan 'Hail to the Motherland'
will rise again.[52]

Ghatate visited Vajpayee in jail. 'So, what's it like being in jail?' he asked his friend, surprised to see Vajpayee wearing warm clothing. 'I'm here at Indira Gandhi's expense,' chuckled Vajpayee. 'Indira Gandhi will feed me, Indira Gandhi will give me clothes. I'm not spending a penny from my pocket!' Vajpayee passed a message via Ghatate to those who were outside, asking them to start satyagrahas. Upon hearing this, Nanaji Deshmukh shot back, 'Let the people inside not tell the people outside what to do.'[53]

The four were being held under the Maintenance of Internal Security Act (MISA), and after almost three weeks in jail decided to challenge the order in court. The petition was posted for hearing in the Karnataka High Court on 14 July 1975. With the help of their counsels, Advani, Mishra and Dandavate argued their own case with Ghatate appearing for Vajpayee. They demanded the right to liberty and that their petitions be disposed of, as a Parliament session had been called on 21 July. The chief justice said the petitions must be heard, because according to practice in England, habeas corpus petitions must be taken up within forty-eight hours and the state must provide reasons for denial of liberty. The next hearing was fixed for 17 July. On the day, after some tense courtroom drama, orders arrived that they were being transferred to Rohtak Jail. Within hours Advani would find himself in new barracks in Rohtak, Haryana. Vajpayee, who had undergone a surgery just a day before at Bangalore's Victoria Hospital, could not be moved because his doctors refused to discharge him. Rohtak Jail was where the maximum number of Opposition leaders were incarcerated, among them Biju Patnaik, Piloo Mody, Sikandar Bakht, Raj Narain and Chandra Shekhar. Advani was later shifted back to Bangalore Central Jail. The shared experience of prison would build comradely ties across party lines and lead to political alliances, for example, between the Jana Sangh's later avatar, the BJP, and leaders of the Akali Dal. Shared jail time even brought the Jamaat-i-Islami and Jana Sangh together. Advani was released only on 18 January 1977, two months before the general elections of March 1977.

While many Jana Sangh leaders were jailed – Nanaji Deshmukh, S.S. Bhandari and K.R. Malkani held in Delhi's Tihar Jail – Vajpayee's role during the Emergency was rather different. He was mostly ill, shifted to various hospitals and then to his bungalow in Delhi at

1 Feroz Shah Road, where, after long stints in hospital, he remained under some form of house arrest for the last months of the Emergency.

On 13 July 1975, just a day before Advani and the others were brought to the Karnataka High Court for the first time, Vajpayee suddenly complained of an excruciating backache, became very ill and had to be taken to Victoria Hospital, where he was operated on for appendicitis. After the operation, doctors realized that his ailment was not appendicitis but a slipped disc and the onset of typhoid. Vajpayee even developed septicaemia. An Opposition politician who was underground at this time told Ghatate to pass on the message to Vajpayee that there was a Parsi gentleman in Mumbai who cured spinal problems by delivering carefully aimed kicks at the patient. When Ghatate conveyed this to Vajpayee, he chuckled, 'Indiraji is already kicking me, why do you want one more person to kick me?'[54] The periodic bouts of ill health that would be his life's bane began around this time. His doctors refused to allow him to be transferred to Rohtak Jail – Vajpayee was instead shifted to the All India Institute of Medical Sciences (AIIMS) in Delhi on 6 August, where he was to remain until he was discharged a few months later. While at AIIMS, Vajpayee asked Ghatate, 'Who is my malik here? In jail I would get soap, toothpaste, here I get nothing.' Ghatate promptly organized supplies. Vajpayee was to later candidly admit, 'Many people went to jail, but I was more in hospital than in jail.'[55]

Critics of Vajpayee within the Jana Sangh, like the irrepressible Subramanian Swamy, have alleged that a 'deal' was struck with Indira Gandhi to get the senior leader out of jail. 'Vajpayee gave an apology letter to Indira and promised not to engage in anti-Congress politics on his release and his illness was only a ruse,' Swamy is learned to have told a confidant. In an op-ed in the *Hindu* newspaper, Swamy maintained that Vajpayee was out on parole for most of the Emergency after giving a written assurance that he would not take part in any programmes against the government. He added that many other Jana Sangh/RSS leaders were released from jail on promise of good behaviour.[56] Swamy himself would earn a reputation as a street-fighter against the Emergency, his 'escape' from Parliament under the nose of a large security presence being seen as one of the defining moments in the battle against Indira Gandhi. The Vajpayee–Swamy relationship would remain hostile. When the Janata Party government was formed in 1977, Swamy was not made a cabinet minister, an exclusion for which he held Vajpayee squarely responsible. The final break would come in 1980, when Vajpayee decided to lead the newly christened Bharatiya Janata Party under the ideological banner of 'Gandhian socialism'.

Did Vajpayee strike a compromise with Indira Gandhi to get out of jail and remain in a hospital during the Emergency? Ghatate stoutly denied this. Whether Vajpayee received any special favours from Indira is a matter of conjecture; the fact is that while Advani stayed in jail, Vajpayee remained mostly in hospital. Stories circulated at this time that during his hospital stay in Bangalore, Vajpayee even fell deeply in love with a nurse and their relationship continued for many months afterwards.[57] 'He used to say Bangalore was the place where he had a rebirth,' recalled Justice Rama Jois, who had represented Vajpayee and Advani in court.[58]

Vajpayee's actions and behaviour during the Emergency reveal him as a politician strategizing for a slice of power rather than strenuously struggling for a cause. He always shunned violence; he was never a protester or on-the-street activist; instead, Parliament and parliamentary deliberations were his preferred workspaces. In the Emergency years, his was no heroic resistance to Indira Gandhi; instead he remained curiously ambivalent towards the daughter of his hero Nehru, and showed a readiness for dialogue and compromise. While he was in AIIMS, he was informed that the 'satyagraha' or protests by RSS leaders who were underground were carrying on apace. Vajpayee sent word that these protests should be deferred. But communication links were difficult, and his message never got conveyed. Laughed Vajpayee: 'So our car is without any brakes – let it go.'[59]

Headlong confrontation was never his style. He was the paramount orator in Parliament, not a blood-spilling roadside revolutionary. A senior BJP leader observed, '*Woh zyada mehnati nahin thhe* [He didn't exert himself much].' He had risen through the ranks by dint of his speaking and politicking talents, not by street agitations, and by the 1970s he belonged more to Delhi's power elite and less to the sangh activist army. Shakti Sinha, the IAS officer who was Vajpayee's private secretary from 1996 to 1999, said, 'His life revolved around Parliament. Vajpayee was never the activist on the street leading a procession.'[60] These characteristics would always mark Vajpayee as a 'moderate' figure, whose general acceptability among all made him a great beneficiary of the post-Emergency Janata Party dispensation.

Through all this time, his personal regard for the Nehru–Gandhis didn't fade, however vigorously he denounced Indira Gandhi. There is a story that, at the height of the Emergency in 1976, Vajpayee met Sanjay Gandhi's crony and minister of state for home, Om Mehta, to keep channels of communication open with the government and work in partnership with it towards the restoration of democracy.[61]

There is another interesting account of how, while his party colleagues endured jail terms, Vajpayee enjoyed shots of whisky and helpings of chicken while lodged in AIIMS. At AIIMS, the private room next to Vajpayee's was occupied by Devi Prasad Tripathi, another poet and litterateur. Tripathi had been associated with the RSS and the ABVP in the past but later gravitated to the left, eventually joining the Congress. One evening Vajpayee asked Tripathi, 'Devi Prasad, what are the arrangements for the evening?' Tripathi immediately understood what Vajpayee meant and procured a bottle of excellent Scotch, while Vajpayee organized chicken dishes and other snacks for a convivial evening in hospital.[62]

As they talked into the night, discussing politics and leaders, Vajpayee said, 'I have never seen a bigger democrat than Nehru.' According to him, Lal Bahadur Shastri, though honest and upright, remained 'a weak man without a hold on his party or on the masses'. Vajpayee grudgingly praised Indira Gandhi, even though so many of his associates were in jail because of her, and confessed to referring to Indira as 'Durga', which he said he regretted because clearly she had learnt nothing from her father. However, he admitted he admired her firm leadership during the Bangladesh war.[63] Such was the hold the Nehru–Gandhis continued to exercise on Vajpayee, wrapped up as he was in the Nehru mystique, that he was unable to ever forget his bond with Panditji in Parliament. He was a Hindu nationalist closer in spirit to the 'secular' leftists than to the street cadres of his own party. A pleasant evening spent with a left-leaning literary figure like Tripathi at the height of the Emergency was no contradiction in Vajpayee's politics of universal friendship.

~

In 1976 in a spooky, stalled 'republic' that was India came a disgraceful judgement, effectively rubber-stamping the Emergency. The Supreme Court, presided over by Indira nominee Chief Justice Ajit Nath Ray, in a bench consisting of, among others, Justices Y.V. Chandrachud and P.N. Bhagwati, in the *Additional District Magistrate Jabalpur* vs *Shiv Kant Shukla Habeas Corpus* case, held that habeas corpus – or right to personal liberty – petitions in high courts were not maintainable during a national emergency. Those detained cannot ask why, nor can courts hold such detentions mala fide or illegal. The one dissenter, Justice Hans Raj Khanna, ruled that accepting a suspension of the right to life and liberty would give the executive 'despotic powers'[64] and the case was not just a matter of the liberty of a few individuals but of the rule of law itself.

It was a tense, unpredictable, strangely perverse and power-worshipping time. The economy stabilized, but durbars coalesced around Indira Gandhi, courtiers hoping for a share of the pie strove for favours, the Opposition was erased from the press, morality counted for nothing and 'access' to the empress's court – even at the cost of self-denigration – was everything. Human nature's dark side settled on India like a treacherous mist.

Sections of RSS workers kept up sporadic agitations; others sent in apology letters with promises to cooperate with the government and acknowledged Indira Gandhi as their leader. The RSS leadership was also accommodating. According to T.V. Rajeswar, former Intelligence Bureau chief and Indira confidant, RSS chief Balasaheb Deoras had established contact with the prime minister's house and declared his support for several measures taken during the Emergency, including Sanjay Gandhi's enforced family planning drive, particularly among Muslims.[65]

Deoras wrote conciliatory letters to Indira Gandhi from Yerawada prison, calling her '*adarniya pradhan mantriji*' and lauding her 'timely and balanced' speech on 15 August. He wrote, 'I pray that you rescind the ban imposed upon the RSS', and promised RSS cooperation in government programmes.[66] Indira ignored Deoras's letters, singling out the RSS for arrests and detentions. RSS sources claimed that tens of thousands of its members were jailed.

As cadres agitated, politicians strategized. By lodging all Opposition politicians in Rohtak and Tihar jails, Indira Gandhi inadvertently gave them an opportunity to meet and deliberate collectively and spurred a fortuitous camaraderie. Many rounds of negotiations began in prison; they would eventually result in the formation of the Janata Party.

On 18 January 1977, nineteen months after the imposition of Emergency, Indira Gandhi suddenly and dramatically announced that fresh elections would be held in March. 'Every election is an act of faith,' she said in her broadcast. 'It's an opportunity to cleanse public life of confusion. So let us go to the polls with the resolve to affirm the power of the people.' Censorship was lifted. Political prisoners were freed. Emergency regulations were relaxed and the Lok Sabha was dissolved. Politics now took off at 'lightning speed'.[67]

Fifty-three-year-old Vajpayee, fully recovered from his ailments, now vital and energetic, made a statement to the press in February:

> Though the ruling party is trying to project its decision to go to the polls as its greatest gift to the nation, it is clear that it has been

> compelled to because of the alarming erosion of its credibility and even legitimacy at home and abroad . . . most of our workers are still in detention, a pall of fear hangs over the country . . . The contest is thus more than ever unequal. Still we have accepted the challenge . . .[68]

The Opposition was exultant. It was now a race against time to forge an alternative to the Dictator-Empress. Within a week, on 23 January 1977, supervised by Jayaprakash Narayan, the Janata Party was officially launched, with Morarji Desai as chairman and Charan Singh as vice chairman. The Janata Party would be drawn from members of the Jana Sangh, Socialist Party, Bharatiya Lok Dal and Congress (O).

It wasn't easy to come together. The socialists were wary of tying up with the so far 'untouchable', 'communal' Jana Sangh linked to the 'fascist' RSS. According to former civil servant M.G. Devasahayam, the Jana Sangh at this time, as a promise to JP, undertook to give up dual membership of the RSS. According to Devasahayam, whom JP confided in, Deoras, Advani and Vajpayee offered to 'wind up the RSS', should they be in a position to form the government. Devasahayam reveals that JP later told him he felt totally betrayed by Vajpayee and Advani.[69]

Several rounds of negotiations were held. The most important doubters to convince were the Jana Sangh party workers, indignant at the imminent demise of the two-decade-old party and its disappearance into the Janata. To convince them, all workers were invited to Delhi, and Vajpayee took the lead in addressing them. He was now in his element, back in the thick of the mainstream politics he loved. Ambitious to start afresh, he said:

> We're building a new India. After the samudramanthan of the Emergency, we're now sinking our 25-year-old Jana Sangh boat into the Janata Party . . . We have made sacrifices and shed blood to build this party, so one eye is full of tears yet the other is full of happiness

> . . . During the Emergency, the lamp of the Jana Sangh [the party symbol of the Jana Sangh was an oil lamp] gave light, but now the sun has risen, it is time to put out the lamp. *Ab surya uday ho gaya hai, deepak bujhane ka samay aa gaya hai.*[70]

In late January 1977, Janata leaders met at Morarji Desai's home. It was decided the Janata Party flag would be saffron and green, and a plough-bearing farmer would be its election symbol. The campaign took off. The RSS deployed its cadres to work for Janata candidates. Vajpayee was seized with a spirit of buoyant optimism. To calm a massive, wildly cheering crowd at Delhi's Ramlila Maidan, he burst into poetry.

Baad muddat ke miley hain deewane,
kehne sunne ko hai bahut afsane,
zara khuli hawa mein saas toh lene do,
kab talak yeh azaadi rahegi kaun jaane.

We friends are meeting after ages,
There are tales to tell and tales to hear,
But first let us breathe deeply of the free air,
For we know not how long our freedom will last.[71]

Vajpayee contested from New Delhi, throwing himself into the Delhi campaign, from where, in 1971, the Jana Sangh had been comprehensively defeated. Vajpayee, the charismatic golden-tongued orator, the 'national leader' and favourite of the crowds, was pitted against Congress's Shashi Bhushan. Through much of his blitzkrieg of ten Lok Sabha wins, he never had a particular bastion or pocket borough, winning from different places in different elections. From 1991 onward, however, he won five consecutive times from Lucknow.

'It's a choice between democracy and dictatorship. We are fighting against those who murdered democracy,' he cried to exuberant crowds, 'those who became arrogant and thought they were bigger than the country'. Posters of a handsome young Vajpayee, his head thrown back and arm upraised in mid-speech, were plastered all over Delhi, reading, 'The Janata's glamour boy – AB Vajpayee. Nation is proud of him, vote and support Janata Party candidate AB Vajpayee.'

Shashi Bhushan dredged up his role in the 1942 Quit India movement, saying he could not last even a week under the colonial government questioning. 'Is this a man you can trust?' Bhushan asked. But the Janata was on song, riding on a tailwind of raw public anger. Writing about his lifelong anti-Congress-party mission, he said, 'For the success of democracy, the party system must be strong . . . and for that a non-Congress government at the Centre is needed.'[72]

On 20 March 1977, the results were declared and the unthinkable happened. Indira Gandhi lost. She was defeated even in her own constituency of Rae Bareli. The Congress crashed to its lowest ever tally of 153 seats. The Janata secured 40 per cent vote share and romped to power with 302 seats, sweeping through North India. Within the Janata grouping, the Jana Sangh secured the highest number of seats – ninety-three. Among all the other parties it had the maximum number of workers and leaders jailed, but had emerged from the Emergency with its organization still holding firm. The Jana Sangh had grown in size and stature, and overall the Janata, a group of old cooks who had stirred up a winning broth, forced the queen out of her castle. After thirty years of unbroken Congress rule, India was set for its first non-Congress government.

After the results, the Janata leaders assembled once again at the Ramlila Maidan for a victory rally. On stage were Morarji Desai, Jagjivan Ram, Vajpayee and the Shahi Imam of Jama Masjid, Abdullah Bukhari. Vajpayee's speech saw the master rhetorician at his colourful best.

'This was not an election . . . it was a peaceful revolution . . .' he declared, smiling and waving his hands, closing his eyes for effect. 'A wave of people's power has consigned the murderers of democracy to the *kuredaan* [dustbin] of history . . . those who had said Indira is India have been proved wrong.'[73]

The speech was as usual replete with mythological references: how the election was a mahateerth that an ancient India had undertaken on the road to modernity; how four great rivers had joined to form the Janata Party; and how the Jana Sangh had sacrificed its identity to dissolve into the Janata Party. 'They said the Bharatiya Jana Sangh was an enemy of the Muslims, but people did not believe this . . . we promise *bhaichara* [brotherhood] . . . we promise *samajwad* [socialism] . . . we promise *sarva dharma sambhav* [religious equality] . . . *vyakti ki swadhinata* [individual liberty] . . . we promise *vikendrikaran* [decentralization].'[74] Charisma can be described as the unique relationship that springs up between leader and crowd, a bond of friendship that grows between a person on-stage and the audience, a sense of identification between speaker and listener, as if the orator is saying, I am you and you are me. This charisma surrounded Vajpayee when he spoke in public, when he sounded as if he was engaging a crowd in frank conversation and talking to thousands as if confiding in a friend. He was relatable and he was funny.

On 24 March 1977 the highly capable and puritanical Morarji Desai, eighty-one years old and recently released from nineteen months in detention, took oath as prime minister. Vajpayee was sworn in as the external affairs minister. L.K. Advani became the information and broadcasting minister, and another Jana Sanghi, Brij Lal Verma, became industries minister in the Janata government. Nanaji Deshmukh had been a ministerial contender, but Vajpayee was reluctant to include Nanaji on the grounds that he was party treasurer and conflicts of interest could arise.

The relationship between Nanaji and Vajpayee started to become mutually suspicious in these years. Later, as Vajpayee took the Jana Sangh towards Gandhian socialism, Nanaji would bow out of active politics, Vajpayee the politician at odds with Nanaji the ideological warrior. When they were together, Vajpayee was not above directing mocking asides at Nanaji for his orthodoxies. Once at a dinner, the host informed Vajpayee that Nanaji would not be eating the chicken, as Upadhyaya had appeared to him in a dream and urged him to give up eating chicken. Joked Vajpayee: 'Arre, Nanaji, such a big personality came in your dream and he did not say anything more important except don't eat chicken?'[75]

Though the Jana Sangh had won the most seats in the Opposition bloc, in its enthusiasm to be part of the Janata, it stayed content with only three ministerial berths. The Sangh Parivar, pariahs on Raisina Hill since 1947, got access to power in Delhi, for the first time in its existence. Throughout the Janata tenure, the RSS, with Murlidhar Deoras, or 'Bhaurao', Balasaheb's younger brother looking after the sangh's political affairs, deployed the strategy of *ghus jao aur wahan chha jao* (enter and spread out). Suspecting the Janata would not last long, this was a strategy by which sangh members would use every opportunity to enter and dominate as many government posts as they could, so they could use whatever access to power they had, to build the organization and strengthen themselves for the future.

The Janata Party, united only by hatred of Indira Gandhi, failed to usher in constructive consensual politics. Soon after coming to power, the Janata dissolved nine state assemblies, and in elections that followed the Janata alliance won decisive victories in seven states. The driving force behind this decision to sack state governments was Law Minister Shanti Bhushan. Interestingly, Vajpayee, always a vociferous protester against the Congress's government-dismissing ways, now stood firmly in support of a similarly imperious step, agreeing with Bhushan, eager to consolidate, at any cost, the Janata's place in India's ruling establishment, eager to take his own place in India's establishment.

Vajpayee wanted to emphasize his legitimate links with the great men of the past and his own particular hero. As he walked to his office in South Block every morning, he once noticed that a photo of Jawaharlal Nehru that hung on the passageway walls of South Block was missing. Assuming that a non-Congress Jana Sanghi minister would not like to see Nehru's photo, his officers had removed the first prime minister's portrait. But as soon as he noticed this, Vajpayee asked, 'Where is the photo that always used to be here?' Nobody replied.[76] The picture of Jawaharlal Nehru, who had been foreign minister as well as prime minister for seventeen years, was put back on the wall, where it continued to hang throughout Vajpayee's tenure. He would not countenance any diminution of Panditji under his watch and would hold aloft the foreign policy that came down to him from the time of his 'rajkumar'. In 1999, he told Parliament proudly: 'I had a lot of disagreements with Panditji. I once told him, his personality was a mix of Churchill and Chamberlain. But I was the one who ensured his photo was put back.'[77]

In 1977, after becoming foreign minister, he even visited the defeated and fearful Indira to assure her that the Janata government would not allow any violent action against her or her family.[78]

~

He wrote a quirky poem on becoming foreign minister: '*Haathon ko Malte*' (Rubbing of hands):

Desh nikala mil gaya, mantrayala foren;
Kootniti ke shastra hain, bain, nain aur sain;
Bain, nain aur sain, churi kaaten bhi chalte;
Pehle haath milate,
Phir haathon ko malte;
Kah kaidi kavirai, laanghna saat samandar;
Lekin pehle shakti jutana ghar ke andar.

Assigned abroad, to the foreign affairs ministry,
The tools of diplomacy are words, eyes and signs;
Words, eyes and signs, plus using forks and knives;

First you shake hands,
Then wring them in repentance;
Declares the poet enchained,
Cross the seven seas by all means,
but first garner your strength in the homeland.[79]

He was chosen as external affairs minister by Morarji because of his many speeches in Parliament on foreign affairs and the fact that he had won the approval of Nehru, architect of India's foreign policy, for his interventions. Excited by his own transition to government after so many years in the Opposition, Vajpayee wrote more ironical lines at this time:

Pehle pehredaar thhe,
ab bhi pehredaar;
tab thhe tevar taante,
ab jhukte har baar;
. . . pehle mad ne aur aajkal,
pad ne jakra.

A watchman earlier, a watchman now;
Earlier proudly arrogant,
now subservient at all times.
. . . Earlier bound by arrogance,
now bound by a post.[80]

In office, he trod Nehru's path, however lustily he may have attacked him in Parliament. In 1957 he had been sceptical of Nehru's policy of non-alignment, saying: 'The word "*tatasth*" literally means to remain on the banks of the river . . . but who can keep standing on the bank? . . . Only that country can remain non-aligned which has national power.'[81] But once ensconced in the ministerial berth, the nationalist harangues were gone, the hawk turned suddenly into a dove, the fiery speeches were revealed as power politics and the perpetual ranter was replaced by a true-blue Nehruvian who declared in Parliament, 'I am a champion of non-alignment,'[82] and later even praised the Soviet Union. Vajpayee in government was a very different being from Vajpayee the man of the Opposition.

The Nehruvian impulse drove him to seek normal relations with Pakistan, shocking those who expected a Jana Sanghi to be a hawkish hardliner. He made an official 'goodwill visit' to Pakistan in February 1978, stepping off the plane at Islamabad looking smart in a bandgala, smiling broadly and briskly shaking hands with Pakistan foreign policy adviser Agha Shahi. Several agreements were signed – among them, allowing for more frequent cross-border visits between Indians and Pakistanis. 'Now India will defeat Pakistan only on the hockey field,' he announced in Islamabad, drawing appreciative applause from his hosts. He termed his visit 'historic'. At a press conference, when asked about Kashmir, he said this could be solved 'later', in accordance with the Simla Agreement. When asked if this wasn't a contradiction from his days in the Jana Sangh when he had rejected the Simla Agreement and termed it a stab in the nation's back, Vajpayee smiled: 'I'm trying to forget my past, and I urge you to do the same.'[83] This Pakistan visit began his long tryst with subcontinental peacemaking and the slow rise of his popularity among India's Muslims. During this time the Pakistani singer Roshan Ara Begum visited India and Vajpayee was invited as chief guest to one of her concerts. As he began his welcome address, he said, 'You have come to listen to sur (tune) and you are forced to listen to my sur (voice), but don't worry I am no asur (demon) that I will harass you with a long speech.'[84]

In 1978, a Pakistan consulate was opened in Mumbai and the Indian consulate in Karachi was reopened with a view to spurring business ties and smoothening visa processes. (Both these are now closed.) 'I hope more and more people will be able to visit the other country . . . I am determined to see travel between India and Pakistan made easier, he informed Parliament.'[85] Revelling in his new role, Vajpayee was moving to write a fresh chapter. He was now living in a gracious, lawn-fringed bungalow on 7 Safdarjung Road – the same road where Indira Gandhi had lived at no. 1 – with his family, the Kauls, around him. He was travelling abroad, clinking glasses with global leaders and making it a point to go sightseeing whenever he could. He belonged to the Partition generation – for his party, born in the fires of religious conflict, Pakistan was the perpetual enemy – yet Vajpayee's repeated shows of warmth towards Pakistan and determined attempts at peaceful contact show a willingness to outrun the clawing demons of his own past.

Indira Gandhi had been a 'special friend of Moscow', and Vajpayee was no less warm in welcoming a Soviet parliamentary delegation in April 1978, himself visiting the USSR in September and lavishing praise on the Soviet Union as India's 'only reliable friend'. He visited China in February 1979 for talks with Chinese premier Hua Guofeng and vice premier Deng Xiaoping, although his visit ended in embarrassment for India. While Vajpayee was in China, on 17 February 1979, China invaded India's friend Vietnam. Vajpayee was forced to abruptly cut short his visit and return to India. As the Opposition berated him for his 'naivete' in trusting China, he defended himself: 'I have no regrets for having visited Peking. My conscience is clear. I believe in taking risks, I believe in taking initiatives.'[86]

The high point of Vajpayee's foreign ministership took place when he addressed the United Nations in Hindi on 4 October 1977. He would later describe it as 'the happiest moment of my life'. Speaking with eloquent energy, he told the UN that India is committed to ridding the country of the fear and terror that had beset it in the Indira years. 'We believe in the vision of vasudhaiva kutumbakam – the world is one family. We in India have all along believed in this.'

The foreign minister loved his job and warmed to his post. He made so many trips abroad – he visited over forty countries – that a newspaper dubbed him 'Shuttle Bihari'. I have now realized how uncomfortable log flights are, he told the press. In fact, through the 1980s and 1990s, Vajpayee – who travelled overseas for the first time at the age of thirty-six – would go abroad almost incessantly on official delegations to Australia, Canada, Japan and Switzerland, and was part of India's teams at the UN General Assembly in 1988, 1990, 1991, 1992, 1993, 1994 and 1996.[87] His travels gave him an open world view, which set him further apart from the provincial narrow-mindedness of many of his ideological cohorts. In a reference to his absences from Delhi and frequent peregrinations abroad, his rivals called him a puppet foreign minister. 'The impression in the country today is that the Prime Minister makes the foreign policy, Mr Jagat Mehta [then the foreign secretary] implements it and you only translate it into Hindi,' shouted Congress's Vasant Sathe in Parliament one day. Such jibes didn't bother Vajpayee. 'Mr Speaker,' he responded smoothly, 'I want to speak in Hindi now because Shri Sathe clearly doesn't understand my English.'[88]

Yet as he flew high, the ground below him was rapidly shifting. A disparate group, a 'motley collection', 'a marriage of convenience', the Janata government rapidly fell prey to internal bickering and ego clashes. On every decision, whether to dismiss Congress state governments or to retain Indira's Forty-Second Amendment, consensus proved difficult. Vajpayee may have vowed to throw her into the 'dustbin of history', but Indira Gandhi still haunted them. Within a year of her crushing defeat, she was back in Parliament after winning the Chikmagalur by-election on 8 November 1978.

The Janata patriarchs had been watching her with rising fury and insecurity, Home Minister Charan Singh sending out the wrathful cry on 28 June 1978 that the Janata was a 'pack of impotent men' for not bringing Indira to justice. Morarji, furious at such language, briefly dropped Charan Singh from the cabinet, only to bring him back again, on the urgings of Advani, Vajpayee and George Fernandes. 'The reinduction wrecked the party,' recalls Advani,[89] particularly because Charan Singh's Lok Dal was a vociferous critic of the RSS.

Back in the government, Charan Singh, perpetually discontent at being denied the prime ministership, began to target Morarji over the corruption charges against his son Kanti Desai. Vajpayee himself had raised the allegations against Kanti Desai as far back as in 1968, when Morarji was deputy prime minister to Indira Gandhi, calling Kanti 'an unworthy son who misled his worthy father'.[90] Morarji was at daggers drawn with his ministerial colleague, and Charan Singh, enraged at the attempt to oust him, huffed about the 'conspiracy' against him. 'Chaudhary Charan Singh can be thrown out of the government but not Atal Bihari Vajpayee – only because he is a Brahmin and I am a Jat!' Charan Singh fumed to Advani.[91]

In the summer of 1979, the rains failed. Protests began at shortages, law and order broke down and for the first time units of the Central Reserve Police Force (CRPF) mutinied. On 11 July, Y.B. Chavan of the Congress (S) – the faction of the Congress that had broken from Indira in 1978 – moved a vote of no-confidence against the Morarji government. Charan Singh's supporters withdrew support, and on 15 July an isolated Morarji resigned. On 28 July 1979, Charan Singh became prime minister with the support of Indira Gandhi, but when he refused to oblige her in withdrawing the special courts that had been set up to try her and Sanjay, she ended her support to the Charan Singh government. Singh resigned on 20 August 1979. As his twenty-three-day-old government collapsed, the Janata experiment juddered to a halt, the President dissolved Parliament and India headed to the mid-term poll of January 1980. As if in profound disillusionment over the Janata's flounderings, on 8 October 1979, its parent and architect, Jayaprakash Narayan, died.

Devasahayam says that at this time, amid the hectic politicking, Sanjay Gandhi had reached out to the RSS and to Vajpayee and Advani, and held several meetings in the Mohan Meakins guest house in Himachal Pradesh to form a government, with himself, then thirty-three, as prime minister, with Jana Sangh support. 'Sanjay had a rightist mindset which fitted well with the RSS,' says Devasahayam.[92]

In 1980, Vajpayee stood again from New Delhi and won easily, but the Janata Party was wiped out. Indira Gandhi won a remarkable victory with 353 seats, galloping to resounding wins herself both in Medak in Andhra Pradesh and in her old constituency of Rae Bareli. On 14 January 1980, she was sworn in as prime minister for the fourth time,[93] 'purifying' her old residence – 1 Safdarjung Road (which had been occupied by Morarji) – by eight days of pujas and chanting.

The Jana Sangh, rocking in the cradle of power for two years, suddenly evaporated from Parliament. The former party's tally within the Janata, from ninety-three, plummeted to just sixteen. With their maverick superstar Vajpayee the only national politician, the Jana Sangh faced near obliteration.[94] Vajpayee called the mid-term fall of the Janata 'disgraceful' and a consequence of the Janata leaders' 'infinite lust for power'.[95]

Yet, because of the *ghus jao and chha jao* strategy, making use of the opportunities provided by access to state power, the Jana Sangh's party organization had grown strong and, as the Janata tumbled, the Jana Sangh emerged much stronger and within months was able to erect its own party.

Humiliatingly defeated by the return of 'Durga', the Janata's squabbling old men exploded into an open blame game. Janata members – who had wanted the dismissal of Vajpayee and Advani for their RSS links even before the government fell – started to openly direct their wrath at the Jana Sangh. The saffron army was accused of undermining and sabotaging Janata candidates. The 'dual membership' issue, simmering for a long time in the Janata coalition, opened up an unbridgeable abyss between the Jana Sangh and others. Socialists like Madhu Limaye and Raj Narain, always acutely uncomfortable with cohabiting with 'communalist' and 'fascist' RSS men, demanded that the Jana Sangh members either give up membership of the RSS or leave the Janata. There could be no 'dual membership'. Negotiations were held, but both sides were unbending. At one of the final meetings of the Janata Party, Advani protested that the Jana Sangh was now being treated like Harijans in the Janata Party and thrown out, whereas when the Janata Party was being formed 'the Harijans were acceptable'.[96]

Advani's outburst did not just stem from rage. It was also smart politics, aimed at creating an aura of victimhood around the erstwhile Jana Sangh. Already, in February–March 1980, aware of the hostility towards them in the Janata, Advani and his party colleague Sundar Singh Bhandari had travelled across India to gauge the popular mood and explore the possibility of forming their own party. Everywhere they went they discovered former Jana Sangh activists resentful about the 'second-class treatment' meted out to them in the Janata Party.[97] The anti-RSS stance of the socialists in the Janata had alienated Jana Sangh/RSS workers, and many did work for the polls of 1980. After the 1980 results, as socialists stepped up their call that the Jana Sangh must quit the RSS, Advani and Vajpayee made it clear that they would not. At the Janata National Executive Committee meeting 3–4 April 1980, attempts at a compromise failed, and on 3 April itself the Jana Sangh quit the Janata Party. Or, as Advani preferred to describe it, 'we were expelled'.[98] The Janata, which had first legitimized and normalized the Jana Sangh by allying with it, pushed it back towards exclusionist Hindutva ideology by then breaking off ties with it.

Now Vajpayee faced a crucial dilemma. Desperate to save the Janata, he had declared in May 1979, even before the Morarji government bit the dust, 'we have left the politics of the Jana Sangh forever. We should forget these things now [large gatherings of swayamsevaks] and get participated in the only nationalist stream of the Janata Party based upon the four principles of nationalism, democracy, religious equality and social equality.'[99] This kind of ideological retreat was not what the RSS and party cadres were fully comfortable with. Responding to the increasing pressures on the Jana Sangh from the left secularists at this time, Deoras held massive annual day celebrations in March 1979, with around 25,000 swayamsevaks attending. It was a show of strength against socialists, which Vajpayee distanced himself from by refusing to sit in the front row at the meeting despite repeated requests. As if embarrassed by his RSS links, he moved away from the leaders to sit right at the back.[100] At this time, noted a press report, Vajpayee 'seems particularly keen to drop his ties with the RSS and is seen fraternising rather cosily with RSS baiters Madhu Limaye and Biju Patnaik', the latter announcing: 'I cannot coexist with these chaddiwallahs.'

Vajpayee the politician and the RSS were intimate adversaries, joined at the hip yet pulling in different directions. Politics demands negotiations, regular dialogue to mitigate differences, necessitating inevitable compromises with ideology. This is how politics advances, wins bigger constituencies and reaches out to those who disagree. Ideologues have no such need. Dialogue is redundant because ideology is always the unassailable truth and theirs is the my-way-or-highway approach. Vajpayee created vital political space and respectability for his party but was always at the receiving end of the wrath of its zealots. At the same time, while taking the Hindu nationalist movement into the 'normal' space, he never frontally challenged the RSS ideologically, because, he remained, at his core, a believer.

With the Janata in ruins, which way would Vajpayee turn: towards Janata culture or RSS culture? Vajpayee, the sanatani traditionalist Hindu and the man of compromise, the parliamentarian who dealt in shades of grey, would now be faced with a black-and-white choice he did not want to make: was he an RSS man first and a mainstream politician only second? He who had so eagerly extinguished the Jana Sangh lamp by announcing 'it is time to put out the lamp', so excitedly rushed to merge his party into the Janata, which way would he go?

He chose the RSS. 'There can be no question of breaking off our ties with the RSS,'[101] he declared. That he was willing to leave his precious Janata formation for the sake of the RSS made known to all Vajpayee's unbreakable ties with the Hindu nationalist parent body.

He was hurt by the 'communal' accusation. In speeches he always lashed out at those who accused him of it. What was wrong in championing the Hindu point of view through politics? Weren't Christian democrats part of politics in Europe? Besides, where would he be without the RSS? Where would he have been without Narayanrao Tarte, U.K. Apte, Golwalkar, Upadhyaya, the Deoras brothers and Advani? He didn't see any contradiction between being a 'rag rag mein Hindu' and being a parliamentary democrat. Wasn't his ideal Jawaharlal also a Pandit from Allahabad? Didn't they share that unacknowledged, implicit fellow feeling of the Hindu Brahmin club?

Vajpayee was the worst sufferer of the Jana Sangh's break from the 'legitimate Opposition'. His ministership was over. His shot at power and a chance to sit at India's establishmentarian high table was over.

His attempt to drown the Jana Sangh in the river of mainstream politics had come to naught. And he was forced to make a choice about his core identity.

His dazzling electability had taken on a momentum of its own; years in Parliament had softened his beliefs; as the quintessential strategic politician, blessed with the art of mesmerizing a crowd, his ambitions would lead him towards an embrace of centrism. If he occasionally wanted to shake off the shackles of the sangh, it was not because he ceased to believe in the saffron parivar, but only because they sometimes got in the way of his politics and in the way of what he wanted most of all – the national centre stage. The RSS needed to understand that he was just as important to them as they were to him, because ultimately it was he who was the elected politician. But leaving the RSS? There was never any question of that. 'I have always had a very deep relationship with the RSS,' he said in 1996 to the news channel News24. 'There are many unselfish nation-building people in that organization. Yes, I have matbhed [disagreement] with them sometimes, but if my disagreements were ever so sharp, there could have been no question of my staying on.' And in 1980 he stayed on with the saffron brotherhood and gave up on the Janata. It was a life-defining decision. It showed that whatever moderate or secular line he genuinely upheld, there should be no illusions about the fact that Vajpayee's home was always the RSS. As the historian of the Hindu nationalist movement Christophe Jaffrelot puts it, 'The differences between Vajpayee and the RSS were always tactical rather than ideological. Vajpayee had been trained in the RSS and remained faithful to them until the end.'[102]

Months before the 1980 split, in August 1979, he had written an article. The article, titled 'We Are All to Blame', was published in the *Indian Express* on 2 August 1979. It was gutsily critical of the RSS, but, like all things Vajpayee, also revealed his customary craftiness about his own image.

Wrote Vajpayee: 'The RSS, claiming to be a social and cultural organisation, should have taken greater pains to demonstrate that they did not seek a political role.' He called for a clear enunciation by the RSS that by Hindu Rashtra it means the Indian nation, which includes non-Hindus as members and said, the RSS should function only as a 'Hindu *religious cum social cultural organisation* [italics author's]', RSS journals should not take sides in the power game, the RSS should not be involved in youth organizations that interact with political parties or trade unions.

Writing in English in an English-language newspaper, marshalling the stature of a mainstream politician to his pen, Vajpayee was telling the RSS to back off, as well as establishing his own non-denominational image, while remaining a part of the RSS. It had the desired effect. A day later, the socialist George Fernandes, who had been vocal about the Jana Sangh's dual membership, wrote a letter to Vajpayee saying, 'I appreciated your article . . . I'm willing to sit with you and work out a solution.'[103] Fernandes would later become a staunch Vajpayee ally. In October 1979, at the RSS's Vijaya Dashami celebrations, Deoras seemed to respond to the article when he said: 'The Sangh has changed in keeping with the necessities of the times, we will keep changing in future too.'[104] In 1980 Vajpayee remained with the Sangh Parivar but also subtly showed his distance from the khaki brotherhood.

After breaking away from the Janata Party, excited as they had been at their first ascent to state power, the Jana Sangh could not easily give up on Raisina Hill. It was time to think of a new way. Advani was fired up about starting a new party, but Vajpayee was not convinced at first and required a lot of persuasion. 'Is there scope for another party in India?' he asked.[105] The Congress was on the march again. The Opposition was fragmented, squabbling, forlorn and even seemed to be heading towards annihilation. A new party at this time looked like an impossible proposition. What would be its name? The Jana Sangh was about to be rechristened and Vajpayee about to embark on the biggest reinvention of his life.

5

Gandhian Socialism Goes Wrong: 1980–1989

A poem for Vajpayee:
A new party, a new identity but a sudden fall,
Indira as martyr, Congress stands tall.
Vajpayee's moderation gives way to Hindutva's rise,
Marginalized, the golden boy's back is to the wall.

Tilting at the Congress, from the 'Gandhian socialist' centre,
That's where his desire lay.
But crushing defeats
shifted the ground from under his feet,
His centrism fell by the way.

~

A grim-faced row of politicians – Atal Bihari Vajpayee among them – sat on the stage at Delhi's Feroz Shah Kotla grounds. Behind them fluttered posters of Jayaprakash Narayan, Syama Prasad Mookerji and Deendayal Upadhyaya. It was a hot April day in Delhi. Soon the grounds were packed with crowds of enthusiastic party workers. They had assembled for the two-day national convention organized by members of the former Jana Sangh, just a day after it broke away from the Janata Party. Over two days, 5 and 6 April 1980, they had a fresh mission: to revive the Jana Sangh through a new party.

Vajpayee, in a white dhoti and kurta, no longer just an angry Opposition man but a former foreign minister, stood up to speak. As the gathered supporters sweated and fanned themselves, he explained why he and his colleagues had broken from the Janata, and also emphasized that there was no going back to the past. 'Nobody should think we are here to form another Jana Sangh,' he said. 'We do not want to revive the Jana Sangh in any way. We will make use of our experience in the Janata Party. We are proud to have been associated with it . . . We look to the future and not to the past, as we begin our endeavour to rebuild our party.'[1] Other leaders spoke too. Striking a note of injured victimhood, the common refrain was that it was the Janata which had 'expelled' the Jana Sanghis because of their proud RSS ties.

For Vajpayee, the way forward was clear: bye-bye Jana Sangh, hello new Janata. Onward towards an ideologically fuzzy, inclusive, party; towards alliances, towards winning elections, and towards putting an end forever to the Jana Sangh–type 'untouchability'. This new party would be different; it would be open to all and hopefully become his long-held dream of a 'national alternative' to the Congress.

The new party's name was the Bharatiya Janata Party, 'Bharatiya' from the Bharatiya Jana Sangh, 'Janata' from the Janata Party. It was decided that the flag would be a variant of the Janata Party's, three quarters saffron and one quarter green. New party symbols were not possible at this time as assembly elections had already been announced for May. Among the party symbols available, Advani chose the lotus.

Vajpayee was elected party president. A suitably diverse team of party general secretaries took charge: L.K. Advani, Sikandar Bakht, a former Janata minister and Congress (O) leader as the party's Muslim face, and the Dalit RSS member Suraj Bhan. The party wouldn't have too much truck with ideology. 'In India, a party based on ideology can at most come to power in a small area. It cannot win the confidence of the entire country . . . whenever the ideology [of the Jana Sangh] was strong, its appeal diminished,' Advani told the RSS journal *Panchjanya* in late 1980, echoing his leader's views.[2] Vajpayee once wrote in an essay that in a diverse country like India – India's incorrigible heterogeneity or vividhita finds constant mention in his writings – just one way of thinking is inadequate and restrictive.[3] A surfeit of ideology constricts a party into a mere pressure group. Instead, to succeed a party needs to be attuned to ground realities. For Vajpayee, the making of the BJP was a cremation of the hoary old Jana Sangh and snatching a new alloy from the flames. The Bharatiya Janata Party when it was first born was a conservative-populist party with a measure of Upadhyaya's society-focused populism and Mookerji's moderation, Vajpayee's tribute to the two mentors he called Upadhyayaji and Doctor sahab.

The addictions of Raisina Hill – speaking at the United Nations, cross-party camaraderie in Parliament, bonding with a cohort of men of state from diverse backgrounds – had moved Vajpayee to a place where the quest for national centre stage mattered more than Hindutva rigidity. Oh, he could do the ideology if it was necessary, but there were so many more rewards to be had if ideology was deployed smartly and strategically. His own ideas were changing; his relationship with the RSS was in flux. The Gandhian socialism that became his calling card in the 1980s had been brewing in his mind since Indira's 1971 triumph. In Parliament and government he had been steeped in India's multiplicity; her many domestic and international challenges had convinced him of the value of dialogue and compromise. In 1980, he was determined that the 'communal', 'fascist', 'Nazi' stigma should be forever deflected and that the party should have a welcoming new identity to attract maximum potential allies.

The animating ideas of the new party would be 'positive secularism' and 'Gandhian socialism' – *Gandhivadi samajwad* – the latter a suitably ambiguous set of ideas designed for maximum openness, to appeal to all and irk no one. Vajpayee had once been part of the Hindu left or the Hindu socialists in the early 1970s when he had strongly resisted Madhok's free-market views, insisting that the Jana Sangh should never be seen as pro-rich. In 1980, 'socialism' established the party's pro-poor line; 'Gandhian' stood for freedom and was designed for universal acceptability. A 1971 speech in Parliament reveals his mind on deriving ideas of economic equality from socialism and ideas on individual freedom from Gandhi's views on personal liberty.

> Is there no dividing line between the yogi [the free individual] and the commissar [state power]? Does India want to eliminate economic disparity by sacrificing individual freedom? Do we want to make a monster of the State? . . . What is India's genius? What is India's tradition? We will have to achieve a confluence of individual freedom and economic equality.[4]

The two words 'Gandhian socialism' stuck in the craw of former Jana Sanghis and RSS men. Some fiercely questioned the name Bharatiya Janata Party. The word 'socialism' raised hackles. The word Janata caused annoyance. 'Many in the sangh found the name "Janata" completely unacceptable. They had wanted to revive the Jana Sangh,' Balraj Madhok recalled.[5] Fumed Vijaya Raje Scindia: 'This is nothing but a photocopy of the Congress.' Nanaji Deshmukh, who had been disapproving of the loss of ideological identity even when the Jana Sangh merged with the Janata Party, bid adieu to politics at this time, unable to stomach Vajpayee's ideas.

Gandhian socialism – Gandhivadi samajwad – was all about Vajpayee, centred on his persona as the party's karta-dharta (head). He was excited and hopeful about the new concept and, intellectual that he was, explained it thus: Socialism snatched away freedom, capitalism promoted inequality, but Gandhian socialism would herald equality and freedom, both bread and liberty. As the party moved to draw in new members from the anti-Emergency movement – among them the Janata law minister Shanti Bhushan and the lively, garrulous lawyer Ram Jethmalani – Gandhian socialism became the big tent idea to hold them all.

The results of the BJP's first election test – the assembly polls of 1980 – were discouraging. Within a month of its birth, barely stopping to catch its breath, the BJP put up candidates in assembly elections to nine states in May. When Indira Gandhi returned to power in 1980, she dismissed nine Janata governments and ordered fresh elections, the surfeit of polls dubbed a 'mini general election'. Vajpayee announced that these elections were again a fight between 'democracy' and 'dictatorship', but the Indira-led Congress raced through as the clear winner in all states except Tamil Nadu. Again in the shadow of a dominant Indira, Vajpayee's political start-up got off to a shaky beginning.

But Vajpayee's hopes were high. The future stretched ahead like the shimmering sea. With the ocean as a backdrop, a gigantic crowd, over 40,000-strong, gathered in Mumbai in a 7,00,000 square foot area covered by pandals, and lit up by row upon row of 1500 neon lights. From 28 to 30 December, the newly born BJP held its first mahadhiveshan or first plenary session in Mumbai's Bandra Seaface, renamed 'Samtanagar', for the occasion. Party members gathered from several states, the largest numbers from Jana Sangh strongholds in North India.

The mood was upbeat. In a spotless white dhoti and kurta and scarf, Vajpayee, the cynosure of all eyes, the 'future prime minister' was as ever-smiling and urbane as always. Fifty-six years old, he was an impressive man at this time: seasoned, charming, resolute and ambitious, an adult in every sense of the word. Yes, he now required reading glasses when he occasionally glanced at his notes while speaking, but his words were still mesmerizing. In the evening, as the sea breeze blew in, he roared dramatically, 'With the Constitution of India in one hand and the banner of equality in the other, let us plunge into the struggle . . . I can say this with confidence about the future: . . . *andhera chhatega, suraj nikalega, kamal khilega* . . . darkness will be dispelled, the sun will rise, the lotus will bloom.'[6]

The well-respected Muhammadali Currim Chagla, jurist and former minister in both Nehru's and Indira's cabinet, a distinguished member of civil society, had been invited to burnish the secular credentials of the function. Chagla, an Ismaili Khoja Muslim, had appeared in court for Vajpayee and Advani during the Emergency and in a book foreword had lavishly praised Vajpayee's 'sincerity, eloquence and love of humanity'. 'My father deeply admired Vajpayee the parliamentarian and never believed he could be communal,' recalls Chagla's son Iqbal Chagla.[7] At the end of a long speech, Chagla asked, 'Who says there is no alternative to the Congress in the country? I see the alternative right in front of me in the form of the Bharatiya Janata Party. And in Atal Bihari Vajpayee, I see the alternative to Indira Gandhi.'[8] The crowd burst into applause, cheering: '*Pradhan mantri agli baari, Atal Bihari, Atal Bihari*.'[9]

Inordinately popular, already a personality cult, Vajpayee had been hailed as a future prime minister since his Jana Sangh days. After the Mumbai mahadhiveshan the journalist Janardan Thakur wrote, 'Atal Bihari Vajpayee will be the next prime minister. I am not saying he *may*, I am saying he *will* . . . both man and party have blossomed [author italics].'[10]

But under the bright neon lights in Mumbai, there was tension, disagreement and frustration. At the mahadhiveshan Vijaya Raje Scindia tore into the concept of Gandhian socialism and received loud applause as she did so. 'I thought the expression "Gandhian socialism" had a false ring to it,' Vijaya Raje Scindia told the press. 'That it was dangerously close to the "socialism" of the other Gandhi [Indira]. I did not want my party to be born in hypocrisy.'[11] Vijaya Raje later withdrew her objections, but subterranean grumblings remained. Nanaji Deshmukh had distanced himself from Vajpayee's party and was absent from Mumbai. 'He was the one most adamant on leaving the Janata, now he stays away from us,' said Vajpayee irritatedly of Nanaji.[12] Another former Jana Sangh veteran told *India Today* magazine: 'We supported the Jana Sangh because it was the only party upholding majority interests, whereas the Congress and communist parties were only championing minority interests. I don't like to see Vajpayee borrowing the same phoney vocabulary as the secularists.'[13] 'Those who came out of the Janata and formed the BJP were our swayamsevaks,' the RSS's K.S. Sudarshan would say in 1989, 'when the party turned to Gandhian Socialism, our swayamsevaks felt differently.'[14] The former Jana Sanghis and RSS had learnt a bitter lesson during the Janata interlude: they had sacrificed ideology and identity to merge with the Janata. And what did they get in return? Only the collapse of the Janata and the election disaster of 1980.

Among fifty-one national executive members, as many as thirty-one were from the RSS, and of fourteen special invitees, eleven were RSS members, revealing the dominance of the RSS in the BJP. But Vajpayee was still confident he could take the newborn baby in a broadly progressive direction: 'Our party was born in 1980; the Jana Sangh in 1951; the RSS in 1925. These are separate events. No one can be the other.'[15]

Yet the decade would conspire against Vajpayee and his hopes of a new centrism. Within three short years of the Mumbai mahadhiveshan, in 1983 Vajpayee would deliver such an incendiary communal speech that it was later blamed for causing barbaric communal killings.

The 1980s was India's most violent decade, a decade in which India's political and social fabric ruptured, a decade which plunged India into the fiery flames of caste and religious conflict. A dozen major riots between Hindus and Muslims erupted, from Moradabad to Bhiwandi to Ahmedabad to Kota, Meerut and Muzaffarnagar. There was a savage massacre in Nellie, Assam, and anti-Sikh riots in Delhi. Almost 4000 people were killed in communal riots between 1980 and 1987.[16] In Punjab and Kashmir, armed militancy reared its head. A prime minister was assassinated. In this bloody decade, Vajpayee's party began a violence-scarred, bloodstained march away from Vajpayee's Gandhian socialist dream.

In the fiery turbulence of the 1980s, Gandhian socialism failed badly at the ballot box. Vajpayee the Gandhian socialist lost his Midas touch. In assembly elections in the early 1980s, the new centrist-moderate BJP kept losing, and losing badly. Workers were unmotivated to work for the 'secular', 'socialist' party; voters were lukewarm. Buffeted by defeat, Vajpayee would gradually give up on Gandhivadi samajwad and make his peace with a lexicon of militant Hindutva that he had been trying to outpace.

~

In the initial years after Mumbai though, a hopeful Vajpayee poured his energies into the new party, engaging in a battle of wits with the RSS old guard to overcome latent antagonisms, launching a publicity campaign to show off a 'high-profile' identity, attempting to reorganize and modernize the party, going on padyatras and holding a study camp in Vrindavan, where strategy papers on foreign policy were circulated. The paper spoke of a peacemaking attitude to Pakistan and dwelt on defence policy – even quoting the ancient Roman philosopher Lucretius on public images and propaganda. 'The BJP has matured,' said Ram Jethmalani, 'due to the influence of the people who joined after 1980 who were neither from Jana Sangh or RSS backgrounds.'[17]

Smarting from the failures of the Janata, frustrated at Indira Gandhi's spectacular return, Vajpayee was determined to pursue his life's mission: trying to create the 'national alternative' to the Congress. He had always believed that democracy needed strong, real parties, based on clear programmes, organized workers and social constituencies. Parties must be 'based on policies, observe democratic norms, have regular membership, hold regular organisational elections and go before the people with clear cut manifestos', he wrote.[18] To make Indian democracy strong by challenging the Congress was his bounden duty. But destiny played a trick on him: the moderate centrism he espoused proved too feeble to take on the Congress.

In 1981, one event set the tone for the decade and became the starting point of the 'Hindu revolution' of the 1980s. Meenakshipuram is a small nondescript village in Tamil Nadu inhabited mainly by small farmers and rural labourers. For years the village had been racked by the torture and humiliation of lower castes. On 19 February 1981, about a thousand Dalits in Meenakshipuram converted to Islam. Sangh Parivar outfits, having tasted power in the anti-Emergency movement and now on the lookout for rallying cries, erupted in outrage. Majoritarian Hindu sentiments were already beginning to rise with sectarian terrorist violence in Punjab and Kashmir. The Vishwa Hindu Parishad (VHP), established by the RSS in the 1960s with the aim of protecting the 'Hindu fold' from Christian missionaries, Islamic proselytizers and the 'westernized class', had been inactive for two decades. But now the VHP took the lead in actively spreading 'Hindu rage' and organizing sadhus for Hindu causes.

After Meenakshipuram the VHP stepped up a shrill campaign against conversions, claiming that Hindu society was 'under siege'. The BJP too created a commotion in Parliament and Vajpayee went on a visit to Meenakshipuram. Meenakshipuram would become the point from which the politics of Hindutva would take off. Vajpayee would look on as his party set off down dirt tracks lined with mandirs and masjids when he had been trying to wrench his party towards the calm of the seaside. In 1982, Vajpayee suspended a party member accused of communal riots, but so outraged were his party men that the suspension had to be revoked against his wishes. He played this snub down in the press. 'We are all like a family, and there is bound to be a little dissent in a democratic party.'[19]

The Indira-led Congress played its part in the collapse of Gandhian socialism. In the years that Vajpayee was trying to chart an inclusive centrist course, in a curious role reversal, the Congress was turning towards cultivating the 'Hindu vote'. After her return to power in 1980, Indira Gandhi had suddenly turned deeply religious and visited dozens of shrines. In an astonishing shift, the secular Indira began to play the politics of Hindu vote banks to deflect what she perceived as the communalist challenge to the Congress. The Indira-led Congress even moved imperceptibly closer to the RSS, so much so that by the elections of 1984 many in the RSS supported Rajiv Gandhi.[20] In the process she imparted a new legitimacy to non-secular politics and began the process of what has been called 'competitive desecularization' and rubbing secularism out of public life.

In Parliament Vajpayee at this time was unleashing a fusillade of attacks at his old enemy, Indira. Punjab and Assam were in turmoil. Sikh militancy in Punjab was taking a daily toll of lives and in Assam anti-migrant agitations were roiling the state in violence and panic. Vajpayee was perpetually on his feet in the House, hurling speech after speech at the Indira government. 'All India Radio has the permission to sing the praises of Smt. Indira Gandhi for 12 mins, in a news bulletin of 15 mins,' he yelled in Parliament. 'Change the name of All India Radio to All Indira Radio.'[21]

But for all his verbal power, he couldn't score at the hustings. Three shocks hit the fledgling 'Gandhian socialist' BJP at the beginning of 1983. In the Andhra Pradesh and Karnataka elections, the party put in a poor performance winning just three out of 294 seats in Andhra Pradesh and scoring slightly better in Karnataka with eighteen out of 224 seats. In the high-prestige Delhi civic polls – including in his own constituency New Delhi – the BJP lost so badly that the Congress shouted, '*Atal Bihari atak gaya, kamal ka phool latak gaya* [Atal Bihari is stranded, the lotus flower is drooping],' and demanded Vajpayee's resignation from the Lok Sabha, mocking him for 'wasting time on jokes and jugglery'. The RSS, suspicious of the BJP's increasingly 'secular', coalition-friendly tendencies, had mostly stayed away from the BJP's Delhi campaign and its workers had not worked for BJP candidates.

The poll defeats alarmed the BJP. 'Our performance did not show any signs of an early take-off,' recalled Advani.[22] 'The BJP has a tendency to play down its Hindu character,' snapped the RSS mouthpiece *Organiser* in an angry article. 'Nobody need quarrel with its efforts to attract non-Hindus. But many may also view it as a weakening of character.'[23] After the January polls came the Assam assembly elections of mid-February 1983. These violence-ridden Assam polls, misguidedly held by Indira Gandhi at the height of communal tensions, brought out Vajpayee in a strangely militant avatar, one he would often deploy like a warlock's lethal weapon if the battle was desperate enough. In February 1983 Vajpayee accused Indira of playing vote bank politics in Assam in openly religious language: 'The Prime Minister of India concluded her speech with khuda hafiz. What does it mean? I have no quarrel with khuda hafiz. But is this the way to maintain goodwill and communal unity by talking like this at election time?'[24]

This speech was nothing compared to the incendiary words he himself used in Assam during the campaign. In early February, Vajpayee travelled to Assam and said, 'Foreigners have come here and the government does nothing. What if they had come into Punjab instead? People would have chopped them into pieces and thrown them away.'[25] Bringing this speech to the attention of the Lok Sabha, on 26 May 1996, CPI MP Indrajit Gupta addressed the House in these words: 'I submit that in the atmosphere prevailing at the time for a responsible leader to make a statement like this that they should be chopped into pieces and thrown away is nothing but inflammatory. Soon after this the Nellie massacre took place in Assam. Mr Vajpayee contributed to creating this atmosphere . . . this is very different from the speech he made here [in Parliament].'[26]

Days after Vajpayee's Assam speech, on 18 February 1983, over a thousand Bengali-speaking Muslims (unofficial figures put the dead at 3000) were hacked to death with machetes, others burnt alive in their homes in Nellie. The party's rout in Andhra Pradesh in January may have pushed Vajpayee towards virulent Hindutva rhetoric in

February in Assam. But where did this leave 'Gandhian socialism' and the Mumbai moment?

'Politician Vajpayee' had several arrows in his quiver. The '*rag rag mein Hindu*' arrow was one of them, to be shot off whenever necessary. The bellicose Hindu identity that Vajpayee regularly displayed, like a flash of menacing lightning in a seemingly placid sky, was integral to his political persona. The democrat and parliamentarian was never willing to entirely abandon the Hindu mobilizing platform, seeing it as a brahmastra to stun the Congress. Yes, he was wary of the militant hotheads and extremist foot soldiers. Yes, he yearned for the inclusive centre. But he repeatedly revealed he was also willing to ride the Hindutva tiger in his speeches because he thought, obviously with great self-deception, that he could dismount when he wanted. He fatally underestimated the power of religious extremism and militancy to overwhelm the same Indian democracy that he so prized.

Vajpayee's infamous '*Ab Hindu Maar Nahin Khayega*' (Hindus will no longer be beaten) speech in Parliament a decade ago on the 1970 Bhiwandi riots is worth noting here. Taking part in a debate in the Lok Sabha on 14 May 1970 on communal riots, Vajpayee cried: 'Not all Muslims want communal riots. There are also patriotic and peace-loving people among Muslims . . . But there is certainly a section of Muslims – and this needs to be said without mincing words – that wants to bring communalism into the country . . . our Muslim brethren are getting more and more communal, and as a reaction Hindus are getting more and more aggressive. Nobody made the Hindus aggressive . . . *Ab Hindu maar nahin khayega*. Hindus will no more take a beating in this country. Hindus will not start, Hindus will not initiate. If you promote Muslim communalism, the other feeling will run high.'[27]

He had for long railed against the shortcomings of Nehru's and Indira's secularism. In 1961, he shouted: 'All rules must apply equally to all . . . in Punjab, police cannot enter a gurudwara, but in Chandigarh police can enter an Arya Samaj mandir.'[28] In 1969, he argued, 'Prime Minister Smt. Indira Gandhi went to launch a ship built in India.

She performed the ceremony by breaking a coconut. "Communal" papers objected to this saying a coconut cannot be broken in a secular state . . . Our revered president [Dr Zakir Hussain] garlanded Sardar Patel's picture. Some Muslim papers wrote a Muslim president must not garland a picture . . . as these are Hindu customs. I say . . . it is part of a culture which has grown out of the soil of this country and we cannot break with it.'[29]

When he was uttering these words, could Vajpayee have foreseen a time when India's parliamentary democracy would wilt under religious majoritarianism? Weaned on the Nehruvian enlightenment of the 1950s, he underestimated the power of religion to overwhelm politics and the democratic institutions he prized. Perhaps this is why he often publicly played the Hindu card.

A lifelong struggle against brute Congress dominance led to a desperate and calculating search for potent, electrifying causes which could dent the Nehru–Gandhi edifice. Hindu nationalism was one of them, its use justified because it had killer potential to strike body blows on the ruling leviathan. The morality of it may have bothered him, which is why he kept trying to move away from it or make contradictory statements, yet he would never turn his back on a cause that could generate so much mass support and become a golden ticket to the ballot box.

For example, at the height of Advani's rath yatra in 1990, the then chief ministers of Bihar and Bengal, Lalu Prasad Yadav and Jyoti Basu, came to visit Vajpayee and told him that Advani's rath yatra was causing too much instability in their states and must be stopped. Vajpayee called Advani. 'Advaniji, perhaps you should call your yatra off now? Problems are being created, *ab ise band kar dijiye.*' Advani hotly turned him down saying that the yatra was turning out to be extremely popular and huge crowds were flocking to him in the villages and towns. 'Atalji, you have no idea how popular it is,' Advani argued. 'Popular, is it?' mused Vajpayee. 'All right then, please carry on.'[30] If a platform was publicly popular, it acquired its own morality.

The stumbling blocks that Gandhian socialism was to encounter deepened this very particular Vajpayee ambivalence about Hindu nationalism and constitutional democracy and the two worlds Vajpayee straddled. In 1980 he attempted to chart a new course for his party based on openness and plurality. But, unable to give it electoral muscle or substance, he saw that modernist dream dissolve into primeval religious war cries. On occasion he himself succumbed to Hindu nationalism's darker side.

In April 1983 Vajpayee was again elected president of the BJP. This time he was the reluctant supremo, striking a resigned note after the election defeats, and said in his presidential speech, 'If a man stays in a post for too long, he loses the capacity for fresh ideas. He becomes a prisoner of stale ideas and tiredness and can't give of his best to the party.'[31] Apprehensions were boiling in his party, as the BJP faced successive routs in elections, and Gandhivadi samajwad was turning into a shrivelling balloon.

Later in 1983 came a 'particularly demoralising setback'.[32] In the Jammu and Kashmir elections in October, Indira Gandhi played Hindu politics in Jammu and accused Farooq Abdullah of being a secessionist and of being in league with Islamist hardliners, emphasizing the discrimination faced by Hindus in Kashmir and warning of the separatist threat. In this election, the BJP failed to win a single seat – even Hindu-majority seats in the Jana Sangh stronghold of Jammu went to the Congress. If its prized Hindu voter had deserted it in Jammu, perhaps Hindus were deserting it across India? The RSS stepped up its criticism of the BJP. Vajpayee's party sank further into gloom.

He desperately needed an election win for his leadership and vision to be firmly consolidated. He had tried hard throughout the pre-1983 period: constituency-level task forces were set up, workers meetings were held in tehsils and the BJP's 1982 Vrindavan study camp had even come up with some innovative suggestions to gain favourable press coverage. But electoral success was not to be for the flickering lamp of Gandhivadi samajwad.

In 1984 came the body blow. Indira Gandhi was assassinated. In general elections after her death the Congress stormed to its biggest ever win of 404 seats. The BJP was wiped out and Vajpayee lost his own seat. Gandhivadi samajwad was unceremoniously buried. In three short years from 1980 to 1983 Vajpayee made a schizophrenic journey from the Mumbai moment to the Assam downfall. That hope-filled Mumbai moment, that passionate charting of a moderate, inclusive line, that brief moment beside the shimmering sea, began to look tragic. The woman he could never defeat in life almost extinguished his political career with her death.

~

His leadership was being questioned in his party, but in his home life, in his rambling 6 Raisina Road bungalow, he was the benevolent paterfamilias of the Vajpayee–Kaul establishment. He rejoiced in his adoptive family, 'Baapji' to his beloved adopted daughter Namita or 'Gunu'. Family friends say his relations with Rajkumari's older daughter, Nandita, were somewhat cooler. There was some talk that Nandita, a psychiatrist married to a US-based software engineer, Ashok Nanda, was not too happy with Vajpayee's role in her parents' life and preferred to maintain a distance. There are almost no recorded instances of Vajpayee talking about or meeting Nandita, except once reportedly attending her birthday celebrations in America in 2001. There are no publicly available photos of Nandita with Vajpayee, as there are of him with Namita. However, friends say that when Vajpayee was in New York, Nandita and her husband regularly visited him. It is also said that Namita and her husband, Ranjan, had their marriage ceremonies in 1983 in Nandita's home in upstate New York. 'Vajpayee and Mrs Kaul had a complex relationship and the relationships around them were also invariably complex,' says a family friend.

Former president Pranab Mukherjee, then a Congress politician, lived at this time at 2 Jantar Mantar Lane and his house shared a boundary wall with Vajpayee's. The two – one an Indira-baiting RSS man and the other the Indira-adoring Congress man – would often step out for after-dinner strolls. Mukherjee remembers the household as tension-free, informal and welcoming, although on one occasion Mukherjee's dog Daku snapped at and bit Vajpayee. Later Vajpayee in Parliament held up his bandaged hand for Mukherjee to see. Mrs Suvra Mukherjee and Rajkumari became close friends and Vajpayee – who loved all kinds of fish dishes – relished Suvra's expert culinary creations, often sending the Mukherjees home-grown vegetables from his own Raisina Road garden.

In 1983, Rajkumari's younger daughter, Namita, educated at Delhi University's Daulat Ram College, married her college friend Ranjan Bhattacharyya, a hotelier. They met when they were both students and she was secretary of her college. 'Namita used to regularly come and play in our place in her younger days, come rushing in to taste our pickles and when Namita's marriage was decided, my wife helped in preparations as the groom was a Bengali,' Mukherjee recalled.[33]

In 1985 was born the apple of Vajpayee's eye, his adoptive granddaughter Niharika, nicknamed Neha. He held an annaprashan ceremony for her at Delhi's Constitution Club, inviting his many friends from all parties, including Rajiv Gandhi and Najma Heptullah of the Congress. As the guests prepared to start on the meal laid out outdoors, it suddenly began to rain. Instantly Vajpayee began to rush around, escorting guests out of the rain, helping to bring the banquet indoors and making sure all the guests were looked after and well fed. The Ghatates were regulars in his social life. One birthday – in days when his birthday was not celebrated with pomp by party men – Ghatate presented him with a cake. Asked by doctors to follow a restricted diet, he grimaced at the cake and said to Ghatate, 'Et tu Brute.'[34]

His wisecracks came in a steady flow, whatever the circumstances. After caste killings in Uttar Pradesh's Sadhupur in January 1982, Vajpayee went on a high-profile padyatra. When asked how long the padyatra would continue, Vajpayee responded: *'Jab tak pad nahin milta, yatra karenge* [I will walk until I get the position – a play on the Hindi word 'pad' meaning both foot and post].' In 1988 in America for his kidney ailment – a trip made possible by then prime minister Rajiv Gandhi – a cancer test produced worrying results. He wrote a poem at this time, '*Maut Se Thann Gayi*', as if welcoming death. The poem was circulated in India and caused a flutter of consternation in party circles about his mortality. It later emerged that his ailment was not serious and could be easily managed. When he returned to India, he was surprised to see thousands of BJP and Sangh Parivar workers at the airport to meet him. Said Vajpayee, sotto voce, to his aide Shiv Kumar: '*Yeh pooch rahe hain ki maut ka dastavez likhkar bheja tha, toh zinda kyon laut aye?*' [They're all asking, after sending us a message of his imminent death, why is he now returning still alive?]'[35] He could be light-hearted even after tortured parliamentary debates. In 1970, after his Bhiwandi speech, Indira Gandhi raged: 'Mr Vajpayee uses forceful Hindi but there is naked fascism behind his words.'[36] Vajpayee later told friends, I better not attract her attention because every time she sees me, she sees Hitler. Vajpayee was a voluble and jokey person in his youth, recalls Ghatate. But over the years he became much less talkative as he became more experienced in politics. As prime minister, Vajpayee barely spoke and became vigilantly cautious about his words.

By 1983, Indira Gandhi was weakening. Opposition politicians like N.T. Rama Rao and Farooq Abdullah were making serious efforts to cobble together an Opposition front, holding meetings in Vijayawada in June 1983 and in Srinagar in October. Advani as BJP general secretary attended the Vijayawada meeting. But at this time, as mounting poll defeats took their toll on party morale, differences emerged between Vajpayee and Advani about alliances with other Opposition parties. While Vajpayee was, as always, enthusiastically in favour of alliances, Advani maintained that there was need to establish the BJP's separate identity first and that it would be hara-kiri to try to align with parties which only a few years ago had ostracized the Jana Sangh for 'dual membership' in the RSS. There was even talk at this time that Vajpayee was reportedly keen to deny Advani a third Rajya Sabha term (which Advani got from Madhya Pradesh).

In 1984 as Punjab went up in flames, Vajpayee lashed out against Indira Gandhi's ordering of Operation Blue Star to capture the Golden Temple: 'This is the last time the army should be sent into a religious shrine . . . why did things come to such a pass that the army had to be called?'[37] In early October at a party meet in Pune, he fulminated: 'There is a martial law–like situation in Punjab. Democracy is being destroyed in the name of fighting terrorism. The prime minister is playing a dangerous game by dragging the army into politics.'

His party, however, seethed with uneasiness. The RSS was uncomfortable with the Vajpayee personality cult and its impatience with Vajpayee's leadership sharpened. Just as the Jana Sangh was done out of the 'nationalism' plank by the Congress in 1971, now Indira Gandhi seemed to be snatching away the BJP's own Hindu plank from under the BJP's feet.

On 31 October 1984 Indira Gandhi was killed in her home by her own Sikh bodyguards. Almost immediately, brutal anti-Sikh riots tore through Delhi. Sikhs were mercilessly attacked and after three days of frenzied violence almost 3000 Sikhs lay dead. There was a taxi stand outside Vajpayee's Raisina Road bungalow, which was ransacked during the riots. Some of the Sikh taxi drivers rushed into Vajpayee's home, imploring the lone security guard to let them in. Upon hearing the commotion, Vajpayee hurriedly emerged and placed himself between the drivers and mob, standing with the drivers until police arrived to take the drivers to safety. He vociferously condemned the brutal attacks on Sikhs. 'A young Sikh man, a BJP karyakarta, came to meet me at night,' he said in 1984. 'I couldn't recognise him because his hair was cut. I asked what have you done to yourself? He said I can't come during the day, I have sacrificed my hair. We must share this pain.'[38] Some members of the RSS met Vajpayee and expressed their disapproval of his comments, given that Sikh terrorists were targeting Hindus in Punjab. 'Whatever I felt I expressed without hesitation,' Vajpayee told the RSS men. 'Killing of innocent Sikhs is as condemnable as killing of innocent Hindus in Punjab.'[39]

He was horrified at what he called Indira's 'diabolical', 'dastardly' and 'tragic' murder. 'I often clashed with Indiraji in Parliament . . .' he writes. 'But she never let political differences affect personal relationships. Her dastardly and tragic assassination suddenly removed from our midst a personality that will not only be remembered as the worthy daughter of a worthy father but also for her own ability, dexterity, decisiveness and firmness.[40]

He had been one of the first to visit her when her son Sanjay was killed in 1980, saying he was 'inexpressibly disturbed'. He had burst out emotionally, 'Indiraji, in this moment of great travail, you will have to show great courage.'[41] He greatly prized a 1971 photo of himself with Indira, in which they are seen immersed in conversation and she is holding an umbrella. When a collection of his speeches was being readied for publication, he insisted the photo be included.[42]

As India mourned the martyrdom of the heroine-prime-minister, the general elections held after her death in December 1984 became akin to a memorial, a funeral procession – a 'shok sabha election', not a Lok Sabha election. The Congress, now led by Indira's son Rajiv Gandhi, harnessed a hurricane, winning over 400 seats. On 31 December, forty-year-old Rajiv Gandhi took oath as prime minister. The BJP was able to get only two seats. In a sensational shock result, the invincible Vajpayee was humiliatingly defeated in Gwalior by the Congress's Madhavrao Scindia.

During the 1984 campaign, as BJP party president, he took his party to the polls under his secular moderate banner. In mustard bandgala and black karakuli cap, he delivered a grave TV broadcast. 'India is a land of diverse religions, diverse languages . . . they are bound to clash . . . if a diverse land has to be taken forward *takrav ki rajneeti* [politics of confrontation] must be forsaken,' he said. He asked for votes for a government of 'aarthik nyay' (economic justice) and 'samajik samata' (social equality).[43]

On the campaign trail he attempted to fire up workers. '*Hum kabaddi khele hain*,' he yelled, '*marne ke baad bhi zinda hona jaante hain* [We have played kabaddi, we know how to come to life even after we've died].'[44]

He chose to contest from his home town Gwalior, from where he had won in 1971, not because he 'was in search of a safe seat . . . but because while discharging the responsibilities of an all India campaign, it was not possible to give more time to New Delhi'.[45] It was a mistake to vacate his New Delhi seat. In Gwalior he stayed at the home of his old friend N.K. Shejwalkar and campaigned hard. But he was outwitted, cleverly lulled by the Congress into believing that the Gwalior prince Madhavrao would not be contesting from Gwalior, when that was exactly what Scindia did, filing his papers at the last moment to take Vajpayee by surprise. Helter-skelter, the BJP tried to rush Vajpayee to Vidisha to file his papers from there, but the deadline had expired. The 'secrecy and cleverness with which the whole strategy to tie me down in Gwalior came to light only later', he recalled. 'Because of the sympathy wave as well as the personal influence of Shri Scindia, my defeat was a foregone conclusion. If a former ruler knocks at the door and solicits votes, it becomes very difficult for people to say no to him . . . It is an incontrovertible fact that he [Madhavrao] was fielded from Gwalior at the last minute only to defeat me.'[46] It was Vajpayee's first poll defeat since 1962.

His defeat was also the result of his lifelong devotion to the Scindia family. In the thick of the campaign, Advani came rushing to Gwalior to urge Vajpayee to shift to another seat – Kota in Rajasthan – as he had heard the Congress was planning to put up Madhavrao from Gwalior. Vajpayee refused. He told Advani that if he, Vajpayee, refused to contest, Vijaya Raje may be compelled to go up against her own son, and in no circumstances would he allow bad blood between mother and son to be spilled on the streets of Gwalior. 'The rift that has developed between mother and son,' he recalled, 'has never been liked, least of all by me. Political differences were one thing . . . bitterness in the inborn, natural and tender relationship between mother and son is absolutely another . . . I always had a natural affection and respect for Shri Scindia.'[47]

Vajpayee was glamour-struck by India's leading families, from the aristocratic Nehru–Gandhis to the princely Scindias. Journeying from shabby Shinde ki Chhawani, via the RSS to Parliament to Raisina Hill, he, hailing from a party of local 'notables' like the Jana Sangh, was impressed by India's old elites, both for their deep roots in India and for the social eminence they represented. Decades later, as prime minister, he would inaugurate Shining India, but new money and sharp business deals never dazzled him. Instead, it was the cultural wealth and grand lineage of the traditional old clans and their attractive young scions that would continue to capture his romantic imagination. Nehru, Indira, Rajiv, Vijaya Raje Scindia, Madhavrao Scindia, all find glowing and repeated mention in his memoirs. His RSS and BJP compatriots feature only rarely. In 'I Recollect', he mentions with a note of pride that it was he who had once enrolled Madhavrao Scindia into the Jana Sangh and records that after the 1984 results it was a matter of pride for him that the prestige of the Scindias was maintained even if he had lost.

During the campaign, that whispered voice of his sixth sense which he always seemed to hear through his long electoral expedition led him to immediately sense the mood. Indira Gandhi's ghost haunted the polls, a hovering phantom which had no living opponent. 'Appa, I am losing,' Vajpayee told Ghatate at the end of the campaign. 'I can smell it in the air. Did you notice how at the Khatipur polling station nobody even wished me? I'm going back to Delhi. Please ask Advaniji to stay and wait for the results.' Ghatate stayed on in the Gwalior counting hall until 1.30 a.m., when the last round of votes was counted. As soon as he knew of the results, he took the first train to Delhi to inform Vajpayee. Vajpayee was reclining in bed, reading a newspaper. 'Out with it, Appa, *kya main 60,000 votes se haara?*' inquired Vajpayee. '*Nahin Atalji, aap ek lakh chalis hazaar voton se haare,*' replied Ghatate. '*Hat teri ki* [to hell with it]!' expostulated Vajpayee, throwing aside his newspaper and sitting up in bed, looking furious.[48]

Vajpayee the golden boy of elections, as the BJP's party president, had been able to bring his party only *two* seats. And he lost his own. So shattered was he that his home town chose its erstwhile prince instead of their own 'Atalla' from Shinde ki Chhawani that he never fought an election from Gwalior again. The assassination of Indira dealt the BJP a punishing rout. Just four years after its birth, Vajpayee's party now lay dying. Winner of ninety-three seats in 1977, it was now down to two, even lower than the Jana Sangh's first Lok Sabha launch in 1952 at three seats. It was necessarily the end of Vajpayee's leadership of the BJP. At the tail end of gloomy 1984, he journeyed to Mumbai. At a jam-packed rally in Shivaji Park to celebrate that he had recently turned sixty, Vajpayee surveyed the teeming crowds, paused for a second and said, '*Haara hua Vajpayee kaisa dikhta hai yeh dekhne ke liye itni bheed?* [Such a huge crowd has come to see what a defeated Vajpayee looks like?]'[49] Immediately a hush descended on the crowd. Subsequently, Vajpayee departed for the hills. He spent a few days wandering through Garhwal, and visited Gangotri. He also spent time at one of his favourite spots, the Jaipuria ashram, in Hardwar.

'I take full moral responsibility for the failure of the BJP in the Lok Sabha elections, and I shall gladly be willing to undergo any punishment the party decides,' he declared at a BJP national executive meeting in Calcutta in March 1985. The party obligingly rejected his resignation offer but set up a committee to study the results. The report of this committee noted that, in spite of the gigantic loss in seats, in terms of vote share, from 1980 to 1984, the Jana Sangh–BJP vote had come down by only 1 percentage point, from 8.6, when the previous election had been fought as part of the Janata alliance, to 7.6 now. Yet a change of guard was now inevitable. The party now concluded that Gandhian socialism, already an unpopular concept, had been a terrible mistake. It had 'blurred the ideological distinctiveness of the BJP', noted Advani.[50]

Chastened and badly defeated as Vajpayee was, he still remained irrepressibly droll. On being informed that a party worker in Karnataka had died of heart failure after learning of Vajpayee's defeat, he immediately rushed to condole with the family, afterwards remarking, 'Now, how come this poor man got a heart attack when I'm the one who lost the election?'[51] In the same election, the former Congress stalwart and Uttar Pradesh chief minister H.N. Bahuguna lost badly to then superstar Amitabh Bachchan in Allahabad, Bachchan defeating Bahuguna by close to 2 lakh votes. On spotting the veteran politician, Vajpayee quipped, 'Why so worried, Bahugunaji, you lost to an actor, the voters must have just come to see him, since they wouldn't come to see you.'

A fortnight after the election results, the BJP filed into the Parliament Annexe building in Delhi for a three-day conclave for a brainstorming on the rout. Unusually for disciplined cadres, the infuriated younger members loudly challenged the leadership for its alliance-seeking and moderate style and demanded that the BJP build its own identity. Thirty-five-year-old Pramod Mahajan asked why the BJP was trying so hard to reach out to other Opposition parties when it was time to carve out a separate, independent place for itself. The politics of consensus and coalitions was trenchantly attacked, and coalition-friendly man Vajpayee found himself at the centre of the storm. 'There is no doubt we have to offer something fresh to the people, beginning with faces,' Vajpayee told the press.[52]

A bigger traumatic question loomed: had the party lost the Hindus? Vajpayee pointed to the positives – that minorities had voted for the party – and said, 'The Hindu vote will come back to us on its own.' He tried to strike an optimistic note: there was no need for despair, the party had, after all, come second in 101 constituencies. But the defeat was too numbing and the mood was too dark. 'Have we seen the worst now, or will there be further humiliation for us in the assembly elections?' wondered BJP Rajya Sabha MP Jaswant Singh.[53]

In assembly elections in 1985 in Maharashtra, Gujarat and Uttar Pradesh, however, the Congress did not do as well as was expected and the slide in its vote share gave Vajpayee hope. 'The Lok Sabha elections were an aberration, a drunken folly, a bad dream caused by the pressure of calamity, a chapter that had better be forgotten,' he said.[54] He had kept up his mocking of the Congress through the campaign for the assembly elections, his wit and repartee making his audience warm to him. At an election rally, when the BJP candidate declared, '*Main Atalji ko haar bhent kar raha hoon* [I am presenting a haar (a garland) to Atalji],' Vajpayee responded in a flash with a pun: '*Main haar lene ke liye nahin aya, main jeetane ke liye aya hoon* [I'm not here to take a haar (a defeat) but to make you win].'[55] When he arrived late for a rally, he apologized, saying, 'I am late because the roads built by the Congress government are such that I didn't know if there were potholes on the road or if the road was to be found in potholes.'[56] But in these elections, the BJP was again badly defeated, in spite of Vajpayee's brave good humour.

Too many poll defeats were piling up and the RSS sent a clear message: if the BJP did not stand forth as the protector of Hindus, it had no future. Gandhian socialism must be junked in favour of cultural nationalism. The Vajpayee formula – Gandhian socialism, moderate parliamentary politics and a distancing from ideology – disappeared. The BJP would now seize upon a completely different campaign. It would be a return to its RSS roots – the RSS's goal of founding the Hindu Rashtra, the cause of its ancestors Savarkar and Golwalkar. It would be ideology, ideology, ideology.

In May 1986, L.K. Advani was elected as BJP party president. The party still needed Vajpayee's commanding parliamentary talents, and on 30 June 1986 he entered the Rajya Sabha from Madhya Pradesh. But now he was kicked upstairs, the chairman emeritus to Advani as the hands-on CEO.

Vajpayee, now the former MP and a former BJP president, went to Pune in 1986 to attend a function in honour of V.D. Savarkar. In a bow to his party's new ideological line, he raved about Savarkar in passionately elaborate prose. At the end of the speech he said, 'I'm quite free now to propagate the works of Savarkar. In fact, I'm looking for work. *Gwalior walon ne meri chhutti kar di hai*, the people of Gwalior have given me a holiday, the people of my party have relieved me of my responsibilities. I can go wherever you want me to.'[57]

He was back to being the man of Opposition, delivering speeches with gusto on the continuing violence in Punjab to the 1984 Bhopal gas tragedy, skewering the Rajiv government for bending 'on its knees before Union Carbide' and failing to obtain a proper settlement.

Party president Advani now set about leading the BJP's fightback from ruination. He appointed three RSS veterans as general secretaries. He also brought in the forty-three-year-old Govindacharya, the RSS ideologue-activist, whom Advani had first noticed during the JP movement in Bihar, as his political secretary. He put in place a team of sharp, young people to shape the party for the reorientation away from Gandhian socialism. Pramod Mahajan was brought in as general secretary; two highly articulate lawyers, both in their thirties – Sushma Swaraj and Arun Jaitley – became part of Advani's team. Andhra Pradesh RSS and ABVP activist M. Venkaiah Naidu, RSS man and BJP's UP chief Rajnath Singh and organizer par excellence and RSS pracharak Narendra Modi, also joined Team Advani. Rajiv Gandhi had begun his tenure with many of his high-ranking aides drawn from his alma mater, the elite Doon School, who were mockingly known as the 'baba log'. By 1986, across the aisle, energetic Opposition warriors – none of them from the Doon School – took up position too.

The BJP under Advani would not only be keenly alive to an ideological mission and ideological 'distinctiveness', but also be on the lookout to ally with grassroots movements that had wide public support. The Vajpayee-led BJP had strayed from the Hindutva path and had alienated the saffron cadres. The Advani-led BJP moved instead to reflect and echo the Hindu nationalist yearnings of the foot-soldier army and to refocus itself on an electorally more compelling plank than the vague, tepid Gandhian socialism. Sounds that had earlier been faint grew louder: the sounds of conch shells and the ringing of temple bells.

~

As we have noted, after the Meenakshipuram conversions, the VHP stepped up its Hindutva mobilization activities. In November 1983, the VHP began the 'Ekatmata Yatras', or rites of unity, in which processions of Hindu activists across India carried holy Ganga water and idols of Bharat Mata – cleverly uniting religion with nationalism – to various temples, all caravans congregating at the RSS headquarters in Nagpur. 'We make no distinction between Atal Bihari Vajpayee and Indira Gandhi,' said a VHP activist. 'Both are bad, both are politicians.'[58]

But the Ekatmata Yatras didn't quite click and the VHP began to look for a more potent emotive issue. In April 1984 in Delhi, three years after Meenakshipuram, the VHP organized its first 'Dharam Sansad', or religious parliament, a gathering of Hindu akharas and maths. The Dharam Sansad also took an important pledge: from now on the VHP would work for the 'liberation' of the Ram Janmabhoomi in Ayodhya. A month later, the VHP created its militant arm, the Bajrang Dal. This new 'people's movement' was to be directed against the Babri Masjid.

The Babri Masjid, a small mosque in Ayodhya built in the sixteenth century, had been the centre of disputes between Hindus and Muslims since the nineteenth century. Hindus claimed the masjid stood on the location of Lord Ram's birth and over the years sporadic clashes had been breaking out between Hindu pilgrims and Muslim clerics at the mosque. On the night of 23 December 1949, when idols of 'Ram Lalla' (the infant Ram) and Sita appeared inside the mosque, Prime

Minister Nehru ordered swift action. The property was attached by the government, and the shrine was locked. Hindu pilgrims and Muslims had continued to offer prayers at the site until 1949 and local legends of a Ram temple and a Sita-ki-rasoi (Sita's kitchen) – structures believed to have been demolished to build the mosque – circulated. Claims and counterclaims on the ownership of the land were placed before the court in Faizabad, and in 1989 the Allahabad High Court ordered a status quo, the same year that the VHP attempted a 'shilanyas' or a foundation-stone-laying ceremony at the site. Ayodhya, birthplace of Lord Ram, soon became the birthplace of the biggest religious divide between Hindus and Muslims since Partition, a battlefield of Hindu sadhus, Muslim clerics, rabble-rousing demagogues and unwise, reckless politicians.

Tasked by RSS chief Deoras to build the Hindu vote, the VHP lighted upon the disputes around the Babri Masjid as the ideal rallying mission, full of tantalizing possibilities of 'Hindu victimhood' and mass action. In September 1984, the VHP organized a Jan Jagran Yatra from Sitamarhi in Bihar (where Sita is supposed to have 'appeared') to Ayodhya to agitate for the opening of the locks of the Babri Masjid. It was an initial testing of the waters and it yielded a resounding response. With murders of Hindus in Punjab now making front-page news every day and the prime minister herself playing to Hindu fears of the threat of Sikh militancy, 'Hindu emotions' were easily roused. Enthusiastic, chanting crowds lined the route of the yatra. The astute and calculating Advani, looking to grow the BJP and lure the Hindu cadres back into its own arms and away from a dangerous drift towards the Congress, became convinced that here lay the answer to the BJP's woes and the potential for a people's movement from below.

By the time the Rajiv Gandhi government was sworn in, the agitations to 'liberate' the Ram Janmabhoomi had acquired momentum, and Rajiv soon handed the BJP two issues that Advani used to further galvanize his cadres. In February 1986 Rajiv Gandhi caved in to Muslim orthodox opinion and overturned a landmark Supreme Court order. The Supreme Court order had awarded alimony to a Muslim divorcee, Shah Bano, and dismissed her husband's appeals to Sharia law. On 27 February, the government introduced the Muslim Women (Protection of Rights on Divorce) Act, 1986, ruling against awarding of alimony to Shah Bano and instead upholding tenets of Sharia law. By doing so, the Supreme Court judgement was fundamentally diluted. Rajiv's actions came on the back of widespread Muslim agitations demanding protection for Sharia law, a sectarian response to the growing Hindu mobilization at this time.

To balance this move towards the Muslim right, a naive and ill-advised Rajiv attempted to assuage majority anger over the Shah Bano case and swung to pander to the Hindu right. At the height of the Shah Bano controversy, on 1 February 1986, the Rajiv Gandhi government now allowed the locks of the Babri Masjid – so wisely placed there by Nehru – to be opened. The VHP had been demanding this, and now Hindu prayers started inside the Babri Masjid, the ceremonies telecast live on state-owned Doordarshan, with millions across India watching transfixed. Across the religious divide, Muslim leaders took up position. Syed Shahabuddin, Janata MP and head of the All India Majlis-e-Mushawarat, said, 'The unliteral seizure of the Babri mosque has shocked the Muslims beyond measure and eroded their faith in secularism.'[59]

Rajiv's moves had a twofold effect. The overturning of the Shah Bano judgement allowed Vajpayee and Advani to immediately claim that the government was trying to appease fundamentalist Muslims by upholding Muslim personal laws. The allowing of prayers in the Babri Masjid gave the opportunity to the VHP to step up its campaign for a full return of the Babri Masjid–Ram Janmabhoomi area to the Hindus.

The BJP, recognizing both planks as effective mobilizing platforms, sprang forward, all guns blazing, Advani in the saddle as BJP president, Vajpayee still at the fore in creating public opinion. 'The Congress's secularism . . . has left the impression in the minds of the Hindus that they are not being treated well,' wrote Vajpayee. 'The Shah

Bano case wounded the psyche of the Hindus. The challenge to the integrity and solidarity of the country in Kashmir and Punjab has also agitated the Hindu mind.'[60] With the party getting ready to win elections Vajpayee was not one to be left behind in climbing the most convenient bandwagon, however sidelined he may have been. As far as his own views on the Ram Mandir movement are concerned, he may have been put off by the violent agitation, but he kept maintaining the self-justificatory line that as long as politics is played from the masjid it will inevitably be played from the mandir. He wrote about the 'acute feelings of the majority community' over the Ram temple and the agitation in the 'Hindu mind'[61] and how Congress governments and other secular governments had failed to understand this. Forcible conversion, which he believed was a threat to poor Hindus, was one of his own personal bugbears, and during his 1981 Meenakshipuram visit he had supported 'reconversion' programmes.

Today, the term 'pseudo secularism' is widely used to target India's secularists. It is interesting to note that the term was used first by Vajpayee in 1969 and not, as is commonly assumed, by Advani.[62] In fact, Vajpayee's early views on secularism are worth noting here:

> According to Hindu polity, the State came into being for the fulfilment of earthly functions . . . Unlike in the west, in Bharat there was no conflict between the State and the religious order. Secular does not mean anti-religious or non-religious. In fact the people of India can never be secular in this sense. Secularism just means an impartial attitude of the State towards all modes of worship . . . .
>
> At present some elements which are trying to draw us away from our glorious past, our noble ideals of life and from our great men and seers in the name of secularism are gaining strength. But we must remember that if we break with our past we would neither be able to face the challenge of the present nor have strength to build the future.[63]

He also expressed his suspicions that Muslim organizations like the Jamaat-i-Islami were trying to sow separatism and declaring that Muslims can only be happy in a state run according to the Sharia.

Vajpayee was a moderate and a parliamentary democrat, and abided by reason and rationality, yet all his life he remained committed to his own particular theoretical version of Hindu nationalism.

Around this time – in the late 1980s – he was invited to visit a mango orchard owned by a Muslim landowner. The host invited twenty other Muslim orchard-owners to dine with Vajpayee. One of the guests asked him, 'Vajpayeeji, isn't it true that Hindus convert to Islam to marry and maintain several wives? Then why do they want to change our laws?' Vajpayee thought for a while and said elliptically, 'The best way is that you should decide against conversion of Hindus to Islam,' and went back to eating his mango.[64]

By May 1986, swathes of India were gripped by high-pitched Hindu militancy and muscle-flexing organized by the RSS, VHP, Bajrang Dal and a myriad other Hindu groups. The theme of all these demonstrations was more or less the same: Hindus were victims in their own land as the government was bending over backwards to please Muslims. The VHP stepped up its rath yatras, processions, street protests and all-night jagrans and kirtans. Luridly decorated raths lurched across the countryside, both rickety and menacing. Hoardings appeared across North India showing a muscular Ram drawing his bow and arrow, and of the Ram Mandir with a huge 'Om' at the centre. Giant depictions of Ram in a cage were held aloft in processions. 'It is as if God himself is going to the people and beseeching them to unshackle him,' intoned the VHP's Ashok Singhal.

India was awash in systematically whipped up 'Hindu rage', and lakhs participated in the VHP's melas and yatras. In Gujarat, RSS workers began house-to-house awareness drives. 'We cannot cope with the work people want us to do now,' said then Gujarat RSS leader Narendra Modi. 'There is so much of public involvement and demands made on us.'[65] In Uttar Pradesh, the Babri Masjid Action Committee vowed to wrest the masjid by force while the Bajrang Dal announced Jan Jagran yatras in the state.

Hindus and Muslims fought pitched street battles in several parts of North India. Between March and June 1987, vicious riots broke out in Meerut and the village of Maliana in Uttar Pradesh. In a horrific incident, in the Hashimpura locality in Meerut, police lined up and shot Muslim youths in cold blood. (In 2018, 16 Provincial Armed Constabulary [PAC] personnel were convicted for the Hashimpura massacre.) In January 1987, Doordarshan had begun broadcasting the phenomenally popular TV series *Ramayan*, created and directed by the film director Ramanand Sagar. The serial was such a sensation that across India people abandoned work or study to watch it, streets emptied out and markets fell silent. *Ramayan* on TV added exponentially to the growing Hindu consciousness, one that was being yoked for a political aim. TV serial and politics waltzed together to create the nationwide 'Hindu' mood.

In a speech in Mumbai on 15 February 1987, Vajpayee suggested that Muslims should give up their claim to the Babri Masjid and hand it over to the Hindus as a gesture of goodwill and respect for their sentiments, and that Hindus in turn should reciprocate by allowing the Babri Masjid structure to stand as it is while constructing a temple adjoining it befitting Ram Janmabhoomi. 'Sadly no one listened to my suggestion at this time,' Vajpayee wrote in a letter to Hiren Mukherjee, 'as both sides became rigid in their positions and the government did not find a solution, probably because it wanted to use the Mandir–Masjid dispute for electoral purposes.'[66] He ended his letter by saying that Hindus despite being the majority are beginning to feel as if they are victims of injustice and these fears must be allayed.

Rajiv Gandhi's failure to resolve the Ram Janmabhoomi–Babri Masjid dispute played into the VHP's hands. In the gathering Hindu storm, the Advani-led BJP found its moment. The VHP-led Ram Janmabhoomi movement was, for the BJP, the ladder to climb out of the deep ditch of two seats. Vajpayee may have bravely declared in 1980 that the BJP would not resurrect the Jana Sangh, but now in 1986 the BJP returned not just to the Jana Sangh (with its anti-cow-slaughter programmes) but to the radical Hindu plank of the fringe parties from which the Jana Sangh had once kept its distance.

Vajpayee sat on the edges of this Hindutva steam bath. He was still vital to confer the BJP respectability and build bridges with other parties if needed, and whenever required, he stepped forward, ever the frontman, to sway crowds with his winning tongue. He swung back into his '*rag rag mein Hindu*' avatar, which was always part of his menu, sometimes as an hors d'oeuvre, sometimes as the main course and sometimes as a small dessert. Just six years earlier he had promised moderation and inclusivity; now he borrowed from the VHP's lexicon. He argued in Parliament:

> Can such parties [Muslim League, Majlis-e-Ittehadul Muslimeen, Majlis-e-Mushawarat] not be prevented from fighting elections as they don't have their doors open for every Indian? Encouraging one type of communalism is not the way to fight another type of communalism. The tendencies now rising in the Hindu community make me worry. If the Hindus leave their generosity and become narrow-minded, the future of this country is plunged into darkness . . .[67]

On 6 March 1987, speaking at a kisan rally in Lucknow, Vajpayee again echoed the VHP line and declared that no comparison could be made between Ram and Babur: Ram was 'rashtra mahapurush' and the other was an invader who came to assault and torture. 'Babur destroyed temples as a political move. He wanted to insult, he wanted to crush Hindus.' Vajpayee went on to say that if there were any masjids across India that had been built by destroying temples, they should all be returned to the Hindus.[68]

Ah, the paradoxes of our slippery hero! One day a moderate, the next day sounding like a hardliner, one day arguing for pluralism, the next day harking to Hindu sentiments. Anything to beat the Congress, to tear away at its smothering dominance, to haul his party up a notch or two on the steep climb towards the summit of power.

~

Within two short years of the humongous mandate of 1984, the Rajiv Gandhi government began to flounder. Terrorism and violence in Punjab continued to spike. In 1985, the much-hailed peace accord between Rajiv Gandhi and Akali Dal leader Harchand Singh Longowal came unstuck with the assassination of Longowal less than a month after the accord was signed. In April 1987, the Bofors scandal hit. National Swedish Radio reported that in 1986 when a contract had been signed to purchase 400 155-mm Howitzer guns from the Swedish arms manufacturer Bofors AB, crores had been paid to ruling party politicians as bribes or kickbacks. A thunderstorm broke around Rajiv, at the centre of which was Rajiv's defence minister, the thin-moustache-sporting fifty-six-year-old corruption buster V.P. Singh. As defence minister he had ordered a probe into the Indira Gandhi government's decision to buy submarines from the German HDW shipyard in 1982. Having ordered the probe, Singh faced an uproar in his own party and was publicly accused of trying to embarrass Rajiv. V.P. Singh resigned from the government on 11 April 1987, in the same month as the Bofors firestorm exploded, and was subsequently expelled from the Congress. Soon afterwards, V.P. Singh started his own political movement, the Jan Morcha, and won the 1988 Allahabad by-poll in a prestige battle with the Congress. He formed his own party, the Janata Dal, in October 1988, which joined the coalition of seven Opposition parties in the National Front that had been formed in August. The BJP was excluded from the National Front, as V.P. Singh, proud of his secular image, was deeply wary of the 'communal' party.

The Bofors scandal saw Vajpayee at his mocking, sarcastic best in Parliament. Blasting a parliamentary committee on the Bofors deal, he snapped: 'I am sorry that the committee spent more time than necessary proving that Bofors guns are good. Even if the guns are good, does it mean the scandal associated with them is also good? . . . The gun fires in Sweden and the boom is heard in India. It fires on the border of Rajasthan and shakes up Delhi . . . these guns will remain hot.'[69]

Bofors was hot, but V.P. Singh was cool towards the BJP. In the Opposition unity moves against Rajiv that V.P. Singh initiated, he kept the BJP firmly out. For its part, the Advani-led BJP remained aloof too. With general elections just a year away, 1988 was a year of hectic politicking. The BJP launched a 'satyagraha' across India demanding the resignation of Rajiv Gandhi. Vajpayee was on the streets of Delhi, leading BJP workers on a march. Advani led a similar march in Lucknow.

The BJP may have been left out of V.P. Singh's 'secular' front, but its championing of the VHP and the Ram Janmabhoomi movement brought it a new crucial ally – the other bellicose Hindutva party, the Shiv Sena. Advani was re-elected BJP president in March 1988, and under his leadership the party reached out to the Sena. The Sena responded, and in October 1988, at a rally in Mumbai's Shivaji Park, Sena chief Bal Thackeray openly invited the BJP for an alliance. With a 'secular' club coalescing on the one side, a 'Hindu' alliance took shape on the other. The Janata Party's Mrinal Gore wondered out aloud: 'How will a fine man like Vajpayee feel sitting next to Bal Thackeray?'

But 'fine man' Vajpayee was unlikely to raise any objections not only because he always fell in with the party line, but because ultimately Hindu nationalism was still an essential part of his core identity. The party was supreme, and if it had decided to embrace Hindutva, he would not lag behind. Tenacity and patience are the strengths of the long-distance runner. He may have become the discredited leader, but he would not stop running the long race he had joined while still a schoolboy, in a movement with which his ties were emotional and laden with boyhood memories.

The BJP continued in its new 'ideological' direction. 'The Hindu vote is going to be politically important in the coming decade,' wrote the *Organiser* approvingly. 'The BJP should have no shyness complex to organise its idea of Hindu renaissance.'[70] As greater links began to develop between the Ayodhya agitation and the BJP, the party's upper-caste profile began to change, with an influx of backward castes and communities from the Ram Janmabhoomi movement. Vajpayee's Brahmin–Bania-dominated party started to give way to broader groups as boisterous kar sevaks and sadhvis, preachers and prelates, took the place of the ascetic RSS pracharaks and Jana Sangh notables. Backward caste leaders like Uma Bharti and Kalyan Singh, the latter having been in the Jana Sangh, now rose to prominence. The Ram movement hurled the BJP to the shikhara (tower top) of power, but changed its character forever.

On 1 February 1989, crowds of pilgrims, sadhus and members of temple organizations gathered on the banks of the Ganga at the Kumbh Mela in Allahabad. The VHP gave the twin calls for 'shila pujan' and 'shila yatra' – bricks with 'Shri Ram' embossed on them would be 'consecrated' in villages and then brought to Ayodhya from thousands of villages and towns across India, and in November there would be a grand shilanyas at Ayodhya. The response was immediate: a steady stream of 'shila' bricks began to arrive in Ayodhya, the process organized by units of the Ramjanmabhoomi activists and Hindutva cadres which had fanned out across the country.

In May 1989, keenly aware of the growing strength of the BJP, V.P. Singh finally reached out to the saffron party for seat-sharing deals. He met Advani and Vajpayee at Advani's residence in July 1989 for a four-hour dinner meeting where he conveyed that he wanted seat-sharing arrangements in all states except Bihar and Uttar Pradesh for fear of alienating the Muslims. Advani disliked the 'hypocrisy' of this caveat, yet the BJP, conscious not to split the anti-Congress vote by being ideologically rigid, wanting to capitalize on the 'anti-Rajiv wave', and thirsty for an election win, was open to allies. Mindful not to alienate any Muslim support, V.P. Singh was clear: there would be no joint rallies with the BJP.

Some of the initial meetings between V.P. Singh and RSS and BJP leaders took place in the Delhi home of Singh's lawyer and advocate, Raian Karanjawala. The BJP and RSS were represented on different occasions by Advani, Vajpayee, Murli Manohar Joshi and then RSS sarkaryavah Rajendra Singh or Rajju Bhaiya, who would later succeed Deoras as sarsanghchalak. Karanjawala recalls that while Vajpayee was in on some of the initial meetings and may have been consulted in the background, there is no doubt 'that the seat negotiations were primarily Advani's show and very often the person who participated in depth in these talks was Govindacharya'.[71]

Vajpayee, the universally liked bridge-builder with friends in every party, was needed to smoothen out the edges between ideological adversaries, but the nuts-and-bolts tough talking was done by Advani and 'Advani man' Govindacharya, in a clear indication of who the new BJP karta-dharta was. In an autobiographical collection of interviews, V.P. Singh says that at this time when Vajpayee was at a low point, some had even suggested to him that he join the Janata Dal.[72] But Vajpayee denied that he ever even considered this.

He was never in any doubt about his RSS identity and he would never give up on the party he had co-founded or the Hindu nationalist identity it represented. In his essay 'The Sangh Is My Soul', he said: 'I wrote "Rag Rag mein Hindu, Hindu Tan-man Hindu Jeevan" when I was studying in the tenth class. I had said *koi batlaye Kabul mein jaakar kitni masjidein todin*. (Can anyone tell me if a Hindu has ever gone to Kabul to destroy masjids?) I still stand by my words. But we [Hindus] did pull down the structure in Ayodhya. It was the first incident in history when we Hindus demolished their worship place themselves. It was a reaction to the Muslim vote bank. I wanted to solve this problem through negotiation and legislation.'[73]

After the seat-adjustment pact with the Janata Dal was completed, Vajpayee hit the streets with enthusiasm at the same time as other

National Front leaders such as V.P. Singh, Devi Lal and NTR, courting arrest, leading demonstrations and addressing meetings. In the course of the campaign, at a press conference attended by both V.P. Singh and Vajpayee, a reporter asked Vajpayee, 'If the BJP emerges as the single largest party after the polls will you become a candidate for prime minister?' Vajpayee replied with a resigned smile, 'In this baraat, V.P. Singh is the bridegroom.'[74]

The voice of his electioneering instinct, that uncannily accurate assessment he was always able to make of people's hidden responses at election time told him that a surprise lay ahead. The atmosphere was uneasy, unpredictable. The face of Rajiv Gandhi, once glowingly handsome, was becoming shadowed with an unkempt stubble.

Vajpayee may no longer have been in his party's driving seat, yet he was still his party's most recognizable public face and committed above all to the party's collective will. He brought his stature and credibility with rivals to staunchly defend his party's ideological turn. In September 1989, Vajpayee had a famous exchange of letters with Hiren Mukherjee, his colleague in Parliament since the 1950s. Mukherjee wrote to him expressing his anguish about the growing communalism in the country and suggested a 'national memorial' at the disputed Ayodhya site. Mukherjee addressed Vajpayee as 'My dear Atal', and Vajpayee addressed Mukherjee as 'Dear Hiren-da', revealing the long friendship between committed parliamentarians that was possible in an India in which ideological opponents were unafraid of dialogue.

In a letter dated 24 September 1989, Vajpayee wrote:

> Hiren-da! . . . I have never been in favour of destroying the Babri Masjid. Like you I want this matter to be settled peacefully . . . but in such sensitive matters which has touched the sentiments, and religious sentiments of a large number of people, a court decision will be difficult to implement . . . if there is to be a national memorial,

> the question arises, what kind of memorial will this be? What will it commemorate if not religious fanaticism – destroying a place of worship of one faith and building one of another faith in its place . . .[75]

In another letter to Mukherjee, Vajpayee wrote, 'I have never said that the masjid should be brought down, nor do I believe this nation can only be seen as a Hindu Rashtra.'

These letters written in September 1989 show that Vajpayee had made his peace with the Ram Janmabhoomi agitation that his party had embraced. Earlier that year, in June 1989, had come a defining moment for Vajpayee and for the BJP.

In Himachal Pradesh, surrounded by the Dhauladhar ranges, sits the hilltop town of Palampur. At its national executive meeting held here from 9 to 11 June 1989, the BJP's alliance with the Shiv Sena was finalized and the BJP passed a resolution which it hoped would help it scale mountains. It was a resolution that committed the party to throwing itself into the Ram Janmabhoomi agitation. Dated 9–11 June 1989, the Palampur Resolution stated:

> The National Executive of the Bharatiya Janata Party regards the current debate on the Ram Janma Bhoomi issue as one which has dramatically highlighted the callous unconcern which the Congress(I) party in particular, and the other political parties in general, betray towards the sentiments of the overwhelming majority in this country – the Hindus . . . the nature of this controversy is such that it just cannot be sorted out by a court of law . . . The sentiments of the people must be respected and the Ram Janmasthan must be handed over to the Hindus if possible through a negotiated settlement or else, by legislation.[76]

This was the pivotal Palampur Resolution with its explicit words: *Ram Janmasthan must be handed over to the Hindus.*[77]

Until now the Ram Janmabhoomi movement had been led by non-political outfits like the VHP and Bajrang Dal. With the BJP now joining the Hindu insurrection and giving it a political voice, the VHP-led movement gained saliency and clout. The Palampur resolution cast the BJP's way forward in stone: the party had now officially adopted the Ram Janmabhoomi movement. The Vajpayee line was officially dead. Vajpayee's close friend and ex-military man, Jaswant Singh who had never been in the RSS, opposed the Palampur resolution and urged Vajpayee to speak up against it, but it was passed without objection. Subdued and mortified by election defeats, Vajpayee offered little resistance to his own marginalization. In September 1989, at the BJP's national executive in Mumbai, the Hindutva alliance of BJP and Shiv Sena was formalized. At Mumbai's Shanmukhananda Hall, Shiv Sena President Bal Thackeray was invited to address the BJP in a packed hall ringing with slogans of Hindu unity.

Vajpayee's Gandhian socialist party became Lord Ram's party as the Ram Janmabhoomi movement gathered pace. 'Ramshila' processions and street demonstrations led to several bloody riots, one of the worst in Bhagalpur in Bihar where a procession had been taken out chanting, '*Hindi, Hindu Hindustan, mullah bhago Pakistan* [Hindustan is Hindu, let the Muslims go to Pakistan].' The Bhagalpur riots were a bloodbath: over a thousand were killed, 900 of them Muslims. In September 1989, thirty died in communal riots in Badaun. The VHP stepped up Ramshila pujans across North India, and in the first week of November 1989 almost 1.5 lakh bricks arrived in Ayodhya. Desperately seeking to use the Hindu tide for his own ends, Rajiv Gandhi began his 1989 election campaign on 3 November from Faizabad, declaring Ayodhya–Faizabad as 'the land of Ram, this holy land'. In another well publicized flourish of Hindutva by a mainstream politician, Rajiv also held a meeting with the Hindu mystic Devraha Baba at this time. On 9 November 1989, the Rajiv Gandhi government allowed the VHP to perform a shilanyas in front of the Babri Masjid. A pit, 7 feet long, 7 feet deep and 7 feet wide, was dug by the VHP, the first step towards mandir construction.

The Palampur Resolution brought the BJP to the front lines of the barricaded, sand-bagged, heavily policed streets of decrepit Ayodhya. The BJP now stood with the armies of Ram, raising fists, flags and trishuls against the Babri Masjid. The Palampur Resolution was the moment when the Advani-led BJP gave up all pretence of secularism and went to stand shoulder to shoulder with the VHP.

Golwalkar's golden boy, the Jana Sangh's unchallenged Parliament celebrity, was forced to take second place to someone who had once been his assistant and who now took centre stage.

6

The Ascendance of Advani: 1989–1996

A poem for Vajpayee:

Raising dust clouds of history, the masjid falls,
Lord Ram's army surges ahead.
As moderate Vajpayee's pale saffron palls,
Advani's sun glows blood red.

As parliament's hero, great orator,
He watches from a distance, thunderstruck.
His rival seizes the crown,
His political stock is down,
With mass frenzy he never did have much truck.

~

6 December 1992. Down Ayodhya's winding, narrow streets, on a grassy hillock, stood the three-domed Babri Masjid. The small mosque was in the eye of a storm, the focal point of hysterical rage on one side and defiant assertion on the other. Railings, barricades, steel fences and ropes ringed the controversy-ridden structure. A thin line of police

stood against an advancing wave. Thousands of self-styled 'kar sevaks', mobilized and galvanized over two years by the VHP, Bajrang Dal and other Hindu organizations had descended on Ayodhya.

By early morning on the 6th, angry crowds gathered some distance away from the Babri Masjid at Karsevakpuram, the camp that had been created for them. Shouts and cries rose: 'It is time for kar seva at the Babri Masjid, it is time to seize the Babri Masjid, it is time to destroy the Babri Masjid.'

Wiry, bright-eyed young men, some with 'Jai Shri Ram' tattooed on their chests, jumped and jostled, waving saffron flags and trishuls, their voices high-pitched. '*Jis Hindu ka khoon na khaule, woh khoon nahin pani hai* [The Hindu whose blood doesn't boil, doesn't have blood in his veins but water].' '*Jai Shri Ram, mandir yahin banayenge* [We will build the Ram temple right here].'

Gathered at a nearby dharamshala, BJP, VHP and Bajrang Dal leaders watched the oddly excited crowds with a growing sense of unease. Today, Sunday, 6 December 1992, was the day they had set for a 'symbolic' kar seva, to establish the presence of the Ram temple at the disputed site. The leaders hoped the 'Ram bhakts' or kar sevaks would gather at the puja and that their planned public meetings would divert the crowds away from the masjid.

But the kar sevaks had other plans. As early as 6 a.m. they began to arrive in front of the 2.77-acre disputed area where the masjid stood. 'If the leaders do not allow kar seva, they will face our maar seva,' shouted one of the kar sevaks. Police stood at the ready, guarding the security cordon around the mosque. PAC jawans patrolled the barrier. RSS volunteers wearing armbands stood in single file alongside the police.

At 10 a.m. L.K. Advani, Murli Manohar Joshi and the VHP and Bajrang Dal leaders arrived at the site and went to the Ram Katha Kunj, 150–200 metres from the disputed site, where a raised dais had been placed. They began their speeches. But who cared about the leaders and their orations? This was the hour of the kar sevak, the moment of historical vendetta, the time to unleash pent-up and well-mobilized fury. The kar sevaks had their eyes fixed on the masjid, as the leaders speechified in vain. The leaders were irrelevant. The crowd took charge.

Some youths began to push against the barricades and security cordons. In big groups, they shoved aside the police and RSS volunteers and lunged at the metal fences, some attempting to clamber over them. The police fell back.

At around 11 a.m., one youth emerged running from the crowd. He pushed aside the constable trying to stop him and jumped clear over the barricade. There was a split-second pause, then others followed him, racing towards the security line and vaulting over the barrier at several places. A scream rang out: '*Mandir yahin banayenge.*' The RSS men scurried after them, trying to stop the flow of running, leaping kar sevaks, but the kar sevaks powered on, deftly dodging the cops. As the PAC looked on helplessly and units of the CRPF quietly departed the scene, groups of kar sevaks broke free of security.

Behind the masjid another group of kar sevaks pulled themselves over the barricades. When police and some RSS volunteers tried to stop them, the gathered crowd began to hurl stones, providing a cover for those pushing forward towards the masjid.

As stones and brickbats pelted down, the police melted away and hundreds of kar sevaks breached the barricades and streamed towards the Babri Masjid. A slightly built youth leapt up the steel railings encircling the structure like a 'circus acrobat'. Others gathered at the base of the masjid and, using ropes and grappling hooks, clambered to the top of the middle dome 'as if they were trained mountaineers'. On the ground someone planted a saffron flag. The crowd action didn't seem like a sudden insurrection; instead it appeared well planned and executed by an able-bodied infantry.

RSS general secretary H.V. Seshadri's voice came over the loudspeaker, appealing to the kar sevaks in several different languages not to damage the masjid. But by now the crowd was shrieking and chanting so loudly that he could barely be heard. Well equipped with pickaxes, chisels, huge blacksmith's hammers and shovels, the kar sevaks, holding up saffron flags, climbed to the top of the masjid. They swarmed all over the three domes as riotously as a colony of bees shaken from their hive. Advani, looking flustered, asked Uma Bharti to try to pull the kar sevaks away from the masjid. Trying to draw them off the masjid and towards the kar seva site, Uma Bharti cried, '*Ram bhakton se meri appeal hai ki kar seva ka samay ho gaya hai . . . wapas aa jayen* [I appeal to the Ram devotees that it is time for the kar seva, they must come back].'

The same Uma Bharti would be pictured hours later beaming before cameras after the domes were demolished when she said: 'Today is the most blissful day of my life.'

The mob was working to its own rhythm, deaf to the leaders' pleas. An almighty battering and bashing began. The kar sevaks worked with maniacal energy in coordinated teams, as if well trained for the task. Some hammered, some chiselled, others slithered down ropes for tool supplies. Clouds of dust mixed with columns of dark smoke which began to billow from mosques and homes in Ayodhya town that had been torched by the crazed kar sevaks. At Ram Katha Kunj, Sadhvi Rithambara, dressed in flowing saffron, began to sing and dance, like a high priestess of doom, her eyes half closed, a smile playing around her lips: '*Ek dhakka aur do, Babri Masjid tod do* [Give one more shove, bring the masjid down].' Gangs of kar sevaks waving saffron flags stood on the domes of the Babri Masjid, like a ragged pirate army aboard a conquered vessel. The scene flashed into the camera lenses of gathered journalists, some of whom were beaten and had their cameras smashed.

As the masjid began to crumble, kar sevaks held up bricks – 'Babur's bricks, Babur's bones,' they yelled – as if they were trophies. All of a sudden, at 1.55 p.m. the first dome collapsed. Some kar sevaks fell and were buried under the rubble; they were extricated and rushed to hospital. Others attacked the base of the other domes with long wooden poles. A four-centuries-old structure, weather-beaten by time, could not withstand this ferocious demolition squad working as if possessed by supernatural spirits. Within hours the other two domes of the masjid broke apart and fell to the ground. By five that evening, in a cloud of blood-red dust, the Babri Masjid came crashing down.[1]

'The Republic Besmirched', thundered the *Times of India* in a front-page editorial the next day: 'The pernicious features of Hindutva espoused by the Sangh Parivar have been exposed . . . the hate, bigotry and prejudice'.

It had taken a little over five hours to flatten the Babri Masjid and to arrive at that fraught moment of its demolition had taken five years of a systematic campaign of religious hatred. A decade later, the VHP's president Ashok Singhal said in an interview: 'Ever since the movement began, it was certain from the first day that the masjid was bound to fall.'[2]

~

In Delhi, Vajpayee was, initially, aghast. He was the only top leader of the BJP not present in Ayodhya at the time of the demolition, part by calculated design, part by political instinct, part by a personal recoil from the spectre of violence, and part because of wanting to remain loftily aloof from sharing the stage with a gaggle of VHP and Bajrang Dal leaders. On 5 December evening he had said in Lucknow: 'I wanted to go to Ayodhya, but I was told to go to Delhi and I'll respect that order.'[3] A day after the demolition he expostulated outragedly in Delhi: 'This is the worst miscalculation my party has made.'[4]

Ghatate met Vajpayee shortly after the demolition, to find him visibly annoyed. 'How misguided people can be,' Vajpayee said when told that BJP leaders were distributing sweets in Delhi's Bengali Market after the demolition, 'our state government is now gone [after the masjid was brought down, Prime Minister P.V. Narasimha Rao dismissed the Uttar Pradesh government on the same day] and they're celebrating?' Pramod Mahajan telephoned Ghatate to say, 'Please try and control Vajpayee.' When Ghatate asked Mahajan how the demolition had happened, Mahajan told him, 'There was not one general at Ayodhya, but so many generals.' When Ghatate mentioned this to Vajpayee, he snapped, 'That is why the Marathas lost the battle of Panipat in 1757.'[5] Ghatate believed that even if some people had worked to a pre-agreed plan to tear down the masjid, Vajpayee was completely unaware of it.[6]

Subsequently, Vajpayee appeared on NDTV in an interview with Prannoy Roy. 'What happened in Ayodhya should not have happened,' he told Roy. 'We tried to prevent it. But we did not succeed. We are sorry for that. A section of kar sevaks went out of control and they did something which was not to be done. A clear assurance was given that no damage will be allowed to be caused to the disputed structure. And that assurance was not kept up. That's why we are sorry.'[7]

Yet Vajpayee did not speak for his party, many of whom were seen gleefully rejoicing after the demolition. In the late 1980s and through the early 1990s, he was the former superstar of the BJP, the also-ran. In these years, it was L.K. Advani, not Vajpayee, who was the BJP's supremo. Vajpayee had relinquished the party presidency in 1986 to Advani, and would never again become BJP president. Advani would go on to be party chief three more times, in 1988, 1993 and 2004–05. In 1986, Vajpayee, badly wounded in the 1984 polls, entered Parliament through the Rajya Sabha and took up his usual position as the eloquent pugilist, hollering away at the Rajiv Gandhi government. But it was Advani who steered the BJP forward as the Hindu 'hriday samrat' (king of the Hindus hearts).

After the abyss of the 1984 results, armed with the Palampur Resolution, the Advani-led BJP embarked on a complete reinvention for the 1989 elections. Fully backed by the RSS, Advani pushed the BJP deeper into the Ram Janmabhoomi agitation and towards a reinvigorated Hindu hard-line, built strong links with grassroots Hindutva groups and encouraged a full mesh with the RSS. Hindutva cadres across North India worked hard for BJP candidates. Unlike in 1984, when a disapproving RSS had stayed away from the Gandhian socialism–inclined BJP, now the RSS sent out wave upon wave of swayamsevaks to build the 'Hindu vote'. Advani's five-year plan was one of embracing the Hindutva plank, calling openly for the Ram Mandir in one voice with the VHP, steering clear of the messy goings-on in the Opposition ranks of alliances and coalitions and instead working painstakingly to cultivate the party's own constituencies among tribal, rural and lower-caste communities. Secularism was buried. The power of violence – both physical and in language – was accepted as a norm, and the battle for survival was won.

Team Advani played its part. The indefatigable Govindacharya, as special assistant to Advani, worked to re-energize local party units across North India. The suave Arun Jaitley played a leading role in raising finances and overseeing the publicity campaign. Bhaurao Deoras (brother of Balasaheb) kept up a constant dialogue between the RSS and the BJP and the politically shrewd Balasaheb Deoras strategized with Advani regularly. An energetic RSS activist, Narendra Modi, took over as BJP organizing secretary in Gujarat.

Advani's hard-line strategy paid off. The results of the general elections of November 1989 were electrifying for the BJP. From two seats in 1984, the party surged to an impressive eighty-six seats and became the third largest party in the Lok Sabha. The humiliation of 1984 vanished. Vajpayee watched from the sidelines as Advani took the BJP to unprecedented success. He writes about the 1989 elections:

> If in 1984, the Indira wave had given the Congress a massive majority in the House, the anti-corruption wave, of which Bofors was a symbol, forced the Congress to lick the dust . . . In 1989 the government of Rajiv Gandhi, which just five years ago the people had, by conceding over 400 seats out of a total of 517 seats, given a massive mandate to rule, was in a way swept off its feet by the same electorate . . . [this is] the decisive power of the ballot.[8]

In analysing the 1989 results, Vajpayee doesn't mention the role played by hard-line Hindutva in upping the BJP's seats. Instead, he announced with smooth sophistry after the elections: 'This time we were determined not to let the Congress play the Hindu card.'[9] So it was not the BJP which had turned communal, it had only acted preventively to stop Congress communalism, was Vajpayee's fanciful conceit. The Congress shrank dramatically. With 197 seats, it was unable to cross the majority mark and was wiped out in the Hindi belt. The 1989 election was thus a significant milestone for India's democratic journey: it marked the end of Congress dominance and laid the foundations for two and a half decades of coalition politics.

Paradoxically, as Vajpayee's own stardom within his party began to fade, it would be the universally acceptable friend-to-all-enemy-to-none Vajpayee who would become indispensable to the BJP as it pursued power-sharing arrangements in the era of coalitions that lay ahead. As the opprobrium of the masjid demolition dogged the BJP, it was Vajpayee the misfit, Vajpayee the marginalized soft-liner, who became his party's go-to man.

In 1989, Rajiv Gandhi's bête noir, V.P. Singh, and the National Front, came to power in Delhi. With outside support from the Left Front and the BJP, Singh took oath as prime minister on 2 December 1989. As a vital column holding up the new V.P. Singh government, the BJP was now a tall saffron-coloured pillar on Raisina Hill.

Smarting from the 1984 rout, Vajpayee had not contested the 1989 elections, but led the campaign in many places, letting fly his captivating speeches, subtly echoing the new Hindu line from Mumbai to Lucknow. In 1989, Advani won his first Lok Sabha seat from New Delhi. The party went all out for its president. Advani's campaign was accompanied by troupes of bhangra dancers, caparisoned horses and drummers parading through the streets. After his win Advani took out a victory procession, travelling through Delhi in an open van with his smiling wife, son, Jayant, and daughter, Pratibha, heavily garlanded and thronged by cheering crowds.

What a harsh lesson in the ups and downs of democracy for Golwalkar's original golden boy! Vajpayee had never thought of

Advani as competition. Vajpayee as the people's leader and Advani as the faceless organizer had always been the power balance of their association, Advani careful to keep Vajpayee in good humour by always calling him 'my leader'. Now as the party and the RSS celebrated Advani's leadership, and Advani became a popular Hindutva leader in his own right, an overshadowed Vajpayee became increasingly glum and morose. Falling into spells of bitterness, in private conversations he would describe the Ram Mandir movement as 'drama', a 'natak', and sometimes condescendingly refer to Advani as 'saien'. 'From the late eighties to 1995, the BJP was Advani's party, Advani was the unquestioned face and the Hindu hero,' recalls Sudhanshu Mittal. 'It was Vajpayee's lowest time.'[10]

Their leadership styles were studies in contrast. Advani, the self-effacing man of the organization, an inexhaustible builder of the BJP network who remembered the first names of district and village workers. Vajpayee, the big-picture man with little inclination to work hard at organizing the party, and with a constant problem in remembering people's names, sometimes even referring to Govindacharya as Dronacharya and once in Parliament when he was prime minister even forgetting Jaswant Singh's name when the latter was foreign minister.

A BJP leader says theirs was always a 'tense relationship' and tensions between them were sometimes fuelled by their respective 'camps'. In Advani's case his family was known to resent that Advani was doing all the hard organizational work while Vajpayee walked away with the public glory. Vajpayee's family was worried about the BJP's hard-line lurch under Advani, convinced it was damaging the party. The mocking epithet 'Ram Avatar' was known to be used for Advani in the Vajpayee household, a typically sardonic Vajpayee-style put-down.

Vajpayee's chosen 'family', the Kauls, were a world away from the Sangh Parivar. Rajkumari's daughter – and Vajpayee's adoptive daughter – Namita and her husband, Ranjan Bhattacharyya, were a well-educated, cosmopolitan and sophisticated couple. The smart young Bhattacharyyas started out as hoteliers, Namita as an executive at ITC and Ranjan with the Oberoi Group. A graduate of the Shri Ram College of Commerce, Ranjan, known for his tastes in sharp suits, Yezdi motorbikes, fine wines and cigars, was a far cry from the austere greybeards of the saffron brotherhood. Vajpayee's personal life choice of living with Rajkumari and her family further distanced him from the RSS.

Yet even in low periods, his irrepressible good humour rescued him from any prolonged melancholy. His jokes and wisecracks abounded. When a group of party workers came to complain to him that the milk in Delhi was being adulterated with soap to make it thicker, he responded: 'What's the problem with that? Now we'll be clean from outside as well as inside.'[11] Suffering from a stomach ache late one night, he dialled AIIMS to ask for medical advice, saying, 'I am Atal Bihari Vajpayee speaking.' 'Oh really,' snapped the nurse on the other end in disbelief, 'then I'm Hema Malini speaking.' Vajpayee dialled again only to get the same response, finally waking Ranjan Bhattacharyya to exclaim that he was in great pain and was trying to call a doctor but the nurse kept assuming he was making a joke.

At this time, Ghatate began to compile Vajpayee's Parliament speeches towards a published collection. Vajpayee gave Ghatate reasons to include even some of his shorter ones, saying, '*Main sansad mein bakwas nahin karta hoon* [I don't talk nonsense in Parliament].' After publication, book covers had to be reprinted because Vajpayee's middle name had been printed as 'Behari' and not 'Bihari', which he was particularly sensitive about.[12]

Two incidents reveal Vajpayee's predicament in his party at this time. The first was in 1990, when journeying from Gwalior to Bhopal by train a group of kar sevaks met him at the station. As soon as they saw him, they began to raise slogans of '*Ram Lalla hum aayenge, mandir wahin banayenge.*' Quick as a flash, Vajpayee barrelled through the crowd and clapped his hand on the mouth of the sloganeer, later saying he did not want party activity to be stained by any form of fundamentalist madness.

The second is an event senior journalist H.K. Dua recalls. In late 1990, after the 30 October kar seva in Ayodhya, the BJP's V.K. Malhotra held a dinner at his Delhi residence, where an argument broke out between Dua and Advani. Dua said that press coverage of the kar seva had done damage to India's image. Advani argued that India's image could only be rebuilt if the country grows stronger and resolute.

When dinner was announced, Vajpayee let Advani walk on ahead, drew Dua aside and in a sly dig at Advani said, 'Duaji, you were rather argumentative tonight.'

'But you stayed completely silent,' answered Dua.

'*Kuchh logon ko khamosh rehna hi theek rehta hai* [For some people it is better to stay quiet],' said Vajpayee expressionlessly.[13] It was an important signal about his reservations about the kar seva. By this time Advani's destabilizing political adventure, or rath yatra of September 1990, had cut a swathe of riots and killings across India, and Advani himself had been arrested. Both events catapulted the BJP to new heights.

In this period Vajpayee was a taciturn party elder, who took to visiting the BJP party office at 11 Ashoka Road regularly to try to stay in the thick of the action. Apart from these visits, Ghatate remembered how Vajpayee had a lot of free time in these years and would sit alone at home for hours, visited only by a few loyal karyakartas. 'Yes, my speeches are well received,' he said wryly, 'but one speech of mine was ruined once when the then home minister Zail Singh told me if you make a good speech, it is published in the newspapers the next day, but a day after, a rickshaw puller uses the paper to wrap his pakodas and then throws the paper away.'[14] In the public he remained popular. In 1994, on a train journey from Gwalior to Delhi, the railway staff went to the extent of changing the platform number of the train so that Vajpayee, afflicted with painful knees, wouldn't have to climb an overbridge. But within the party, very few came to wish him even on his birthday. In his circle, he confessed to friends that Advani's Ram Mandir theatrics were neither politically valuable nor sustainable. According to an editor who knew him well, he privately 'cursed' his party for adopting the Ram movement.

'Vajpayee's passions were elections and Parliament,' says Mittal, 'and as such he was never fully in support of the Ram Janmabhoomi agitation. He believed strongly in the construction of the Ram Mandir and in the integrity of the people's demand for it. But he believed this should be achieved peacefully through negotiation, not through agitation.'[15]

Always an elite politician, never one for disruptive andolans (protests), he was unnerved by the fearsome march of Lord Ram's rough army as his comments to his friends in these years show. Conjuring up religious phantoms from the past for present-day politics disturbed his modernist dreams and theoretical political debates on secularism. But he was in a minority of one, ranged against his entire party throbbing with the excitement of rath yatras. Advani's leadership cult dispirited him. Attaching the BJP to the mandir movement had been Advani's marketing campaign. His own sales pitch – Gandhian socialism – had simply not delivered. He had been sacked as CEO, watching with annoyance as his replacement turned the company around, where he had only driven it into losses. He was too strategic a politician to let himself be forgotten and clung to the party line by weighing in with high-voltage speeches. But it was plain to see that in the Hindu nationalist biopic, he was the character actor to Advani's leading man.

'Vajpayeeji, are you marginalized in your party now? Are you on the margins?' asked the journalist Neena Vyas at a press conference in Jaipur in February 1991. Never one to let his lively sense of the ridiculous desert him, Vajpayee seized on the word 'margin' for a comeback: 'Sometimes you need the margin if you have to make corrections.' 'His tone was light and funny, but you could make out it was laden with hidden meaning,' recalls Vyas.[16] It was an accurate prediction. Soon Vajpayee's marginalization in the Ram movement would be the very thing that would become his biggest asset.

~

The V.P. Singh dispensation that took office in December 1989 was, like the Janata Party of 1977, beset with internal rivalries and ego clashes. In 1989 the septuagenarian Haryana strongman 'Tau' Devi Lal, whose party had supported V.P. Singh, was appointed deputy prime minister. Devi Lal kept interfering in Singh's decisions. On 1 August 1990, in a political crisis just eight months into his tenure, Singh sacked Devi Lal from his cabinet. Devi Lal responded by announcing that he planned to stage a mammoth farmers' rally later in August, as a show of strength against V.P. Singh. Two days before Devi Lal's kisan rally, to checkmate Devi Lal and aiming to cast a wide electoral net over the rural farmers' vote, V.P. Singh hit back by exhuming a document that had been gathering dust for ten years. This was the Mandal Commission report.[17]

On 7 August 1990, V.P. Singh announced in Parliament that his government would implement the Mandal Commission report, recommending that 27 per cent of all government jobs be reserved for OBC communities, taking the total percentage of reserved jobs for Scheduled Castes (SCs), Scheduled Tribes (STs) and OBCs to 49 per cent (a cumulative reservation of 22.5 per cent already existed for SCs and STs). In a country where unemployment is of epidemic proportions, a massive chunk of available government jobs would now be out of reach for youth belonging to the upper, or the 'forward', castes. Singh calculated that not only would this move bolster his populist, pro-poor credentials, but with castes taking up cudgels against each other, the Hindu monolith, or the single community of Hindus being sculpted by the BJP, would crack apart.

A firestorm of protests flared through North India. Police lathi-charged and fired on protesting crowds. In September, a Delhi

University student, Rajeev Goswami, set himself on fire, prompting others to do the same in several cities, in a deadly new innovation of violent student resistance. Once his most enthusiastic supporters, the urban middle class went into open revolt against V.P. Singh, and his minority government began to wobble. 'The havoc the politics of reservation is playing with the social fabric is unimaginable,' fulminated the RSS journal *Organiser*,[18] well aware that caste could work as a speed-breaker to the Hindutva juggernaut.

Already disappointed with the V.P. Singh government, the BJP took to the warpath. The 'Mandal monster' threatened to shatter the Hindu fortress, tearing upper and lower castes apart, and the saffron party sprang into red alert. At a party conclave in September, Advani huffed: 'The government can't go on ignoring us and take our support for granted.' In Parliament Vajpayee raised objections: 'Self-immolation is new to the North . . . there is something that touches the innermost recesses of youths' hearts . . . the youth are asking questions, I have no answers . . . Where are the jobs that are being fought for? Where are the jobs that you are going to give?'[19]

Upper-caste voters in turmoil, Hindu poised against Hindu over caste reservations, and Ram Mandir threatened with an eclipse, the BJP had had enough of V.P. Singh. Lord Ram had hurled the mythological brahmastra at his foes, and now a new political weapon lumbered into the landscape – the rath.

~

On the morning of 25 September 1990, after first offering prayers at the Somnath temple in Gujarat, L.K. Advani started out on his Ram rath yatra. The Somnath temple, for the Sangh Parivar, stood as a symbol of the rebuilding of 'Hindu pride' after its bloody sacking by Mahmud of Ghazni in the eleventh century. In 1951 it had been rebuilt with much pomp. Now the BJP's reigning ideological helmsman, sixty-three-year-old Advani, dressed in a crisp silk kurta and white dhoti, stepped aboard his rath or a decorated, air-conditioned DCM-Toyota van. This 'chariot' would carry him across 10,000 kilometres in a yatra from Somnath to Ayodhya, arriving in time for the VHP's planned kar seva in Ayodhya on 30 October. The rath was designed to look like Arjuna's chariot from the *Mahabharat* tele-serial, a richly decorated political wagon hung with saffron flags and posters, and marked with tilaks.

Advani's Ram rath yatra changed forever the battle lines of Indian politics. After the 1989 general election results, eager to remain part of the VHP's ongoing Ram Janmabhoomi movement, Advani had already announced to his party that there would be no turning back from the path of the Ram Mandir. 'The BJP believes in positive secularism . . . Positive secularism means justice for all, appeasement of none.'[20] Justice for all and appeasement of none sounded innocuous enough; in reality, on the ground, it released murderous rage and translated into bloody street battles against Muslims, or the so-called descendants of Babur.

A modern-day chariot churning up waves of religious fervour under its wheels had been high-tech wizard Pramod Mahajan's idea and off went Advani, powering through India from west to east, to an overwhelming public response all along the yatra route from Gujarat to Uttar Pradesh.

Sword-brandishing youths pranced in front of the rath and women came rushing out of their homes to throw flowers in front of it, hailing Advani as an incarnation of Lord Ram. Urban religious fervour, the reflexive by-product of unemployment and social instability, was ratcheted up to dangerous levels. In Ahmedabad, a Bajrang Dal member applied a tika using his own blood on Advani's forehead, and in Jeptur, near Rajkot, Bajrang Dal members offered Advani a container full of their blood. Advani held press conferences by day and addressed jam-packed rallies by night. Hindus in towns like Ajmer turned out in large numbers to welcome the yatri, even as Muslim areas remained in terrified lockdown. As Hindu activism and Muslim fears began to boil along the yatra route, tensions developed within the ruling alliance, within the National Front and among members of the Janata Dal. Bihar and Uttar Pradesh Chief Ministers Lalu Prasad Yadav and Mulayam Singh Yadav, the rumbustious secular chieftains in the Lohia-ite mould, made noises threatening Advani's arrest if the rath yatra entered their states. Warned the BJP: if Advani is arrested, we will withdraw support to the V.P. Singh government.

An aggressive Lalu Prasad Yadav would brook no argument, his own Muslim, lower-caste support base now roiled in anxiety about the rath yatra. On 23 October 1990, when Advani's rath rolled into Bihar, Lalu Prasad Yadav arrested Advani in Samastipur and sent him to five weeks' custody, albeit to a comfortable government guest house near the Massanjore Dam. Advani's rath was thus blocked from entering Uttar Pradesh. With communal outbreaks spurting everywhere, Mulayam Singh Yadav, not to be outdone by Lalu, fortified Ayodhya, barricading the road leading to the Babri Masjid. At dawn on 30 October, almost 40,000 kar sevaks[21] gathered at Ayodhya, some even swimming across the Saryu river to gain access to the town. In a sudden flurry of activity, a Naga sadhu commandeered a police bus in an attempt to burst through the police barricades. As kar sevaks stormed through the gap and began to run helter-skelter around the masjid, some even planting a saffron flag on the masjid's dome, the Mulayam Singh government ordered the police to open fire. Guns blazed, and by the end of the day several lay dead. The kar sevaks returned the next day to attempt another assault on the masjid. This time the police first used tear gas and then fired again, leading to more deaths. There are conflicting figures of the dead. Official figures say six died, while the VHP claimed the number of dead as fifty. On the second day official figures put deaths at fifteen, while the VHP claimed fifty-nine.[22]

Bloody violence erupted across Uttar Pradesh in the weeks that followed. The VHP took out ashthi kalash yatras, processions bearing urns containing the ashes of the kar sevaks who were killed, waving trishuls and threatening anyone who came in their way, raising the slogan '*Ayodhya ke shahidon ko zindabad!*' Later in the year, in December, more than a hundred were killed and thousands injured in Hindu–Muslim riots in Hyderabad, and there were riots in several parts of Uttar Pradesh.

High political drama unfolded in tandem with the communal outbreaks. As soon as Advani was arrested, a BJP delegation led by Vajpayee marched to Rashtrapati Bhavan and presented President R. Venkataraman a letter withdrawing support to the V.P. Singh government. On 7 November 1990, V.P. Singh lost a confidence vote in Parliament and, after eleven shaky months in office, his government collapsed.

~

Vajpayee never openly criticized the rath yatra but found ways to make his displeasure known. After the 1989 elections, when the VHP announced its plans to hold its kar seva in Ayodhya in October 1990, a suggestion was made to undertake four ekatmata yatras – to be led by Vijaya Raje Scindia from Guwahati, Sikandar Bakht from Mumbai, Advani from Kanyakumari and Vajpayee from Jammu. Vajpayee turned down the suggestion point-blank, saying, 'I don't believe in nautanki of this kind.' Vijaya Raje Scindia and Bakht too refused.

Subsequently, when the party asked Vajpayee to lead the welcome when Advani's yatra entered Lucknow, he again flatly refused, and agreed only after much persuasion. Vajpayee was canny enough to realize the direction of the wind within his party. If the Ram movement was leading to greater electoral rewards, he would not shy away from the bandwagon and he had no hesitation in flagging off the rath yatra from the Constitution Club when the yatra passed through Delhi, even though he later grumbled to friends, 'It's wrong to think we gained too many seats in 1991 because of the rath yatra. Maybe we got ten–twelve more seats. Nothing more.'[23]

In his essay 'I Recollect', however, Vajpayee mounts a vigorous defence of the rath yatra as a salve for the Hindus' 'wounded psyche', which, he claims, had developed as a result of the overturning of the Shah Bano judgement, terrorism in Kashmir and Punjab and 'the politics of vote' pursued by the Congress and the left. The objective of the rath yatra, he writes, was not to bring down V.P. Singh's government but to mobilize wider support across the country for the building of the Ram Mandir. And the rath yatra, he adds, showed what a deep emotional chord the temple issue struck with 'the majority community'.[24] Vajpayee also adds that V.P. Singh should have tried to 'convince Muslims' to adopt a 'conciliatory attitude' on the Ayodhya dispute, because the Ram temple resonated even with 'backward classes'. 'Forty years of Congress rule . . . have left an impression on the minds of Hindus that they are not being treated well . . . the rath yatra became a symbol of their [Hindus'] disenchantment,' Vajpayee writes.[25]

He may have been edged out of centre stage, but he clung with all his might to the party line, supplying intellectual heft to the argument that it was the communal politics of the Congress that necessitated Hindutva politics.[26]

Vajpayee was also unhappy about the BJP's decision to withdraw support for the V.P. Singh government. Before Advani's arrest, at a meeting of the BJP's national executive in Delhi on 17 October, as related earlier, the party had decided that it would withdraw support if Advani's rath was stopped. At this meeting, Vajpayee remained silent and grim-faced throughout. When Pramod Mahajan asked if he supported the party's ultimatum to the government, Vajpayee urged the party to listen to what his friend Ghatate had to say. Ghatate spoke up: 'After the yatra passes through UP and Bihar, it will enter Bengal. What if the yatra is stopped in Bengal, will we still withdraw support?' (The Jyoti Basu–led CPI(M) was a supporter of the V.P. Singh government.) The master of equivocation and elliptical suggestion had spoken through his best friend, to convey that he was not in favour of withdrawing support to the V.P. Singh government and wanted to give it more time. He was intent on making a non-Congress government work and not fall apart like the Janata Party. But again, he was alone and, true to form, didn't take a stand.

Vajpayee writes that at this time, rather than risk another general election, he had 'publicly welcomed' the idea of the formation of a national government of different parties, to which the BJP also agreed. This was an idea developed by President R. Venkataraman, who even held discussions with different leaders to see if this national government could be achieved. But relations between the Janata Dal and the BJP had become so 'embittered' that nothing came of the initiative.[27] Vajpayee was disappointed that such a government could not be formed, and writes, 'I remain of the view that to strengthen and bring prosperity to this large country with many diversities, it is essential to evolve a consensus . . . no single party or group of parties can fulfil the demands of development.'[28]

When V.P. Singh's government fell, the Janata Dal split, a rump of sixty MPs rallying under the leadership of the bearded, low-profile Janata leader Chandra Shekhar. Hurrying into the breach and sensing a triumphant return to power, the Congress quickly tied up with Chandra Shekhar and extended him support, and the mandate-less Chandra Shekhar was sworn in as prime minister on 10 November 1990. As Congress workers danced and roared around in open jeeps, flaunting posters of Indira and Rajiv Gandhi, Vajpayee, perpetually nursing his dream of a non-Congress government, looked on in dismay. 'The historical experiment of a second non-Congress government at the Centre was ruined in 1990 . . . the non-Congress leaders were more responsible for this . . . The recommendations of the Mandal Commission were used as a weapon in a hasty and clumsy way . . . the parties supporting the government were not taken into confidence,' writes Vajpayee bitterly.[29]

One Sunday afternoon, after taking over as prime minister, Chandra Shekhar came to visit Vajpayee at his Raisina Road home. They were good friends. Welcoming Chandra Shekhar with a broad smile,

Vajpayee said: *'Aap toh pradhan mantri ki gaddi par baith gaye* [You are now sitting on the prime minister's throne].' To which Chandra Shekhar replied, '*Gurudev, yeh sab aapki kripa hai. Yadi aapka rath nahin chalta toh V.P. Singh ki sarkar nahin girti aur main pradhan mantri nahin banta* [It's thanks to you. If your rath hadn't started rolling, V.P. Singh's government wouldn't have fallen and I wouldn't have become prime minister].' Musing on this, Vajpayee admitted regretfully, *'Aap ki baat mein kuchh satya hai* [There's some truth in what you say].'[30]

Chandra Shekhar's government lasted for only seven months, yet it made brisk efforts to solve the Ram Janmabhoomi–Babri Masjid tangle by bringing the two sides together and arranging the first official meeting between the VHP, the All-India Babri Masjid Action Committee and a group of chief ministers, to present all sides of the dispute. Vajpayee wholeheartedly but invisibly supported these negotiations, one of the negotiators being his close friend Bhairon Singh Shekhawat, a Vajpayeesque moderate, entrusted to persuade the Hindu side, while Maharashtra chief minister Sharad Pawar worked on the Muslims. However, the Chandra Shekhar government proved short-lived as the Congress withdrew its support and Chandra Shekhar resigned on 6 March 1991, fed up with the Congress's 'tantrums'.[31] Within a year and a half of the BJP's impressive gains in the 1989 polls, India trundled off once again towards general elections, scheduled for May 1991. Speaking about the BJP's adoption of the Ram Mandir plank at this time, Chandra Shekhar presciently remarked, 'Once you ride this tiger [communalism] you won't be able to get off.'[32]

In 1991 Vajpayee was eager to take a crack at the polls again, to depart once more for his well-loved election landscapes, for those heaving rallies, mud-scented dirt tracks and flood-lit crowded maidans. Initially he professed to be disinclined to contest: 'I was a member of the Rajya Sabha and had announced I would not contest the Lok Sabha election.'[33] But the disingenuous artist of doublespeak was eager to throw himself into the poll action and a story goes that when party general secretary Govindacharya initially said no to Vajpayee's candidature, Vajpayee immediately dashed to Lucknow and filed his nomination papers, returning to Delhi before his party had time to react. In any event, the BJP subsequently threw its weight behind him and, careful not to take any chances, he contested from two seats – Lucknow and Vidisha. Uttar Pradesh was in the throes of the Ram Janmabhoomi movement and the BJP was anxious to form a government in the state. 'To boost the election campaign, it was necessary to field a person who could muster public support,' Vajpayee writes, '. . . the astrologers made their contribution . . . I had my old contacts in Lucknow and had contested elections thrice from there.'[34]

Back in the Lok Sabha fray for the first time after the humiliation of 1984, he was desperate to win from high-prestige Lucknow. He campaigned hard, holding rallies and meetings late into the evenings. '*Yadi aap hamein seva ka mauka denge, hum aapko shikayat ka mauka nahin denge* [If you give me an opportunity to serve you, I will give you an opportunity to bring your complaints to me],' he assured the crowds. He let loose a broadside or two at the Ram bhakts in his party. One hot May afternoon, when he returned from the campaign to his room in the Circuit House to find then BJP state chief Kalraj Mishra dozing on a sofa in air-conditioned comfort, Vajpayee said mockingly, '*Arre yeh kya ho raha hai? Yahaan Hindu Rashtra so raha hai. Kaise kaam chalega?* [What's going on here? The Hindu Rashtra is sleeping here, how will our work get done?]' Hectically touring Lucknow, Ghatate once lost his shoes at a public meeting and had to come back to Delhi barefoot. Vajpayee counselled him: 'Be like the Muslims when they go to prayer and carry your shoes in a cloth bag. That way shoes won't get lost or stolen.'[35]

In 1991 his rival parties had obligingly put up a range of non-entities against him, but he was still on alert against his opponents' tricks. Since general elections and assembly elections were being held at the same time, his opponents raised the slogan: '*Oopar se vote Atal ko do, magar neeche se vote humko do* [Give the national vote to Vajpayee but the state vote to us].' To this Vajpayee hit back: '*Kurta mujhko diya aur dhoti doosreko di to mera kya haal hoga?* [If you give the kurta to me and the dhoti to another, then what will become of me?]'

On polling day, a party youth came running up to Ghatate and informed him that booths were being captured. Ghatate rushed to tell Vajpayee who became intensely agitated. 'Why did you not tell me immediately?' he cried, surging out of his room in a flurry. '*Mera sansaar loota ja raha hai* [My world is being looted].'

He was possessive about Lucknow. It was here, as a schoolboy, that he had recited his poem '*Rag Rag Mein Hindu*' to applauding audiences. It was from here that he had already contested three elections.[36] It was in Lucknow that he had been a new RSS recruit and had worked in Deendayal Upadhyaya's magazine *Rashtradharma*, and then become founder-editor of the RSS journal *Panchjanya*.

The city was in his blood, it was his political home and his artistic inspiration. Lucknow – known for its nawabs, for its Ganga–Yamuni tehzeeb, and, like Gwalior, never known for communal conflagrations – was the city of his political birth and remained part of his life for fifty years. By the end of his career he would be a five-time MP from Lucknow, winning every election from Lucknow from 1991 to 2004. He recalled the city later in evocative words:

> Biryani, makhan malai, rose and chameli petals . . . these are my memories of my Lucknow. The tehzeeb of the nawabs, strolling and chatting with friends on Aminabad street; wandering in Bara Imambara, Rumi Darwaza and Bhool Bhulaiyan with tourists from all over the world; cucumber vendors crying '*Majnoon ki haddiyan, Laila ki pasliyan le lo*' [Majnoon's bones, Laila's ribs] . . . what a scene it used to be. *Tokri mein phoolon ki pattiyan rakhi huyi, beech mein mombatti jalti hui* [Baskets of flower petals, a candle burning in their midst].[37]

This was the city where he had first heard Nehru speak in public, at Jhandewalan Park, and was awestruck by the prime minister's eloquence; this was the city where 'the makhan malai was so light and fluffy, even Indiraji used to ask for it when she visited Lucknow', as he would muse years later.[38] Today in Lucknow, in crowded mohallas and streets, on smoky evenings when the air is filled with the fragrance of the rose and jasmine that he loved, jokes and stories about Vajpayee still abound. Residents talk about how he often stopped to chat with them on the street. In the 1950s he lived for a while in a hostel named Kalantri Niwas in Marwadi Gali in the Aminabad locality. The place was a meeting place for Jana Sangh politicians and it was here, locals say, that it was decided that Vajpayee would contest the 1955 by-poll. After he retired from politics in 2005, and before he fell ill, he planned to write a book set in Lucknow.[39]

On the day he filed his papers from Lucknow he also needed to file his nomination from Vidisha. On the way to Vidisha, while waiting at Lucknow airport, an airport official informed Vajpayee that Amitabh Bachchan – hero of the Allahabad election in 1984 – could be Vajpayee's challenger in Lucknow. When gathered journalists asked Vajpayee for his response, he retorted with a line from one of Bachchan's hit songs, '*Mere angne me tumhara kya kaam hai?* [What business do you have in my courtyard?]' Bachchan later refused to contest against Vajpayee.

The 1991 elections were called the 'mandir–mandal' elections. The BJP went to the polls on a radical Hindutva plank, kicking off its campaign with a rally at which BJP leaders Advani, Vajpayee and Murli Manohar Joshi (now BJP president) sat alongside the RSS representative K.S. Sudarshan, the VHP representatives Ashok Singhal and Vishnu Hari Dalmia, along with mandir activists Uma Bharti, Sadhvi Rithambara and Mahant Avaidyanath. The party distributed leaflets which played to Hindu victimhood, which read: 'Ever since we earned our freedom, we have been in fear of losing it. Fear of separatism, fear of terrorism, fear of exploitation, fear of losing one's cultural identity.'[40]

Tragedy struck midway through the 1991 campaign. On 21 May

in Sriperumbudur in Tamil Nadu, Rajiv Gandhi was killed by a Tamil suicide bomber in an explosion so powerful that his body parts scattered across the rally grounds. Vajpayee was shocked by Rajiv's slaying. He recalled: 'I saw Shri Rajiv Gandhi in many forms . . . it is true we had differences . . . but he did not allow these differences to sour personal relationships. [In 1988] I had once fallen ill . . . he immediately made arrangements [for me to go abroad] . . . it was a small thing but it touched the heart. So long as Indian democracy has this mutual respect and affection, it can gather the strength to face assault by murderers.'[41] Vajpayee was down with a kidney ailment in 1988. Hearing about this, Rajiv had included him in his official delegation to the UN, telling him to use the time in the US to get medical treatment. This was when Vajpayee wrote his poem '*Maut Se Thann Gayi*', which we noted in the previous chapter.

He had warmed to Rajiv from the start, just as he always did to the gilded princelings of India's elite families. In the Indira Gandhi years, alighting from a plane once, the smart young captain in his cap had greeted him with a charming 'namaskar'. Not recognizing him at first as the prime minister's son, Vajpayee later said he was touched that Rajiv had greeted him so respectfully. 'Prime Ministership greatly changed his informal and simple nature . . . his decisions at times bordered on impropriety . . . he committed many grave mistakes . . . [but] he was always particular about etiquette. Whenever he met anyone, did so heartily,' Vajpayee recalled.[42] In another interview he said: 'Rajiv Gandhi is the reason I am alive today . . . Today I'm in Opposition and people expect me to speak like an opponent. But I can't. I only want to talk about what he did for me,' later even calling Rajiv his 'younger brother'.[43]

The Nehru–Gandhis, his lifelong object of fascination from 'rajkumar' Jawaharlal to 'Durga' Indira Gandhi and 'informal and simple' Rajiv, occupied a special place in Vajpayee's heart. The better part of his political life was spent in the shadow of this 'dynasty' which he was transfixed by, however much he mocked, attacked and targeted its members. Upon each of their deaths, the outpouring of emotional and warm tributes from Vajpayee reveal an intimate attachment to the Nehru–Gandhi family.

Chandra Shekhar had warned the BJP about the dangers of riding the Hindutva tiger, but in 1991 the tiger brought in a breathtaking haul of seats. Just seven years after the suicidal two-seat showing in 1984, the party now swelled to a remarkable 121 seats. The BJP became the second-largest party in the Lok Sabha. It had taken giant strides, commanding arcs of support across North India. It was an ashwamedha horse, spurred forward by the militancy of the Ram movement, cantering across territories unimpeded, as if set for even bigger wins. Vajpayee won handsomely from both Lucknow and Vidisha, later giving up Vidisha. In the Uttar Pradesh assembly polls, the BJP zoomed to power, winning 221 seats as the Congress collapsed. Upper castes turned against the Janata Dal because of the Mandal report. The Ram Mandir movement created a gigantic Hindu vote bank across the state. Across India the Congress – benefiting mid-election from a sympathy undercurrent after the killing of Rajiv Gandhi – emerged as the single largest party, with 244 seats. On 21 June 1991, the Congress's P.V. Narasimha Rao, one of Vajpayee's long-term parliamentary colleagues and trusted friends, was sworn in as prime minister.

At a time when Vajpayee was perceived as shunned by his own party, Prime Minister Rao sympathized with his friend Vajpayee and made it a point to praise him publicly. When Vajpayee was presented the Best Parliamentarian Award 1994, Rao said at the presentation function:

> [Vajpayee and I] have always sat on opposite sides of the Well. I have always found his interventions intellectually stimulating . . . His political convictions run deep but in the true parliamentary spirit, he operates within the parameters of the democratic process . . . he is willing to listen to other person's views and has an unshakeable faith in the need to ensure that all disputes be resolved through discussion

> . . . Young parliamentarians can learn from him the art of conducting a debate and containing differences in a parliamentary system.[44]

The qualities that made Vajpayee alluring to the Rao-led Congress did not endear him to his own Sangh Parivar. In 1991, the BJP became the largest Opposition party and Vajpayee, its most distinguished parliamentary face, should logically have been made leader of the Opposition, a prestigious post not only for the Opposition party, but for Parliament as a whole. But it was a post Vajpayee was denied by the RSS. His own saffron parivar rebuffed him and opted for Advani. According to Govindacharya, Advani did not even want the post and sent him to the RSS headquarters in Jhandewalan to inform the RSS's Rajju Bhaiya that Vajpayee, in all fairness, deserved to be the leader of the Opposition. But Singh refused, saying the matter had already been settled. Relations between the Vajpayee and Advani families became tense at this point, with Vajpayee's family of the firm belief that the BJP had grown to its present size only because of Vajpayee and that Advani's militant image was bringing the party a bad name. But for the RSS it was Advani who had brought the BJP its electoral windfall, it was Advani who was Nagpur's favourite, and it was Advani who should be leader of the Opposition. From this point onward, Vajpayee began to grow increasingly bitter about Advani and angry and mistrustful of Govindacharya. Says Govindacharya: 'I had only been the messenger from RSS and had gone to Jhandewalan to convey that Advani was actually on Vajpayee's side.'[45] Vajpayee never fully trusted Advani after 1991, and later in government would try to counterbalance Advani's importance by promoting his own men like Brajesh Mishra. It was a role reversal indeed. In 1991 Vajpayee, the BJP's most famous parliamentarian, was abruptly displaced by Advani, a Lok Sabha novice who had entered the lower House for the first time only two years earlier.

~

Vajpayee had fallen out of favour with the saffron parivar, but staunch party soldier that he was, in Parliament he remained his party's stormy petrel for the mandir cause, raging, yelling, interrupting and arguing on the rightness of the Ram movement, the justness of the mandir demand and accusing the Congress and its allies of playing the politics of 'minority communalism'. The ghosts of the Babri Masjid and Ram Janmabhoomi encircled Parliament at this time, filling the House with vengeful, angry spirits. Tempers were frayed, and compromise looked difficult. A cyclone was circling, about to make landfall.

Throughout 1992, the year of the Babri Masjid demolition, Vajpayee made blistering 'Hindutva' speeches. On 17 July 1992 he said:

> If politics in this country is played from the masjid, from the church, from the Gurdwara, then it cannot be stopped from reaching the door of the temple . . . those who took politics to the Gurdwara, to the mosque . . . are the people who go to the mosque during elections to take orders from the Imam . . . I have never been to any Shankaracharya to seek blessings during elections . . . one-sided action will not do, there can't be one-sided battle against fundamentalism . . . there was nothing like majority communalism in this country . . . there cannot be different yardsticks to measure communalism.[46]

Soon he would go much further in Hindutva rhetoric.

As described earlier, through 1992, wave upon wave of kar sevaks, mobilized by the VHP and Bajrang Dal and other Hindu groups, converged on Ayodhya. In a tacit admission of the growing strength of Hindu demands for the mandir, Narasimha Rao told the Babri Masjid Action Committee in October, 'I can fight the BJP, but I cannot fight Lord Ram,' implying that the Ram temple may have to be built but the government would protect the mosque.[47] However, talks between the two sides broke down, and by the end of November the VHP announced a new date for a kar seva at Ayodhya: 6 December 1992.

On 5 December, just a day before the fall of the Babri Masjid, Vajpayee addressed a crowd of kar sevaks at Jhandewala Park in Aminabad, Lucknow. It was a speech replete with double meanings, hidden layers and sneaky allusions. This was his notorious '*Kam Se Kam Vedi Toh Banegi*' (At least we will build a platform) speech.[48] It was a speech similar to the inflammatory words he used in Assam days before the Nellie killings. Once again, in this instance, in the place of Vajpayee the smiling moderate democrat, he appeared in a rather different avatar: this was Vajpayee the roguish, sharp-eyed demagogue. Said Vajpayee in strident and sarcastic tones:

> Even the Supreme Court decision does not stop the kar seva . . . the court has shown us the path to do kar seva . . . [cheers from the crowd] By doing kar seva in Ayodhya we will not be disrespecting any court order . . . It's true that as long as the Lucknow bench of the High Court does not come to a decision, the Supreme Court has asked us not to start any construction work. But the court has told us that you conduct bhajan kirtan programmes. And bhajan is not done by one person, bhajan is done together with others . . . and bhajan and kirtan is not done while standing . . . There were sharp stones that came out, no one can sit there [cheers from the crowd], the ground has to be levelled . . . arrangements for a yagya will be done so there will be some construction . . . at least there will be a platform made.[49]

He ended his speech by saying, 'The kar sevaks will decide together . . . I don't know what will happen there tomorrow.' When a journalist asked him if the kar seva would pass off peacefully in Ayodhya the next day, his answer was typically cryptic: '*Aasha hai, aashanka bhi!* [There are hopes, but there are also fears!]'[50]

What was Vajpayee trying to convey here? Was he sending out a tacit signal to 'construct'? What were these 'sharp stones' he was referring to, and why did he specifically say the 'ground must be levelled' for the yagya? The Ram movement was bringing the BJP bumper harvests of seats and, shrewd harvester of votes as he was, Vajpayee was not one to reject the juicy fertilizer that was making the fields turn saffron with ripening produce. He would sow, he would farm, he would harvest. A wily sixth sense told him to stay away when the fire truly began to burn. But he would make an incendiary speech or two, even while taking care not to be seen on the same stage as Uma Bharti or Vinay Katiyar. Soon after the demolition, Vajpayee made a speech in which he said the 'Babri Masjid was a symbol of shame and has been erased'.[51]

Vajpayee the supreme tactician, Vajpayee the ruthless politician with an unerring instinct about which way the mood was swinging and what the 'mahaul' was, would never allow himself to become isolated. Whatever his personal inclinations, he knew how to play politics much more expertly than others, when to be visible and when not to be, and how to stand out as the Hindutva dove among the hawks. Shakti Sinha provides an interesting insight: 'Vajpayee always knew that if he did not go along with the party line he would become irrelevant. And then he would not be able to play any role in stabilizing his party.'[52] To retain his own leadership and identity in the party, Vajpayee would convincingly defend the party line, but at crucial moments also smartly publicize his divergence with it.

Weeks of blood-curdling riots followed the demolition. Riots erupted in Delhi, Ahmedabad and Kanpur, 2000 dying in the immediate aftermath of the demolition. Riots torched Mumbai in 1992–93, in which approximately 900 were killed. After the riots, on 12 March 1993, bombs went off across Mumbai, killing over 200. Advani, Murli Manohar Joshi, Ashok Singhal, Uma Bharti and others were arrested. The RSS was banned for a few months, and the VHP too was briefly banned. The Jamaat-e-Islami Hind and Islamic Sevak Sangh were also banned. On 16 December Rao sacked three BJP state governments – Madhya Pradesh, Himachal Pradesh and Rajasthan, having already dismissed the Uttar Pradesh government – for failing to protect law and order in their states. Uttar Pradesh remained submerged in the boiling cauldron of Hindu–Muslim tensions.[53] But in the assembly elections of 1993, the ghost of the Babri Masjid seemed to laugh in vengeance. In Uttar Pradesh two backward caste parties – the SP and BSP – fighting in alliance worsted the BJP. Hindutva crashed elsewhere too. In 1993 the BJP lost badly in Madhya Pradesh and Himachal Pradesh and only scraped through in Rajasthan on the leadership of Bhairon Singh Shekhawat, although the party won in Delhi. Advani was again elected BJP president in 1993 and began to gear the party up for the 1996 Lok Sabha polls, but the ruined masjid cast a shadow on the BJP's acceptability. Advani, who always maintained that the masjid was demolished because the movement was 'undermined by those who took the law into their own hands', later also wrote that 6 December was the 'saddest day of my life'.[54] He subsequently resigned as leader of the Opposition.[55] As the Ram Mandir tide began to recede after its 1992 apogee, Advani, the 'Ram Avatar', sat alone on a rock of his own making.

Vajpayee, back as the lion of the Lok Sabha, recently elected from Lucknow, sprang into fightback mode, raging and blustering. On 17 December 1992, he brought a vote of no-confidence against the government, cleverly turning the tables, blaming the ruling party for failing to protect the masjid and attacking the Congress's secularism. He regretted the demolition, but unleashed a tirade about the 'intensity of the sentiments of the majority community'.[56] Vajpayee said:

> Shri Advani was very sad when the structure was demolished. He was in tears . . . Whatever happened there, we regret the incident . . . When Shri Advani went on the rath yatra, I had my reservations . . . when I expressed my feelings the press said the BJP has worn two faces . . . sometimes moderates and sometimes hardliners . . . but even Pandit Nehru wrote that the present Hindi translation of the word 'secularism' is causing trouble and confusion . . . we had not performed the 'shilanyas'. It was performed during the Congress government . . . will the government put us behind bars only because of this?[57]

In July 1993 – after the stock market scam of 1992 came to light – the stock market trader Harshad Mehta levelled the sensational allegation that he had paid Rs 1 crore to Prime Minister Narasimha Rao. Vajpayee demanded Rao's immediate resignation, shouting, 'corruption has become a part of the system, it has become a way of life . . . bribe is not called a bribe in Uttar Pradesh, it is called a *suvidha shulk* [facility fee] . . . where have we reached, where are we heading to? We are not in politics for this'.[58]

In 1995, he cried angrily, 'Please leave alone the Bharatiya Janata Party. The more you dub us communal, the more people will repose confidence in us because the definition of communalism is changing.'[59]

Yet Narasimha Rao was no pushover and after surviving a no-confidence motion in 1993 (although by sordid means as three Jharkhand Mukti Morcha MPs were given bribes to vote for the government) his government slowly strengthened itself. 'Manmohanomics', or the liberalization of the economy in 1991, under Finance Minister Manmohan Singh, had a dramatic impact and there was talk of an 'economic miracle in India'. Vajpayee and the BJP supported the 1991 liberalization. In Parliament, Vajpayee said he hoped the poorest would not have to wait as long for their share of prosperity as one has to wait for hair to grow. In a hilarious reference to Sardar Manmohan Singh's 'zulf' or long hair, he remarked, 'By the time the grief [of the poor] reaches you a lifetime would go by. Sardarji actually has *zulf* [hair], so we don't know what would happen to us by that time.'[60]

Unstoppable in Parliament, he galloped out as head of his party's cavalry, marshalling every argument possible to protect his disgraced flock. The BJP faced all-round condemnation. As widespread revulsion at the masjid's demolition grew, Vajpayee's own image of the good man in the bad party, the friendly man in the unfriendly party, the-hail-fellow-well-met Hindu nationalist who loved his Scotch almost as much as he loved Hindu sanskriti shone. The leader they had once shunned during the Ram Mandir euphoria began to become a lifeline for a party rapidly becoming an 'untouchable' again.

Ghatate pointed out: 'After the demolition of the Babri Masjid, the others looked upon the BJP with fear and the party became even more of an untouchable. In this situation of untouchability only one man could bring the BJP back into the mainstream, and that was Vajpayee.'[61] Advani resigned as leader of the Opposition after the Babri demolition and Vajpayee took over the post.

As the acceptable statesman, Vajpayee basked in the prime minister's welcoming friendship. Between P.V. Narasimha Rao and Vajpayee there was something like an old-school bromance. Separated by only three years (Rao being the elder), they shared the unspoken kinship of the Pandit brotherhood. Prime minister and Opposition leader were both consensus-seekers, both played the politics of reconciliation, both were bookish and prided themselves on their literary compositions. In Vajpayee's dining room in his Raisina Road residence a framed photo of Narasimha Rao had pride of place. They hailed from a cohort of politically conservative, erudite Hindu men who made their debuts in the 1950s and carried the memory of the most sophisticated Pandit of them all – Jawaharlal Nehru – as their lifelong inspiration. Mani Shankar Aiyar once described Vajpayee as 'one of the best Congress prime ministers we never had' and Rao as the 'first BJP prime minister', in a telling insight about how their identities merged.[62]

Warming instinctively to fellow Brahmins was a unique Vajpayee trait. He often mocked and directed self-deprecating teasing humour at the Brahmin identity in general and his own in particular. Whether making fun of Lok Sabha Speaker M. Ananthasayanam Ayyangar's Sanskritic name or jokingly telling a crowd during a 1950s election rally, just after then chief minister Govind Ballabh Pant had finished speaking, 'you were listening to one Pandey, now listen to another Pandey'[63] ('Pandey' being a synonym for Brahmin), or referring to CPI MP Chaturanan Mishra as 'Panditji', Vajpayee revelled in a Brahmanic affinity with many of his close friends from Ghatate to N.K. Shejwalkar to Rajkumari Kaul to Rao. In July 1992, he raged against Ram Vilas Paswan in Parliament: 'Throughout the country he [Paswan] is saying the President is a Brahmin, Vice President is a Brahmin, and the Prime Minister is also a Brahmin. He said the leader of the Opposition is also a Brahmin. I did not know the caste of Shri Advani . . .' Advani was not a Brahmin, to which Vajpayee made this glancing reference.[64]

Rao and Vajpayee were at loggerheads in Parliament, but outside the House, Rao not only showered accolades on Vajpayee but in 1994 appointed him leader of India's delegation to the UN Human Rights Council in Geneva, where Pakistan had brought a censure motion against India's human rights violations in Kashmir. 'The Pakistanis were astounded to see me. Where has he come from? In their country Opposition leaders do not cooperate with the government, they try to bring the government down,' Vajpayee told Parliament in 1996. 'They thought perhaps it was a ruse, that if anything went wrong, the prime minister would blame me and my party. They did not understand that it is this which is the strength of India's democracy.'[65]

Vajpayee's Geneva intervention was a great success. A forceful Indian delegation swung the UN in favour of India – Vajpayee in the lead, the Congress's Salman Khurshid and former Jammu and Kashmir chief minister Farooq Abdullah by his side – and Pakistan was forced to withdraw its censure motion. The delegation returned home in glory and the popularity of Vajpayee as the wise national elder who had led India to an international triumph bounded upwards. 'Vajpayee was full of self-confidence in Geneva, he was wonderful,' recalls Khurshid. Khurshid remembers how the Hindujas, the industrialist brothers with whom Vajpayee had a long association, had established contact with Vajpayee in Geneva and invited him to a dinner. Vajpayee was reluctant to accept. 'He asked us repeatedly if we should go for the dinner.' Khurshid agreed to go as they were an all-India delegation and not partisan, and together they attended the Hindujas' dinner. On another occasion, the two went shopping for a doll for Niharika, Vajpayee specifying he wanted to buy a talking doll. 'The shop attendants were most surprised to see two Indian gentlemen searching for a doll,' says Khurshid. On the way back on the Air India flight, Vajpayee and Khurshid sat side by side in first class and Vajpayee, partial to the chotta peg, asked Khurshid, '*Aap kuch piyenge?* [Would you like a drink?]' Khurshid chose a cola and soon dozed off. When Khurshid woke up, he found Vajpayee was missing from his seat. Khurshid looked around and discovered Vajpayee in the bar on the upper deck of the plane, chatting with a group of people. After their return to India, Khurshid went across to Vajpayee's home for press briefings of the trip where *India Today* magazine clicked a photo of Vajpayee and Khurshid in a warm embrace. The magazine used it as a cover picture. 'This photo was used against me in the 1996 election campaign in Farrukhabad,' says Khurshid, 'saying I had sold out to the BJP!' Khurshid lost the election, and when he later told Vajpayee about how the photo may have been the cause of his defeat, Vajpayee burst into loud laughter.[66]

There was another turning point in 1994. One Delhi evening at a large gathering in Delhi's FICCI auditorium, there was much excitement in the air. VIPs entered one by one, first top ministers and then none other than the prime minister. The occasion was the launch of Vajpayee's book *Meri Ekyavan Kavitayen*. After the launch function, admiring groups gathered around the poet-politician, asking for his autograph and requesting him to recite a poem from his book. Rao and Vajpayee chatted cheerfully. Ministers exchanged jokes with Vajpayee. 'This book launch was a turning point for Vajpayee,' recalls Sudhanshu Mittal. 'Everyone, all the VIPs, came across to Vajpayee, they all wanted to talk to him and meet him. He was the centre of attention. Advani stood isolated in another corner, no one went up to him and barely anyone spoke to him.'[67] It was the first glimmer of the end of Vajpayee's decade-long marginalization and a return to the limelight. The book launch of 1994 was a kind of rebirth at the age of seventy, when Vajpayee's Ambassador car would start to edge past Advani's rath. When asked in 1996 why he chose Prime Minister Narasimha Rao to release his book and not someone from his own party, he replied: 'Only because Rao is a litterateur and I wanted to present Rao's literary side.'[68] But his intent was clear: at a time when his party was isolated and ostracized, he wanted to demonstrate his own high standing.

The 1993 election losses were partially recouped with a two-thirds majority win in 1995 in Gujarat and a BJP–Sena alliance government in Maharashtra formed in March 1995. With a year to go for the general elections, this time it would not be Advani but Golwalkar's golden boy who would be the party's spearhead.

~

In November 1995, Advani made a crucial decision. It was a decision that revealed not only his political astuteness but also his sharp appraisal of his own limitations and the direction the party now needed to take. Advani was the face of the mandir movement but he was seen as too hard-line and extreme to attract a broad range of voters or lure allies. A lifelong man of the organization who gave his entire life, like Upadhyaya, to building the BJP, Advani was able to put the party above himself. With general elections a year away, Advani realized that the Congress – defeated the previous year by the TDP in Andhra Pradesh and the Janata Dal in Karnataka – was going into the elections badly weakened. The BJP had made gains but the demolished Babri Masjid millstone hung around its neck. To take another shot at Raisina Hill, Vajpayee, the respectable bridge-builder-poet, the man his rivals had described as 'basically a Congressman', would be invaluable to win over allies and present a non-communal and harmonizing face for the BJP. So Advani decided that it would be Vajpayee who would be the BJP's prime ministerial face for the 1996 Lok Sabha polls.

In September 1995, Vajpayee once again proved how indispensable he had become as the BJP's reconciling elder statesman. In assembly polls in Gujarat in 1995, the BJP scored spectacularly well, winning the state for the first time and gaining its first chief minister there.

But the big win plunged the party into a crisis when the Jana Sangh–era stalwart Shankarsinh Vaghela rebelled against the chief minister installed from Delhi, Keshubhai Patel. Vaghela threatened to break away from the party with forty-seven MLAs, but Vajpayee rushed to the rescue, smoothened feathers, gave a rousing speech and even burst into tears in the Delhi party office. Immediately, others, including party general secretary Venkaiah Naidu, also wept openly, and a reconciliation was achieved and the government saved. 'Vajpayee is a man in whom there is widespread confidence within the party . . . certainly more confidence than in me,' admitted Advani.[69] Vajpayee's stature swelled after his Gujarat success; the individualist iconoclast showed that only he could unite disputatious factions with his disarming emotionalism.

On a bright November afternoon in Mumbai, the BJP began its three-day mahadhiveshan. On the evening of the second day, 12 November 1995, party workers crowded into Shivaji Park to hear the party president's speech. Advani made a game-changing announcement: Atal Bihari Vajpayee would be the BJP's prime ministerial candidate for the Lok Sabha elections of 1996.

The audience was astonished. The BJP had never before declared a prime ministerial candidate. No one was more startled than Vajpayee himself. '*Kya ghoshna kar di aapne, kam se kam mujhse toh baat karte* [How could you announce this? You could at least have first talked to me],' he told Advani. '*Kya aap maante agar hum ne aapse poochha hota?* [Would you have agreed if I had asked you?],' responded Advani.[70] Vajpayee smiled in joy. He had been prime-minister-in-waiting for a long, long time. From being described as a promising politician by Nehru, declared as a potential prime minister in 1980 in Mumbai by M.C. Chagla, to fielding questions about whether he would like to be prime minister during the 1989 elections, the exceptionally clever, ambitious, tenacious, tactical Vajpayee had bided his time for decades, perhaps driven forward by a sense of his manifest destiny that one day his turn would come. For the politician who is a long-distance runner, patience is indeed the mother of all virtues.

For Advani 1996 was a year of scandal and setback, as his name figured in the diaries of two Bhopal-based businessmen allegedly involved in 'hawala' (money laundering) transactions. The 'Jain hawala' scam was called the 'biggest scam of post-Independence India' and Advani's name in it cracked the BJP's moral high ground on corruption. The hawala revelations against Advani were rather fortuitous for Vajpayee. Advani promptly resigned as BJP president and from the Lok Sabha, and announced that he would not contest elections until his name was cleared, which it eventually was. As Advani's arc began to swing downwards, Vajpayee's began to curve upwards. The sudden leaking away of Advani's political capital came as a shot in the arm for Vajpayee. When asked about his own image, he replied, 'The party has nominated me [to contest from Lucknow] . . . The entries [in the Jain diaries] are donations. Suppose I had been on my way to Lucknow to contest the election and Jain had come to me and told me to take Rs 1 lakh. Would I have refused it?'[71] At this he laughed loudly.

The summer general elections of April–May 1996 were described as an 'issue-less' election, in which Chief Election Commissioner T.N. Seshan's stern orders on electioneering took away much of the carnival gaiety and frolic from the campaign. Nevertheless, giant cardboard cut-outs of politicians still sprang up in Tamil Nadu. Camels and elephants sashayed down the streets and a horse decorated with BJP flags and posters trotted along in a procession when Vajpayee went to file his nomination papers in Lucknow. Prime Minister Narasimha Rao campaigned hard, criss-crossing the country alone in his special Air Force plane, aiming for a second term. Vajpayee campaigned energetically too, contesting from both Lucknow and Gandhinagar as state units sent out the message to party headquarters that they would rather have Vajpayee than Advani leading the campaign. It was Vajpayee's face, and not Advani's, which was displayed on posters, banners, badges and TV ads. A poster captioned 'Chunavi Dangal 1996' showed Vajpayee's face with a muscle-ripped wrestler's body, slamming his opponents on to the mat.[72]

Seen as ineffectual during the Gujarat crisis and hit hard by not only the hawala scam, Advani had suffered a setback. In March 1996, he embarked on rath yatra II from Ernakulam to Delhi, accompanied by the usual cries of 'Jai Shri Ram', a yatra that was projected as not ideological, but aimed at personal redemption. Vajpayee was quick to distance himself from this yatra at the outset. 'It is Advani's programme, not the party's. To undertake the trip was his personal decision. He had not consulted the party executive before announcing his decision.'[73]

On the campaign trail Vajpayee kept up his entertaining, crowd-pleasing style, flying across India in an eight-seater Beechcraft plane or driving in a fleet of air-conditioned cars with a pilot jeep clearing the way. Crowds at political rallies, accustomed to politicians' monotonous droning, thrilled to this politician-cum-master-entertainer, full of parables, gags and witticisms, making audiences laugh as he slipped in his broadsides against the Congress. Now shouting, now whispering, with his characteristic head-inclining, gesticulating style, he was the insightful comic, biting yet very funny. 'I was going somewhere when I saw a pit. I asked, where's the road? In the pit, they said. I asked, where's the pit? In the road, they said. A man was riding a scooter on the pit, sorry the road. He kept poking his wife who was sitting behind him. I asked him, why are you doing that. He said he was making sure she had not fallen off.' The crowd roared.

This time Vajpayee the prime-minister-in-waiting had an air of a seen-it-all election veteran, obliging journalists with quiet one-liners. In his speeches, he dwelt on topics ranging from the degradation of politics to Congress corruption and Rao as the 'most corrupt prime minister'; he objected to the hawala allegations and dialled down on Ayodhya, rarely referring to Ram Mandir. He never ended his speeches with the chant 'Jai Shri Ram' as Advani did; instead he gravely informed journalists that 'the BJP's majestic isolation is over'.

Unlike Advani's frenzied non-stop campaigns, Vajpayee set himself a much more comfortable pace, beginning his day at a relaxed

7 a.m. and addressing his last meeting at sunset, secretly relieved at the Election Commission's ban on late-night meetings. After his meetings, back in the plane, he would scour newspaper reports and party briefing notes, often taking journalists along for the ride. Food was very important: whether it was kachoris, sabzi and rasgullas from a roadside dhaba or more elaborate fare at a party worker's home, he ate with gusto, gulping cups of chai and ice-cold cola. He was full of optimism about the results. The BJP grandly declared that if the party got fewer than 200 seats, it would not even stake a claim to forming the government.

In an April 1996 opinion poll, while 29 per cent favoured Rao as prime minister, Vajpayee came a close second with 27 per cent.[74]

Among the cognoscenti, opinion on Vajpayee as prime minister was divided.

'Atal Bihari Vajpayee and Advani are possibly good alternatives as prime ministers, only I wish they were not communal minded,' opined jurist Nani Palkhivala.[75]

'Vajpayee is lazy,' said editor Sham Lal, 'incapable of putting in the 16/17 hours a day the job requires.'[76]

'I have reservations about his party, but Vajpayee is a person of integrity,' asserted author Nirmal Verma.[77]

The 1996 polls produced a hung Parliament. But it was a watershed moment for the BJP. For the first time in history, the Congress lost its dominance and the BJP emerged as the single largest party with 161 seats, the Congress came down to 140. The BJP did not cross the 200-seat mark – in fact the BJP never crossed 200 in Vajpayee's time – nonetheless, emerging as the single largest party was a thrill. A legal debate was ignited about whom the President should invite to form the government – the single largest party, the BJP, or the 'United Front' of a group of parties consisting of the Janata Dal, DMK, TDP, Samajwadi Party and left parties, claiming larger numbers? Legal minds like Nani Palkhivala and H.R. Khanna insisted it was the BJP's right to be invited first.

On 12 May 1996, the BJP met President Shankar Dayal Sharma to make a formal request that Vajpayee be invited to form the government. But there was a delay in the President's call, leading an anxious Vajpayee to nervously joke, 'The would-be prime minister might become the would-have-been prime minister.'[78] On 15 May, victorious from Lucknow and Gandhinagar, the soon-to-be prime minister held a meeting with BJP leaders in his 6 Raisina Road home. Outside, security agencies were at work setting up an emergency security post, as the Intelligence Bureau does for all prime minister designates. At one-forty that afternoon Vajpayee drove out of his home to keep his appointment with the President. The long wait for the politician-poet from Shinde ki Chhawani was about to end.

7

The Man India Awaits: 1996–1999

A poem for Vajpayee:

It was happening, it was real, he was prime minister,
He now had to prove he could rule.
A balancing act and a legacy to foster,
And in government, to create a big talent pool.

In the crescent's light,
His thoughts took flight,
Soaring into the realm of fancy.
Could this political man, this bus-riding man
Shake off the burdens of history?

~

'The President has fed us some laddoos,' exulted Vajpayee on the phone to Advani.[1] President Shankar Dayal Sharma invited him to form the government and he would be prime minister. Decades of Congress failures, insurgencies in Punjab and Kashmir, short-sighted religious politics and the deftly calculating leadership of Advani and

Vajpayee had enabled the BJP to stand forth as the Congress's 'national alternative'. The saffron flag now ascended Raisina Hill. However, the presidential laddoo rapidly crumbled into a ball of ash. Vajpayee took oath on 16 May 1996. But the BJP could not find enough support to form a government. The Ram Mandir party, covered in the blood-red dust of the demolished Babri Masjid, was unable to get allies, and without the numbers needed it could not prove its majority in the House. After just thirteen days in office – the shortest tenure ever for any Indian government – Vajpayee's government fell.

The absurd drama of being the single largest party but being unable to form a government, of being the universally popular Vajpayee but heading such an 'untouchable' party that no one would be his ally, the frustration of such a long odyssey in politics, the slogan '*Agli bari Atal Bihari*' ringing in his ears for years, being so rudely interrupted, echoed in his famous resignation speech in Parliament on 27 and 28 May 1996. It was the most emotional and dramatic resignation speech a prime minister had ever made in Parliament, a sprawling harangue that set the stage for his return.

In India's midsummer, it was a day of hot parliamentary drama. The Lok Sabha was packed to capacity. For the first time the proceedings of a no-confidence vote were to be telecast live. Streets emptied across the country as people gathered in front of TV sets. Debate and accusations raged. The CPI's Indrajit Gupta attacked the prime minister to show exactly why he faced such a trust deficit and why nobody would ally with him. Vajpayee's 'liberal' image was fake, said Gupta:

> Sir, my friend Shri Vajpayee who is a very very old friend of mine and I think we are on very good terms with each other. We have seen one face of him here in this debate. All the media, the Press and everybody have definitely been very much impressed by his sobriety, his calmness, his appeal to everybody, his reasonableness etc. etc. But I regret to say that Shri Vajpayee on occasions also has a very different face. This is the trouble . . . [his speech in Assam] was nothing short of inflammatory . . .[2]

Then came Vajpayee's resignation speech. The thirteen-day-old prime minister delivered colourful theatre, replete with moments of comedy, erudition, taunts, irony and a ringing sense of hurt. Part meltdown, part stump speech, part diatribe, all of it designed for live TV, it was a speech which laid the foundations for a future BJP win and conferred upon Vajpayee the halo of a wronged yet gallant general who deserved to win but didn't because of his petty, scheming rivals. The BJP would exploit this image to the hilt particularly for the next general elections in 1998.

Dressed in a full-sleeved silk kurta and dhoti, Vajpayee was in fighting form, strongly asserting Vajpayeeism. He was no street warrior for Ram, no, he was the nationalist-conservative parliamentarian, with four decades' experience in the House. He drew his political lineage from Mookerji and Nehru; he was the former foreign minister, the former Gandhian socialist, the distinguished Best Parliamentarian. Was he, *he*, really so communal and so unacceptable? Vajpayee said:

> The BJP does not stand for uniformity. We recognize the celebrated Indian plural multi-religious, multi-lingual, multi-ethnic character . . . I have been accused. And these accusations have pierced my heart. I have been accused of being greedy for power. I have been in Parliament for 40 years. Members have seen my behaviour, my character. I will never do anything wrong because of greed for power . . . the refrain is heard, Vajpayee is good, but the party is bad. Now if that's a good thing to say, what do you intend to do about it? What are you going to do for this good man?

He declared grandly: 'If parties are to be broken and opportunistic alliances are to be made just for power, I do not want to even touch power even with a cheemta [tongs].'

He sought the moral high ground: 'Lord Ram has said: *Na bhito marnadasami kevalam dashito yashaha.* I don't fear death, if I fear anything I fear a bad name.'

He became dramatically confessional: 'My 40 years in public life are an open book . . . when the people made the BJP the single largest party, should the people's will be scorned? When the President asked me to form the government and prove my majority by the 31st, should I have run away from the maidan and fled? . . . where is the greed for power here? Where?'

He turned reproachful and accusatory: 'You want to keep us out at all costs. You are talking about the birth of fascist forces . . . I have been in Parliament for 40 years, we are working as a party, on the basis of democracy. We go among people. We fight elections. You have all abused each other but now you want to get together to abuse the BJP. Such moves do not strengthen the health of democracy, I am warning you.'

In a comradely nod to the RSS, he said: 'You can differ with the views of the RSS, but if RSS works among poor and Adivasis, they should be helped. Those who are wise know that the RSS works for the good of the nation.' He quoted the views of H.D. Deve Gowda (now chosen leader of the United Front) on the RSS working for the good of the nation.

He drew a contrast between his own lofty goals and his rivals' small-minded politicking: 'We are willing to sit in the Opposition. Mr Speaker, when I came to politics I never dreamed I would ever be an MP. I was a journalist. And the politics I see today, I have no interest in it. I want to leave politics, but politics does not leave me.'

Classic Vajpayee-speak: addicted to politics, yet always claiming he didn't want it. 'I became an Opposition leader. Today I am prime minister. After a little while I will no longer be prime minister. When I became prime minister it's not as if my heart jumped in happiness . . . even when I leave all this, I will not be too affected.

'And now Mr Speaker,' Vajpayee declared ending his speech, 'I am leaving to give my resignation letter to the President.' With a wave of his hand, and before the Speaker knew what exactly was going on, off he marched towards the exit door.[3]

Indians watched transfixed. A government had crashed to an articulate, emotional death, on live TV. Vajpayee's wounded soul was candidly laid bare. He had tried hard to win sarva sammati (the agreement of all). He had even approached his old friend P.V. Narasimha Rao for support, but everyone (except pre-poll allies Shiv Sena, Haryana Vikas Party and the Samata Party, and post-election supporters, the Akali Dal) turned him down. Rival 'secular' parties had rushed to form the 'United Front' with the express aim of keeping the BJP out. Cut to the quick by that old 'untouchable' tag, he revealed his anguish openly and stagily. The speech was deliberately spun out for maximum impact. Vajpayee stood on the national stage as a targeted, misunderstood and principled leader who would not manufacture a majority by foul means simply to seize power. 'To say the BJP veteran leader stole the show is an understatement,' said the *Indian Express* in an editorial on 29 May. 'He was not merely achieving political martyrdom. He was elevating himself to the role of a folk hero.' The speech became his claim to become prime minister again and the BJP went into battle in the general elections of 1998 and 1999 with the slogan 'Vajpayee, the Man India Awaits'.

Two short-lived United Front governments followed – the first with H.D. Deve Gowda as prime minister, the other headed by I.K. Gujral, both brought down by the Congress withdrawing support. The United Front was a messy experiment, the period marked by intense bickering, conflict and instability. The fractured eleventh Lok Sabha saw three prime ministers sworn in and felled within two years, before Parliament was finally dissolved in December 1997 and by early 1998 India was in the throes of general elections.

The BJP embarked on Mission Vajpayee. In 1996 the party was humiliatingly isolated. Now in 1998 the BJP aggressively and hard-headedly courted allies and pushed towards the moderate centre symbolized by Vajpayee, the universally popular bridge-builder whose wordily ambiguous and lyrical sanatani Hinduism could be skilfully deployed to hew a middle path through the thicket of ideological contradictions.

The BJP was within touching distance of power, and the Man India Awaits was going to leave nothing to chance. 'I will be a decisive prime minister,' said Vajpayee at the start of the campaign, 'and we are a middle-of-the-road party . . . we have adversaries, there are no enemies. The concept of the enemy is against the democratic spirit . . . We are branded communal except when others can't do without us. We were part of SVD governments, the Janata Party, and without us it would not have been possible to defeat Rajiv Gandhi in 1989. Still we are called untouchable.'[4]

From 1996 onward, he had begun to speak more cautiously than before, and his manner had become more reserved. 'People scrutinize every word I say,' he complained. 'I can't go and eat in a dhaba the way I used to or go wandering in a market.'[5] '*Atpata lag raha hai* [I feel awkward],' he said in an interview after the 1996 results. 'We have won the people's trust but it's not a clear verdict . . . rival parties are saying BJP *ko roko* [stop the BJP]. Why roko? Didn't we get a majority? . . . *Main bahut bandha hua anubhav karta hoon* [I feel hemmed in]. I feel like a prisoner. Why so much security? The roads around me are closed, it feels like a hartal. Citizens can't come and meet me, karyakartas can't come near me.'[6]

Attracting allies being the primary goal this time, he forcefully emphasized that the BJP would not take up more temple agitations in Kashi (Varanasi) or Mathura. 'They are not on our agenda. Full stop.'[7] In May 1997, Advani embarked on another yatra, this time named the Swarna Jayanti Yatra. This was no Ram rath yatra hurtling through fired-up crowds but a limousine driving sedately down the middle of the democratic road. Throughout the yatra, Advani praised Gandhi, Nehru, Ram Manohar Lohia, K. Kamaraj, Sardar Patel and Netaji Subhas Chandra Bose, attempting to establish Vajpayee as the inheritor of the founding fathers' mantle.

Vajpayee himself set about putting as much distance between himself and the Ram Mandir agitation as he could. After the Gujral government fell in November, on the day the eleventh Lok Sabha was dissolved, 4 December 1997, Vajpayee was reciting Urdu couplets at the BJP's first all-India conference for Muslim youth. 'The Congress should realize,' he told the crowd , 'that after 110 years, its historical role is coming to an end . . . if Congressmen want to leave a sinking ship . . . [they should] come to a strong ship.'[8]

The BJP, it seemed, had come full circle, not quite back to Gandhian socialism, but back to the Vajpayee line. To those potential allies, terrified by the saffron madmen chanting '*Har Har Mahadev*' and '*Mandir Yahin Banayenge*', Vajpayee sent out the calming message: '*Main hoon na* [I am here].' Yet Vajpayeeism was a bitter pill for sections of the RSS. Before he took oath in 1996, there was talk that while he was the prime ministerial candidate of the BJP, it was Advani who was the prime ministerial candidate of the RSS. The strains in his relationship with the RSS and the Sangh Parivar remained deep. He was still locked in a power tussle with the orthodox and extremist sections of his own party, still the tightrope-walking, middle-of-the-roader Nehruvian individualist. A year after 1996, this gulf would be publicly revealed and make him very angry.

Govindacharya, Advani's close deputy, was the BJP's powerful general secretary at this time, a diehard proponent of the Hindu left or populist ideas which combined Hindutva avidity with anti-corporate, anti-MNC fervour. On 18 September 1997, in a conversation with two British diplomats and a British High Commission staffer, when the diplomats asked Govindacharya to name candidates for the post of BJP president, Govindacharya reportedly gave them a list which did not include Vajpayee. One version of this conversation is that when the diplomats asked why Vajpayee's name was missing, Govindacharya said, 'Vajpayee is our PM candidate and our most popular leader.' Another, and more widespread, version of the conversation is that Govindacharya actually called Vajpayee a mukhauta, or mask. On

6 October, an article written by former *Panchjanya* editor Bhanu Pratap Shukla was published in a number of Hindi newspapers. It was titled '*Vajpayee mukhauta hai: Govindacharya*'. The article reported Govindacharya as saying: 'Vajpayee is not the internal strength of the BJP, merely a mask. A mask is useful only for theatre.'[9] The *Times of India* published a report on this four days later[10] and Vajpayee as 'mukhauta' became a media cause célèbre.

Atal Bihari Vajpayee a mukhauta? A mere mask? Shock waves rippled through the BJP, which has always prided itself on inner-party discipline. Advani immediately telephoned Govindacharya and demanded an explanation. On being told by Govindacharya that he had not used the word 'mask', Advani insisted on a public denial. The British High Commission too sent a denial, saying the article was fabricated, but Shukla stood by his column, refusing to retract it. The mukhauta fracas was an acutely embarrassing public put-down of the BJP's main man from within his own party.

Vajpayee hit back with a powerful force that showed how unsparing he could be with challengers to his authority. Returning from a trip to Bulgaria and hearing about the article, Vajpayee was furious and immediately telephoned RSS pramukh K.S. Sudarshan. Sudarshan summoned Govindacharya to say that Vajpayee had informed him that the conversation in question had been taped. In fact, no such tape existed. Vajpayee wrote infuriated letters to Advani and Govindacharya. To Advani he wrote: 'On returning from my foreign trip I read an interview given by Shri Govindacharya. You must have read it as well. Vijayadashami greetings to you.' Vajpayee asked Govindacharya for an explanation. At a BJP leader's book launch Vajpayee asked loudly, 'I wonder why I have been invited here when I am only a mask?' At a BJP youth convention – from which Govindacharya reportedly exited as soon as Vajpayee began to speak – he cried belligerently: 'It is not the party that makes a prime minister. It is the people who do so.'[11] Vajpayee and Advani acolyte Govindacharya had never had warm relations. In 1992, at a party meeting Vajpayee had asked openly, in a clear reference to Govindacharya's publicly expressed admiration for Advani: 'I have one question for Govindacharya. If you want to honour one leader, is it necessary to denigrate the other?'[12] Behind his rage there was a niggling sense of doubt: was he thought of as nothing more than an ineffectual mask, simply a showpiece at the prow of a ship he neither steered nor really controlled? The old tug of war, that inner-party battle he had fought since the 1965 Jana Sangh Vijayawada session again surfaced. Ideological zealot versus the elected politician was the long bout of kushti (wrestling match) he had been engaged in for many bruising years.

Today, Govindacharya stoutly denies that he used the word 'mukhauta':

> In my conversation with the British High Commissioner I said, 'Vajpayee is our most popular and well-loved face with whom we are certain to win elections . . . The word 'Face' became the word 'chehra' which became the word 'mask'. The word 'mask' does not exist in the British High Commission's minutes of the meeting. I denied it strongly, I wrote a 17-page rebuttal of the report. Yet Vajpayee did not refute the allegation strongly enough in all forums, instead gave evasive answers which strengthened the perception that I had used that word. It showed that he was excessively touchy.[13]

The 'mask' controversy shows Vajpayee's own prickliness about the way the Sangh saw him – his own uncertainty and insecurity about his relationship with the RSS blew the 'mask' incident into a full-blown crisis.

There was no surviving the supremo's wrath. Govindacharya's career in the BJP soon came to an end. Already in 1992 when it had come to light that he, an RSS pracharak, had planned to marry the BJP MP Uma Bharti, eyebrows had been raised and he had been deputed to Tamil Nadu. Now he was systematically sidelined. In 2000 he stepped down as general secretary and embarked on a period of study leave. In the same year when Govindacharya was attending a function of the Swadeshi Jagran Manch, one of the speakers referred to Vajpayee as 'the most *nikamma* [useless] prime minister'. There could be no comeback for Govindacharya any more and in 2003 he resigned from the BJP. 'If anyone needs an example of what a tough politician Vajpayee could be, they need to look at his treatment of Govindacharya,' said Ghatate. 'Vajpayee ran the party, there could be no argument on that.' Acceptance of disagreement was fine, insubordination or any open challenge to Vajpayee's supremacy was not. The 'mask' controversy, coming months before the 1998 polls fought by the BJP on 'The Man India Awaits' plank, was hurriedly buried. The Nehru-idolizing, 'half-Congressman', who often made it clear he preferred the word 'Bharatiyata' to 'Hindutva', was his party's biggest electoral asset, yet for many in his own saffron parivar he was still something of a pariah, too secular and too mainstream for their comfort, not enough of a man of the sangathan (organization). Vajpayee fiercely guarded this careful ambiguity to weld a party in his own image and give it constitutional respectability, notwithstanding his own forays into militant speechifying. His tightrope walk and balancing act was a reflection of what he was – a politician with a laser-sharp focus on his own image and a real sense of how to pursue power.

He was an elected politician, a politician who had won seats with big mandates and placed his status as an elected representative far higher than those in the RSS who had never contested elections. For Vajpayee, those who had proved their electability should be the decision makers in a political party. The cultural missionaries grumbling in their shakhas must not attempt to interfere in politics when they had never fought elections. The nub of his dismissiveness towards the RSS lay here: what did the Hindutva puritans know about fighting for and winning seats? What did they know of being accountable to Parliament?

'When I met Vajpayee subsequently, he was always affable and friendly,' says Govindacharya. 'He offered me tea and samosas. I will always remember him as an *upypukt rajneta* [the perfect politician] who trusted people, which is why people trusted him.'[14]

The 'mukhauta' tag stuck to Vajpayee though. In 2004 the Congress's Jaipal Reddy mocked, 'It is during election time that Vajpayee dusts off his *mukhauta*,' meaning we see Vajpayee's real face in his rabble-rousing speeches during campaigns.[15]

Vajpayee's small circle of close friends, Bhairon Singh Shekhawat, Jaswant Singh and Appa Ghatate among them, were all moderates, Jaswant Singh known for his suspicion of the RSS. It was with them that he would sit to eat his favourite Chinese food, recite poetry or exchange perspectives on his favourite subject of foreign affairs and weighty global matters. 'Vajpayee was an extremely shy person,' revealed Shakti Sinha. 'Shy to the point of being socially awkward. He had a high comfort level with only very few, the closest to him being Appa Ghatate.'[16] Appa was an RSS insider, but he was not a saffron ideologue or a dhoti-clad pracharak. A PhD from the US, often in a jacket and tie and working as an advocate in the Supreme Court, Appa was an urbane and sociable Delhiite. He was also a prolific author and someone who began his legal career as a junior to Nehru's defence minister V.K. Krishna Menon, when Menon worked in the Supreme Court. Ghatate's father, M.N. Ghatate or Babasaheb, had been one of RSS founder Hedgewar's comrades as well as a Hindu Mahasabha leader and was one of Vajpayee's early gurus in the RSS. But Appa himself was no Hindutva activist and it is revealing of Vajpayee's own persona that it was the cosmopolitan and dapper Appa Ghatate and the educated and sophisticated Rajkumari Haksar Kaul who were his best friends for over fifty years.

In 1997 Vajpayee set up a trust in his father's name in a small section of the family's home in Shinde ki Chhawani, aimed at providing education for women and girls. He took great care over the invitations to the inaugural, writing them himself by hand. Ghatate purchased a screen from Delhi's Kerala Emporium to screen off the trust rooms from the rest of the house. Vajpayee contributed one lakh, but wouldn't accept more than Rs 11,000 each from others as donations. Ghatate's wife, Sheila, became a trustee. When the news of the setting up of the trust came out, he was pleased with the caption. 'Trustworthy Vajpayee Forms Trust' said the *Times of India*.

In 1998 he was seventy-four, but set on another shot at elusive Raisina Hill. He yearned to forget about the thirteen-day farce, to take his place among the greats. Hadn't he served Parliament for four decades, and fought election after election since Independence? Hadn't he known and worked with prime ministers from Nehru to Morarji Desai? Fate had chosen him for big things and it was his turn now, the prime ministership was rightfully his.

After 1996 an all-out courting of allies was bringing some successes. The BJP entered into a power-sharing pact with the BSP's Mayawati in Uttar Pradesh. In early 1997 the BJP–Akali Dal alliance swept to power in Punjab. For the 1998 polls, Vajpayee filed his nomination papers from Lucknow in a carefully orchestrated display of secular pluralism. First he offered prayers at a havan, sitting cross-legged in his cream silk kurta before a fire, heavily garlanded and sporting a red tilak. But the Hindu havan was only one part of the programme. After filing his papers, Vajpayee hurried to Lucknow Christian College and released, to enthusiastic applause, an Avadhi translation of the New Testament. That evening, he stepped smilingly into an iftar party, hosted by the Lucknow elite, and munched heartily on samosas. 'My religion is different but my dharma is the same,' he announced grandiloquently.[17]

He shared a personal rapport with the fourth RSS sarsanghchalak, the physics professor from Allahabad University Rajju Bhaiya, who had taken over from Deoras in 1994. But he was quick to draw the red lines: 'It is ridiculous to say that the RSS will remote-control a BJP government,' he declared in interviews. 'The RSS has views of its own. The BJP has views of its own. And the BJP is changing, adjusting to a more real situation.'[18] Echoed Rajju Bhaiya: 'They have their programmes and priorities, we have ours.'

The 1998 campaign took off. Posters, slogans and even hot air balloons bearing the BJP symbol were let off. Vajpayee campaigned hectically across India focusing on the need for healthcare and education in India as his new secular mantra and targeting the United Front as a '*kaheen ka eent kaheen ka roda, Bhanumati ne kunba joda*', a strange collection of odd items. The Ram Mandir and Article 370 were rubbed out from his speeches.[19] The BJP trumpeted its battle cry: 'Vote for a stable government' and 'A stable government and an able prime minister'. 'He [Vajpayee] is not a person who claims leadership by birth or in relationship with any dynasty,' claimed the 1998 BJP manifesto.

When the results were declared in April, India had voted in yet another hung Parliament, the fourth since 1989. The BJP, however, showed a spectacular rise, jumping to 182 seats (from 161 in 1996), its vote share crossing 25 per cent for the first time and almost equal to that of the Congress, which tumbled to 141 seats, the United Front falling to eighty-six. For the first time, the BJP won seats in Tamil Nadu, West Bengal and Assam. In a rebuff of its 'Brahmin–Bania' image, the BJP won twenty-four SC and fourteen ST seats and galloped through Uttar Pradesh, scooping up fifty-seven out of eighty-five seats. Vajpayee came roaring in from Lucknow.

The BJP-led front with its allies was established as the principal pole of Indian politics. The Congress increasingly looked like a party in seemingly terminal decline, trapped in leadership wars and factionalism. The vacuum created by a faltering Congress was filled in by a resurgent BJP.

In sharp contrast to the BJP's ostracism in 1996, now half a dozen parties lined up to ally with Vajpayee's party. Vajpayee's 7 Safdarjung Road home – which he had moved into as leader of the Opposition – began to buzz with activity. The victorious Good Man held court, unleashing a steady stream of wisecracks and keeping his guests supplied with samosas, jalebis and cups of tea. Where in 1996 only four parties had joined hands with the BJP, now a thirteen-party NDA – or National Democratic Alliance (so named by Advani) – took shape, with allies ranging from the AIADMK to the newly formed Odisha party Biju Janata Dal (BJD). The TDP pledged outside support. Just two years earlier, the TDP's Chandrababu Naidu and the BJD's father figure, Biju Patnaik, had pushed for a non-Congress, non-BJP United Front. Now, Naidu and Bijubabu's son Naveen Patnaik happily switched sides. 'Vajpayeeji's charming persona was the only reason to be attracted to the BJP,' the genteel anglophile Naveen would remark later. In 1998 the 'untouchable' party of just two years ago enjoyed untouched leadership.

The BJP created a Common Minimum Programme – later called the National Agenda for Governance – with which it would negotiate with its allies. In it, issues repellent to the allies, such as the Uniform Civil Code, construction of the Ram Mandir in Ayodhya and repeal of Article 370, were left out. The triumphalist war cries of the Ram Mandir were firmly muzzled. Vajpayee had already reassuringly declared during the campaign that no law would be brought in to build the mandir. Instead he said, 'We will resolve the issue through dialogue – the same way we resolved the Azadari dispute between the Shias and Sunnis of Lucknow. A law will not be needed.'[20] The sun set on Ayodhya and rose over the grounds of Rashtrapati Bhavan.

On the morning of Thursday, 19 March 1998, in the forecourt of Rashtrapati Bhavan with the presidential palace steps stretching behind him, Vajpayee stepped up in white dhoti, beige kurta and raw silk jacket. He took oath as prime minister for the second time.

~

'When we formed the government in 1998 we knew there was no alternative to our alliance,' Vajpayee later recalled, 'but problems came from our own camp, not from outside . . . I was, to some extent, affected by my experience as a thirteen-day prime minister, yes, I used to worry a lot.'[21] He had reason to worry.

To form the government Vajpayee was dependent on two

unpredictable allies: Mamata Banerjee and her seven MPs from Bengal and the formidable Jayalalithaa and her eighteen MPs from Tamil Nadu. President Kocheril Raman Narayanan delayed for ten days his invitation to Vajpayee to form the government, and when he did so he demanded letters of support from allies, which the BJP could not present in time. The time lag allowed J. Jayalalithaa to set stiff conditions for her backing, including appointment of her chosen nominee, Subramanian Swamy, a long-time Vajpayee baiter, as finance minister. When this was turned down, she set other conditions, keeping the BJP hanging for almost two weeks. Vajpayee's buddy Jaswant Singh rushed to Chennai to build bridges with the prized Tamil Nadu ally and she was eventually won over, but the thirteen-party government rested on a parchment-thin majority in a deeply divided Lok Sabha.

The saffron parivar's attitude to Vajpayee was almost as unpredictable as that of his allies. The night before the swearing-in, as Vajpayee sat quietly at home with his family, reading and chatting as he prepared for his oath-taking, came another reminder of the hidden presences around the prime ministerial chair. In Advani's Pandara Park residence that evening, Advani and his aides began to telephone all those who had been selected as ministers, and who would be taking oath with Vajpayee. In the list were former military man and deputy leader of the BJP parliamentary party 'Major sahib' Jaswant Singh, who, implicitly trusted by Vajpayee, had been finance minister in Vajpayee's thirteen-day government, and Pramod Mahajan. Many had raised objections about both Singh and Mahajan, particularly because in 1998 Singh had lost from Chittorgarh, the seat he had won in both 1991 and 1996, and Mahajan had lost from Mumbai North-East. But Vajpayee held firm and both Jaswant Singh's and Mahajan's names were sent to Rashtrapati Bhavan on the evening before the swearing-in.

As the evening wore on, a slight, bespectacled figure appeared out of the darkness of the night. Vajpayee had a surprise visitor. He was an unassuming figure but had a bright, fixed gaze: it was the RSS leader

K.S. Sudarshan. Sudarshan sat with Vajpayee for about twenty minutes, then quickly took his leave. Within seconds Vajpayee telephoned Shakti Sinha asking him to return to Vajpayee's home. 'I went back to his house that night, and retyped the list of ministers,' recalled Sinha.[22] The list was resent at the last minute to the President's secretary Gopal Gandhi. The RSS had laid down the law to Vajpayee: those who had lost the elections could not be included in the cabinet. In the final list, Jaswant Singh and Pramod Mahajan had both been dropped.

'Vajpayee would never stick his neck out for anyone,' recalls Sudhanshu Mittal, 'and he didn't stick his neck out for either Jaswant Singh or Pramod Mahajan. He did not fight for them.' Singh and Mahajan were free-market-inclined, worldly-wise 'Vajpayee men'. The aristocratic, English-speaking Jaswant Singh was at this time perceived as backed by industrialists of the 'Bombay Club'. Mahajan was the flashy tech whiz who flaunted his big-money Mumbai connections. The sangh regarded both with disapproval, seeing them as enemies of the Hindu left's swadeshi orientation and the diametrical opposites of the sangh's chappal-and-crumpled-dhoti-kurta-clad cadres.

Vajpayee gave in to Sudarshan that night, but the Vajpayee style was as outwardly conciliatory as it was manipulative, a style he would use to good effect in his years in government when his differences with the RSS began to mount. He bowed to Sudarshan's wishes before the swearing-in, anxious that it should go off without a hitch, but once his government was installed, he appointed Jaswant Singh as deputy chairman of the Planning Commission and brought in Pramod Mahajan as political adviser. Jaswant Singh believed that Vajpayee would have fought against his 1998 exclusion if Advani had backed him. 'Vajpayee was keen to appoint me, but Advani did not support me. He stayed silent and put the blame on the Sangh Parivar, when Vajpayee wanted to fight them on my candidature.'[23] The late-night wrangling over appointments, the seeming helplessness of both Vajpayee and Advani faced with RSS diktat, did not bode well for the prime minister's ability to exert his authority with autonomy.

The new government won a crucial confidence vote on 28 March but it was balanced on a knife edge. Jayalalithaa was all too aware that the government could not survive without her. Vajpayee was at pains to sound as if he was fully in control: 'As long as I am Prime Minister and my government is there, the National Agenda of Governance will not be diluted . . . the RSS's decisions are not imposed on us,' he said bravely.[24] Memories of the thirteen-day disaster still fresh, Prime Minister Vajpayee could not afford to fall again. He needed a show of strength, not only for its allies and voters but also to command world attention. A bold signal was necessary, a big bang.

Over two decades ago, another beleaguered government had had the same idea. In 1974 Indira Gandhi, cornered by mass protests, failed monsoons and a massive strike by railway unions, had ordered the testing of nuclear weapons at Pokhran. Conducted on Buddha Jayanti day, the tests were code-named 'Smiling Buddha'. Now, another shaky, firefighting government, hamstrung by moody allies, and a testy party organization, again tested nuclear weapons. Two months after Vajpayee took office, between 11 and 13 May, the Buddha smiled for the second time. Vajpayee's nuclear tests were named Pokhran II.

After a long period of political uncertainty and petty squabbling, an escape into a grand narrative was needed so that trifling everyday disagreements paled into insignificance, so that grander vistas opened up, in this case a giant mushroom cloud. Besides, if this precarious government also fell and a mid-term poll arrived, the tests would give the BJP an election advantage.

Atomic weapons had always been part of the Jana Sangh's ideology. In a 1964 speech in Parliament on what India's response should be to a Chinese atom bomb, Vajpayee had strongly argued, 'Do not talk of morality, non-violence and Gandhiji . . . The Government must acquire the weapon that can save the country . . . I want the government to seriously consider manufacturing the atom bomb.'[25]

Yet as Vajpayee ordered Pokhran II, he could not have forgotten his own poem *'Hiroshima ki Peeda'* ('The Agony of Hiroshima'), which he had composed a long time ago.

Kisi raat ko
Meri neend achanak uchat jati hai,
Aankh khul jati hai,
Main sochne lagta hun ki
Jin vyagyanik ne anu astron ka aavishkar kiya tha:
Ve Hiroshima-Nagasaki ke bheeshan narsanhar ke samachar sunkar,
Raat ko soye kaise honge?

Sometimes at night,
Suddenly, sleep deserts me,
My eyes open,
I begin to ponder –
Those scientists who invented nuclear weapons: On hearing of the gruesome human destruction,
Of Hiroshima and Nagasaki,
How did they ever sleep at night?[26]

Poet and politician facilitated each other in Vajpayee's persona; agonies about nuclear wars and the necessity of testing nuclear weapons both came from political impulses, each with its own poetic logic. In an interview two years later, hitting back at a question about whether he was too 'soft' and 'weak', he said: 'Do you think the decision to go nuclear and to test nuclear weapons was not a difficult decision? But I took that decision. I knew what was coming. I knew there would be attempts to isolate India, that there will be economic sanctions. I took a bold decision.'[27]

Three prime ministers before Vajpayee – P.V. Narasimha Rao, Deve Gowda and I.K. Gujral – had considered the nuclear option but had rejected it for fear of America's wrath and economic sanctions. But Vajpayee, demoralized and fatigued, irritated at RSS pressures on him and often at a loss over his unwieldy coalition, with rumours spreading that he was ready to resign, badly needed a shot of political adrenalin. The tests produced an immediate image shift: a 'tired' prime minister became a 'bold' prime minister. He was now a decisive strongman and nationalism spiked to a 'Viagra high'. The so-called Hindu nationalist bomb silenced, for a while at least, the restive cadres in the RSS.

Internationally, there were immediate and negative consequences. The world community recoiled in anger and shock. India had successfully kept the tests a complete secret. The Clinton Administration declared it was 'deeply disappointed' at India's actions. Britain expressed its 'dismay'. UN chief Kofi Annan declared his 'deep regret'. Pakistan cried out about a subcontinental arms race and the US clamped a range of trade sanctions on India. The World Bank indefinitely postponed promised loans of over $850 million.

A year later in Parliament Vajpayee hit out at his critics:

> I was in Parliament in 1974 when Indira Gandhi conducted nuclear tests, we welcomed them even though we were in the Opposition. Because it was about the country's security . . . Do we not have a right to be *atmanirbhar* [self-reliant] in matters of defence? . . . Pokhran II was not to show off . . . *purusharth ki prakatikaran ke liye nahi tha* [it was not just to show off our efforts] . . . We must have a minimum credible deterrence . . . But let me make it clear, we will not use nuclear weapons first. No first use. We will not use these weapons against those who do not have them . . . we have conducted these tests to *prevent* war.[28]

In this speech, made a year after taking office, after the Kargil war, after it was evident that the tests had clearly failed to prevent Pakistani aggression, and also after the US's economic sanctions had taken their toll on India, he sounded rattled and self-justifying. Pokhran II created a patriotic surge, but did not in the end stave off serious challenges to the Vajpayee government through 1998 and well into 1999.

On Independence Day 1998 he appeared on the ramparts of the Red Fort, the karta-dharta of the nationalist Indian family, but under pressure from trade sanctions on India and threatening noises from ally Jayalalithaa. He reached for higher ground by linking himself to the prime ministers who came before him. 'Lal Bahadur Shastri said Jai Jawan Jai Kisan . . . I have added a new aspect to this "Jai Vigyan" . . . I have never compromised on principles in pursuit of power and I will never do it. Being in and out of power is the same for me.'[29]

He recited his own verse '*Raah Kaunsi Jaun Main*' ('What Road Should I Go Down?')

Chauraahe par luttaa cheer,
Pyaade se pit gaya vazeer,
Chalun aakhiri chaal, ki baazi chhod virakti rachaun main
Raah kaunsi jaun main?

Honour lost at busy crossroads,
Knights defeated by pawns:
Do I make my final move, or do I withdraw from battle?
What road should I go down?[30]

He ended the speech on a fighting note, reciting his famous lines:

Haar nahin manoonga,
raar nahin thanunga.
Kaal ke kapaal par likhta-mitata hoon
geet naya gaata hoon.

I will not give in,
I will wage a new fight.
On time's brow I write and erase as I go along,
I sing a new song.[31]

He had little to sing about at this time. At around the same time as bombs went off in Pokhran, another explosion was gathering steam, this time not underground but in public view in Tamil Nadu. Jayalalithaa began to present him with a list of demands for her continued support. Jaswant Singh had been pressed into service to reassure Jayalalithaa, but she was firm about her conditions: all cases against her must be withdrawn and the Karunanidhi government in Tamil Nadu must be dismissed forthwith. Throughout 1998 the tug of war continued – a constant reminder to Vajpayee that his government was on a short fuse.

Internationally there was trouble for Vajpayee. Clinton was furious at India's nuclear tests, and relations between India and the US took a nosedive. To find an entry into talks with America, Jaswant Singh turned to his old friend, the former *TIME* magazine journalist Strobe Talbott, who was deputy secretary of state in the Clinton Administration. Singh and Talbott began a wide-ranging series of talks, within a month of India's nuclear tests, with Singh trying to soften US attitudes and explain why India had decided to conduct the tests. The closed-door dialogue between Jaswant Singh and Talbott was conducted over two years, the two meeting '14 times in 10 locations in 7 countries on three continents', and became the basis for opening of doors to a new phase of US–India ties.[32]

Talbott in his memoirs describes Vajpayee as the most silent politician he had ever met. 'Vajpayee's pauses seem to last forever . . . I had never met a politician so laconic.' Vajpayee's instructions to Jaswant were clear. 'He [Jaswant],' writes Talbott, 'was under instructions from Vajpayee to serve as a discreet and, if necessary, secret channel to Washington to be used for anything sensitive that the US leadership wished to convey to the prime minister.'[33] Talbott's brief was to get Jaswant Singh to use his influence to get India to sign the Comprehensive Nuclear-Test-Ban Treaty (CTBT), but when India refused to sign, the talks petered out. The Jaswant–Talbott talks failed to deliver for the US but still contributed to friendly atmospherics when Clinton visited India in March 2000. But now in the immediate aftermath of Pokhran II, with US disapproval glaring down on India, with trade sanctions biting, there was pressure building globally on the Vajpayee government to make peace with Pakistan. And he did so spectacularly.

~

Saturday, 20 February 1999 was a crisp and sunlit winter day in Delhi. It was a day when a gleaming deep-gold-coloured luxury coach, with the Indian and Pakistani flags and the name of the bus – Sada-e-Sarhad (Call of the Frontier) – painted on its front, rolled towards the border between India and Pakistan. Slowly, it drove towards the Radcliffe Line, that blood-drenched line drawn by retreating British imperialists in 1947 which separated the mortal enemies who had fought three wars. In the bus sat India's Prime Minister Vajpayee and twenty-five chosen celebrities, from actors Dev Anand and Shatrughan Sinha to cricketer Kapil Dev, sculptor Satish Gujral, lyricist Javed Akhtar, danseuse Mallika Sarabhai and Akali Dal leader Prakash Singh Badal. Vajpayee was crossing into Pakistan on a bus. He was inaugurating the Delhi–Lahore bus service, on the invitation of Pakistan Prime Minister Nawaz Sharif. A prime minister from a Hindu nationalist party, head of a government that had just tested nuclear weapons, was journeying towards his Muslim counterpart, the head of a government of an Islamic republic, which had also recently tested the atomic bomb.

It was an act of assertive risk-taking Vajpayeeism, part of the long arc of subcontinental 'Nehruvian' peacemaking he had begun as Janata foreign minister. In November 1998 the BJP had been badly routed in assembly elections. The Congress swept to a record win in Delhi, bringing Sheila Dikshit to power as chief minister; it retained power in Madhya Pradesh, with fifty-one-year-old Digvijay Singh at the helm; and it streaked to a two-thirds majority in Rajasthan, Ashok Gehlot felling BJP stalwart and Vajpayee's friend Bhairon Singh Shekhawat.

The BJP was taken aback by the defeats, and sangh hardliners again fumed that it was an overdose of 'Vajpayee-type secularism' and departure from Hindutva dogma which was damaging the party and alienating its core supporters. Sections of the sangh even grumbled it was time to set up another Jana Sangh. In December 1998 the RSS affiliate the Swadeshi Jagran Manch held a dharna against Vajpayee in Delhi, shouting out its objections to reforms in the insurance sector. It was BJP vs BJP, as swadeshi stormtrooper Uma Bharti, minister of state in Human Resource Development (HRD), and RSS ideologue and trade unionist Dattopant Thengadi, fire breather of the Swadeshi campaign, vowed to oppose Vajpayee's reformist moves in the economy. Vajpayee had already clearly spelt out his economic agenda before becoming prime minister in 1998. 'We are for the acceleration of reforms in the true sense of the word. We criticised the Congress [about] the lack of conviction on the part of the "reformers" and the direction of the reforms. There can be no going back to the days of licence-quota raj. There are still large areas in need of de-bureaucratization, especially at the state level.'[34]

As prime minister, Vajpayee was set on getting his way. The hand-wringing BJP party president Kushabhau Thakre was summoned and given an earful from the PMO about government being supreme over party. Thakre was warned about those making noises against Vajpayee and instructed to ensure the party fully backed the government on the economy. 'We are elected representatives of the people,' Vajpayee said impatiently. 'We are accountable in Parliament. Decisions have to be taken by us.'[35] The *elected representative of the people* – this was Vajpayee's argument clincher with his party radicals.

Under siege from both the saffron brotherhood and his allies – and troubled by the election losses – Vajpayee knew it was time again for a narrative-setting moment.

Setting off for Pakistan from Delhi early on 20 February 1999, Vajpayee was in a state of excitement and also a little nervous. So much so that ten minutes into the ride to the airport, he suddenly turned to Shakti Sinha to say, '*Hearing aid chhoot gaya*.' He had forgotten his hearing aid at home, without which the seventy-five-year-old was almost completely unable to hear. The prime minister's motorcade travels fast, speeding through traffic lights without stopping, and to turn it around is impossible. Another car was quickly dispatched to fetch the hearing aid, resulting in a few minutes' delay in the flight to Amritsar, where Vajpayee would board the bus to Pakistan.

Awaiting Vajpayee's arrival in Amritsar's Raja Sansi airport was the golden-hued Sada-e-Sarhad. A military band struck up '*Saare Jahan se Achcha*' as Vajpayee landed. Stepping off the plane, Vajpayee boarded and off drove the bus towards the Wagah border post. 'Balle balle,' shouted bhangra dancers leaping in front of the bus. Schoolchildren waved flags. Even BJP president Kushabhau Thakre was at Wagah to wish the prime minister. Vajpayee kept waving to the crowds as the bus arrived at the border post. Slowly, the bus headed for the iron gates that separated India and Pakistan. Masses of officials stood gathered on both sides of the border. On either side of the gates, military and police bands struck up tunes. The Pakistan Rangers' musical band belted out such catchy tunes that people on the Indian side danced to their beat. As the bus reached the gates, India's Border Security Force and the Pakistani Rangers rose up in coordinated goose-steps, throwing open the two gates in unison. The gates opened, the bus pulled through, and in thirty seconds India's prime minister had entered Pakistan. For the first time ever, an Indian premier had travelled by road to Pakistan. The bus stopped in Wagah. Out stepped Vajpayee, watching his steps, yet endlessly smiling, caught up in this date with history.

As he alighted, Pakistan Prime Minister Nawaz Sharif stood waiting on the red carpet. They embraced, and shook hands vigorously. A twenty-one-gun salute boomed. Crowds of journalists on both sides watched, their dispatches rocketing out to the world. Here, in the golden winter sunlight of the northern subcontinent, a little after 4 p.m., India and Pakistan were making peace in the biggest act of détente since 1947. 'It is with a sense of elation that I find myself on

Pakistani soil after twenty-one years,' gushed Vajpayee. 'I bring the goodwill and hopes of my fellow Indians who seek abiding peace and harmony with Pakistan. I'm looking forward to a substantive programme and talks with Prime Minister Nawaz Sharif. I'm conscious that this is a defining moment in South Asian history and I hope we will be able to rise to the challenge.' Dev Anand, returning to Lahore, the city of his student days, was overcome with emotion. 'It has been too long a wait. This is the moment of the century.'[36]

The idea for the bus journey had not been begun as a grand plan but had fallen into place bit by bit. In July 1998 Vajpayee and Nawaz Sharif had met in Colombo, shaking hands stiffly, making no progress in talks. The mood lifted considerably in September 1998, when they met in New York during the UN General Assembly session and Vajpayee hosted Sharif for lunch. Vajpayee served his Pakistani guest a deliciously elaborate five-course Mughlai and Punjabi meal, the highlight being a masala lobster curry. The UN General Assembly sessions were Vajpayee's stamping grounds; he had attended them regularly since 1988 and loved being there. Away from excoriating domestic politics, in New York he reverted to his smiling, gregarious self, unlike the withdrawn, grim visage he wore at home, catching up with old friends like Israeli Prime Minister Benjamin Netanyahu and others.

As Vajpayee and Sharif warmed to each other, both speaking in fluent Hindustani, Vajpayee said to Sharif, '*Arre sahab, jhagde ki baat hi kahan hai? Hum to apki cheeni kha rahein hain. Bahut meethi hai* [Where's the question of a quarrel? I am eating your sugar – a reference to Pakistan's sugar imports to India].'[37] Sharif for his part nostalgically recalled his visit to India in 1982, when he, with a known fondness for fast cars, drove his own car to Delhi to watch the Asian Games. There was talk at that time of establishing a highway link and a regular bus service between the two countries.

In early 1999, in an interview to *Indian Express* editor Shekhar Gupta, Sharif said, 'Vajpayee is an extremely decent man,' and invited him to Pakistan, promising to show him a hospitality 'so great the people will not forget it for a long time . . . I will even be happy to go back with him . . . we will solve 50% of our problems, make 50% progress on all issues on the way.'[38] Before the interview, Sharif had told Gupta that he would be extending this invitation on condition that he didn't lose face and wasn't rebuffed. Gupta had conveyed this to Vajpayee and had received a yes to Sharif's invite. On the morning that the interview was published, Vajpayee landed in his constituency, Lucknow. When the press asked about Sharif's invitation he said, 'Yes, I would like to have a bus ride to Pakistan.' 'By accepting Sharif's invitation immediately and open-heartedly, Vajpayee left no space for the hesitations of the MEA [Ministry of External Affairs] and diplomats to come in,' recalls Gupta.[39]

But in Pakistan, passions were aroused and the hard-line Jamaat-e-Islami made threatening sounds. The Pakistan authorities told the Indian side that once Vajpayee arrived in Pakistan, it would not be safe for him to travel all the way to Lahore by bus, and so from Wagah Vajpayee left the bus and travelled to Lahore by helicopter. As the helicopter carrying Vajpayee and Sharif lifted off for Lahore, multicoloured kites shot into the air, dancing airborne escorts for the two peacemakers.

In Lahore, Sharif had arranged a grand official banquet at Lahore Fort. He had spared no effort and had personally supervised the arrangements. At the banquet Sharif recited Vajpayee's line '*Jung naa hone denge*' (We will not let war happen). In the magnificent Diwan-i-Khas in the Lahore Fort bedecked with lights, the mood was festive but outside it was belligerent. The Jamaat, with a strong presence in Lahore, was bitterly opposed to the visit of the Hindu nationalist Vajpayee. It had called a hartal that day, and across Lahore traders downed shutters. The veteran journalist Kuldip Nayar, who had been sitting behind Vajpayee on the bus, recalls that Vajpayee had entered Pakistan as a worried man. 'He beckoned to me and informed me that he had received news about the killing of 26 Hindus by militants in Jammu.

He was anguished and wondered whether there was any use in further talks.' Nayar tried to reassure him by saying that the militants were only desperate to stall the talks, but Vajpayee said he was unsure how Indians would react to his visiting Pakistan after these killings.[40] In Lahore, Jamaat cadres attempted to block Vajpayee's convoy. Jamaatis swarmed around the fort and pelted stones at some diplomats' cars. Some held up banners saying 'Vajpayee go back'. 'Don't worry about this,' Vajpayee reportedly told Nawaz Sharif, with whom his rapport was growing warmer by the minute, 'these things happen everywhere.' In spite of the protests, the visitor was charmed.

Vajpayee had come bearing gifts: shawls for Kulsoom Nawaz and CDs of Hindi film classics like *Pakeezah* and *Mughal-e-Azam* for his counterpart. Ghatate recalls how before his trip Vajpayee had asked Brajesh Mishra what he should say. 'Read your poem "*Jung Naa Hone Denge*",' advised Mishra. So Vajpayee did. But first, on the morning of 21 February, throwing protocol to the winds, and against the advice of the foreign ministry, in an unprecedented move, Vajpayee visited the Minar-e-Pakistan in Lahore.

This seventy-metre-tall tower was built at the site where, in 1940, the All India Muslim League called for a separate homeland for India's Muslims. For Vajpayee, member of a party which has always rejected Partition and called for an 'Akhand Bharat' or undivided India, to visit a monument to a separate Muslim nationhood and to the two-nation theory, was decidedly out of the diplomatic box. Not only did Vajpayee visit the Minar-e-Pakistan, but he wrote in the visitor's book there, 'A strong, stable and prosperous Pakistan is in India's interest. Let no one in Pakistan be in doubt. India sincerely wishes Pakistan well.'[41] At the glittering Governor's reception that evening, he would enthral the Pakistani elite by saying:

> When I go back home some people in my party will say that by going to the Minar-e-Pakistan I have placed my mohar on Pakistan. *Kya Pakistan meri mohar se chalta hai? Pakistan ki apni mohar hai, aur woh*

chal raha hai [Does Pakistan need my seal of consent? Pakistan has its own seal and it works]. Suspicions are so deep . . . Pakistan is a reality, we want it to grow and thrive . . . there has been so much enmity, let's give friendship an opportunity . . . In these 24 hours I feel the distance between Delhi and Lahore has become a little less . . . we must bring all of Pakistan and India closer.

He quoted from his poem '*Jung Naa Hone Denge*'.[42]

Jung naa hone denge!
Vishva shanti ke hum saadhak hain,
Jung naa hone denge!
. . . Kafan bechne vaalon ko kah do chilla kar,
Duniya jaan gayi hai unka asli chehra, kamyaab ho unki chaalen, dhang naa hone denge.
Jung naa hone denge.

We shall not allow war!
We are devoted to peace
We shall not allow war!
. . . To those who sell shrouds we must say,
We have seen through your game, you will not succeed.
We shall not allow war.[43]

The audience leapt to its feet in a standing ovation. Vajpayee was in his element, the heady atmosphere infusing him with a new energy. He began to recite the beautiful lines of poet Ali Sardar Jafri:

Tum aao gulshan-e-Lahore se chaman bardosh,
Hum aayen subh-e-Benaras ki roshni lekar,
Himalaya ki havaon ki taazgi lekar,
Phir uske baad yeh poochein ke kaun dushman hai.

You come from the gardens of Lahore laden with flowers,
We come bringing the light of a Banaras morning,
The fresh breezes from the Himalayas,
And then together let us ask, who is the enemy.[44]

As the silver-haired peacemaker recited, guests wiped away tears.

He loved every minute of his visit. He was on a high, eager to make history, carried away by his own role in demolishing decades of mistrust. He had always believed he was a man of destiny, that doors had opened for him for a reason, and now here in Pakistan a bubbling self-confidence took over. He was a rider on the bus, and a rider on the crest of a wave soaring towards certain peace. The high-emotion summit ended with the Lahore Declaration of 21 February 1999, emphasizing the need for people-to-people contacts and the need to avoid the use of nuclear weapons.

But the romanticism of Lahore was soon revealed as a shimmering mirage, an illusion that floated seductively over the harsh, bloody realities of the continuing clash of Indian and Pakistani nationalisms. As Vajpayee headed back to Delhi from Lahore and made plans to announce his peace deal to his voters, another man was already executing a very different plan which had been in the works since the middle of January 1999. This man was Pakistan Army Chief Pervez Musharraf. As Vajpayee flew back to Delhi, Musharraf too boarded a helicopter. In an act of personal 'daring', he flew along the Line of Control (LoC)[45] to meet his troops. Musharraf was here to tell his soldiers that the Lahore Declaration between Sharif and Vajpayee did not mean very much. It was still full speed ahead for Operation Badr, also called Operation Koh-e-Paima. Operation Kargil.

~

On his return from Lahore, applause for Vajpayee rang out, at home and around the world. The world's press paid glowing tribute to the audacious act of peacemaking in the shadow of nuclear tests, and

Vajpayee revelled in the accolades. But his political rivals were waiting to strike.

In January and February 1999, in Bihar, the Ranvir Sena – an armed upper-caste militia – swooped down on Dalit communities in Shankarbigha and Narayanpur in Bihar and slaughtered over forty Dalits, including women and children. The chief minister of the state at this time was Bihar people's idol Lalu Prasad Yadav's wife, Rabri Devi. In an astoundingly unconstitutional act, Lalu Yadav had simply installed her as chief minister after he was forced to resign on corruption charges. The Vajpayee-led government loudly lamented the collapse of law and order in Bihar over the Shankarbigha and Narayanpur killings, and Advani as home minister decided to move for dismissal of the Bihar government. On 12 February, while Vajpayee was abroad attending the G15 summit in Jamaica, the Rabri Devi government was dismissed and President's Rule imposed on Bihar. The dismissal of an elected government was a fundamental overthrow of Vajpayee's own long record of robustly opposing central takeovers of state governments seen in the way the Congress repeatedly imposed President's Rule on states. He had stormed in Parliament against the dismissal of BJP governments after the Babri Masjid demolition. As far back as in 1959, he had protested vociferously against the dismissal of the Kerala government, and in 1967 he had raged about President's Rule in Rajasthan. And now the same Vajpayee, ferocious fighter against the Congress's use of Article 356, had unhesitatingly deployed the same weapon he had criticized so vehemently.

The dismissal of the Bihar government caused pandemonium in Parliament. The Congress voted against the proclamation (dismissing the Bihar government), and since the Vajpayee government did not have a majority in the Rajya Sabha, the dismissal order could not pass in Parliament. In a big embarrassment to Vajpayee, the dismissal order was revoked and Rabri Devi was again sworn in as chief minister in March 1999. Fresh from the triumph in Pakistan, Vajpayee was disgraced over Bihar. In Pakistan his reconciling nature had won the day. But on Bihar he damaged his own image by allowing himself to be led by the demands of his Samata Party allies – George Fernandes and Nitish Kumar – who wanted the Lalu–Rabri dispensation fired.

Keeping the precarious thirteen-party coalition going was proving to be almost impossible. The restless Jayalalithaa, egged on by her associate Subramanian Swamy (dubbed the 'one-man demolition squad' against the Vajpayee government), began to play hardball. She was angry that the Vajpayee government was not meeting her demand for the dismissal of the Karunanidhi government. Swamy's intense dislike for Vajpayee led him to stitch an uneasy alliance between the AIADMK and the Congress leadership. On 29 March Jayalalithaa met Sonia Gandhi at a much-publicized tea party at Delhi's Ashoka Hotel to give out the impression that she may switch sides any time. Jayalalithaa had several demands, apart from immediate dismissal of the Karunanidhi government. She also wanted the reinstatement of Navy Chief Vishnu Bhagwat, who had been sacked in December 1998 for allegedly defying the government. All attempts to mollify Jayalalithaa failed. On 14 April she sailed up to Rashtrapati Bhavan and handed President K.R. Narayanan a letter stating that she and her block of eighteen MPs were withdrawing support to the Vajpayee government. Once again, Vajpayee's government toppled.

Its majority lost, the President asked Vajpayee to prove his majority in the House. Three days later, on 17 April 1999, came the most famous no-confidence motion in the history of the Indian Parliament. Vajpayee launched another impassioned tirade: 'I sometimes wonder, as there was no issue, was the fact that we were doing everything possible to make India strong . . . that the government was sought to be brought down?' His well-networked crisis manager Pramod Mahajan was pressed into action once again. Armed with the latest model of cell phones, Mahajan tried to persuade a range of parties, from Mayawati's BSP to even a section of the Congress, to back Vajpayee in this hour of crisis. Mahajan was confident that he could get a large group of disgruntled Congress MPs who didn't want fresh elections to switch sides at the last moment. 'We worked the phone lines till the last minute before the vote, a number of individuals were ready to support Vajpayee but were too scared to go against the party line,' Mahajan recalled later.

The vote brought numbing anguish. Vajpayee was defeated by one vote, a single vote – 269 to 270 – the single clinching vote being that of Orissa Chief Minister Giridhar Gamang, who voted even though propriety demanded that he quit his Parliament membership once he had become a state chief minister. A government that had tested a nuclear bomb and made historic, globally visible peace with Pakistan was defeated by one measly vote. After dreams of rosy dawns came enveloping darkness. Vajpayee was shattered. Sitting in his office in Parliament, his face ashen and his eyes moist, he kept repeating, 'One vote. We lost by one vote.' The Nationalist Congress Party leader Praful Patel recalls how hard the Vajpayee government worked in the days before the vote, talking to all parties to somehow save the government. 'They spoke to all of us, every party was approached,' recalls Patel.[46] Patel points out it was not just Gamang's vote, but Mayawati's last-minute betrayal that brought Vajpayee down, because having promised support to Vajpayee at the last minute Mayawati and the BSP voted against the government. 'I saw a red-faced Pramod Mahajan rush across to Mayawati in Parliament and ask, *kya hua, kya hua* [what happened, what happened], but she remained impassive.'

'In 1996, Vajpayee was laughing, he expected the government to fall,' said Shakti Sinha. 'But in 1999 he almost cried in front of everybody, his face was ashen, he was broken.'[47] In the days that followed he sat moodily at home, snapping into the phone. One evening when the caller addressed him as 'pradhan mantriji', Vajpayee replied curtly: '*Arre goli maro pradhan mantri ko, kaho kya kehna chahte ho* [Oh to hell with the prime minister! Tell me whatever you wanted to say].' He later became calmer, and told Ghatate, '*Chinta mat karo, jo hota hai achche ke liye hota hai* [Don't worry. Whatever happens is for the best].'[48]

By the end of April, in spite of Sonia Gandhi's naive boast that she had the support of '272 MPs', it was clear that no party was in a position to form a government. President K.R. Narayanan dissolved Parliament and India was again set on course for snap general elections, this time for the thirteenth Lok Sabha, scheduled for September–October 1999. But before the election, Vajpayee's defeated caretaker government faced the prospect of another defeat hurtling down from the high mountains like a deadly avalanche.

~

In mid-May 1999, Brajesh Mishra came rushing into Vajpayee's room. 'Please come quickly. The army wants to brief you,' was all he said. Vajpayee hurried to meet the Director General of Military Operations (DGMO) at his office in South Block. 'There's an infiltration, sir, in the Kargil sector,' a military officer told Vajpayee, 'it's probably mujahideen.'

The mountain town of Kargil lies 200 kilometres east of Srinagar surrounded by the high Himalayas. Intruders from Pakistan had been digging themselves in at heights of 16,000–18,000 feet in the mountains above Kargil since early May. In India realization dawned only much later that it was not the mujahideen but units of the Pakistani army, armed to the teeth, which was dug in above Kargil. Aiming to cut Kashmir off from Ladakh, the intruders began to pound the strategically vital Srinagar–Leh highway.

Vajpayee was bewildered. Hadn't he just returned from Lahore, riding the crest of the peace wave? Hadn't his poetry conquered hearts?

From May to July 1999, Pakistan and India fought the Kargil war. The army began its gruelling fight to push back Pakistani forces in the merciless terrain of the high mountains. Deadly gunfire and shelling rained down from mountaintops, hitting Indian soldiers full blast. Soldiers clawed their way up sheer rock faces in the cover of night inch by inch in sub-zero temperatures as howling winds whipped past, to take on the Pakistani forces dug in far above them.

Savouring the romance of the Lahore Declaration and initially believing that the Indian army was engaged only in a routine counterterror operation, Vajpayee erred badly in thinking India–Pakistan peacemaking could just be about sublime poetry. A vital meeting of the Cabinet Committee on Security was held only on 24 May, when the number of deaths was already very high. 'Vajpayee didn't once ask why so many were dying, nor was he alive to the urgency of what was happening,' says military analyst Pravin Sawhney.[49] In early May, Defence Minister George Fernandes had told the press that the conflict was nothing but a counterterror operation which would be over in forty-eight hours. For the first few weeks of the war the government was clueless about what was going on. Vajpayee clung to the Lahore spirit. The then army chief V.P. Malik records how, while determined to expel the intruders, Vajpayee took the principled stand that India should not and would not cross the international border.[50] But the war quickly started to become a fiasco. Bodies were piling up, the absurdity and organizational failure of the Indian response was revealed in the fact that no one in the government thought to urgently call the Army Chief back from his overseas trip, from which he returned only at the end of May.

During the two-month-long Kargil war the scam-entwined Bofors howitzer rose to the occasion on the battlefield. Able to fire three rounds in twelve seconds, it pummelled sheets of precision gunfire at its targets. But the greatest heroes of the Kargil war were India's young officers and soldiers, who with raw courage beat back the intruders peak by painful peak, sometimes in brutal hand-to-hand combat operations. It was in one of these close fights that the daredevil warrior twenty-four-year-old Captain Vikram Batra was killed while leading his unit. He was shot in the chest and hit in the head by shrapnel as he faced his attackers head on. After weeks of this 'long freezing hell', with more than 500 Indian soldiers dead, after India had recaptured the strategic Tololing and Tiger Hill and Pakistan was running out of fuel and supplies, on 4 July Nawaz Sharif flew to the US. He asked President Clinton to intervene. Earlier, on 12 June, a visit to India by Pakistan foreign minister Sartaj Aziz had failed to make headway, and Sharif was now desperate for a face-saving way to end the punishing war. A 'perplexed' Clinton, under the impression that India and Pakistan were moving towards peace, delivered a firm admonishment and demanded that Pakistan immediately withdraw to its old positions behind the LoC. On 11 July Pakistan finally began its withdrawal, and on 14 July Vajpayee declared Operation Vijay a success. The war ended by the end of July.

Vajpayee was shocked by Kargil. Having staked his entire being on the peace process with Pakistan, he considered Kargil the rudest possible jolt. He kept repeating, it can't be Nawaz Sharif who has done this, it can't be. Knocked off his feet, he failed to provide decisive leadership in the first flush of the invasion, but later rushed to the front and toured hospitals to visit wounded soldiers. 'How are you feeling?' he would ask them worriedly. 'What can I do for you?' 'Please get us lighter weapons and equipment which we can carry on these mountains more easily,' answered one of the jawans.[51] In June, Vajpayee declared in a shaking voice: 'Have confidence in the ability of our armed forces, they will accomplish this task and ensure that no one dares to indulge in this kind of misadventure in future.'[52] However, the Indian establishment's failures during the war were evident, and in one instance Vajpayee was intensely discomfited when, referring to the glaring lack of modernized equipment, General Malik told the press, 'We will fight with whatever we have.' General Malik was summoned to the PMO, where Vajpayee told him not to use such language, but the general insistently pointed out how badly equipped and vulnerable the jawans were. After the war, the Kargil Review Committee, which inquired into why India was so ill-prepared for the Pakistani attack, concluded: 'There is overwhelming evidence that the Pakistani armed intrusion in the Kargil sector came as a complete and total surprise to the Indian government, army and intelligence agencies.'[53]

Whatever happened to the '*jung naa hone denge*' spirit? He had sunk too deeply into the rose-tinged dream of peace through poetry. The canny realism of his younger days – about threats to subcontinental peace – had dulled. A disconnected romanticism had taken over, centred on his own place in India's destiny. Had the Lahore moment been a cruel trick of fate? After a visit to the Kargil battlefront in June, Vajpayee insisted on calling Sharif from Srinagar. The lines from Srinagar to Pakistan were blocked and Bharat Sanchar Nigam Limited had to specially remove the block so the prime minister's call could go through. '*Mian sahab yeh kya ho raha hai, aap kya kar rahe ho* [what's going on, what are you doing], you need to sort this out,' he said to Nawaz Sharif. Sharif pleaded that he had been kept completely in the dark by Musharraf. Five years later, in exile in Jeddah, Sharif recalled, 'I remember my old friend Atal Bihari Vajpayee well. A sincere and good man. A well-meaning man. Vajpayee and I had planned 1999 as a year of peace . . . Vajpayee and I would have resolved Kashmir. But Musharraf betrayed us both.' On Kargil he insisted, 'I had no idea of it. In fact I heard about it from Vajpayee when he first called to tell me.'[54]

Lost in the illusions of his own preordained mission, Kargil had revealed Vajpayee's dangerously slipping grasp of India's security environment. As we shall see later, in the hijacking of IC 814 and in Operation Parakram, Vajpayee appeared dithering and uncertain.

In 1999 Vajpayee went into the general elections as the strong nationalist, armed with nuclear tests and victory in the war, the figurehead of post-Kargil nationalism. The BJP had actually wanted the elections to be advanced so the Kargil momentum would remain with it, but the Election Commission decided on elections in the latter part of the year. 'Tried, tested and trusted' was the BJP slogan for Vajpayee this time, now the seventy-five-year-old all-too-human father figure, the measured, benevolent consensus man who held allies together, who kept the religious madmen at bay and brought respectability and conservative good sense to his party. His leadership had ended the BJP's untouchable tag, and a broad-based pre-poll alliance shaped around his persona. Centred entirely on his image as a statesman-politician, in 1999 the BJP's slogan was '*Sapne adhoore, karne hain poore*' (We have to fulfil our unfinished dreams). Vajpayee's cabinet had been conservative-nationalist rather than extremist Hindu, Murli Manohar Joshi the only minister seen to have openly pursued the Hindutva agenda as Union HRD minister. But even though Advani took charge of the campaign as head of the campaign committee, Hindutva was pushed off the menu and nationalism was the main course.

The 'nationalism' card in the 1999 elections had another dimension. Sonia Gandhi had taken over as Congress president in March 1998 after leading a 'bloodless coup' against the ineffectual octogenarian Sitaram Kesri. Sonia's ascent split the Congress, with a section of the party led by Maharashtra leader Sharad Pawar questioning her credentials to lead the country because of her 'foreign origins'. 'Foreign origins' became the BJP's cry too. The party propaganda machine designed the 1999 election as a contest between the 'foreign', inexperienced Sonia Gandhi and the 'Bharatiya nationalist' Vajpayee, the tried and tested steady hand at the wheel. Print media ads pumped up the foreign origin theme: 'Don't vote for him because HE was born in India. Vote for him because YOU were. He doesn't have to go around saying this is his country and that he loves his country' ran one of the full-page ads that the BJP took out.[55] 'What next,' asked Arun Jaitley, 'will we have some Kargil intruder wanting to be prime minister?' In response the Congress's Ghulam Nabi Azad shouted: 'How does the PM have a son-in-law without being married? Whose son-in-law? Who is married to whom?' Vajpayee himself never directly brought up Sonia's antecedents; instead, he cleverly played the victim to the Congress's counterattacks. Responding to Sonia Gandhi's charge that he was a traitor, he struck an injured note: 'I can't speak the language Sonia is speaking. Let there be criticism but it should not be baseless allegations. *Meri zindagi khuli kitab hai* [My life is an open book].'[56]

On the campaign trail, Vajpayee was not able to travel as hectically as before. His health was declining, his knees gave him trouble and he tired easily. He addressed only three rallies a day and travelled cocooned in the prime ministerial Boeing, accompanied by his son-in-law Ranjan Bhattacharyya, Sudheendra Kulkarni and Shakti Sinha.

His speeches, earlier high on energy and packed with jokes, were now more serious, sermonizing and measured.

He again stood from Lucknow. '*Humne Lahore mein dikha diya ki hum shanti ke pujari hain. Lekin jung mein hum toh tod jawab dete hain* [In Lahore I was the devotee of peace. But in war we showed that we will give a devastating response],'[57] he said at a rally.

Vajpayee won the day for the BJP. This time the NDA – the BJP going into elections for the first time with a pre-poll alliance – won a decisive mandate with almost 300 seats (including support from the TDP) although the BJP's own tally remained at 182. In 1998 the BJP had thirteen allies; this time it had a whopping twenty-four. Interestingly though, in spite of Kargil nationalism, the BJP buckled in Uttar Pradesh, winning a measly twenty-nine seats, and Vajpayee's victory margin in Lucknow shrank significantly. The BJP on its own failed to breach the 200-seat mark, a jinx, as we have noted, Vajpayee was never able to break. The Uttar Pradesh results were a reminder of the limitations of the party organization at the ground level in the country's most populous state, in the face of the challenge being thrown up by the more regionally rooted, caste-based SP and BSP. The limits of Vajpayee's ability to punch above his party's weight on his home turf would come to haunt the BJP five years later.

However, with the BJP-led alliance winning a clear mandate, a collective sigh of relief went around the country, as the curse of fractured verdicts over the last four elections seemed finally to be over. The Congress slid to 114 seats from 140, its worst-ever showing. The CPI won just four seats and lost its status as a national party. In 1999, Vajpayee was the country's Neta Number One by some distance – 'tried, tested, trusted'. It was an election based not around Hindutva ideology but around him and what he represented, and he had won it on the strength of his own popularity, a fact of which he was acutely conscious. He, 'Stable Atal', the weather-beaten madhyam-margi (middle of the roader), represented security, stability and a focus on development. The chord he was able to strike with crowds brought him goodwill that none of his rivals could match.

Indian elections were turning presidential and based around personalities. Fifty-three-year-old Sonia Gandhi, with her bobbed hair held in an Alice band and still speaking hesitant Hindi, was seen as far too inexperienced to match Vajpayee's national stature. The Third Front withered away after its brief tryst with power. A range of allies in southern and eastern India now had their tents firmly pitched with the BJP, making Vajpayee appear even more unassailable.

On 13 October 1999, in the forecourt of Rashtrapati Bhavan, seventy-five-year-old Atal Bihari Vajpayee, dressed in a brown raw silk jacket and crisp dhoti-kurta, was sworn in as prime minister for the third time. But this time he wasn't going to be a prime minister living on monthly oxygen from allies. This time he was determined to live up to his image as the Man India Awaits.

In return, as his reward from the people, he was loved for his tireless effort. Enduring an embarrassing thirteen-day government, a besieged thirteen-month government, lumbered with fickle allies and foreign policy defeats, the stooping, careworn, overweight poet-humorist, the battle-weary but reassuring father figure who loved his food and drink, the wizard speechmaker, once the RSS's favourite, later its bête noir who made the occasional militant speech, but whose oeuvre was generally moderate, his difficult life's ups and downs, compromises and stumbles spooling before the public like a gritty, intimate film, attracted for Vajpayee an emotion among the public that prime ministers seldom do: an indulgent love. Love for a plodding familiar protagonist, from a people sympathetically reconciled to his many years of toil and failures, a man for whom the line *at least he tried* so often rang true. Success came his way only after years of patient endurance; after he had weathered attacks from all sides. He was crowned only at twilight when he stood blinking, fallible and flawed, in the rays of the setting sun.

His first government had lasted for thirteen days, the next for thirteen months with thirteen allies, and now, after elections to the thirteenth Lok Sabha, he was sworn in on 13 October. Would unlucky thirteen prove lucky for him?

8

The Dominant Vajpayee: 1999–2002

A poem for Vajpayee:

Did it matter that Hindutva was shelved and shunned
When stock markets boomed and soared,
When cell phones, TVs and cars rained down
Instead of plans for mandirs, however grand

Never mind the shouts, it was a shining moment,
For many even a Camelot.
Prime Minister Vajpayee, a centre-right exponent,
Pulling off what many 'impossible' thought.

~

A forest of flags fluttered at Delhi's Ramlila Maidan on 16 April 2001. A massive crowd raised its fists and chanted loudly. 'Vajpayee is the weakest prime minister in history,' bellowed Dattopant Thengadi, once Vajpayee's Jana Sangh colleague in Parliament and now leader of the Sangh Parivar's labour union, the Bharatiya Mazdoor Sangh (BMS). The BMS and another sangh outfit, the Swadeshi Jagran Manch, had congregated to protest against the Vajpayee government's liberalizing economic policies. Important sectors had been thrown open for foreign direct investment by finance minister Yashwant Sinha. disinvestment minister Arun Shourie had put up certain government undertakings for sale. 'This particular finance minister [Yashwant Sinha] is an *apradhi* [a criminal],' bellowed Thengadi, 'and he has committed a crime by encroaching upon the legitimate jurisdiction of the labour ministry.' Thengadi called for mass protests against the Vajpayee government, saying the government was pursuing anti-poor policies. 'Our rally will not push out the government. The government is pushing itself out,' Thengadi told the press. Thengadi also said the government was following policies which were in 'virodh' of the national interest, a statement which was later reported as Thengadi calling the Vajpayee government 'desh virodhi' or anti-national.[1]

The BMS rally was part of the continuing protests, agitations and seminars that the Sangh Parivar was staging against Vajpayee, the BMS rally at Ramlila Maidan taking place after the Tehelka revelations hit Vajpayee and further emboldened the Sangh (see later section for the Tehelka exposé). The anti-Vajpayee front was led by a troika of saffron malcontents: the RSS's K.S. Sudarshan, the BMS's Dattopant Thengadi and the VHP's Ashok Singhal. 'Vajpayee's government is anti-Hindu and pro-videshi [pro-foreigner]. It has come to power in spite of the RSS not because of it. I wouldn't mind if it collapses,' a senior RSS leader told *India Today* in 1999.[2] The Swadeshi Jagran Manch in its December 1998 rally had cried, '*Yeh Yashwant Sinha arth mantri nahin anarth mantri hai* [This finance minister is a disaster].'[3]

The blossoming Vajpayee line in the government – the Ram Mandir on the back burner, a lunge towards privatization and globalization, attempting to bring in liberal labour laws, peacemaking with Pakistan and in Kashmir – had sent the Sangh Parivar into outraged rebellion against its own government and against Vajpayee, the self-confessed 'swayamsevak' and '*rag rag mein Hindu*'. 'Thengadi on economic policy and Singhal on Ram Mandir attacked Vajpayee from every angle, he didn't like it but preferred not to get into a slanging match,' recalled

Appa Ghatate. Vajpayee as prime minister faced more attacks and insults from the Sangh Parivar than the original liberalizing prime minister, P.V. Narasimha Rao.

When the newspapers reported that Thengadi had called him a 'criminal', Yashwant Sinha, the strapping former IAS officer who had become Vajpayee's finance minister in 1998 and held the portfolio until 2002, was shocked. He immediately informed Advani that he would send his resignation letter to Vajpayee. Hearing about this, Vajpayee called in Sinha to his office. '*Nahin, nahin, aisa mat kijiye*,' Vajpayee told Sinha, '*yeh log aise hi hain, hum logon ke liye bahut embarrassing situation create kar diya hai* [No, no. Don't do that – these people have created a very embarrassing situation for us].' Vajpayee then insisted that Sinha accompany him to a party meeting, where he made a speech praising the government's economic policy, ending by saying, '*Virodh hota hai to hoye, humein chinta nahin karna chahiye* [We shouldn't worry about opposition to our policies].'[4]

The Vajpayee-led NDA struck out towards the free market more boldly and more decisively than any government had ever done before. Where P.V. Narasimha Rao and Manmohan Singh had left off, Vajpayee sent the horse galloping forward. Swadeshi economics was fully overthrown. 'India *cannot* be an island,' Vajpayee stressed in an interview, 'we have to move in this competitive world.'[5] As a result, the sangh's swadeshi Hindu left armies like the SJM and BMS began an excoriating war against Vajpayee, actively encouraged by the RSS's K.S. Sudarshan himself. Ironically it was these same populist Hindu socialist cadres that had rallied around Vajpayee's leadership in the 1960s and 1970s and isolated Balraj Madhok. 'Vajpayee dealt with the RSS very deftly, keeping them at arm's length,' recalls N.K. Singh, former secretary in the Vajpayee PMO. 'But it is true that his relationship with K.S. Sudarshan [a Hindutva and swadeshi hawk who became sarsanghchalak in 2000] were never as good as they had been with Rajju Bhaiyya.'[6]

Even within the government, liberalizers on one side and swadeshi ministers on the other clashed continuously. Vajpayee's method of settling disputes was to hear everyone out and resolve matters by setting up a committee, but then insisting on a decision. 'I used to oppose Yashwant Sinha in every cabinet meeting,' recalls Murli Manohar Joshi. 'But Vajpayee was a very astute politician. He let everyone have their say and let a consensus emerge naturally,' recalls Joshi. 'On the disinvestment of oil marketing companies, for example, he called Shourie and me together. I let fly at Shourie. Then Vajpayee set up a committee and told me, *aap samadhan karenge* [you will find a solution]. Decisions were taken through committees so everyone felt involved.'[7]

By the time he became prime minister, Vajpayee had long surpassed his ideological parent body, both intellectually and in terms of his own national fame and profile. 'In government, Vajpayee was not an RSS man,' says Yashwant Sinha. 'His thinking matured a great deal. He did things that he knew would annoy the RSS but he didn't care. He was a genuine liberal on the economy, rooted in the BJP's original right-of-centre ideas of a belief in private enterprise and growth through people's efforts and not state action. He had seen the folly of the state taking over the commanding heights of the economy during the Nehru and Indira years and his natural inclination was pro-business.'[8]

In 2001, after the Ramlila Maidan rally, *Organiser* editor Seshadri Chari, who had good relations with both Sudarshan and Vajpayee, organized a hush-hush peacemaking lunch –the first such lunch – between Vajpayee and Sudarshan at the prime minister's house. The set date turned out to be Ekadashi and Sudarshan was fasting. Vajpayee asked Chari what kind of fasting food he should have prepared, Chari replied that *sabudana khichdi* (sago mix) and fruit would be best. Vajpayee then asked Chari to instruct his kitchen accordingly, so Sudarshan was served exactly the right sort of food. During the lunch, Vajpayee jokingly said to Chari that since he wasn't fasting, why didn't he eat Sudarshan's quota of the meal? There was mango and ice cream for dessert. Sudarshan ate the mango but refused the ice cream, punning, 'I don't scream.' At which point Vajpayee pressed Chari to eat more of the ice cream. After lunch, Vajpayee spent half an hour talking to the RSS doyen. The prince of Nepal had just a few days ago gunned down his family members and so, initially, they talked about Nepal. After this lunch relations between Vajpayee and Sudarshan became considerably less tense. Chari subsequently organized another meeting between the two at teatime, during which Sudarshan, who drank neither tea nor coffee, sipped only water, but Vajpayee drank a cup or two of tea. 'Not many knew about these meetings, but they helped in creating an understanding between the two,' recalls Chari.[9] 'The RSS has the freedom to its own views,' Vajpayee said in an interview in 2000, 'but there should be a lakshman rekha, a self-imposed limit. Nothing should be said that has an unsettling consequence. This would apply to all of us in public life.'[10]

Another meeting between BJP ministers and the sangh at the home of BJP MP Sumitra Mahajan was not so civil – in fact, it was particularly stormy. 'Arun Shourie lost his cool and shouted at the sangh fellows,' recalls Sinha. Shourie says he became angry at the absurdities uttered by the Sangh Parivar members, including Sudarshan's demand that foreign exchange reserves be held in Indian currency. 'Sudarshan didn't seem to understand that India held its reserves in a basket of internationally acceptable currencies, the proportions of which were kept secret. I thought his arguments were totally without any foundation and I said so,' recalls Shourie, who says that Vajpayee was openly dismissive of the RSS attempts to interfere in policy.[11] On one occasion when Shourie offered to talk to Sudarshan about the proposed amendments to the patents law, Vajpayee said sarcastically: '*Arre bhaiya kyon unka samay aur apna samay barbaad kar rahe ho, woh toh sarvagyani hain* [Don't waste your time or his time, Sudarshan fancies himself as the all-knowing].'[12]

'The RSS was constantly at our throats,' recalls Yashwant Sinha, 'but Vajpayee didn't let us in the cabinet feel the RSS heat. He would say: "*Aapke upar bahut dabav dala hai in logon ne, usko kabhi mat maniyega* [Don't let yourselves be affected by the RSS]." He threw his weight behind us and never let us feel the severe pressure being put on him by the RSS. Instead, he internalized everything.'[13] N.K. Singh concurs. 'Vajpayee was a great delegator,' says Singh. 'His great strength was he didn't micromanage.' Singh says because Vajpayee was confident of his leadership he gave his ministers free rein. 'There was lots of criticism of him, but he would absorb it all and move on.'[14]

Occasionally, though, he lost his patience. At a 2001 RSS meeting in Mumbai, a senior RSS functionary was surprised to suddenly receive a call from none other than the prime minister. Vajpayee sounded angry. 'The way some in the sangh are talking about me, makes me wonder what I should do,' he snapped. 'Should I resign?'[15] The resignation threat was always his trump card: he knew well his own irreplaceability and how badly such a threat could upset the entire RSS–BJP apparatus. Another time he burst out at a BJP parliamentary party meet: 'You always complain about me. But I too have complaints about you. You are not effectively countering opposition propaganda against our government.'[16]

Vajpayee's punishing battles with the Sangh Parivar on the economy paid off. The economy fizzed upwards. A dizzying range of consumer choices became available, from gadgets to new homes; *Kaun Banega Crorepati* making a technicolour debut in 2000. In the new century, Indian techies and infotech companies were in high demand globally to sort out Y2K, the millennial bug that could affect data storage. Shares of infotech companies soared and the Indian stock market zoomed. Middle-class salaries went higher than they had ever been, part of a trend since 1991. In 2000 India boasted 2765 models of televisions; 183 types of washing machines; 233 kinds of refrigerators; seventy-four models of cars; over fifty satellite and cable channels; a rapidly burgeoning cell-phone network. There were still 100 million families without water supply at home and 150 million households without electricity, but industry cheered and the urban middle class whooped. Upwardly mobile India was becoming addicted to that once-forbidden pleasure: the good life.[17]

Amid controversy, the telecom sector was overhauled through the Telecom Migration Policy. The monopoly of government telecom companies was ended and private telecom given impetus; a fixed fee for using airwaves was waived, and instead companies would pay a percentage of revenues. The government got a share of the telecom companies' profits and competition among private companies led to lowering of call tariffs, foreign companies arriving in India and improvement in telecom quality. 'Vajpayee grasped that telecom was in trouble, he told us *rasta nikaliye* [find a way out],' recalls N.K. Singh.[18] To do it Vajpayee even shifted out communications minister Jagmohan and took over the sector himself. The sacking of Jagmohan was controversial and allegations were levelled that it was done at the behest of the government's powerful cronies who owed vast sums to the ministry. Nonetheless, many saw the Telecom Migration Policy as Vajpayee's biggest achievement and he was hailed as the 'father of modern telecom in India'. Mobile phone connectivity surged forward as millions of Indians acquired cell phones.

Arun Shourie forged ahead on privatization of public sector enterprises. 'Vajpayee's thinking on the economy was like P.V. Narasimha Rao's – he believed socialism does not work,' says Shourie. 'Yes, the state had a duty of welfare, but the state should not be dominant in the economy. Even when the early BJP adopted Gandhian socialism as its slogan, this was socialism in the Gandhian sense, meaning welfare for the last man.'[19] Between 1999 and 2004 Arun Shourie's disinvestment department, which in 2001 became a full ministry, pushed the strategic sale of Videsh Sanchar Nigam Limited (VSNL), Hindustan Zinc, Balco, IPCL, several ITDC hotels and Modern Food Industries, fetching the government over Rs 6000 crore. The Vajpayee government also began to divest its holdings in Maruti. Vajpayee started an ambitious road-building project. Construction was begun for the 'Golden Quadrilateral', or four-lane highways, spanning over 5000 kilometres, connecting India's major cities.

The government of a massive coalition was run with a light touch.

Delicate balances had to be struck in allocating ministerial portfolios and Vajpayee's reconciling tendencies were to the fore as he kept the jumbo alliance afloat by a non-interfering style. But this same autonomy-giving method fell short in tackling national security crises. His let-my-ministers-work-freely approach succeeded brilliantly in igniting the economy and he managed well the politics of liberalization, but the same Vajpayee failed during security crises when his responses became weak and fumbling. Vajpayee kept shying away from tough decisions and kept calculating the political risks. His failures in crisis situations are seen in two instances – the hijacking of IC 814 in 1999 and in Operation Parakram in 2001.

~

The story of the doomed aircraft flight number IC 814 deserves retelling as it reveals glaring gaps in Vajpayee's leadership and how incapable he could sometimes be of quick and firm decision-making.

On 24 December 1999 Indian Airlines IC 814 from Kathmandu to Delhi was hijacked by a Kashmir-based terrorist group. The pilot was first ordered to fly to Lahore, and when Lahore refused it permission to land, IC 814 touched down in Amritsar at 7 p.m., with only 20 minutes of fuel remaining. The plane was hijacked a little after 4.30 p.m., but an emergency cabinet meeting in Delhi got under way at Vajpayee's residence only at 6 p.m. Vajpayee was away in Lucknow at the time of the hijacking. He was not immediately informed of the seizure of the plane as he was en route to Delhi and was able to join the emergency meeting only at 7 p.m., more than two hours after the plane was captured. It was the end of December. The new year would herald a new century and Vajpayee had been looking forward to his seventy-fifth birthday and the party planned for him in Chennai by Pramod Mahajan. IC 814 crashed into his year-end reverie and he was unable to gather his wits in time.

As news of the hijacking spread, wailing relatives of IC 814 passengers gathered in front of the prime minister's residence at 7 Race Course Road. TV news went into overdrive, broadcasting their anxious laments round the clock. When IC 814 was on the ground in Amritsar, the government's Crisis Management Group (CMG) and Cabinet Committee on Security erupted into the Tower of Babel. Views and counterviews kept being interchanged. At one point, foreign minister Jaswant Singh snatched the phone, telephoned the Punjab police chief and ordered that the plane be immobilized on the runway by means of a trolley or a truck. But the Punjab police did nothing as the Punjab chief minister kept insisting that passengers should not be harmed. Vajpayee sat listening in silence, taking no decisions, only occasionally and plaintively asking about the passengers' plight. A chattering, arguing Vajpayee government and a silent, indecisive and passive prime minister failed to take the initiative to immobilize IC 814 all the while – almost 50 minutes – it stood in Amritsar. The hapless plane, unable to refuel due to airport missteps, again took off for Lahore, where it landed and refuelled, then landed at a military airbase near Dubai at around one-thirty the next morning. At Dubai, India reportedly readied a commando-style operation but the local authorities didn't cooperate and again India failed to take any decisive action. The hijackers had stabbed and killed a passenger, twenty-five-year-old Rupin Katyal, and in Dubai his body was flung out of the plane in a chute. In Dubai twenty-seven passengers – women and children and some injured – were released. Someone from the government was needed to bring the twenty-seven back from Dubai. Civil aviation minister Sharad Yadav immediately volunteered but confessed he had no passport. The demands of alliance politics had led Vajpayee to appoint as civil aviation minister a rustic political warhorse who had never flown on an international flight. A passport was hastily arranged for Sharad Yadav – the visit becoming his first overseas trip – who received the released hostages in Dubai. Meanwhile the grief-crazed relatives kept up their 24x7 hysteria on TV and high-decibel pressure kept building on the government, which

Vajpayee couldn't withstand. A shamefaced India meekly gave in to the terrorists' demands and released three wanted terrorists being held in jails in Delhi, Jammu and Srinagar. Taking off from Dubai at 6.20 a.m. on 25 December, IC 814 now flew to an undisclosed location, landing in Taliban-controlled Kandahar at 8.30 a.m. to remain on the tarmac for six days while the Vajpayee government and hijackers negotiated. Jaswant Singh staked his own credibility and offered to fly with the released terrorists to Kandahar. After Jaswant Singh's plane had taken off, Vajpayee whispered in a weak and exhausted voice, '*Kya woh chale gaye*? [Has he gone?]',[20] the phrase encapsulating the prime minister's plight as a helpless bystander through the entire sordid saga. After Jaswant Singh had delivered the terrorists to the Taliban, the remaining hostages were freed and returned to India on the evening of 31 December, after six days of torment. The sight of a union minister of the apparently strongly 'nationalist' India, which had only that year declared victory in the Kargil war, escorting terrorists to their freedom was a shameful disgrace.

The IC 814 hijacking episode had been a fiasco, and all the top officials in the Vajpayee government, from Brajesh Mishra to A.S. Dulat to the director of the National Security Guard (NSG), Nikhil Kumar, came in for scathing criticism. Cabinet Secretary Prabhat Kumar 'took his time calling the CMG'; Brajesh Mishra 'sent confused signals'; Dulat 'should have pre-empted the hijack', and Nikhil Kumar 'could have ensured the NSG reached on time', said media reports.[21] Vajpayee became a victim of his own consensual style: the taking-everyone-along, delegating, hands-off approach meant government became paralysed by a cacophony of decision makers. The 'friendly, happy government headed by the easy-going prime minister' had failed abysmally at a time when swift hard decisions needed to be taken.

Operation Parakram in 2001–02 too was dubbed a 'strategic fiasco'.[22] The operation began as a result of events that took place on 13 December 2001. That morning the Vajpayee government faced a volley of attacks from the Opposition in Parliament. 'Coffingate', or an alleged scam in the purchase of coffins from a US-based company during the Kargil war to transport soldiers' bodies, rocked both Houses. '*Kafan chor, gaddi chhor* [Coffin thief, leave the throne],' shrieked Opposition members rather tastelessly, creating such a ruckus that both Houses were adjourned. Around 11.40 a.m. a white Ambassador car came speeding into Parliament. Five heavily armed men leapt out, shouting 'Pakistan Paindabad [Long live Pakistan],' as they sprayed bullets and lobbed grenades. Nine security staff were killed and the gunmen – suspected Pakistan-based terrorists – all died. Outrage rippled across the country that India's Parliament itself should be targeted, and the Vajpayee government mobilized for war with Pakistan. By January 2002 masses of Indian troops stood along the India–Pakistan border. Operation Parakram had begun. Parakram was yet another example of the Vajpayee government's running theme of fumbling on national security while being sure-footed on the economy.

Vajpayee seemed confused about what he hoped to achieve by Operation Parakram's show of strength. As it turned out, the incredibly long ten-month troop build-up on the border became what former navy chief Sushil Kumar called 'the most punishing mistake for the armed forces'[23] because, having mobilized the army, Vajpayee didn't know what to do. Humiliatingly enough for India, while full army mobilization was on, gunmen dressed in Indian army fatigues struck Kaluchak near Jammu on 14 May 2002 and gunned down thirty-four. After international pressure on Musharraf, tensions began to dissipate and the operation eventually ended, but almost 800 soldiers were tragically killed in battle accidents, more casualties than the dead in Kargil.[24] Crores worth of ammunition went to waste.

~

Vajpayee was visibly tiring. His voice was becoming softer and his knees ached constantly. During his 1998 Independence Day speech he had stumbled towards the Red Fort lectern in a daze, wearing only a single shoe, leaving the other one behind in the car. By 2000, he had undergone two cataract surgeries, was unable to hear without his hearing aid, and had been living on one kidney since 1984. His blood pressure was a not unhealthy 78/130 and his heart was in good condition. But his love of food began to catch up, and at 5 feet 6 inches, he weighed a hefty 83 kilos. In March 2000 when Bill Clinton came visiting, exuding energy and charm, the contrast between the youthful US President and the stooped, shuffling Indian prime minister couldn't be greater.

At his Independence Day address in August 2000 he enthused that the new century would be one of youth, that India was a 'Yuva Rashtra' (young nation) and congratulated the inhabitants of the newly created states of Chhattisgarh, Jharkhand and Uttaranchal. But his voice quavered, he kept clearing his throat and after the speech had to be helped to his car. At a BJP National Council meeting, party cadres, expecting yet another rousing Vajpayee speech, saw that he was unable to stand up and had to speak sitting down. The gesticulating, grandiloquent, now grave, now comic, expansive speaker was seen crouched in his chair reading prepared speeches. 'Atalji, you reading a prepared speech is like Shivaji riding a scooter into battle,' Arun Shourie told him bluntly. When a planned trip to America in 2000 was cut short and official meetings cut by a third, rumours of his ill health spread like wildfire. He was quick to dispel these and declared in an interview: 'Apart from arthritis I have no problems, if the media wants to speculate about my health, there's nothing that can be done about it . . . arthritis is not uncommon for people of my age.'[25]

After the Kargil war, he seemed to recover some of his old fighting spirit and for the 1999 polls joked that the slogan '*Agli bari Atal Bihari*' should be '*Teesri bari Atal Bihari*'. '*Jab bhagwan Ram ke raj tilak ki tayaari ho rahi thi*,' he said dryly, '*tab unko chaudah saal vanvaas jana pada tha* [When people were preparing for Lord Ram's coronation, he was sent into fourteen years' exile in the forest].' But it was evident he had trouble walking. He underwent two knee replacement surgeries in 2000 and 2001 at the Breach Candy hospital in Mumbai but his gait improved only slightly. The pressures on him were constant and his indispensability had become a burden, even a curse. He was the sole reconciler between government and party/RSS and the single-handed enabler of a diverse coalition. The demands pushed him into a shell and he became more taciturn and desperate for privacy than he had ever been, retreating into a small group of close friends. Sensing his isolation, Ghatate made it a point to visit him over breakfast, even though breakfast time was when political decisions were taken. After one of Ghatate's regular breakfast visits, Vajpayee joked, '*Ghar me khana pina nahin milta kya?* [Don't you get food at home?],' but was always visibly relieved to be able to spend time with his most trusted friend.

~

Vajpayee's easy-going, delegating ruling arrangement was beset with vulnerabilities. On 13 March 2001, in a sensational exposé the website Tehelka.com screened a hidden camera sting operation, dubbed 'Operation West End', which showed in suggestively grainy images then BJP party president Bangaru Laxman accepting a cash bribe of Rs 1 lakh and Jaya Jaitly, then Samata Party chief, the party to which defence minister George Fernandes belonged, also in a conversation about an alleged donation, while seated in her office in the defence minister's residence. Dubious money transactions by politicians had been routinely blamed as the bane of India's democracy. Now for the first time, in dramatic and shadowy hidden camera pictures, politicians were actually shown on TV talking about and accepting hard cash. Parliament and media erupted. The Opposition shouted 'chor'. Bangaru Laxman resigned as BJP president, Jaya Jaitly stepped down as Samata Party chief and George Fernandes resigned both as defence minister and NDA convenor. Fernandes, the spirited former trade union leader, was Vajpayee's trusted troubleshooter, his secular-socialist image valuable to reassure NDA allies.

A crucial ally said a humiliating goodbye: railway minister Mamata Banerjee, chief of the Trinamool Congress, had been chafing for a while, uneasy about Vajpayee's liberalizing policies. Vajpayee made repeated attempts to placate her, once even dropping in at her Calcutta home. Warmly greeting Mamata's mother, Gayatri Devi, he bent down and touched her feet. 'Your daughter is very naughty and gives us a lot of trouble,' he smiled, instantly mollifying Banerjee. 'I was very grateful he did that,' Banerjee later recalled.[26] He had a soft spot for this lone warrior-woman tilting against the mighty Left Front. '*Aap toh agniganana* [fiery woman] *hain*,' he said when he first met her. Waiting to receive him at the airport once, she bent down to touch his feet when he arrived. But grasping her midway, Vajpayee enveloped her in a fatherly hug, leaving her with a lifelong affection for the septuagenarian charmer. But Bengal assembly elections were approaching. Mamata's demands for the dismissal of the Buddhadeb Bhattacharya government were falling on deaf ears. In the storm over the Tehelka exposé, Banerjee resigned and withdrew the support of her nine MPs from the NDA.

After Tehelka, an opinion poll gave a punishing thumbs down to the government – 42 per cent said the impact of the Tehelka revelations on the Vajpayee government was 'very serious', 39 per cent said 'serious'.[27] There were already whisperings and rumours that the liberalization process was only benefiting select people. Vajpayee's son-in-law Ranjan Bhattacharyya was a good friend of Pramod Mahajan and part of his glamorous circle, which included shady tycoons and backroom operators. A Goa-based former BJP leader recalls that Mahajan was the go-to person for all election funding. 'Pramod ji had this team of people who would meet us in five-star hotels where the financial transactions would be worked out. For many of us in the BJP, it was the first time we were exposed to the power of big money,' he says.

Bhattacharyya, who became Vajpayee's Officer on Special Duty (OSD) in 1996, was his constant companion on foreign tours. In the Tehelka tapes, Bangaru Laxman mentioned Bhattacharyya as a key dealmaker in 'projects'. Vajpayee's close officers in the PMO were also targeted for allegedly tweaking telecom policies to suit friendly corporates. In the tapes, Bangaru Laxman suggested that the real power in the PMO was the formidable Brajesh Mishra, known to run the PMO with an iron hand and having a vice-like grip on Vajpayee. Mishra's relations with the BJP's top leadership like Advani and Sushma Swaraj were chilly. Advani detested Mishra's closeness to Vajpayee and Vajpayee deviously used Mishra to keep Advani in his place. The BJP top brass and the RSS were profoundly irritated that Mishra imperiously ran the PMO exactly the way he wanted with Vajpayee's full backing. After the Tehelka revelations whispers against Mishra became louder. 'The Congress has declared war,' cried Vajpayee as the Opposition attacked him daily in Parliament, 'and we have accepted the invitation.' 'Instead of declaring war on the Congress, Vajpayee should have declared war on corruption,' shot back Anand Sharma of the Congress.[28]

Vajpayee's relationship with the grim-faced Brajesh Mishra was a long one that stretched for many decades. Vajpayee knew Mishra's family well – Mishra's father, D.P. Mishra, was former Congress chief minister of Madhya Pradesh, Vajpayee's home state, as well as a poet and writer. Many evenings spent with the hard-drinking Mishra as well as Vajpayee's natural and everlasting affinity for the Brahmin brotherhood, created a trusting comradeship. Mishra controlled almost all bureaucratic appointments in the government. Yashwant Sinha recalls how Economic Affairs Secretary E.A.S. Sarma was suddenly transferred and subsequently resigned from the IAS. Sarma later gave an explosive interview to *Outlook* magazine alleging that certain business houses were being favoured by the Vajpayee PMO.[29] When IAS officer Ajit Kumar's name was proposed for finance secretary, Yashwant Sinha received a call from Ranjan Bhattacharyya: '*Baapji [Vajpayee] nahin chahte.* If his name comes up, *aap virodh kijiyega* [Father doesn't want it. If his name comes up oppose it].' Sinha duly protested, but Mishra had his way and Ajit Kumar was appointed.

'Vajpayee never wanted to confront Mishra,' says Sinha. Sometimes though he didn't give in to Mishra, as in the case of extending the tenure of Foreign Secretary Kanwal Sibal, to whom Mishra was keen to give an extension. '*Kya aap chahte hain ki Sibal ko extension mile?* [Do you want Sibal to get an extension?]' Vajpayee asked Sinha. 'Yes I do, he's a very competent officer,' replied Sinha. But with a mischievous glint, Vajpayee replied, '*Brajesh ji ki har baat maanna zaroori nahin hai* [It's not necessary to do everything that Brajesh wants].' Sibal didn't get an extension and Shashank became foreign secretary, reportedly also because Vajpayee's dear friend Bhairon Singh Shekhawat, then vice president, put in a word for Shashank.[30]

'Vajpayee was always proud of his clean personal record. A contractor once approached me for a deal, which I mentioned to him. He rounded on me fiercely and said, "Appa, never do that."' Ghatate revealed that Vajpayee was never completely comfortable with Ranjan's friendship with Pramod Mahajan. Once when Namita and Ranjan were going to Mahajan's house for dinner, Vajpayee told them, ' Go for the dinner, but keep your mouth shut and your ears open.'[31] Vajpayee loved life's pleasures, but retained the early RSS's zealous vigilance against personal corruption all his life. In his half a century in politics, he was personally untouched by corruption allegations, losing his grip only towards the end of his tenure with those surrounding him. At lunch with Ghatate while he was prime minister, Vajpayee told him, 'When someone gives money, his hand is at the top and the receiver's hand is at the bottom. When the money is given under the table, the giver's hand is at the bottom and the taker's at the top.'[32]

Money power in elections had always worried him. 'The manner in which money is used to win elections can become a big problem for us in future,' he said to NDTV in 2004. Talking about the Tehelka exposé and Bangaru Laxman accepting money, again in 2004, he told *India Today*, 'Elections are increasingly becoming costlier. Where does the money come from? Who gives it? These things influence politics. It is a big problem in our democracy.'[33] But Tehelka got his goat and his retribution was fierce: Tehelka's offices raided by the Central Bureau of Investigation and cases filed against its reporters.

Allegations were levelled in the same year, 2001, by *Outlook* magazine when it published sensational reports in two cover stories, 'Rigging the PMO' (5 March) and 'The PM's Achilles Heel' (26 March), which alleged that a small group of business houses in collusion with Mishra, Bhattacharyya and Singh – who were all featured in a cover photo – were dictating economic policies. Wrote *Outlook*:

> The clout wielded by Ranjan [Bhattacharyya] is also demonstrated by the durbars he holds. A senior BJP leader from Rajasthan who happened once to visit 7 Race Course Road was surprised to find Ranjan having a drink along with a Union cabinet-rank minister and a minister of state in the anteroom next to where Vajpayee was meeting a delegation of foreign diplomats. The BJP leader mentioned this incident to Vajpayee, who apparently gave his son-in-law a dressing down.[34]

The problem with the Vajpayee PMO was that it did not respect the role of the cabinet and cabinet secretaries, the former bureaucrat E.A.S. Sarma told *Outlook*.

It must be pointed out here that no solid or specific evidence has ever been produced linking either Bhattacharyya or Vajpayee's PMO bureaucrats with any illegal or under-the-counter transactions. But in a liberalizing economy, the narrative of a suave, whisky-drinking son-in-law leading a ritzy lifestyle, and sharp-suited bureaucrats with big money connections made for tantalizing gossip, particularly among the insular sections of the Sangh Parivar. The fact that the three men in the eye of the allegations – Mishra, Bhattacharyya and Singh – were not exactly RSS favourites meant that the rumour mills churned ever faster.

Did Vajpayee have a moral centre, asks *Outlook* editor Vinod

Mehta, and answers: that's a question mark question. Vajpayee and Mehta shared a jokey rapport built over many years and used to meet regularly. Mehta often referred to Vajpayee as a 'naughty old boy' who did all kinds of 'naughty things' when he was overseas and far away from the RSS gaze. When Mehta, of all people, published reports of corrupt practices among Vajpayee's most trusted men, the Vajpayee government came down hard. In May the office premises of *Outlook*'s proprietor, Rajan Raheja, were raided by income tax authorities, computers taken away and journalists' bags searched. Immediately Mehta made a statement accusing Vajpayee of muzzling the press 'in the spirit of thuggish vendetta'. He never received a response about the raid, Mishra maintaining that neither he nor Vajpayee knew anything about them. Corruption allegations robbed Vajpayee somewhat of his sheen as the clean alternative to the Congress, and as if sensing growing public disillusionment, he retreated more into his glum silences. The rosy romance between Vajpayee and his voters which began with his one-vote fall in 1999 began to dwindle after the charges levelled by Tehelka and *Outlook*.

Congress's Jaipal Reddy once remarked that Vajpayee showed more cynical disregard for political morality than any other prime minister in India.[35] While this is an overstatement, Vajpayee's fierce drive through his entire political life to be the alternative to the Congress and to take the Congress's place led him on occasion into moral pitfalls and murky power play. As an Opposition leader he railed against Indira's dictatorship, but in government he showed he was capable of being just as draconian as Indira on state action against the press. Like Indira Gandhi, he had begun to believe that whatever he did was good for India, because, after all, he was Atal Bihari Vajpayee. The self-belief resulted in his dynamism during the 1999–2002 period – a time which, chiefly because of the energy created in India's economy despite the saffron detractors, can be described as the time of the Vajpayee Dominance.

If the economy was Vajpayee's no. 1 achievement, his second biggest achievement was his reach-out to Kashmir, Pakistan and to India's Muslims. To create an inclusive government, and a legitimate competitor to the Congress, wrenching the BJP away from the Hindutva stranglehold was his great passion; 'Respect for difference', 'have to take everyone along', 'everyone is entitled to an opinion' were lines he repeated in almost every interview. 'We have proved through our governance and actions how misplaced the views about the BJP being anti-minority or anti-Muslim are,' he declared. 'There has been increasing support for the BJP among Muslims. We will now build on that to carry our inclusive world view to its logical conclusion.'[36]

Solving the Kashmir tangle was a test of this inclusivity, Vajpayee realizing early that there could be no breakthrough in Jammu and Kashmir without peace moves with Pakistan. The way forward, therefore, was to win hearts through open dialogue with all. Militancy was on a slow burn in Kashmir in 2000, and Vajpayee now made a significant and unexpected move. On the eve of Ramzan, 19 November 2000, he offered a unilateral ceasefire in Jammu and Kashmir. The Government of India would forthwith cease all combat operations against militants in Jammu and Kashmir during Ramzan. The offer was immediately rejected by militant groups and denounced by Pakistan as 'tactical manoeuvring by India'. But some Kashmiris warmed to the offer, which was intended as a stepping stone to dialogue and negotiation, calling it a great opportunity which should not be lost at any cost.

Of course, the Vajpayee brand of inclusivity must also be tempered with balancing acts. At this time, in a typically clever Vajpayee tightrope walk, he threw the Sangh Parivar a mithai: on 6 December 2000, the anniversary of the demolition of the Babri Masjid, he said the agitation for the Ram Mandir was a national movement, *kaam adhure reh gaye* (our work is unfinished). Vajpayee later admitted, 'NDA leaders were unhappy at what I said,' but the point had been made.[37] Vajpayee has bared his 'fascist saffron soul', shouted the left. Uttar

Pradesh elections were only two years away and RSS cadres, already becoming alienated, could not be antagonized. Besides, whatever the demands of coalition politics, Vajpayee the strategic politician would never fully jettison the Hindu cause, nor would he ever entirely stop believing in Hindu nationalism as a force for positive change. By letting it slip now and then, he played a skilful guessing game, giving himself room to manoeuvre. In ambiguity and doublespeak lay Vajpayee's claim to liberalness.

Visiting the communally torn Dangs in Gujarat in 1999, he didn't criticize the VHP (which was thoroughly hostile to Vajpayee), but instead called for a 'national debate on religious conversions'. However, on Mahatma Gandhi's death anniversary on 30 January 1999, Vajpayee fasted for a day in memory of the Christians who had been attacked as well as in memory of the missionary Graham Staines who was burnt to death with his two sons on 23 January 1999. With Dara Singh, allegedly with links to the Bajrang Dal, charged with Staines' macabre slaying, Vajpayee asserted: 'Let no one be under any illusion. The laws of our land are clear and they will be enforced without exception.'[38] In June 2000 Vajpayee met the Pope in the Vatican City and vowed to take action against those attacking churches, but in an interview to NDTV he defensively asked, 'How can our government be blamed for what happened in Orissa?' When announcing the Kashmir ceasefire, he used the words 'holy month of Ramzan'.

Two years after the Ramzan ceasefire came another defining chapter in Kashmir's history when Vajpayee oversaw what was widely hailed as a free and fair state assembly election in October 2002. Kashmiris, cynically habituated to rigged polls, experienced the thrill of a free vote. 'Vajpayee was a messiah for Kashmir,' Mehbooba Mufti recalled years later. 'He understood our agony.'[39] The polls sent out an important signal: democratic India was determined to restore elected government in Kashmir. The government began to mull a dialogue with the Kashmiri separatist leaders of the Hurriyat Conference. When L.K. Advani asked, '*Kaun baat karega?* [Who will talk to them?],' pat came Vajpayee's reply: *'Aap baat karenge* [You will talk to them].' Subsequently, in January 2004 it was Advani the nationalist hardliner who was sent into dialogue with New Delhi's most trenchant separatist opponents.

In 2004 an interviewer asked him to name what his biggest achievement as prime minister had been. 'If the process of normalization of relations with Pakistan becomes a permanent process, then I will see that as my biggest achievement,' he replied.[40] Beginning as foreign minister in 1977 to his bus ride to Lahore and the continual efforts by the Hindu nationalist former Jana Sanghi to reach out to the Islamic Republic of Pakistan, all were marks of his straining at the Sangh Parivar leash, attempts to leap out of the box of Hindutva politics and seize the Nehruvian torch. A few months after being battered by the Tehelka and *Outlook* allegations, the Vajpayee government struck out towards a rallying national moment, a moment which would grab eyeballs and focus the country's attention on something other than the wearying catalogue of wrongdoing at the top. With the Taj Mahal as the backdrop, this high-visibility event would become a TV spectacle and a display of the persona of Peacemaker Vajpayee. This was the Agra Summit between India and Pakistan, held in Agra in July 2001.

Elaborate arrangements were laid out in Agra for the two-day summit over 14–16 July. General Musharraf and his team were housed in the ultra-luxurious Oberoi Amarvilas hotel. Vajpayee and his entourage moved into the slickly modern Jaypee Palace hotel, which was also the venue of the summit because of the prime minister's painful knees. He was struggling to walk and it was thought best to have him stay at the venue. An assemblage of senior ministers stood at the ready: ranged alongside Vajpayee were external affairs minister Jaswant Singh, finance minister Yashwant Sinha, commerce minister Murasoli Maran, information and broadcasting minister Sushma Swaraj and the ubiquitous Brajesh Mishra.

Agra city was given a thorough sprucing up, with flowering plants arranged everywhere. Along with the potted plants, another entity was flowering at this time: 24x7 TV media. Aaj Tak had just been set up and NDTV had started 24x7 broadcast. The Agra Summit became the first full-scale summit in the age of TV news in India. The TV camera was not only a witness, but also a participant: it spoke loudly, amplifying and sensationalizing even minor details.

The talks began on 15 July but hit a wall. Musharraf was insistent on first resolving the Kashmir dispute, Vajpayee pressed for a composite dialogue on eight points, among them cross-border terrorism. There was no meeting of minds. On the morning of Monday, 16 July, Vajpayee's ministers assembled in the prime minister's room in the Jaypee Palace hotel. Jaswant Singh showed them all a draft of a joint statement he had prepared with his Pakistani counterpart Abdul Sattar. Advani strongly objected to this document, asking where the reference to cross-border terrorism was. Jaswant Singh 'suddenly lost his cool' and grew angry.[41] As the ministers talked in Vajpayee's room that morning, a bombshell exploded on the television screen. Some startling images appeared on TV: lo and behold, Musharraf was holding a breakfast meeting with top editors.

At the meeting Musharraf appeared truculent, unbending and even hostile. He refused to accept the existence of cross-border terrorism from Pakistan, refused to speak on Kargil and was almost dismissive of the Simla Agreement and the Lahore Declaration. Recalls NDTV editor-in-chief Prannoy Roy, who attended the breakfast meeting: 'Musharraf came across as uncompromising, unashamed and unapologetic about fighting for Kashmir.'[42] The media contingent had not been allowed into the breakfast gathering but as soon as the meeting was over, Roy noticed that a PTV cameraman had filmed the entire interaction. He walked over to the cameraman, asked for the tape, and then 'literally ran' to the NDTV OB van at Agra, and uplinked the tape for immediate telecast.

The effect of the broadcast was sensational. An aggressive Musharraf was seen forcefully laying out his own agenda and signalling that for him there would be no compromise. The collective jaws of the gathered ministers dropped. 'We watched in horror from Vajpayee's room,' recalls Sinha.[43] Advani lapsed into stony silence. Musharraf had effectively thumbed his nose at India.

Vajpayee was downstairs at the conference venue, holding one-on-one talks with Musharraf. He was now handed a transcript of the general's tirade. As soon as he read it, his face crumpled. Musharraf had spilled the beans about his own thinking: he was not ready to accept the existence of any cross-border terrorism, refused to budge on Kashmir and insisted there could be no moving forward until Kashmir was resolved. TV played the meeting in continuous loop. In India's first made-in-media summit, Pakistan seized the airwaves. Taken completely aback, the Indian side was in no mood for compromise. Television images of Musharraf's 'breakfast offensive' wrecked the Agra Summit.

Nirupama Rao, MEA spokesperson at the time, recalls: 'As a government we were completely unprepared for a summit in the glare of 24x7 news . . . The Agra event was planned as a retreat, which means seclusion, but it became a jamboree, with a huge media presence. The Pakistanis ran away with the media narrative, because we simply did not understand how to communicate strategically. More than an air attack or sea attack, in this case, the ground was literally being dug up under our feet.'[44] 'With a country like Pakistan, every dot, every comma should be in place before the principals meet,' says Yashwant Sinha. 'We were ill-prepared.'[45] However much Vajpayee desired a history-making breakthrough, his cabinet said a resounding no to the joint statement. The Agra Summit became a grandly televised, high-profile dud.

In his memoirs, Musharraf writes about his final meeting with Vajpayee, in Vajpayee's room, when he told India's prime minister that 'there seemed to be someone above the two of us who had the power to overrule us', and that both of them had been humiliated. Vajpayee listened to him without saying a word. Concluded Musharraf: 'Vajpayee failed to grasp the moment and lost his moment in history.'[46]

Musharraf left Agra in a huff on the night of the breakfast debacle, cancelling his planned Ajmer visit, calling the summit 'a sad and ridiculous episode'. Vajpayee didn't even see Musharraf off to his car nor was there a farewell handshake between prime minister and general. Vajpayee too drove out of Agra that night, saying, '*Koshish jaari rahegi* [Our efforts will continue].' After Musharraf's book was published in 2006, Vajpayee said the reason the Agra Summit failed was Musharraf's insistence that those whom India called 'cross-border terrorists' be described as 'Kashmiri freedom fighters'.

In Parliament Vajpayee faced attacks and tried to make light of the failed summit, saying with his usual self-deprecating wit: 'The guest came with his own karma, our karma was such that this was what we had to face.' He made the House laugh, as he always did, but he was now becoming a recluse, closeted away with a small inner circle, mainly his household and a few others. The once jovial jokester with a sense of humour unusual in politicians was often gloomy, keeping his eyes closed at meetings, saying almost nothing.

In August 2001, at a meeting of the BJP parliamentary party, Vajpayee unexpectedly switched on the mike and before anyone could stop him said:

> I find myself unable to run the NDA cohesively, and being prime minister I own full responsibility for this. I want to quit and you should choose somebody else in my place. I am told I have grown old and that I am also unwell. Before people tell me it's time to go, I want to retire on my own.

Within minutes the news leaked, and Aaj Tak galloped into breaking news: 'Vajpayee offers to resign.' The foxy politician had deployed his familiar weapon of the resignation threat and had rallied his support base, as he always did when he felt besieged. Again, the gambit worked. Senior leaders rushed to cajole him to take back his words; threats to his position and criticism of him were staved off for the moment.

In spite of RSS disapproval, despite the failure at Agra, Vajpayee refused to give up on subcontinental peacemaking. In April 2003 Vajpayee arrived in Srinagar to deliver a speech that became one of the highlights of his prime ministership. The Sher-e-Kashmir Stadium was packed to capacity on that bright afternoon of 18 April. Dressed in a black bandgala, Vajpayee spoke from behind bulletproof glass in a slightly quavering but assertive voice, his speech sprinkled with Urdu words. He reached out to Musharraf for talks: 'I went with the message of friendship to Lahore, but they attacked in Kargil. We again invited General Musharraf to Agra, but it was incomplete. I am again extending the hand of friendship.' To Kashmiris he said: 'Let's talk on the basis of *insaaniyat* [humanity] . . . let's move forward on the basis of *jamhooriyat* [democracy] . . . *jamhooriyat*, *insaaniyat* and *kashmiriyat* [democracy, humanity and the Kashmiri tradition] need to be saved.'[47]

Jamhooriyat. Insaaniyat. Kashmiriyat. Vajpayee the Hindu nationalist had started his political journey with Syama Prasad Mookerji in Jammu and Kashmir; now his words opened the hearts of Kashmiris to Vajpayee. On 6 January 2004, at the SAARC summit in Islamabad, Vajpayee and Musharraf met again, this time the talks resulting in a successful joint statement in which Pakistan affirmed it would not allow any territory under its control to be used to support terrorism. The 2004 joint statement was a last milestone in Vajpayee-style peacemaking. But by this time, his government did not have long to live.

As 2001 drew to a close Vajpayee could not have known that his political innings was coming to an abrupt end with an unexpected election defeat, and that the beginnings of the ultimate demise of his government would be sown in 2002, a year that would dramatically change not only his prime ministerial tenure, but Indian politics as well. The golden hue of Vajpayee's dominant years would dissolve into an area of darkness.

9

The Beginning of the End: 2002–2004

A poem for Vajpayee:

Malevolent spirits from times past
Ran wild and threatening, as he looked on aghast.
His carefully balanced poise,
His time to rejoice
Now looked as if they were fading fast.

~

The year 2002 was Vajpayee's annus horribilis. It was the year in which many things began to go wrong and when the Vajpayee dominance came to an end. The year became the turning point of his prime ministership, and brought his own personal Waterloo. It was a year which, as he had once written, concealed snares in moments of salvation.

His poem '*Geet Nahin Gaata Hun*' ('No Longer Do I Sing') encapsulates a sense of helplessness at what destiny had in store for him.

Benakaab chehre hain:
Daag bade gahre hain.

Tootta tilism, aaj sach se bhay khaata hun.
Geet nahin gata hun . . .
Peeth me chhuri saa chaand
Rahu gaya rekha phaand
Mukti ke kshanon me baar baar bandh jaata hun
Geet nahin gata hun

The masks have dropped away:
These scars run too deep.
The spell has broken, I face the terror of truth.
No longer do I sing . . .
The moon is a scimitar in my back,
Rahu's fury knows no bounds;
Every moment of salvation conceals a snare.
No longer do I sing.[1]

In 2002 bugles sounded for the all-important assembly elections in Uttar Pradesh scheduled for February–March. In Uttar Pradesh, the BJP had been cast into the poll wilderness after the demolition of the Babri Masjid, pushed against the wall by the rampaging elephant of the BSP and the fast-pedalling cycle of the SP. Repeatedly trounced in elections in Uttar Pradesh through the 1990s, the BJP entered into alliances with Mayawati in 1995 and 1997. The Mayawati–BJP power-sharing arrangement broke in 1997 and the BJP's powerful backward caste leader Kalyan Singh cobbled together a government by splitting the Congress and BSP. The BJP's showing in Uttar Pradesh in the Lok Sabha polls of 1999 had been disastrous; even in the flush of post-Kargil nationalism the party floundered, falling to twenty-nine seats from fifty-seven in 1998. In 1999 the BJP in Uttar Pradesh was in a free fall, discontent was rife and Kalyan Singh, the BJP's first backward caste Hindutva face in Uttar Pradesh, was expelled from the party.

Like Govindacharya, Kalyan Singh became another target of Vajpayee's wrath. Kalyan Singh, a Ram Mandir warrior and OBC chieftain, had never had warm relations with Vajpayee. Always a part of the BJP's brahmanical social elite, Vajpayee was never fully comfortable with fiery backward caste politicians or backward caste assertion. While Advani embraced the plebeian groups who emerged into leadership roles during the Ram Mandir movement, Vajpayee by contrast was never fully at ease with anyone outside the upper-caste fold. Kalyan Singh, always an Advani acolyte and distant from Vajpayee both socially and intellectually – Vajpayee's Uttar Pradesh circles dominated by Brahmins and Banias – suspected that Vajpayee had tried to stall his chief ministership in 1997 during the BJP–BSP power-sharing government. Kalyan was given to making off-the-cuff remarks about the veteran. During the 1999 polls, Kalyan complained bitterly about his 'marginalization', stayed away from campaigning and openly mocked Vajpayee by saying: 'Before becoming PM, Vajpayee must first become an MP,' and 'Vajpayee is a tired leader led by retired bureaucrats.' The 1999 campaign in Uttar Pradesh had been spearheaded by members of Vajpayee's upper-caste Uttar Pradesh clique Lalji Tandon and Kalraj Mishra (both Kalyan's detractors), and the 1999 losses were a personal setback for the prime minister. Kalyan was accused of sabotaging the polls and was thrown out of the party in December 1999. Vajpayee was slow to anger, but when he did lose his temper, he launched a no-holds-barred onslaught. Like, Govindacharya, Kalyan was determinedly neutralized.

In 2002, with the Uttar Pradesh polls ahead, Ram's armies were growing restless. Desperate to assert their presence, thoroughly disenchanted with Vajpayee's liberal economics and peacemaking moves with Pakistan and in Kashmir, Hindutva entities stepped on the accelerator. Led by the VHP, Hindutva groups restarted campaigns to begin construction of the Ram Mandir in Ayodhya. The VHP announced 15 March 2002 as the date when bhumi puja for construction would begin, and in scenes reminiscent of 1992, thousands of Ram Mandir activists descended on Ayodhya. A tense stand-off between the saffron brigade and the Vajpayee government ensued. Vajpayee was the object of their fury: why was their own Sangh Parivar prime minister ignoring them, treating their demands with disdain and obstructing their Ram temple plans? 'Hindu anger is growing,' bellowed the VHP's Pravin Togadia, 'and the Ram Mandir is more important than any government.'[2] Another Hindutva leader, Ramchandra Paramhans, openly blasted 'secular', 'half-Congressman' Vajpayee. 'Vajpayee will have to pay a price for hurting Hindu sentiments,' he declared. 'We gave him a chance but he has shown his true colours.' BJP MP Swami Chinmayananda fumed: 'Vajpayee cannot be trusted. He says something on the floor of the House then goes back on it. *Yeh rajpaat nahin, raj part kar rahe hain* [He is not ruling the country, he is dividing it].'[3]

Familiar malevolent ghosts again circled the centrist prime minister. Once again, he looked in danger of being overpowered by the street-fighter zealots as he had been in the 1990s. Luckily, a court order brought reprieve. On 13 March 2002, the Supreme Court ruled that 'no religious activity of any kind will be held at the disputed site'. After the Supreme Court ruling, the Vajpayee government, saying no puja could be allowed before the court verdict, slammed down a massive police presence on the twin towns of Ayodhya and Faizabad. The kar sevaks were rounded up and bundled out of Ayodhya, and the crisis of yet another shila puja was averted. There was a reason for Vajpayee's determination. The reason was the bloodstained burning streets of Gujarat and the February–March 2002 Gujarat riots.

On 27 February 2002, as Hindu kar sevaks and local Muslim groups clashed at Godhra railway station in Gujarat, a railway coach was burnt, killing fifty-nine kar sevaks. Communal sentiments boiled over, leading to three days of brutal communal riots in which, according to official figures, 1267 were killed and an estimated 1,50,000 lost their homes. Media reports began to emerge of administrative collusion and of the Narendra Modi–led government not having acted swiftly enough to stop the violence but in fact having been complicit with the rioters. Fact-finding missions found that people had been butchered and burned beyond recognition, and children speared and thrown into flames. The rioting finally ended after the army marched through the streets and shoot-at-sight orders were announced. Narendra Modi was the hand-picked chief minister of the BJP 'high command', sent to Gujarat by Vajpayee and Advani. In fact, Vajpayee was responsible for Modi's return to India from the US. In 2000, when Prime Minister Vajpayee, on a US tour, met Modi and some American NRIs, he told the fifty-year-old RSS pracharak: '*Aise bhagne se kaam nahin chalega. Kab tak yahaan rahenge? Dilli aao* [It won't do to keep running away like this. How long will you stay here? Come to Delhi].' Now Chief Minister Modi staunchly defended his government: 'Where was the delay? I restored sanity in a record seventy-two hours.'[4]

National Human Rights Commission (NHRC) head Justice J.S. Verma and team rushed to Gujarat on 19 March. After two visits, Justice Verma wrote a five-page letter to Vajpayee:

> A serious travesty of law will occur with potentially grave consequences to the reputation of the country in case our nation falls short in rendering justice to the victims and their families of the Godhra train-burning incident on February 27, 2002 and the riots that followed . . . I am profoundly concerned whether the perpetrators of the violence will be punished and whether victims will be allowed to avail legal remedies they are entitled to.[5]

Former IAS officer P.C. Sen, who as secretary general of the NHRC had accompanied Justice Verma to the Gujarat relief camps, recalls their shock at seeing the camps. The conditions in the Shah Alam Camp were horrifying. Among countless other victims, they met a mute fourteen-year-old girl who had lost her power of speech after being raped. 'The NHRC produced detailed reports on Gujarat,' says Sen, 'but there was no feeling of fear and intimidation that we could not write and document exactly what we saw, even though Mr Vajpayee was from the BJP.'[6]

With Gujarat riots on one side sparking tensions across India and the VHP's shila puja mobilization in Ayodhya on the other, which road was Vajpayee to go down? NDA allies, outraged by the Gujarat riots, would pull his government down if he pandered to the VHP but cracking down meant risking the volcanic wrath of Hindutva cadres already in an implacably anti-Vajpayee mood. All his political life, through guile, shrewdness, ambiguity, and his own stature, Vajpayee had kept the sangh out of the highest echelons of government and away from crucial decision-making. But the Gujarat riots and the subsequent systematic build-up of Hindutva sentiment weakened his hand. Once again Ram's army came galloping on towards the beleaguered prime minister.

Meanwhile, NDA allies fulminated and the Opposition shouted for Modi's resignation. Lok Janshakti Party leader Ram Vilas Paswan resigned. Sharad Yadav, Vajpayee's long-time associate, also threatened to resign but was mollified. NDA ally Chandrababu Naidu publicly declared that Modi must resign. The Opposition brought a censure motion against the government in Parliament over the Gujarat violence, and attacked the government so vociferously that Doordarshan was not allowed to telecast it.[7]

Vajpayee made double-edged statements. He declared that the events in Gujarat had brought shame to the entire nation but also castigated the media for showing 'exaggerated' images of the carnage and for misquoting him, and rejected pleas by rights activists to ban the VHP or Bajrang Dal.[8] Trapped in a hard place between NDA allies and sangh hotheads, Vajpayee mysteriously did not visit Gujarat in the first weeks of the Godhra incident. Instead, he mentioned Godhra and the riots in one breath, saying, 'From Godhra to Ahmedabad, in so many places, there are so many incidents of people being burnt alive, including helpless women and children. This is a blot on the nation's forehead and has grievously harmed India's image in the eyes of the world.'[9]

Just as Indira Gandhi, when she started playing Hindu politics, had delayed visiting communal riot–torn Moradabad in 1980 for fear of being seen as sympathetic to Muslims, Vajpayee, once MP from Gandhinagar, kept delaying his visit to the burning grounds of Gujarat. Nor did he censure the Gujarat government or say a word against the chief minister's inability to maintain law and order, or restrict or ban the Bajrang Dal and VHP. The same NDA which had moved with such alacrity to impose President's Rule in Bihar in 1999 on grounds of 'breakdown of law and order' took no such step in Gujarat, where bloody riots raged for three days. Appallingly, on Gujarat, Vajpayee the calculating politician prevailed over Vajpayee the constitutional moralist.

Grim disapproval glared down from Rashtrapati Bhavan. President K.R. Narayanan, progressive and secular to the core, wrote letters to the prime minister. In an interview to the Malayalam monthly magazine *Manava Samskriti* in March 2005, Narayanan spoke of 'governmental and administrative support for the communal riots in Gujarat'. He said:

> I gave several letters to Vajpayee . . . I met him personally . . . But he did not do anything effective. I requested him to send the army to Gujarat and suppress the riots. The military was sent, but they were not given powers to shoot. Had the military been given powers to shoot, the carnage in Gujarat could have been avoided. I feel there was a conspiracy involving the state and central governments behind the Gujarat riots.[10]

The angry letters that Narayanan wrote on the Gujarat riots have never been made public because of a high court order, and they could have been the reason why the Vajpayee government denied Narayanan a second term. In the same interview, Narayanan also talked about how he had objected to the BJP's saffronizing agenda in education and had raised objections to some of the university vice chancellors that the BJP had appointed. An old friend of Vajpayee was also anguished by the Gujarat events. 'I feel broken, shattered, desolate . . .' wrote the communist leader Hiren Mukherjee to President K.R. Narayanan in April 2002. 'I cannot write to Atal for whom I have had much affection, because as Prime Minister he has chosen to condone and explain away cruelties that almost out-Hitler Hitler.'[11]

In 2002 came another setback to his leadership. The Uttar Pradesh assembly results came in. The BJP's fortunes took a nosedive: the assembly was hung, with BJP finishing third with eighty-eight seats, to the BSP's ninety-eight and the SP's 143. The defeat cast the BJP into disarray, its declining organization and lack of leadership humiliatingly on display. After a period of President's Rule, BSP chief Mayawati was sworn in as chief minister, with outside support from the BJP, the party propping up the mercurial bahujan supremo for the third time, she who had ditched Vajpayee in the 1999 one-vote-loss no-confidence vote. The power sharing was ruinous for the BJP, its upper-caste votes draining away to the BSP, which stepped up its Brahmin jodo sammelans (gatherings aimed at getting Brahmins to join the BSP) and sarvajan samaj (united society) campaign. Uttar Pradesh was lost again. The sangh seethed: the secularizing Vajpayee-fronted BJP had paid for deserting the Hindu cause. Vajpayee-style moderation was not winning elections, and cadres strained for a full-blooded return to Hindutva and 'core values'.

A crown of thorns for our hero who wanted to be loved by all! With the multiparty, multi-voiced NDA to manage, he could not openly encourage the VHP, but if he clamped down on the mandir programme he faced a revolt from within. He fell back on a familiar ploy: offering to resign. In March 2002, during a Parliament session, Jaswant Singh received an urgent call from Pramod Mahajan, asking him to come immediately. Jaswant Singh burst into Vajpayee's office in Parliament House to find the prime minister with pen and paper in hand. 'He's writing his resignation,' cried Mahajan. Jaswant Singh grabbed Vajpayee's hand to stop him. 'What are you doing, don't do this,' said Jaswant Singh. Vajpayee kept trying to write and Jaswant Singh kept persuading him not to, until Vajpayee finally gave up and they all went to Vajpayee's home. 'We were able to defuse the situation,' recalled Singh.[12]

On 4 April 2002, several weeks after the riots began, Vajpayee finally arrived in Gujarat, saying he had come with a 'broken heart' and that 'I had wanted to come earlier but I was told things were not okay'.[13] His first stop in Gujarat was Godhra, where he went to the train station and pensively stepped into the charred S-6 train compartment of the Sabarmati Express in which the kar sevaks had died. He then flew to Ahmedabad and visited riot-affected areas and relief camps where thousands of desperate Muslim families languished. At the Shah Alam Camp, he burst out emotionally: 'You [Muslims] are not alone in this time . . . It is heart-wrenching to see you as refugees in your own land . . . with what face will I go abroad after what has happened here.'[14] At a joint press conference at Ahmedabad airport, sitting side by side with Modi, Vajpayee said:

> India commands a lot of respect internationally. Muslim countries are also present in the world. I am wondering with what face will I go there? The people in the camps must be looked after, the orphaned children and widows must be looked after, we must heal the wounds; along with the government social organizations must also come forward.[15]

Yet, bowing to the BJP–RSS line he also referred to Godhra as a 'pre-planned conspiracy'.

A journalist asked Vajpayee, 'Prime Minister, what's your message to Chief Minister Narendra Modi?' Replied Vajpayee: 'My one message to the chief minister is that he should follow *Rajdharma.* Rajdharma [ethical governance] . . . *yeh shabd kafi sarthak hai*, this word is meaningful. I keep trying to live by it. A ruler should not practise any discrimination between his subjects on the basis of birth, caste or religion.' Modi, sitting next to Vajpayee, responded in a low tone, 'I am also doing that, sir.'[16] Vajpayee, after one of his long pauses, said, 'I am sure Narendrabhai is doing this. Thank you.'

Vajpayee's words were hardly overly censorious. On the Gujarat riots he never took a clear or hard stand. Yet the word rajdharma burst into the media and the word haunted Modi. To counter his failures to live up to his rajdharma, Modi now let loose the roar of 'Gujarat asmita', or 'pride of 6 crore Gujaratis', and as a result of this openly jingoist, parochial cry, his popularity began to steadily grow.

'Vajpayee desperately wanted Modi to take moral responsibility and resign at this time,' says Yashwant Sinha. 'That is what he would have preferred. And if Modi had resigned, the NDA would not have lost the general elections of 2004.' 'Vajpayee was terribly upset with Gujarat,' says Sudheendra Kulkarni. 'He was upset on two counts. It lowered the image of India in our own eyes and it hurt him politically.' Ghatate recalled how troubled his friend was. 'After the Ram Janmabhoomi movement, this was the next big disagreement that Vajpayee had with Advani,' says Ghatate. 'He wanted Modi to step aside of his own accord.' Vajpayee wanted Modi to go, yet Advani remained Modi's unswerving supporter. For Vajpayee, with the much-vaunted inclusivity of his image and government at stake, Modi's resignation was almost a necessity, and he held meeting after meeting in April–May 2002 – six in all, with L.K. Advani, former party president Kushabhau Thakre and RSS leader Madan Das Devi and others – and in every one of them he pressed for Modi's resignation. But Thakre, and even George Fernandes, spoke up strongly against sacking Modi. Thakre, the RSS's Rajju Bhaiya and H.V. Sheshadri tried to get Vajpayee to change his mind, but the prime minister kept insisting that the Gujarat chief minister must quit.

There are those who seek power by trampling upon dead bodies, Vajpayee once wrote in a poem, '*Satta*' ('Power').

Masoom bachon
boodhi auraton
jawan mardon ki lashon ke dher par chadhkar
Jo satta ke singhasan tak pahuchna chahte hain
Unse mera ek sawal hai:

Kya marne walon ke saath unka koi rishta natha?
Na sahi dharm ka naata
Kya dharti ka bhi sambandh nahin tha . . .

To those who try to reach
The throne of power
Over mounds of dead bodies
Of innocent children
Old women
Young men,
I have a question:
Did nothing bind them
To those who died?
Their faiths differed;
Was it not enough that they too were of this earth . . .

Children charred by fire
Women savaged by lust,
Houses reduced to ash
Constitute neither a certificate of culture
Nor badge of patriotism.[17]

The poem was written years earlier, but perhaps the same question could be asked of those in his own party who rioted and rampaged in the name of religion: '*Was it not enough that they too were of this earth?*'

Vajpayee was once again at odds with the saffron groundswell in his party. Wildfires had begun that could engulf the frail sailboat of Vajpayeeism. If the Hindutva forces grew too powerful, he was in danger of becoming an irrelevant and dispensable back number. Vajpayeeism or reformist economics and secular accommodation were seen as election flops by the party. Cadres were resentful at ideological dilution. In 1998 and 1999, the BJP had been the single largest party in Parliament, but the party had won 182 seats both times, unable to increase its tally. Something was going wrong. Advani, preoccupied in government, had stepped down as BJP president, to be replaced first by the lacklustre Kushabhau Thakre, then by Bangaru Laxman; who was felled by Tehelka, and then by the ineffectual Jana Krishnamurthi. The party was adrift; the prime minister was a world statesman and beloved national leader but he couldn't win them a big election victory. There started a quest for a new platform, a new leader. Atal–Advani were the greying ancien regime and there was a search for new, younger captains, with some suggesting Pramod Mahajan. But Mahajan was lumbered with the big disadvantage of being far too flashy for the sangh. A new leader was waiting in the wings, but nobody knew it yet. Once this new leader emerged as the unquestioned darling of Ram's army, the leadership of Vajpayee began its slow fade towards irrelevance. In 2002 the rise of Narendra Modi spelled the fall of Atal Bihari Vajpayee. Vajpayeeism was defeated by Moditva.

In 2002 the BJP was further demoralized. Not only were Uttar Pradesh and Uttaranchal lost, the BJP was well and truly routed in its bastion Delhi in municipal polls. Vajpayee was shaken. He had come to detest the constant interference by the dirigiste RSS, with the SJM and BMS bashing him openly and haranguing him on the wrongness of the privatization programme and demanding that it be rolled back immediately. In March 2002 he snapped at his critics publicly. At the book launch function of his party colleague K.R. Malkani, Vajpayee delivered these enigmatic lines: 'When Swami Vivekananda spoke of Hinduism, nobody called him communal . . . but now some people have defined Hindutva in such a manner that it is better to keep a distance from it.'[18] He had grown distant from the party, hadn't visited party headquarters since he became prime minister, and his relationship with Advani was tense, each camp jostling for power and planting stories about the other in the media. The old informality between the two old-timers, when they would drop in at each other's homes for lunch, was disappearing. There was a growing gulf between 'Pandara Park' – where Advani lived and 'Race Course' – where Vajpayee resided.

Both Ranjan Bhattacharyya and Namita were known to be wary of the chaddiwallahs and saw Vajpayee as the one person standing for sanity in the saffron ocean. The Sangh Parivar not only viewed Vajpayee as not Hindu enough, but saw damaad Ranjan as a far too flashy 'enemy' figure. In 2000 there had even been talk of floating a new Jana Sangh. In October 2002 RSS leaders met Vajpayee to complain that, under the influence of a 'handful of advisers', Vajpayee's government had grown distant from the Sangh Parivar.

~

12 April 2002 was the date set for the BJP's national executive meeting in Goa where matters regarding Modi's resignation would come to a stormy head. Advani would later write that though he himself was not in favour of it, he knew that Vajpayee wanted Modi's resignation.[19]

On the two-hour flight from Delhi to Goa, en route to the party's national executive on 12 April, Vajpayee was accompanied by Advani, Jaswant Singh and Arun Shourie, the last at Brajesh Mishra's request. Shourie provides a highly revealing account of the journey and what subsequently transpired.[20]

Between 7 and 11 April 2002, just after returning from Gujarat, Vajpayee visited Singapore and Cambodia. On the flight to Singapore, Ranjan Bhattacharyya approached Shourie, who was travelling with Vajpayee, to say, '*Baapji ke paas jaiye, bahut down hain* [Please go to Atalji, he is feeling very down].' Shourie went across to the prime minister's first-class luxury cabin to find Vajpayee slumped in his chair, his arms hanging down limply. He gestured to Shourie to take a seat and burst out furiously, '*Main kis mooh se wahan jaa raha hoon?* [Why am I being taken there (abroad)? My face has been blackened (after the Gujarat riots). How will I show my face there?]' Shourie, taken aback by the outburst, advised him to call Advani and ask him to tell Modi to offer his resignation. To which Vajpayee replied, '*Arre, itna aasan hai kya* [It's not so easy]'; no call took place between Vajpayee and Advani during the trip. As the prime minister's entourage returned to Delhi, Brajesh Mishra inquired of Shourie if he was going to Goa for the BJP national executive. He told Shourie, '*Atalji ke plane mein jao. Tumhara aur Major [Jaswant Singh] ka duty hai, woh baat nahin karenge, baat karvao* [Advani and Vajpayee will not talk, it's your duty and Jaswant's duty to make them talk].'

In the prime minister's plane to Goa, the atmosphere was frosty. Vajpayee sat by the window, Advani in front of him, Shourie to Advani's left and Jaswant to Vajpayee's left. Vajpayee was completely silent, staring out of the window. A few minutes after the plane took off, he snatched up a Hindi newspaper, opened it fully to cover his face and began to read. Advani also buried himself in a newspaper. Shourie realized he needed to act if there was to be any dialogue. He leaned over, jerked down Vajpayee's paper and said, '*Chaar din se baat karna chahte thhe, ab baat kijiye na* [You've been wanting to talk for four days, now please talk].' Vajpayee put his paper aside as did Advani. For the first few minutes they talked about finding a replacement for the ageing Jana Krishnamurthi as BJP president and about how the younger Venkaiah Naidu would be the best candidate. The conversation then turned to the looming question on everyone's mind: the resignation of Modi. Vajpayee made an unequivocal statement: '*Woh reh nahin sakte* [He cannot stay on]. *Kam se kam isteefa toh offer karte* [He must at least offer to resign].' He also told Advani to convey to Modi that he must announce his resignation and also select a replacement. For his part, Advani later said that he told Vajpayee that there would be much resistance in the party, but 'if Narendra's quitting is going to improve the situation in Gujarat, I'm willing to tell him to offer his resignation'.[21]

When they landed in Goa and gathered at the Marriott Hotel by the banks of the Mandovi, Advani asked Modi to resign, and Modi initially agreed. Journalist Rajdeep Sardesai recalls being told by Brajesh Mishra to prepare for the 'big breaking story'. 'You can flash it in about an hour, Modi will be asked to resign, I will message you when it's formally done,' Mishra told Sardesai. But the message never came. Something had not gone according to plan. Mishra, the eyes and ears of Vajpayee, had on this occasion completely misread the mood in the party over Modi.

At the meeting, Vajpayee, Advani and Jana Krishnamurthi were on the dais when Modi stood up and delivered a thundering speech, arguing how riots used to occur in the past, alluding to Congress rule. 'Adhyakshji, I want to speak on Gujarat,' said Modi. 'There is need for a free and frank discussion, for this I wish to place my resignation before this body.' Within minutes, groups of people rose to their feet in different corners of the room and began to shout: '*Isteefa mat do, isteefa mat do* [Don't resign, don't resign].'

'I was sitting at the back of the room with Yashwant Sinha and Bhairon Singh Shekhawat,' recalls Shourie. 'I could see Vajpayee looking distressed and puzzled.' Watching the prime minister's discomfiture at the sloganeering, Shourie called out from the back, '*Nirnay liya gaya hai* [The decision has been taken (by Vajpayee)].' A few moments of pin-drop silence followed, then again the groups of people began their chants in support of Modi. 'It was a set-up and a clear coup against Vajpayee,' recalls Shourie. 'Modi stayed on against Vajpayee's wishes.' As the chanting continued, Vajpayee looked at his watch and said, '*Achcha, kal baatcheet hogi* [All right, we'll talk tomorrow],' and left, by then convinced that he had walked into a pre-planned trap. He had been outmanoeuvred.

Arun Jaitley then moved a resolution against Modi's resignation, which was supported by Pramod Mahajan. That even Mahajan, his key aide, had gone along with Modi was the last straw for Vajpayee. 'We felt that removing Narendrabhai at this stage would cost us the support of our rank and file,' was Mahajan's explanation to journalists later. Union minister Shanta Kumar, who had openly demanded Modi's resignation, was rebuked and forced to apologize. A year later Shanta Kumar was dropped from the cabinet. The parivar's core Hindutva vote had found a new leader in the man from Gujarat. With his well-timed resignation offer and an orchestrated outcry against it, Modi had imitated and outsmarted the original master of the political resignation.

After the Modi affair at the national executive, Vajpayee confessed to friends that he was fed up and wanted to leave party matters entirely to Advani.[22] But at the same time he dug in his heels and refused to let himself be totally marginalized.

With the Hindu right on the warpath, Vajpayee the antennae-alert politician sensed that the party was shifting away from him. It was time to do what he had done in 1992: get back into the Hindu action or risk being cast by the wayside. But his act of trying to play catch-up with the new, belligerent mood also signalled loss of control. The BJP was shifting slowly towards Modi and the RSS, and away from him. And he sensed it.

Thus, not only did Vajpayee not put his foot down on Modi's resignation, but in an astonishing volte face from his anguished tone in Gujarat, he made a ringing hard-line Hindutva speech at a public meeting in Panaji on the final day of the party executive, blaming the Muslims for the riots:

> Who are these people accusing us? India was secular when Muslims hadn't come here and Christians hadn't set foot on this soil. It's not as if India became secular after they came . . . If the conspiracy to burn alive the innocent . . . had not been hatched, the Gujarat tragedy could have been averted . . . *Aag lagayi kisne? Aag faily kaise?* [Who lit the fire? How did the fire spread?] Islam has two facets. One is that which tolerates others, that preaches the path of truth, that teaches compassion and mercy . . . But these days militancy in the name of Islam leaves no room for tolerance. Wherever Muslims live, they don't like to live in co-existence with others, they don't like to mingle with others; and instead of propagating their ideas in a peaceful manner, they want to spread their faith by resorting to terror and threats.[23]

The Modi effect had hit the veteran. The saffron parivar's impatience and mounting frustration with Vajpayeeism – appeasement of NDA allies, outreach in Jammu and Kashmir and desertion of its core Hindu constituency, believed to be causing defeat after poll defeat – boiled over in Goa and coalesced around the persona of Modi. Mindful of the party's mood, Advani had exercised his veto to save Modi, else the Gujarat chief minister too may have met the same fate as Govindacharya and Kalyan Singh. That April in Goa the BJP and RSS rediscovered aggressive Hindutva, and fiery anti-Muslim rhetoric became the flag of BJP's gen-next. In Goa, as Vajpayee fell in with the party line, Modi got a new lease of life. Within months of Vajpayee's 'defeat' at the Goa meeting, Advani would take over as deputy prime minister.

After Goa, complicated, contradictory Vajpayee attempted another turnaround to stand forth again as the inclusivist reconciler. In Parliament, on 1 May 2002, he tried desperately to control the damage. 'It seems I have lost all I have earned in my life. I have never discriminated against anybody in my life on the basis of caste or religion.'[24] Three months after the riots, Vajpayee wrote a letter to Modi, an unusual thing for the prime minister as he rarely wrote to chief ministers. The letter – obtained through an RTI by the press in 2011 – reveals a worried concern about the Modi government's relief efforts. 'I have been informed,' Vajpayee wrote in a letter dated 1 June 2002, 'that relatives of the dead are yet to be paid compensation as the bodies are yet to be identified . . . this inordinate delay is a matter of concern.'[25] He added that DNA sampling should be used to ensure that compensation reaches the correct people, and displaced persons 'should gain enough confidence' to return to their original residences.

Vajpayee's detailed letter, listing points where he clearly felt the state government had failed in rehabilitation efforts, was a reminder that although Modi had managed to cling on, the old warhorse would not give in easily. Meanwhile, flushed with his victory in Goa, Modi set about on an even bigger win. He embarked on a Gujarat gaurav yatra, with the slogan 'Gujarati asmita' (Gujarati pride), and started directing barbs at then election commissioner J.M. Lyngdoh, who was resisting Modi's insistence on calling early polls. Modi kept bringing up the Chief Election Commisioner's full name, James Michael Lyngdoh, to suggest that a Christian was standing in the way of a proud Gujarati Hindu.

In June 2002 there was another public assault on Vajpayee. *TIME* magazine published a no-holds-barred profile of the prime minister, entitled 'Asleep at the Wheel':

> He drank heavily in his prime and still enjoys a nightly whiskey or two at 74 . . . he takes painkillers for his knees and has trouble with his bladder, liver and one remaining kidney. A taste for fried foods and fatty sweets plays havoc with his cholesterol. He takes a three-hour snooze every afternoon on doctor's orders and is given to interminable silences, indecipherable ramblings and not infrequently falling asleep in meetings . . .

The magazine went on to describe him as 'half dead'.[26]

It wasn't completely inaccurate. At this time Vajpayee began to increasingly stumble while walking, fall into bouts of endless silence and became even more notoriously forgetful of names. With the prime minister looking 'shaky and lost', his friend and bête noire, confidant and competitor, indispensable companion and intimate adversary, his efficient home minister, Advani, described in many quarters as the 'prime-minister-in-waiting' stepped up as the government's dynamic face.

In July 2002 President K.R. Narayanan's term came to an end. The BJP had always disliked Narayanan, not only because of his stalling in inviting the NDA to form the government in 1998, but also because of his strict line on the Gujarat riots of 2002, and was reluctant to give him a second term. During the search for a presidential candidate, sections of the RSS, anxious to be rid of Vajpayee, were inclined to kick Vajpayee upstairs to Rashtrapati Bhavan in order to install Advani as prime minister. The RSS's Rajju Bhaiya approached Vajpayee with this suggestion, ostensibly on grounds of his ill health, saying, '*Aap hi kyon nahin Rashtrapati bante?*'[27] But the canny colossus said neither yes nor no, allowing the suggestion to simply vanish into thin air.

Delhi's bush telegraph at this time was afire with tales of the 'Advani camp' 'planting stories' about Vajpayee's illness. But Vajpayee the long-distance warrior refused to give up, adeptly sidestepping sangh attempts to marginalize him, showing remarkable tenacity and shrewdness in remaining firmly in his chair. For the fourteenth Lok Sabha, Vajpayee was determined to remain prime minister, inclined to cede space only if the party won again in 2004. For this reason, Advani, the next in line to be prime minister, was impatient to get over with the general elections of 2004 as fast as possible.

In June 2002 Advani was appointed deputy prime minister, in a move that suggested a shift in power equations, though Advani vociferously scotched rumours that this would lead to the creation of a parallel power centre, saying the decision had been Vajpayee's and was only a formalization of the work he, Advani, had already been doing. Said the irrepressible Jaipal Reddy of the Congress: 'It's not a promotion of Advani but a degradation of Vajpayee.'[28]

In the Gujarat assembly elections of December 2002, the Narendra Modi–led BJP powered to a big victory, netting 127 out of 182 seats and 49.85 per cent of the vote, getting an almost 10 percentage point lead over the Congress, which was able to win just fifty-one seats. The BJP got an injection shot of saffron elixir: after a long election drought and tepid Vajpayeeism, a hot new Hindutva line had mopped up a much-needed win.

Vajpayee had campaigned in the Gujarat assembly polls on dogged Vajpayeeism. 'God is one,' he told a rally in Vadodara in December, 'but ways of prayer can be different. In our country there is respect for all religions.'[29] But it was Modi with his strident, volatile and hard-line Hindu campaign who had won the match. He had turned on a firehose of sheer vitriol. 'If they can't shout Jai Shri Ram here, will they go to Italy and raise these slogans?' Modi screamed at rallies.[30] He was no longer just a faceless pracharak but a loud, sarcastic demagogue, his provocative words making him even more popular. Predicted an RSS leader: 'If we win Gujarat, we will be able to force the BJP leadership to follow the parivar principles and stop the party from looking for endorsement from those who are culturally, socially and politically opposed to us.'[31]

The Sangh Parivar threw its weight into the Gujarat campaign; Modi's hardcore image as 'Hindu Hriday Samrat' (emperor of Hindu hearts) – or, conversely, 'Muslim killer' – carried the day, and the Modi model, with its massive winnability, became a new model for the BJP, a party desperately in need of sellable ideas, winning tickets, new slogans and new faces. Vajpayee had created the first BJP government at the centre which lasted five years – but at what cost to the party, party men asked? Would it be forever a coalition partner, always in power-sharing with others, always apologetic about itself? Or could it hope to storm to power on its own, even if it meant lethal hate-laced speeches, foul-mouthed slogans and vicious personal attacks on the 'enemy'?

Moditva became the sangh's weapon of choice against Vajpayee. As the VHP's Praveen Togadia yelled during the Gujarat campaign, in a clear dig at Vajpayee, 'Those friends of Miyan Musharraf, *jo Godhra bhula dena chahte hain unko aukat dikhao* [Those who want to forgive and forget Godhra, let's show them the reality].' The Vajpayee government belongs 'to the dustbin of history', wrote *Panchjanya* in a 13 October editorial.[32] Modi's 2002 triumph was the beginning of a turnaround for the BJP as a whole. The 'Modi-quake' created a whole new alchemy of brazenly majoritarian leadership, riding the deep saffron tide and calculated to race through the ballot box.

If Vajpayee had stood up determinedly for Vajpayeeism in Gujarat perhaps he would have attained greatness. If he had mustered all his magical eloquence and coaxed his party to the constitutional path and sacked Modi, perhaps it would have become a turning point in the BJP's path away from Hindutva militancy. He could have forced a crucial change of direction on his army – like Ashoka, standing on the battlefield at Kalinga in the third century BCE, who suddenly changed course, realizing the futility of bloodletting becoming Indian history's greatest example of a genuine change of heart. But the tactical politician in Vajpayee took over; he was too weak, too fixated on staying in power and by now too ill and tired to openly challenge Modi or stop his party's turn once again towards destructive Hindutva. Advani's installation as deputy prime minister in June 2002 was a signal that the Sangh Parivar wanted to clip his wings.

As the eighteenth-century letter writer 'Junius' famously wrote, reproaches and inquiries have no power to affect either the man of unblemished integrity or the abandoned profligate. 'It is the middle compound character which alone is vulnerable; the man, who, without firmness to avoid a dishonourable action, has feeling enough to be ashamed of it.' All through his life, Vajpayee, the 'middle compound character', showed he lacked the strength of character to act against wrong, but still had the sensitivity to be ashamed about his own failings. On 22 December 2002, when he attended Narendra Modi's swearing-in ceremony at the Sardar Patel stadium in Ahmedabad – the first time in India's history that a prime minister was in attendance at a chief minister's swearing-in – he wore a bemused smile.

Through the years, driven by ambition and his own sense of destiny, as he trudged to the top, he had easily destroyed all his rivals, ever the tactical, adaptable political expert who could make lusty speeches even on causes he didn't believe in, a master player in the game of thrones. But now that he had reached the summit, he was faced with a ferociously dynamic challenger who practised bruisingly rough politics and didn't play by the old rulebook to which he, reared in the Nehruvian democracy of the 1950s, was accustomed. As it turned out, once Vajpayee was defeated in the general elections of 2004, the fireballs of Moditva devoured the wavering sailboat of Vajpayeeism.

If Vajpayee had won in 2004 and the BJP got firmly entrenched in the democratic centre-right, today's uber-Hindutva era – when Hindu nationalism's recessive gene dominates – may never have come about.

Yet Vajpayee had a triumphant moment in 2002, a moment he took pride in and considered one of his most important achievements. After the misery of the Gujarat riots, a master scientist who would soon become a beloved Pied Piper for India's children, lifted the country's spirits. On 25 July 2002 Avul Pakir Jainulabdeen Abdul Kalam, of the silvery mop of hair, twinkling eyes and wide smile, was sworn in as President. A Muslim appointed as President was a flamboyant flourish of the Vajpayee line. Vajpayee's original choice had been the former principal secretary to Indira Gandhi, P.C. Alexander, but Sonia Gandhi demurred. Vajpayee's vice-presidential choice, Farooq Abdullah, was rejected by the Sangh Parivar and instead Vajpayee's old friend Bhairon Singh Shekhawat took oath as vice president. 'The way Vajpayee picked a Muslim for President was impressive,' says the Congress's Mani Shankar Aiyar. 'He appeased his followers by pointing to Kalam playing the veena.' In a similar vein, back in 1996, Vajpayee went against his party in reviving the Srikrishna Commission inquiring into the post–Babri Masjid demolition Mumbai riots of 1992–93, which had been disbanded by the BJP–Shiv Sena Maharashtra government. In photographs with Kalam, Vajpayee appears smiling broadly as if in self-congratulation at Kalam ascending to India's presidency just months after the Gujarat riots. With a Muslim as the chosen BJP president, Vajpayee was hoping that the embers of the 2002 riots would be doused and that his image as the great reconciler would dominate over the shrill voices once again being heard at the extreme.

At the end of 2002 he wrote his 'Musings from Goa', the second of his year-ender messages to the country. 'True Hindutva', Vajpayee wrote, is 'forward-looking', 'liberal' and 'reform-minded', and is the 'same as Bharatiyata'. He was scathing about '. . . some people [who] project Hindutva, which presents a *viraat darshan* [broad, all-encompassing view] of human life, in a narrow, rigid and extremist manner – an unfortunate and unacceptable interpretation that runs totally contrary to its true spirit.' In a sharp reprimand to those in the saffron brotherhood who swore by the aggressive Moditva version of Hindu nationalism, the veteran middle-of-the-roader sought to forcefully assert Vajpayeeism. But there was no good news to be had from his ratings among the public. An opinion poll held in 2002 showed that Vajpayee's popularity, although still 13 percentage points ahead of his nearest rival Sonia Gandhi's, had declined sharply.[33]

~

The year 2003 brought a new surge of life. After the annus horribilis there were glimpses of an annus mirabilis. The monsoon was bountiful, stock markets zoomed to a three-year high and economists declared that the economy was booming. In July Vajpayee visited China, signing a slew of agreements, President Hu Jintao even reading out a Chinese translation of Vajpayee's poem '*Jung Naa Hone Denge*'.

Vajpayee was the lone preserver of the twenty-odd-party NDA and the BJP's national face, but with Advani installed as deputy prime minister and Modi as Gujarat chief minister, there were niggling doubts: was the Vajpayee line falling behind the Advani line, was Vajpayeeism falling behind Moditva? Was he the convenient puppet geriatric, the BJP kingdom being expanded on the battlefield by younger knights? An open temper tantrum in June 2003 revealed his anger at any hint of his irrelevance.

On the morning of 2 June 2003 BJP president Venkaiah Naidu invited over 250 party men – ministers and party leaders – to 'Panchvati', the wood-panelled, carpeted seminar hall next to the prime minister's bungalow, to welcome Vajpayee back from an overseas tour. Two days earlier, when Vajpayee was not in India, Venkaiah Naidu had made the highly contentious declaration that drove Vajpayee into a rage: 'We are confident that in the next election we will move forward under the guidance of lauhpurush [Advani, the Iron Man] and vikaspurush [Vajpayee, the progress and development man].' The statement was not entirely innocent. Naidu was an Advani protégé, and the public equating of Advani with Vajpayee was slyly intended to convey that the BJP was led by two men and not by one, a significant break with the BJP's slogan of '*Vajpayee ka naam aur Vajpayee ka kaam*' (Vajpayee's name and Vajpayee's achievement).

Vajpayee, dressed in a Jodhpuri bandgala, sat on the dais with Advani, Jaswant Singh and George Fernandes. The gathering was expecting to be regaled with stories about Vajpayee's foreign tour. Instead, an expressionless Vajpayee said, in a voice both defiant and annoyed: '*Advaniji ke netritva mein vijay ki ore aage badhein* [Let us all march towards victory under Advaniji's leadership].' There was a stunned silence. In a flash Naidu was on his feet to hurriedly bluster: 'Let us clarify this once again. Atalji will lead us in the next elections and he will be our prime minister again.' As everyone busily clustered around Vajpayee, and Advani walked out of the meeting to pace the corridor outside, for now, the threat to his leadership was deflected. Having cast the gathering into a tizzy, Vajpayee settled down to a plate of pakodas, and asked, '*Maine kuchh kaha tha kya?* [Did I say anything?]' In a time of economic buoyancy and an overall change in mood among the public, the political grandmaster had put down any hint of a challenge to his supremo status.

As the political arena at home grew ever more cut-throat, Vajpayee revelled in his overseas tours, which invariably lifted his mood. In the past whenever he visited New York, he would watch Broadway shows and stroll down the streets buying ice cream cones for himself and his security staff. N.K. Singh was with him on one of his annual trips to New York, to the United Nations General Assembly, and found Vajpayee full of energy and verve, back to being his witty self, ready with jokes and anecdotes, in sharp contrast to his withdrawn, grim-faced persona at home. 'I invited him, along with some others, out for a meal in New York,' recalls Singh. 'We went to a nearby Chinese restaurant, all of us around the table, very informal, very relaxed. He was careful about how he looked, his dark bandgalas were always smartly tailored. He spoke optimistically at the dinner. He was very keen to leave behind a legacy.'

In 2003, sensing a return of momentum to the NDA, estranged ally Mamata Banerjee returned to the fold and was reinducted as a minister in September. In assembly elections in Madhya Pradesh, Rajasthan and Chhattisgarh in December, the BJP decimated the Congress and soared to record wins, Vasundhara Raje and Uma Bharti leading the charge in Rajasthan and Madhya Pradesh.

Vajpayee was elated at the election victories and the end of 2003 found him resolute and full of optimism. Despite the Sangh Parivar's grumblings, he was pushing forward towards peacemaking and his international reputation was formidable. To celebrate his seventy-ninth birthday on 25 December 2003 he planned a four-day break in Jaipur with his family and entourage. Fifteen rooms were booked in the Rambagh Palace hotel, in the manner of a sultan's travelling court.

On 24 December he visited his constituency, Lucknow, planning to return to Delhi by the evening, celebrate his birthday at home and then leave for Jaipur. But by the evening of the 24th, North India's dense winter fog closed in and Vajpayee's flight back to Delhi was diverted, funnily enough, to Jaipur. Birthday engagements had piled up in the capital so Vajpayee and his team decided on a late-night drive from Jaipur back to Delhi. This was his famous night-time dash from Jaipur to Delhi, a symbol of his bravura leadership at this point. The prime minister's fast-moving motorcade leapt down the fog-bound highway, sirens wailing, the powerful fog lights and red pilot lights of his limousines and escort jeeps flashing, as the speeding convoy streaked through the mist. Could a bit of fog stop the march of the political Ulysses of his time? En route the clock struck twelve. It was his seventy-ninth birthday. The prime minister's party stopped at Ajmer for an impromptu celebration. Vajpayee cut an Ajmer milk cake, cups of tea were passed around and photographs were taken of a beaming Vajpayee. He made it to Delhi just in time as by early morning thousands of party workers had begun to gather at his residence to wish him. Later that morning, he stepped out among them, cheery and confident. '*Vijay hai, bishram nahin, samay ka mahatva hai* [It's the time of victory, not of rest, time is of utmost importance],' he told them. In the evening he attended an evening of song and poetry organized by Vijay Goel and recited his poem '*Haar Nahin Manunga*' ending with a ringing '*Geet Naya Gata Hoon*'. The audience applauded. The songs began. Tamil Nadu Chief Minister M. Karunanidhi sent birthday greetings describing Vajpayee as 'India's tallest surviving leader'.

It was full steam ahead for the SAARC summit scheduled for 4 and 6 January 2004 in Islamabad and the BJP national executive on 11 January 2004, where it was likely to be announced that general elections had been brought forward to May taking advantage of the feel-good factor. Radiating positivity, Vajpayee cancelled his Jaipur holiday, eager to begin work on his second term, he and his team certain of a fresh new mandate in 2004. 'Are you ready for elections?' journalists asked Vajpayee. 'I am fit and ready. I believe in destiny, I believe in God.'[34]

It was not to be. On 22 May 2004, a different prime minister – the Congress's Manmohan Singh – took oath. Vajpayee, the virat purush (leading man) of politics bit the dust. There would be no more '*Agli bari Atal Bihari*'. He was forced into exile from which he would never return.

~

Five years later

In 2009 the BJP was defeated again. In the same year Vajpayee suffered an incapacitating stroke which snatched away the skill that had built his career and taken him into the hearts of people: his speech. He could no longer speak. He was now mostly bedridden and confined to his new home in 6A Krishna Menon Marg, among his few visitors the ever-faithful Appa Ghatate, Advani and the BJP's B.C. Khanduri. Glassy-eyed, unable to communicate or eat properly (his favourite food – Chinese-style stir-fried prawns – was served to him in tiny amounts), he became unrecognizable.

'Before he lost his speech, he told me, I've spent fifty years in public life, Appa, I now want to fade way. After his stroke, I used to go at least twice a week to see him, sit with him, talk to the family. He couldn't speak, but would try to watch TV or read the newspapers. There were doctors, physiotherapists and nurses there most of the time. I really missed his steady supply of jokes, wisecracks and witticisms,' Ghatate recalled.[35]

On 11 June 2018 he was admitted to AIIMS and placed under the care of his personal physician Dr Randeep Guleria. On 16 August 2018, after a decade of illness, at the age of ninety-three, Vajpayee died.

The physical agonies in his last years symbolized the manner in which the idea he represented – Hindu nationalism trying to operate within the constraints of democracy – was also in its death throes. With his death, that idea – the creed of Vajpayeeism – died too.

10

The Personal and the Political

A poem for Vajpayee:

Bachelor, not celibate, not husband yet lover
The Hindu bohemian was moved by passion's power,
He said 'to hell with convention,
never mind the wrath of the saffron organization,
Like Ulysses I'll drink of life to my last hour.'

But his abiding love was that great Hall,
Where he saw titans rise and fall,
Where his words caused countrywide ripples,
Because in debate and dissent,
Lay great service of the people.

~

Through the changing seasons of his life Vajpayee held one relationship as his anchor and emotional centre: his relationship with Rajkumari Kaul, the married woman he lived with and whose family he adopted as his own. 'You could say Vajpayee loved both Mr and Mrs Kaul equally,' recalled Ghatate. 'Mrs Kaul was his close friend who simply happened to be a woman. I have no idea whether their relationship was purely platonic or not, and frankly it made no difference.' The world saw the living arrangement as an unconventional, even outrageous ménage à trois; to the three protagonists it was a perfectly natural extension of the youthful friendship between Rajkumari and Vajpayee, college friends in Gwalior who grew up together and knew each other's families.

How did he become such an integral part of the Kauls' life? The early preacher-activists of the RSS were family-less bachelors who, striving for the ascetic ideal and having moved away from their own families, often came to live with host families who took them in. They lived peaceably in households as the friendly uncle or visiting guru. In the 1950s Vajpayee was sharing an austere, dormitory-like house at Rajendra Prasad Road with Advani and another MP, Premjibhai Assar. The Kauls' home at Delhi University, a more comfortable and inviting spot, became like a second home for him. Vajpayee would later recall that once, when Brij Narain and Rajkumari visited him at Rajendra Prasad Road, they were shocked to find that he was using a laundry bar as body soap.

Since he had been a fixture in their home for so long, when Vajpayee acquired his own bungalow, 6 Raisina Road, it was perfectly natural for the Kauls to move in with him, although Rajkumari's older daughter, Nandita, moved away early. Friends say, as noted earlier, that Nandita seemed somewhat distant from the Kaul–Vajpayee establishment. The others, however, were a close-knit unit and their harmony created a welcoming home.

The Vajpayee establishment, even when he was prime minister, was very private. Vir Sanghvi, who used to visit the prime minister's household often as the Bhattacharyyas' close friend, recalls that unlike other politicians, in Vajpayee's house, there were never any political workers or party leaders around. Vajpayee would return from work, change into his lungi and kurta, sit in a special chair and be handed a cup of soup. 'It always looked as if he really needed to unwind after a long and tiring day.' Adoptive granddaughter Niharika would chatter and play about while Namita and Ranjan would sit talking with Vajpayee, their conversation never about politics. 'Not only were there no PAs and secretaries there, even the phone rarely rang,' recalls Sanghvi.[1] Diwali would be a family affair, with fireworks in the garden, Vajpayee, the adoring 'Nanaji', taking inordinate pleasure in Niharika's joy with sparklers. 'It didn't feel like Diwali with the prime minister. Vajpayee seemed like just another doting grandfather,' says Sanghvi.[2]

Vajpayee took inordinate pleasure in the world of children. Namita, who later worked as a schoolteacher, would often bring her tiny students to play in the lawns of the prime minister's house. At the age of almost seventy, he so adored a visit to Disneyland that he eagerly went on all the rides, refusing to stop. In New York he would often visit the toy shop FAO Schwarz and carefully inspect dolls and gadgets to buy for Niharika.

Rajkumari ran the house, supervising meals and looking after Vajpayee's daily needs and his medication. 'Every morning she would sit at the table and choose the masalas for the food,' recalls Sheila Ghatate. 'The cook would lay out all the masalas in little portions and she would choose the spices for the day. She taught me how to cook many dishes.' In 1966, when supplies of milk could only be procured through tokens, Rajkumari made sure that she sent across her extra tokens to the Ghatates. 'If you ever need anything,' Vajpayee would tell Sheila Ghatate, 'just ask Mrs Kaul.' Ghatate recalled how, when he was once leaving with Vajpayee for a trip, Rajkumari sent word that Ghatate should come and see her before they departed. When he went to the kitchen just before they set off, she said, 'Please do make sure he takes his medicines, he needs to be very careful.' She would also often call Ranjan on his phone to ask if Vajpayee had taken his tablets.

'When I first visited them, I did feel a bit awkward at the arrangement,' recalls journalist and former BJP MP Balbir Punj, who lunched at Vajpayee's home frequently. 'But they were all so normal and natural with each other that I was put at ease.' When the Ghatates invited Vajpayee and the Kauls over to their home for dinner, they would all come together, Vajpayee, Brij Narain and Rajkumari, and later Namita and Ranjan. 'Vajpayee treated Professor Kaul with utmost respect, as a teacher and guru,' says Punj. A decade older than Vajpayee and Rajkumari, Brij Narain was a respected elder for them both, and they both cared for him equally, as much as they cared for each other.

'All three of them were very mature individuals. In the house they all had separate bedrooms. Vajpayee called Mr Kaul "Kaul Sahab" and treated him as a family elder,' recalls Punj. Brij Narain not only accepted Vajpayee and Rajkumari's friendship, but also remained admiring and constantly solicitous about Vajpayee. 'Has he eaten his lunch yet?' 'How was his speech, did it have enough josh?' were questions he would often ask Punj. Not only did he take an active interest in Vajpayee's speeches, he also often advised him on politics and which direction the BJP should take.[3]

Punj remembers the relationship between Vajpayee and Rajkumari as an informal and jokey one, as well as often argumentative. Punj once arrived for lunch to find that Rajkumari was not at home and that the lunch laid out was a healthy, spartan fare of dry rotis and vegetables. Vajpayee loudly expressed his disgust and proceeded to the kitchen to rustle up his famous speciality: puris deep-fried in shuddh ghee. When Rajkumari arrived and noticed the puris, she flew into a rage, saying, 'What is this? Why are you eating oily puris? How could you use shuddh ghee?' Vajpayee, who hadn't yet begun to eat, responded hotly: 'Well, the food you provide is very ashuddh!'

The noted kathak dancer Uma Sharma, who shared a long and mutually admiring relationship with Vajpayee, recalls Vajpayee telling her that he and Rajkumari had once intended to marry, but as he had got caught up in political life and plunged into RSS and Jana Sangh activism and was busy travelling across India, Rajkumari married and went her own way.

Many of those who joined public life in the heady 1940s, when freedom and liberation – both personal and political – were great romantic fascinations, had unorthodox personal relationships. Gandhi wrote openly about his experiments with celibacy. Nehru as a widower shared close relationships with women friends, and the socialist leader Ram Manohar Lohia was openly disparaging of marriage as an institution and lived with his companion, Rama Mitra, whom he never married. The radical activism of the Independence era promoted and permitted personal freedom to a far greater degree than today, when the media glare and outrage industry force conformism to often hypocritically conventional roles.

Vajpayee always addressed Rajkumari as 'Mrs Kaul'. She was rarely seen in public and was never his official hostess – a role usually played by Namita. But she was a constant presence in his home, a grey-haired, pleasant-faced lady in a sari. Gossip swirled frequently. During a lively press conference in 1978 when Vajpayee was foreign minister, suddenly, a young journalist got up and hurled the million-dollar query: 'Vajpayeeji, forget Pakistan, China and Kashmir, can you tell us about Mrs Kaul?' A stunned silence descended. Unfazed, Vajpayee thought for a while, then replied with smiling eyes, '*Kashmir jaisa maamla hai* [The matter is a bit like Kashmir].'[4] On another occasion, when another journalist asked why he had never married, he replied it was because he was in search of the ideal wife. Did you not find her, asked the journalist. 'Yes, I did find her, but she too was in search of the ideal husband,' responded Vajpayee. In another interview he said, 'My life got taken over by events, I got caught up in them and *vivaah ka muhurat nikal gaya* [the time for marriage passed by].'[5] Did he have any affairs, the interviewer rather boldly asked him. He didn't deny it, just chortled: '*Affair ka charcha nahin kiya jaata hai saravajanik rup se* [Affairs are not spoken of publicly].'[6] Still another time, when asked about his bachelor status, he remarked, '*Main kunwara hun, brahmachari nahin* [I'm a bachelor, not a celibate].' He was inspired by the monk-like life of the RSS's celibate activists Golwalkar and Upadhyaya, but readily acknowledged that he wasn't an exemplar of that type. The journalist Karan Thapar once attempted to reach Vajpayee for an interview.

After several unsuccessful telephone calls to his Raisina Road home, finally Rajkumari came on the line to pleasantly say, 'Oho beta, let me speak to him. Interview *ho jana chahiye* [the interview should happen].' Thapar got his Vajpayee interview, which Vajpayee began by saying, 'Since you have spoken to the High Command, how can I refuse you?'[7]

Vajpayee first met the Haksar family in Gwalior and became a close friend of Rajkumari's brother Chand Haksar. As students at Victoria College in Gwalior, they were immediately attracted to each other. Rajkumari, nicknamed 'Bibi', was the educated, attractive daughter of a well-born family which moved in the town's elevated social circles, someone unafraid to voice her opinions and argue on politics. They were both striking young people, Rajkumari with her flashing dark eyes and Vajpayee a magnetic young man with a captivating charm, burning with the ambition to be noticed. There were very few women in college in those days, and Vajpayee was overawed by Rajkumari. The Haksar haveli in Gwalior was a family mansion in which several generations of Haksars had been born, including Ajit Narayan Haksar, who would go on to become the first Indian chairman of tobacco giant ITC. Growing up together in Gwalior, Ajit Haksar remained a lifelong buddy of Vajpayee's, the two sharing a friendly fraternal bond. As Vajpayee became increasingly distant from his own family in Gwalior, he was a frequent visitor at the Haksar haveli and formed friendships with its younger members. In traditional small-town India where social life generally revolved around siblings and cousins, friendships based on affection were a thrilling new adventure.

Yet, however attractive Vajpayee the college debating star may have been and however much Rajkumari admired him, for the clannish Kashmiri Pandit Haksars, the shakha-going youth from Shinde ki Chhawani was not a suitable boy for Rajkumari. Relationships between young men and women were disapproved of, and a friendship with someone outside the Kashmiri Pandit biradari was strictly out of bounds for a Kashmiri girl. Their 'romance' remained unspoken. There is a story that Vajpayee once left a letter for her in a book in the college library. She replied to the letter and left it in the same book, but for various reasons it never reached him. These were times of the upheavals of Independence, of riots and social disturbances. Worried by the high-spirited Bibi's friendship with Vajpayee, her family hurriedly brought her to Delhi, and her marriage was arranged to the scholarly college teacher Brij Narain, the wedding taking place later in Gwalior. 'Vajpayee had gone his own way, got carried away with his political activities, and in this time Rajkumari was married off,' says Uma Sharma.[8]

Rajkumari settled down in Delhi with Brij Narain Kaul, and as Vajpayee began to forge his way up the political ladder in the Jana Sangh to Parliament, the friendship of their youth was rekindled. 'Today's generation may find it difficult to understand,' says a member of the Haksar family who knew 'Bibi bua' (as Rajkumari was called by the younger members of the family), 'but in those days it was not unusual for educated women from progressive families to have close male friends whom they studied with, who were also friends with their brothers.' In the Kauls' Delhi University home, Rajkumari played the hospitable 'auntie' to Kaul's students. The BJP's Hardeep Singh Puri first met Vajpayee when he was a Delhi University student. '[He was] the young, debonair and fast-rising star in Jana Sangh . . . His leadership qualities reverberated amongst us college students during the dark days of the Emergency,' writes Puri.[9]

Like Ghatate, senior editor Vinod Mehta believed that Vajpayee was just as close to Brij Narain as he was to Rajkumari. Through his life Vajpayee had always bonded strongly and revelled in friendships with erudite Brahmin men, whether it was the strong admiration he had for Nehru, or his close ties with P.V. Narasimha Rao, Brajesh Mishra and Appa Ghatate. Brij Narain was another Brahmin compatriot in whose company he could relax and be himself.

In her only interview – to a women's magazine in the 1980s – Rajkumari said Vajpayee and she had a mature relationship which few could understand and they never had to explain their relationship to her husband. Besides, the friendship that husband and wife shared with Vajpayee was so strong that the nasty rumours never touched them.[10]

Vajpayee, recalled Mehta, 'loved all the good things of life, good food and drink and the company of beautiful and accomplished women. He had a glad eye too.' Uma Sharma was said to be one of Vajpayee's particular favourites. 'I know there was a lot of talk about Atalji and me,' laughs Sharma, a curvaceous beauty with long-lashed eyes and lustrous hair. 'But he was very admiring of my dance, used to regularly come to my dance recitals and visit my dance school. Sometimes he would just call and say, "I am coming to your school," and come across with his security men, to sit and chat. We shared a terrific rapport. There was no formality between us. He had such a wonderful sense of humour. He was a kala premi, a lover of the arts, and we belonged to the same region of Gwalior–Dholpur, we both came from Sanskritized families and spoke the same language.'

Uma Sharma was introduced to Vajpayee by Rajkumari, whom Sharma had met through her original mentor P.N. Haksar, Indira Gandhi's principal secretary. Haksar had close family ties with Rajkumari and sent Uma Sharma to meet her, as Uma was at the time trying to raise funds for her dance academy. Uma had choreographed dances set to the poems of Gopal Das Niraj and Harivansh Rai Bachchan's *Madhushala* and after watching one of her performances, Vajpayee told Sharma, '*Hum par bhi kripa kijiye, Umaji* [Do consider my verses too].'

'I selected his poem "*Maut se Thhan Gayi*", which I danced to,' says Sharma. It was a poem Vajpayee wrote lying in a hospital bed in the US before going in for a major surgery, having come to America with the help of then prime minister Rajiv Gandhi. When Sharma was awarded the Padma Bhushan in 2001, at a tea party after the ceremony, she sat chatting for a long time with Sonia Gandhi before noticing Vajpayee sitting across the room. When she went to greet him he immediately said, '*Umaji, gairon se baat karti ho aur hamse Padma Bhushan leti ho* [You talk to all kinds of people but you take the Padma Bhushan from me].'

'There was a lot of hasi mazak [joking and laughter] between us,' says Sharma. 'I once asked him whether I should contest elections, and he said no, never, elections are not good for you. If you want, come straight to the Rajya Sabha.' Sharma recalls how intense he was about his poetry. 'The way he recited his poetry was remarkable, he would become completely involved and filled with josh . . . He was a very secular person, who loved music, dance and the arts of all communities and castes.'[11]

Some of Vajpayee's poems reflect an erotic, sensual yearning. In his poem '*Rote Rote Raat So Gayi*' (Night's Passage), Vajpayee wrote these rather dithyrambic lines:

Jhuki na alken,
Jhapi na palkein,
Sudhiyon ki baraat kho gayi.
Dard purana,
meet na jana,
baaton mein hi pratah ho gayi.
Ghumdi badli,
boond na nikli,
bichuran aisi vyatha bo gayi.

No cascading hair,
No luminous eyes,
The procession of memories has lost its bearings.
An ancient pain,
The beloved unknowing,
Though we talked through the night and into morning.
Darkening clouds,
not a drop of rain,
Separation has sown such seeds of suffering.[12]

The lifelong RSS man was also a rebel against stifling traditions, never hiding that he drank alcohol or ate meat, and impatient with the deceit that politicians in India practised in their personal lives in contrast to their public image. '*Jaisi ki taisi nahin, jaisi hai, waisi hi sahi* [Be not this or that, be just as you are],' he once wrote. Recalls Sudheendra Kulkarni, 'Vajpayee was socially highly liberated, often irreverent . . . he had no double standards.' The politician who led a party that lectured the public on traditional Bharatiya values was in his own life breezily avant garde. He belonged to a right-wing party, his political views were centrist-conservative, yet he quietly thumbed his nose at social convention and bourgeois family values. He was Golwalkar's golden boy who rapidly outgrew the closed-mindedness of the RSS, a lover of dance, music and literature, and also of personal liberty, and the freedom to change and evolve.

The RSS's strong disapproval of his living arrangement with a married woman blighted his relationship with the saffron patriarchs. Yet they could do nothing against their biggest election star and political grandmaster. But he took care to always be discreet. Rajkumari never accompanied him on his official trips, and it was only once that he accommodated her request during an official programme when, on her express wish, he visited the America-based Nandita on her birthday while he was in New York to attend the UN General Assembly in 2001.

By making the Kauls his adopted family, Vajpayee by extension became close to the Haksar clan. Meeting one of Ajit Haksar's granddaughters once, he said, '*Yeh to meri beti hai* [She is my daughter].' Says a member of the Haksar family, 'Bibi bua always helped us out with many small things.' Once when a young Haksar couple rushed a hit-and-run accident victim to hospital and the cops rounded on them and tried to blame them for the mishap, 'Bibi bua' helped them get out of the police clutches. 'Vajpayee was very jovial and jokey around Bibi bua and always pulled her leg,' says another Haksar family member, 'but I never got the impression that they were a couple.' Arun Shourie remembers meeting Mrs Kaul at AIIMS in the 1970s when he was there for his son's treatment. 'She was helping out with patients as a volunteer, doing a lot of drudge work for them, reading out their prescriptions . . .' Public-spirited and helpful, Rajkumari maintained strong relationships with a wide circle of her sprawling Kashmiri Pandit family.

After Vajpayee's term as prime minister ended, when members of the Haksar extended family visited Rajkumari in Krishna Menon Marg, where Vajpayee lay bedridden and almost comatose, Rajkumari and her sister received guests gracefully, laying out an elaborate high tea. '*Bibi didda, kya Atalji se mil sakte hain?* [Can we meet Atalji?],' one of the Haksar relatives once asked. '*Woh toh humein nahin pehchante, tumhe kaise pehchanenge* [He doesn't recognize even me, how is he going to recognize you],' Rajkumari replied sadly.[13]

When Rajkumari, who had been ailing for several years, died in 2014 at the age of eighty-six in the middle of the general election campaign that year, the press release announcing her death described her as a 'household member' of former prime minister Vajpayee, and the *Indian Express* called her 'the most unknown other half'. That even in the midst of an acrimonious election battle, then Congress president Sonia Gandhi quietly visited Vajpayee's home to pay her last respects to Rajkumari Kaul, that apart from top BJP politicians like Sushma Swaraj and Arun Jaitley, even then Congress worthies like minister Jyotiraditya Scindia attended her funeral, shows that, unacknowledged as she was publicly, she was a respected member of the former prime minister's family. Even the judgemental RSS sent two senior functionaries, Suresh Soni and Ramlal, to her funeral. Vajpayee, bedridden after his 2009 stroke, could not attend.

~

While Rajkumari remained in the shadows, Namita and Ranjan Bhattacharyya, Vajpayee's adopted daughter and son-in-law, were his family's public face. They and their wide circle of Delhi friends called Vajpayee 'Baapji', and the lively and friendly Bhattacharyyas were often spotted in Delhi's hip salons or at five-star watering holes with their pals. When Vajpayee became prime minister, the couple became an acknowledged power centre in the prime minister's household. 'Ranjan and Namita were always charming hosts,' writes Vinod Mehta, also, however, recalling that Ranjan seemed to have some 'seedy-looking' friends with 'flashing diamond rings who reeked of after-shave' and looked like 'cosmopolitan wheeler dealers'. Mehta writes that Namita and Ranjan 'assiduously cultivated the Delhi media'.[14] At functions at the prime minister's house, if asked what her plans were for the day, Namita would often respond with a giggle, 'My plans? Serving chai and samosas to all, what else?' She was known for her suspicion of the 'chaddiwallahs' (RSS types) and 'knickerwallah' (saffron-inclined) journalists and had once even attended a 'secular' meeting against the Ram Mandir movement. Namita was proud that her Baapji was able to keep the RSS at arm's length in government. 'He kept them . . . here,' she once said, stretching out her arm.[15] Namita could often be seen browsing books at Delhi's trendy Khan Market or socializing with college friends at upscale South Delhi restaurants. When a journalist once tried to gently broach the question of Vajpayee's relations with her mother, she retorted with a knowing smile: 'You're not getting any masala from me. Next you will say I look like Baapji!' When a friend once indiscreetly remarked that she looked exactly like Vajpayee, she confronted him angrily at a function, and demanded to know why he had cast doubt on her paternity. Vajpayee adored Namita and doted on Niharika, a fatherly and grandfatherly affection clearly born out of his regard for Namita's mother. When Rajkumari fell ill, Namita quit her job to look after her mother and was soon the dominant force in the household.

Ranjan and Namita met as college students in 1976 and, according to one of Ranjan's friends, Niranjan Koirala, Ranjan and Namita had a small marriage ceremony in 1983 in New York. Koirala, a former Oberoi executive who is now no more, was Ranjan's hotelier colleague and recalled that he was the only guest from Ranjan's side, as Ranjan's parents had passed away and he had very little family of his own. 'I got a call from Ranjan, saying I'm getting married, please come as you are the only person I know from my side, none of my family is here.' Koirala went along with him to a house in upstate New York, where a small marriage ceremony was held, one of the guests being Vajpayee, sitting quietly in a corner. 'Perhaps the reason the ceremony was held in New York was because in India Mrs Kaul would have had to appear in public,' recalled Koirala. Namita, the down-to-earth former ITC Hotels executive and schoolteacher, remains one of Delhi's popular and friendly figures with none of the airs of a daughter of a three-time prime minister.

Ranjan, the polished and sociable graduate from the Shri Ram College of Commerce, Delhi University, hailing from a distinguished Bengali family based in Patna, was a successful hotelier, and after his stint at Oberoi, where he became general manager of the Oberoi hotel in Srinagar, turned entrepreneur, setting up his own Orchid Resorts in Manali, then setting up his own reservation services for hotel chains, and operating out of an office in Delhi's Masjid Moth. Before marriage, the Yezdi-bike-riding Ranjan would often be seen at Delhi nightclubs like The Cellar and Sensation, and was thoroughly intimidated when he first met Vajpayee. His foster father-in-law-to-be didn't speak much at all, but had an 'overwhelming presence'. Namita later told him that before meeting Vajpayee again, he should read the newspapers because of his 'abysmal ignorance on politics'.[16]

In the early years of their marriage, before Vajpayee became prime minister, Namita and Ranjan led a quiet life with their friends, Namita teaching at the Shiv Niketan school and Bhattacharyya socializing with his small group of friends and fellow hoteliers, such as Shiv Jatia, owner of the Hyatt hotels. Low profile and distant from politics, the Bhattacharyyas burst into Delhi's high society after Vajpayee became prime minister, when they became a power couple. In 1998 the Bhattacharyyas hosted a birthday party for Niharika on the lawns of Pramod Mahajan's 7 Safdarjung Road bungalow, which was attended by the who's who. It was their debutante ball. Soon they were part of Delhi's chic set, friends with industrialists like Nusli Wadia, hotelier Lalit Suri and doyens of the chattering class, like journalist Vir Sanghvi and *Hindustan Times* proprietor Shobhana Bhartiya. 'Nusli was close to Vajpayee and was in and out of Vajpayee's home quite a lot,' says a friend of the Bhattacharyyas. 'When Jaswant Singh became finance minister we all congratulated Nusli, as he was close to Jaswant too.' Ranjan and Namita were totally at odds with the puritanical RSS with its swadeshi fixation and hatred of all things 'foreign' and 'corporate'. Namita, sharply observant of people, spoke her mind and encouraged six degrees of separation between the prime minister's household and the khaki-shorts-clad brotherhood. Vajpayee was known to be greatly influenced by her likes and dislikes, and with her friends in the media she was keen to project and protect Vajpayee's image as the lone secular-moderate in a sea of zealots.

When Vajpayee became prime minister for thirteen days in 1996, Ranjan had become his OSD. When Shakti Sinha, married to Namita's first cousin, became Vajpayee's private secretary, the prime minister's household had its own man in the PMO. Vajpayee's family was suspicious of the harm that could be done to him by his party and enemies in the sangh and Shakti Sinha, the affable and informal family insider, could be trusted to protect the vulnerable patriarch. Sinha departed for Washington in 1999, and with his departure Ranjan, along with Brajesh Mishra, and Namita at home became Vajpayee's gatekeepers.

Vajpayee was a 'rasik', says former diplomat Pavan K. Varma, who translated his poems. 'A quintessential Indian term for someone who enjoys the rasas – the senses – to the fullest, music, food, the changing seasons.'[17] The love of life spilled into the way he worked. 'The Vajpayee PMO was a PMO like no other,' recalls Dulat, 'one happy family, easy-going and sociable, an open, chatty place where officers and families would be invited every six months to the prime minister's home for lunches and dinners usually held in the lawns. A wonderful table would be set, there was lots of good drink. Vajpayee would mingle among us freely, cracking jokes, and saying to me, "*Dulat sahab, whisky nahin piyoge? Piyo, piyo* [Dulat sahab, won't you have some whisky? Drink, drink]." Drinks were served freely, there was no hypocrisy.'[18]

N.K. Singh, recalling the hospitable atmosphere at Vajpayee's home, says, 'I was at his residence for a meeting one evening and it stretched into dinner time. Vajpayee looked at us and said, "My food is very restricted, but *in logo ka kya hoga? Inke liye khana ka intezam kijiye* [What about everyone else? Please get dinner for them]," he told his family. Delicious food was immediately arranged for all of us.'[19] Holi at the Vajpayee home was celebrated with much joie de vivre. Dholaks would start up, Namita would welcome the guests with a tika, Sheila Ghatate would arrive with thalis of colours and mithai, and Bhojpuri singers would burst into song. On catching sight of an *Outlook* journalist at his Holi get-together once, Vajpayee pointed at her (me!) and laughed, '*Khatra!* [danger].' Yashwant Sinha, sometimes with a dholak, sometimes singing and playing the manjira (small-sized hand cymbals) with a singing troupe, was often at Vajpayee's Holi bashes. It was quite common to see Vajpayee and ministerial colleagues, their faces smeared with colour, being dragged off to dance while folk songs rang out.

The seductive charm of his youth would remain with Vajpayee for most of his life. 'In 1978, when he was foreign minister, Vajpayee reminded me of John F. Kennedy,' recalls Dulat, who met him for the first time in those years. 'He was highly cerebral, radiated warmth, would quote poetry and philosophy and could charm the pants off anyone, with the way he talked.'[20] Arun Shourie says, 'There was an easy-going sense of comfort you felt with him, you felt you wanted to confide in him, to tell him what you had in your head and heart. Outwardly he gave off the air of a slow-moving poet but his antennae were very sharp and everywhere. That's why he had so many sources of information.'[21]

His capacity for easy interactivity served him well in government.

On many issues Vajpayee would simply pick up the phone and call his ministerial colleagues, party politicians and Opposition leaders and sort out matters directly on the phone. Politics Vajpayee style: pick up the phone and talk things through, and more often than not, work the matter out through dialogue, not grandstanding. That he was a terrific listener, spoke little and had exceptional political judgement meant that his phone calls were rarely in vain.

Vajpayee was careful to maintain interactions even with those who he fell out with. He was furious at *Outlook*'s allegations against his son-in-law and things were never the same again between Vajpayee and Vinod Mehta. 'He called me for a meeting and looked very unhappy,' Vinod Mehta recalled. 'He scolded me mildly and said Ranjan and Mishra were as pure as driven snow.'[22] However, in a later formal meeting with editors, Vajpayee came up to Mehta to say, '*Aaj aap bahut chup hain* [You are very quiet today],' and engaged him in banter. Mehta retained his fondness for Vajpayee: 'There are not many politicians I like personally, but Vajpayee was one of the few I did,' Mehta writes, saying he agreed with jurist Fali Nariman's assessment of Vajpayee, which was: 'In spite of his inconsistencies, I like the old boy.'[23] Ghatate believed the tension points between Vajpayee and Advani were never so great as to damage their regard and respect for each other. Sheila had once worked as Advani's assistant and when Vajpayee was in hospital during the Emergency, Advani wrote long letters to Ghatate from jail inquiring after Vajpayee's health.

'There were never any corruption charges against Vajpayee personally, he was totally free of any kind of wrongdoing,' said Ghatate. 'He would often say he had never seen currency notes of high value and would often sternly warn me about people trying to take advantage of my relationship with him.'[24] He was a lover of life, not of material wealth, the family owning a single TV set and a beat-up Ambassador car until the 1990s. He was deeply shocked and troubled at the allegations against Ranjan, although he didn't believe them. There was no change in Ranjan's role in Vajpayee's life and his son-in law continued to accompany him on his overseas trips as his faithful aide.

With close friends Vajpayee was a most convivial host and raconteur. In the 1970s, Vajpayee, Ghatate, young Namita and Ghatate's little boys went for a family picnic to the Qutub Minar. They walked across to a nearby Moet's outlet for some food and when orders were delayed, Vajpayee called out, '*Bhai, jaldi karo bachchon ke pet mein choohe daur rahe hain* [Do hurry, there are mice running in the kids' stomachs].' They celebrated his birthday sitting by a small stream near the Qutub Minar.

He loved his wine or Scotch in his early days, chivda from Gwalior, magora from Agra, chaat and thandai from Lucknow and fat jalebis from Chandni Chowk. Rasgullas, chicken, kheer, khichdi, stir-fried prawns and fish made up his long list of favourite food. A dosa followed by cold coffee in the Indian Coffee House in Connaught Place, a popular joint in the 1950s, was another treat he indulged in. On overseas trips, chefs from the Taj group would travel in the prime minister's entourage and there would be the three kinds of cuisine he loved: South Indian, continental and Chinese. A former diplomat recalls that at official banquets Vajpayee would help himself to all the desserts on offer. He loved Chinese food so much that as external affairs minister for days before his 1979 visit to China, he kept practising how to eat with chopsticks. At a party meeting in Bhopal, recoiling at the fruit presented to him, Vajpayee exclaimed, '*Arre yeh sab kya ghasphus lekar aye?* [What is all this grass and leaves?] Where are the pakodas, kachoris and namkeen?' On learning that Rajnath Singh was a vegetarian, Vajpayee exclaimed, 'Now what kind of a thakur are you? *Kaatpeet nahin khate*? [You don't eat meat?]'

In New York he would make it a point to eat at his favourite Chinese restaurant, Mr K's, once booking an entire floor for his group. Part of Vajpayee's 2000 trip to Italy, H.K. Dua asked him how the trip was going for him. Commenting on the culinary choices he was being offered, Vajpayee sighed, '*Baingan bahut khana pad raha hai* [I'm having to eat a lot of brinjal].' On a flight to New York, chatting informally with journalists, Vajpayee asked Rajdeep Sardesai: 'Your first visit to New York?' 'No sir, I have been before,' Sardesai replied. 'New York is a great city, and I am sure you must be a pucca non-vegetarian?' When Sardesai replied he was, Vajpayee turned to Brajesh Mishra, 'Brajeshji, tell Rajdeep where he can get the best steak in New York.'

Once a group of rain-soaked Delhi University professors arrived at his doorstep to complain about the delay in their salaries. Insisting that they first dry out and come in and sit at the dining table, Vajpayee instructed the cook to prepare hot rotis, which he served himself, making sure everyone in the group first got a hot meal, before settling down to listen to their complaints. One of his guests remarked that his manner was almost maternal in its concern about what everyone was eating, sometimes bringing out plates of food himself.

The closeness between Vajpayee and George Fernandes, who would bring him a cake from Koshy's in Bangalore on his birthday every year, reveals how Vajpayee's tastes in political allies was as eclectic as his tastes in food. They met during the anti-Emergency movement and were colleagues in the Janata government. Later, the chief of the Samata Party became a staunch Vajpayee ally, despite his aversion to the RSS, and was proud to be known as a 'Vajpayee man'. The bond of mutual trust between the socialist Mangalore Christian and the RSS-bred Hindu nationalist revealed the breadth of Vajpayee's political reach. Today's BJP would probably cast George Fernandes as an 'anti-national'; Vajpayee appointed him not only as defence minister but as convenor of the gigantic NDA. Even though Fernandes, the former trade union leader, often lashed out at the RSS, loudly declaring there was no link between patriotism and a particular religion, he was always protective of Vajpayee. In 2000, when churches were being attacked, Fernandes declared to the press that the protests against the attacks were 'only an excuse to attack the government – the attacks take place in Karnataka and the demonstration takes place in front of Vajpayee's house'.[25] For Vajpayee's part, even after the Tehelka allegations exploded in his government's face, Vajpayee made sure to attend Fernandes's party colleague Jaya Jaitly's daughter Aditi's wedding. He stayed for over an hour at the event and feasted heartily on the Kashmiri wazwan on offer.[26]

~

As prime minister, he followed a fairly regulated routine at home. On normal days he woke up at 6.30 a.m. and helped himself to a glass of hot water with lime and honey. Then the newspapers were brought in, which he read carefully until 8 a.m. From 8 a.m. to 8.30 a.m. he exercised, either walking on his LifeFitness treadmill or going out for a walk with his two fluffy dogs, Babli and Loli, with security men in tow. Like Indira Gandhi, he was a dog lover and even composed a poem about Babli and Loli: '*Babli, Loli, kutte do, kutte nahin khilone do, lambe lambe balonvale, phoole pichke gaalon wale* [Babli, Loli, two dogs, not dogs but playthings, with long hair and chubby cheeks].' After becoming prime minister of the thirteen-day government in 1996, Vajpayee and the Kaul–Bhattacharyyas had moved into another elegant Lutyens bungalow, 7 Safdarjung Road, set amid rolling manicured lawns. Here he had other pets, two dogs named Sassy and Sophie and a cat named Ritu.

After the morning walk with the dogs would follow a quick shower and breakfast of a single-egg omelette, toast or idlis, and fruits like papaya, grapes, watermelon and orange. He loved his moong too. Cups of tea, then work from 10 a.m. onward; then visitors, trips to Parliament, meetings and conferences. He had his lunch at 1.30 p.m., which was usually a light Indian meal of chapattis, with a selection of cooked vegetables and raita, followed by a gulab jamun or kheer. He would then rest until 4 p.m. before beginning the second half of his day, and work until about 8.30 p.m. Tea would be at around 5 p.m., accompanied by cocktail samosas, spicy mixture, kaju or paapri chaat. His evenings were packed – with meetings, visits from foreign dignitaries, receptions, functions, clearing files and settling the agenda for the next day. If he was at home for dinner, the menu was usually a light vegetable soup, prawns or chicken, in the Chinese style he loved, and occasionally kulfi or ice cream and fruits for dessert. Dinner with the Ghatates was a frequent affair. He would relax in their spacious and well-appointed Hailey Road apartment and enjoy a long chat with his closest friend, over Sheila Ghatate's delicious chutney fish.

Through much of his life, Vajpayee was, like his friend Brajesh Mishra, a regular drinker, knocking back the whiskies and often tipsy at kavi sammelans or in the privacy of his home. 'He was a big drinker before he became seriously ill,' recalled Niranjan Koirala. 'When we used to go to their home to meet Ranjan, Vajpayee would sit with us and have many drinks and get quite pickled.' In later years though, especially after he became prime minister, alcohol was strictly forbidden on the doctor's orders because of the medication he was on for his ailments, particularly his knee pain. Pavan Varma recalls that when Vajpayee was on a state visit to Cyprus – where Varma was ambassador – he had organized a dinner for the prime minister at a fine restaurant, with his favourite prawns, lobster and a selection of the finest whiskies. 'Sir, the mahaul [ambience] is right, why don't you have a small drink?' Varma suggested. Vajpayee's eyes lit up, but almost immediately one of his Special Protection Group officers, the Sikkim-born G.T. Lepcha, stepped forward to say, 'No drink, please. Only Sprite, only Sprite,' as if under instructions. Vajpayee held back but looked disappointed.[27]

~

'Out of the crooked timber of humanity, no straight thing was ever made,' the philosopher Immanuel Kant said. There was little that was straight about Vajpayee. He was a contradictory, multilayered figure, full of twisted strands, the only constant in his life being the ambition to leave his mark on India. With a sense of manifest destiny – that he was fated to play a role in the shaping of India – he adopted varied roles at different times, multiple selves coexisting in his variegated personality. He was the flamboyant public speaker who was a shy, reserved introvert in person. Ghatate recalled how they would often sit together or travel for hours without Vajpayee saying a word. He looked like a sleepy grand-uncle, but was a political sharpie, antennae always alert. He professed a desire to escape into the literary life, called politics a kajal ki kothri (a place from which you cannot escape unmarked) but revelled in the cut and thrust of realpolitik. He kept offering to resign and saying he wanted to give it all up, but loved the limelight and wanted centre stage. He was a devoted RSS man, yet in government shunned the RSS, keeping the khaki-clad brotherhood firmly at bay. He made several shrill militant speeches, and came to power on the strength of communally charged street agitations, yet for him parliamentary norms were sacrosanct and he remained deeply uncomfortable with Hindutva militancy. He revered his 'Shri Guruji' Golwalkar, but shied away from Hindu supremacism. He made a revealing statement once when asked about Shiv Sena leader Bal Thackeray's stridently communal speeches. 'Don't judge Thackerayji by what he *says,* but by what he *does*. Are the actions of the BJP–Sena government discriminatory?'[28] It was as if he craved to be understood in the same way: don't judge me by my speeches and my occasional demagoguery, judge me by what I actually do in government.

In the puritanical, disciplinarian, Sangh Parivar, he was the meat-eating, alcohol-drinking, non-conformist oddball, friends with the westernized Jaswant Singh, Brajesh Mishra and Ghatate. Vajpayee's men – Yashwant Sinha, Jaswant Singh, Brajesh Mishra, Arun Shourie – were westernized centrist-right-wingers, yet still firmly rooted in the Nehruvian Enlightenment of reason and rationality. 'Vajpayee's men' weren't religious zealots. They were market-friendly liberals on the economy and impatient with state-control-espousing lefties, their identities focused primarily on opposing Congress definitions of secularism and socialism. Yet, the continuum they represented with the

Congress, particularly with the dispensation of P.V. Narasimha Rao, was very strong. The centre-right challenge that Vajpayee and his men mounted to the Congress was a democratic contest, expressed through Parliament. For them, attempting to delegitimize or criminalize the Opposition was unthinkable.

The Vajpayee years could have become a time when India was pushed to a genuinely bipolar polity, with a left-of-centre progressive Congress and a right-of-centre conservative BJP squaring off ultimately in Parliament. But without Vajpayee's parliamentary centrism, the BJP was taken out of the democratic game and tumbled into the arms of militant, populist nationalists with scant respect for democratic norms and restraints. 'We need to hold fast to Vajpayee's legacy because the challenge to the Congress comes from this constitutional parliamentary Vajpayeeism,' says Yashwant Sinha, 'not from the unconstitutional majoritarianism that Narendra Modi today represents.'[29]

~

At a *Janta ki Adalat* TV interview in 1998, Vajpayee was asked about Khushwant Singh's famous line about him: Vajpayee is a very good man, he's a statesman, he was a good foreign minister, but there's one minus point, he's a good man in a bad party. On hearing the question, Vajpayee laughed but also looked annoyed. 'I have a lot of respect for Sardar Khushwant Singh. I'm grateful for his praise. But I don't agree with his view that I'm a good man in a bad party. If I'm a good man, how can I be in a bad party? And if I am in a bad party, how can I be a good man? If the fruit is good, the tree cannot be bad. People have not properly understood the BJP. We are running state governments, there is no communal tension in any of the states. We believe in sarva dharma sambhav [equality of religions]. What is communalism? Communalism is any kind of discrimination on the basis of religion. The politics of vote banks is communal. We are a rashtravadi party and there's no difference between me and my party.'

After the Babri Masjid demolition, at a BJP national executive meeting in Delhi he was booed and heckled by his own party men during his speech. As he emerged from the meeting, a journalist asked, 'Vajpayeeji, why don't you leave the BJP?' He smiled and walked away, tossing over his shoulder a line from a song: '*Jaye toh jayein kahaan?* [If I leave, where will I go?] It made hard political sense for him to stay with the BJP. It was in the BJP where he stood out and was unique, with the ready backing of the saffron electioneering infrastructure.

Extreme Hindutva was Vajpayee's morally flawed means to achieve Nehruvian ends. In this Vajpayee neglected to heed Gandhi's advice that unless the *means* are just and decent, the *ends* will not be just and decent either; that if despicable means are used to seize power, then power itself will be rendered despicable. This contradiction between means and ends in the BJP would need to be managed by Vajpayee all his political life.

Vajpayee's Hindutva was a political credo, not a personally consuming '*rag rag mein*' zeal. 'His parliamentary speeches and his public speeches were completely different,' points out Ghatate. 'In Parliament he showed tremendous foresight. In public he just tried to sway his audience and could often be a rabble-rouser. When he became foreign minister, he never spoke the way he did when he was trying to whip up a crowd or when he was a backbencher.'[30]

Vajpayee paid effusive homage to Savarkar, father of political Hindutva, at a Savarkar memorial meeting in Pune in 1986. Two years after the BJP's humiliating defeat in 1984, with Advani now installed as party president, it made political sense to deliver a poetic oration about Savarkar, in a strategic rebound to Hindutva after the failure of Gandhian socialism. At the meeting of the Hindu extremist VHP in Staten Island in America in 2000 while on a prime ministerial visit, Vajpayee proclaimed, '*Main pratham swayamsevak hoon, yeh adhikar koi nahin chheen sakta* [I am first a swayamsevak, no one can take away that right from me].' Vajpayee's loud proclamations of being a 'swayamsevak' could have arisen from continuing pique at being stripped of his 'pracharak' rank and downgraded by Golwalkar as far back as 1966. In the RSS, his rank was thus always of the swayamsevak. But importantly, in and around election time a nod to Hindutva brought him the service of the saffron cadres. A year after the Gujarat riots and the triumph of Modi, he again reasserted his Hindutva links. On 26 February 2003 President A.P.J. Abdul Kalam unveiled a portrait of V.D. Savarkar in the Central Hall of Parliament. Vajpayee, along with top ministers stood in line as chants of '*Swatantraveer Savarkar amar rahe* [Long live Savarkar]' were raised. The entire Opposition boycotted the function.

Vajpayee was no godman-visiting Hindu ritualist. He was rarely ever seen in a temple, rarely seen in overtly religious garb and there is no evidence that a regular morning puja was part of his daily routine or that he was openly pious or devout. In 1995, when instances of Ganesha statues 'drinking milk' entranced the country, Vajpayee, recalled Ghatate, laughed uproariously. Vajpayee was a part of what we are calling the Nehruvian Enlightenment of the 1950s and 1960s – that period when India's political leadership, emerging from the 200-year-old relationship with western imperialism, was also uniquely influenced by the seventeenth- and eighteenth-century European Enlightenment ideals of reason, rationality, tolerance, scientific inquiry, debate and argument. This spirit never left Vajpayee; tribal emotionalism of the Hindutva cadres was never his thing. After all it was in Nehruvian constitutional democracy that the young Jana Sanghi's voice was not just heard but applauded.

'Vajpayee wasn't a practising Hindu,' recalled Shakti Sinha. 'I never saw him go to a temple. The word "Hindu" meant the Indian existence, didn't mean a religious belief, it was cultural and civilizational.' His awe of Hinduism's high culture of poetic philosophy, art and metaphysics shaped his desire to create a Hindu-Bharatiya identity against the 'children of Macaulay', yet his own devotion to modern parliamentary practices was highly westernized and modernist. If there was any shrine that Vajpayee, the Churchill- and Toynbee-quoting devotee of parliamentary practices, worshipped, it was Parliament. 'This House is a temple of democracy for me,' he said.[31] As prime minister he would attend the House even on days reserved for private members' bills. '*Prime Minister Parliament mein baitha rehta hai* [The prime minister keeps sitting in Parliament],' his officers would say.[32] In fact, one of Vajpayee's flaws as an administrator was that because he had never worked at the local or municipal level and had always been a national politician, he had a patchy understanding of how to make government processes work or how to actually implement the nuts and bolts of policies. During his tenure, he showed little interest in micro-level healthcare or education initiatives as much as he did in foreign policy stances and big national debates.

It was in Parliament that he was his best self. He was a serious, studious and painstaking parliamentarian who researched his speeches deeply. His friendships with communists Hiren Mukherjee, Bhupesh Gupta and Indrajit Gupta, Dravida stalwarts C.N. Annadurai and M. Karunanidhi, socialist George Fernandes, and a range of Congressmen, foremost among them P.V. Narasimha Rao, were born in Parliament. When he received the award for Best Parliamentarian he said: 'This is an era of democracy . . . we as the world's largest democracy can't fail the test. Whenever I falter, this Award will tell me not to make the mistake of wavering from the path.'[33]

Vajpayee embarked on peacemaking in Pakistan and a reach-out to Kashmir and to Muslims, but always retained a sense of cultural separateness from Islam, a feeling he recognized. He said in Parliament: 'I call Shri [Syed] Shahabuddin my friend. My party members would not like this word. But this is the cultured way of behaviour.'[34] 'He had no religious animosities,' said Ghatate. 'His long-standing driver was a Muslim named Mujeeb.'[35] In 1980 when then Pakistan High Commissioner Abdul Sattar brought him a Pathani suit as a gift from General Zia ul-Haq, he had no hesitation in promptly putting it on. At the same time, there are many speeches in which he repeatedly inveighs against Muslims. In the Jana Sangh's pratinidhi sabha address in 1968, he cried: 'I would, however, request my Muslim friends to ponder as to what exactly is the reason that in 99.9 per cent of the cases, the riots originate with members of the Muslim community.'[36] In his article 'The Sangh Is My Soul', he wrote, 'Islam has yet to learn the art of existing and flourishing in a country where Muslims are a minority. They cannot convert the whole of India to Islam.'

His justification for the politics of Hindutva was always an oppositional argument with the Muslim separatism of bodies like the Jamaat-i-Islami and the Congress's cultivation of the Muslim vote – that if politics is played around mosques, it will also be played around temples. 'The BJP's doors have always been open to Muslims,' he said before the 1998 elections, when he was preparing to lead another coalition. 'We don't see Muslims as a vote bank, but as citizens of India and as children of India.'[37] Within the framework of politics and governance, a reach-out to Muslims, to Pakistan and to Jammu and Kashmir made eminent sense in the all-out quest to be the Congress's national alternative. This constant attempt at bridge-building brought him oodles of goodwill. 'Vajpayee never made any open distinction between Hindus and Muslims,' said Maulana Kalbe Sadiq, the Shia leader. 'He was respected in all countries.'[38] 'Vajpayee's defeat was Kashmir's misfortune,' said a leader from the Kashmir-based Peoples Democratic Party in 2018.[39] Whatever the provocation, Vajpayee simply refused to give up on peace efforts with Pakistan, writes his media adviser Ashok Tandon.[40]

Any talk of the BJP being controlled by the RSS irritated him most of all:

> This allegation of remote control is an injustice to the BJP. Such a big party, such an influential party, can such a party be managed through a single remote control? We are an independent organization, RSS is a patriotic organization, many of us are with them, but this doesn't mean they decide what we do, and everything that is done in Delhi is decided from Nagpur. We take considered decisions on our own.[41]

Electoral success was his crown and trump card. He was *elected*. This electoral success was his own, it did not belong to the RSS, and it brought with it responsibilities and allegiances to the Constitution, to Parliament and to democracy. Once in office, he would attempt to build India like Nehru and Rao before him, not strive to realize the fantasy of a Hindu rashtra.

~

Stories about Vajpayee abound, each showing his many sides. Well-travelled over many years, Vajpayee knew most of India's cities well. He once travelled to Indore for a public meeting. Party men picked him up at the airport and then drove him along a circuitous route, trying to delay his arrival at the meeting. Catching on immediately, he expertly directed the driver to the Circuit House, where he was staying, and asked, 'So not enough crowd at the venue yet, eh?' His humour followed the rule that the best jokes are always pleasant for both listener and teller. In 1968, on a blisteringly hot summer afternoon, H.K. Dua (later to briefly become Vajpayee's press adviser in 1999) was riding his scooter to a Jana Sangh press conference at Vithalbhai Patel House. As he drove along he spotted Vajpayee standing alone outside his home on 1 Feroze Shah Road, briefcase in hand. Surprised to see the very politician whose press conference he had been sent to cover standing in the heat, Dua stopped his scooter and hailed Vajpayee. Without thinking twice, Vajpayee came running towards Dua, jumped on the scooter and the two sped off towards the press conference. As they rode into Vithalbhai Patel House, his party colleagues cried out, 'Vajpayeeji, what are you doing, now tomorrow's newspaper headline will be "Vajpayee Rides H.K. Dua's Scooter".' 'No, it won't,' retorted Vajpayee, 'it will be "Dua Takes Vajpayee for a Ride".'[42] When Vajpayee telephoned Dua to ask him to become his press adviser, he explained why he had called him late at night. 'You know what we politicians are like. When we don't want to meet you, our PA says, "Sahab is in a meeting." When we want to meet you we don't hesitate to telephone you even at midnight.'

Chatting with journalists in the 1970s in Parliament, he directed several broadsides at then prime minister Indira Gandhi. 'Vajpayeeji, how come you are criticizing Mrs Gandhi when in 1971 you called her Durga?' '*Haan, Durga kaha tha, bilkul kaha tha,*' he responded, '*par mujhe kya pata tha ki woh humare hi upar prahar karegi?* [Yes, I did call her Durga, but how could I know she would crush us underfoot?]'[43]

In 1993, accompanied by Punj, he set off for an election rally in Himachal Pradesh aboard a small aircraft. Vajpayee and Punj sat side by side and Vajpayee soon fell asleep. As they were getting ready to land, the co-pilot emerged worriedly from the cockpit to whisper to Punj that they couldn't locate Dharamshala as the navigation system had failed. Unable to land, the plane circled disorientedly, surrounded by unknown snowy peaks on both sides. Vajpayee, who had been asleep, awoke and said, '*Utar rahein hain kya?* [Are we landing?]' 'No,' said Punj agitatedly. 'The pilot can't find Dharamshala. We are lost and we only have four hours of fuel. If we can't find a place to land, we could crash.' 'Oh wonderful!' said Vajpayee. 'Tomorrow's headline will be "Vajpayee dead during election campaign" and I'll travel in a gun carriage.' 'You'll be in a gun carriage but what about me?' cried Punj. 'Oh come on, you and I will go to the afterlife together, won't it be good to have company while we go?' Vajpayee chuckled, and promptly dozed off again. After a few harrowing minutes, the pilot made contact with an Indian Airlines plane which guided him to Kullu.[44] Whether in his unhidden relationship with Rajkumari Kaul or his Lahore bus ride or remaining coolly unfazed about a possible airplane catastrophe, Vajpayee possessed a devil-may-care personal bravery.

His oratory was a magical thing. Former Lok Sabha speaker Shivraj Patil, a Congress stalwart, once recalled how he would travel over 50 kilometres just to hear Vajpayee speak. Performing before live audiences year after year left Vajpayee with a ready instinct for crowd management. At a public meeting in Jaipur's Tripolia Bazaar, speeches went on until 2 a.m. The venue was jam-packed. Suddenly, someone in the crowd let loose a snake. Before the crowd could start to panic, Vajpayee quickly reacted, 'Don't worry, it's a fake snake,' he shouted, sounding so believable and reassuring that the audience settled down. His eightieth birthday was celebrated by the BJP in grand style; a cake was cut and there were rounds of applause. Quipped Vajpayee, 'Saying many happy returns to an eighty-year-old person is indeed an act of bravery.'

When he was prime minister he created the 'Panchvati' hall in the prime minister's residential complex where meetings, book launches and lectures were held, Vajpayee making sure to personally meet all attendees. He lavished respect on writers and literary figures more than on politicians and kept saying in interviews how much he yearned for a life of letters, holding a fond self-image of himself as the poet-litterateur. In 2000 when he arrived in Kerala for his Kumarakom holiday, the bureaucrat Amitabh Kant recalls that he only came with his family and spent time reading, there were no politicians or political hangers-on to be seen.[45]

The desire to grow, to liberate himself, to cast off the shackles of small-town Gwalior and narrow-minded RSS ideas was an ever-present driving impulse. When Rajiv Gandhi became prime minister, he confessed to Ghatate: 'What an inexperienced person has become PM – *mujhko bana ke dekho* [make me PM and see how I will do].' At the same time in his poem *'Unchai'* ('Never Place Me So High'), he observed the lonely barrenness at the top:

Unche pahad par,
Ped nahin lagte,
Paudhe nahin ugte,
Na ghas hi jamti hai . . .
Jo jitna uncha,
Utna hi ekaki hota hai,
har bhaar ko swayam hi ddhota hai,

chehre par muskaan chipka,
mann hi mann rota hai

On a very high mountain
Trees cannot take root
Plants do not grow,
Grass will not survive . . .

A person is as solitary
As the height to which he rises,
He bears his burdens alone,
Wears his smiles and weeps unseen.[46]

'His poetry,' says Pavan Varma, 'is deliberately simple, written in Hindustani with a mix of Urdu words, designed to convey basic emotions while always conscious of his public persona.' Before he became prime minister, he invariably composed a poem on his birthday. When Vajpayee sent word to Varma that he would like him to translate his poems and Varma sent word back that he wasn't too 'khush' (happy) with the BJP, Vajpayee sent another message via Namita, '*Hum apni party se kaunse khush hain?* [And am I happy with my party?]'[47]

He received several awards – the Padma Vibhushan in 1992, the Outstanding Parliamentarian Award in 1994 and the Bharat Ratna in 2015, by which time he was a voiceless, bedridden invalid confined to his home. President Pranab Mukherjee and Prime Minister Narendra Modi arrived at his home to present him India's highest honour. Photographs were strategically clicked only of his face hidden behind tinted glasses.

Two days after his death, his funeral was held in grand style, with Prime Minister Narendra Modi walking behind the hearse, leading the funeral procession all the way to the banks of the Yamuna to the cremation site – the same Narendra Modi whose resignation Vajpayee had sought and whom Vajpayee had reminded about a politician's 'rajdharma'. 'Vajpayee was a *manav shilpi*,' says his long-time assistant Shiv Kumar Sharma, 'a sculptor of human beings. The sculptor makes lifeless statues, but Vajpayee breathed life into people. That was his talent. And that's why the BJP rose to become such a big party.'[48]

In his home in Manali, the garden with its flowering bushes, roses and hollyhocks brought him joy. He was a lover of nature, Hindi movies and Marathi plays. Madhubala, Suraiya, Dev Anand and Dilip Kumar were his favourite stars. While living in Delhi's Feroz Shah Road he once kept a couple of rabbits as pets, and used to feed the baby rabbit milk using balls of cotton. But with his busy work schedule, he was unable to take proper care of the rabbit and it died in the heat of the summer. Vajpayee wrapped it in a white cloth with great care, buried it in the garden and planted a flowering shrub above it.

'I like watching tragedies,' he said in his last interview, sitting in his Manali garden to Zee News. 'I enjoyed watching the film *Devdas*, it's one of my favourites. And as for sport, my favourite is hockey. I used to find cricket tiresome at first because it went on for so long, but I enjoy the new form where it finishes in a day, it holds audiences. And yes, I'm a good cook. I can make good pakodas. I made some recently for a party meeting.'

Vajpayee reached out to opposite ends of the spectrum, because for him all solutions lay in dialogue. And the highest forum of dialogue in India was Parliament. 'You got more than 400 seats in the Lok Sabha . . .' he told the Rajiv Gandhi government in Parliament. 'But the country's problems cannot be solved on the strength of one party. One individual, however popular, cannot find a way out of complicated problems. You need political consensus for that.'[49] India must not only be ruled through consensus, but the best way to govern kaleidoscopically diverse India was from the ideological centre – however ambiguous that centre may be – not from the extremes of any hue.

In parliamentary debate, democracy was protected and strengthened. In vigorous, clever and learned exchanges between a cohort of brilliant, elite men across parties was modern India to be forged. It was in

Parliament that he grew into a man of the world, where he learnt to respect the opposite view, where RSS's absolutism faded and the parliamentary spirit began.

And so Vajpayee took his place among India's great parliamentarians, the men – for, in his time, these parliamentary talents were mostly all men – who used language and ideas in the service of a newly born nation dreaming audaciously of becoming a functioning democracy.

Democracy rests vitally on a set of shared values between rulers and the Opposition, on a shared political culture of respect and restraint. Vajpayee was an integral part of this shared democratic culture. As prime minister, when two businessmen's names were sought to be removed from a government–industry panel because they had been associated with the Congress, he objected: 'If they are reputed people *toh unhe avashya rakhiye, Rajiv Gandhi, Sonia Gandhi ke aadmi hain – yeh bematlab baat hai* [They must be kept, whether they are Rajiv Gandhi's or Sonia Gandhi's people is of no consequence].' In 2002–03, drought struck poll-bound Madhya Pradesh, where the Congress's Digvijay Singh had been ruling for a decade. BJP party folk from the state urged Vajpayee not to send relief because the Centre would be paying and the state government benefiting. 'How on earth can you people think like this?' Vajpayee burst out. 'Relief funds is the right of the people, no matter who the chief minister is. I will release the funds, you please see how you can go about winning elections.' 'Relationships with the Opposition were vital for Vajpayee, and he treated me like a family member,' Digvijay Singh recalled.[50]

In his dramatic speech of 1996, he demanded that democracy be always protected. 'Constitutional democracy is a system, there are *rules,* there are *procedures.* Don't break them.' Once the people's representatives gathered in the House, they had to protect the precious inheritance that gave India life: constitutional democracy.

He began life in a small-town RSS shakha, he joined Hindu nationalist politics and he was a party man all his life. But he rose above his origins to belong to something much bigger. When he had Nehru's portrait put back on the foreign ministry wall, when he trundled in a bus to Pakistan, when he led all-party efforts at UN forums, when he journeyed to Kashmir searching for 'insaaniyat', he was sending an important message. He wasn't just the foreign minister or prime minister of his party, no, he represented the whole country. He was Vajpayee of the Lok Sabha, Vajpayee of Parliament, he was Atal Bihari Vajpayee of India.

Acknowledgements

I faced a heartbreak as I was completing the final drafts of this book. The hospitable, ever-smiling Narayan Madhav Ghatate or Appa Ghatate, Vajpayee's oldest and most trusted friend, without whom this book could not have been written, passed away in January 2021. I am still coming to terms with the fact that Appa will not be able to see the completion of my labours. While writing this biography, I spent hours with Appa in his Hailey Road apartment in Delhi listening to stories, analyses and anecdotes of Vajpayee. Appa even let me have his two unpublished manuscripts about Vajpayee, 'Atalji as a Man' and 'Atalji's Wit & Humour', to draw upon. In lockdown times we would be on the telephone almost every second day and he shared with me his memories in detail and with utmost generosity, helping me with the first drafts of my early chapters. My heartfelt gratitude to Appa for giving me the benefit of the wealth of his experiences with Vajpayee to whom he was almost a constant companion and closest friend for over five decades. 'Your book should be like the biography of Napoleon,' he told me. My thanks to Mrs Sheila Ghatate too for all those cups of tea at her home, as well as for sharing her own insights and memories of Vajpayee.

My thanks are due to those who generously gave me their time and shared with me their valuable perspectives of the former prime minister. My grateful thanks to Arun Shourie, A.S. Dulat, Balbir Punj,

Christophe Jaffrelot, Dorab Sopariwala, H.K. Dua, Iqbal Chagla, Karan Thapar, K.N. Govindacharya, Mani Shankar Aiyar, Maseeh Rahman, M.G. Devasahayam, Murli Manohar Joshi, Neena Vyas, Nirupama Rao, N.K. Singh, P.C. Sen, Pavan Varma, P.D.T. Achary, Praful Patel, Prannoy Roy, Pravin Sawhney, Raian Karanjawala, Salman Khurshid, Seshadri Chari, the late Shakti Sinha, Shekhar Gupta, Sudhanshu Mittal, Sudheendra Kulkarni, Uma Sharma, Vir Sanghvi and Yashwant Sinha. The erudite and free-spirited Niranjan Koirala is no more, he too will not be able to see the book, but I am deeply grateful to Niranjan for sharing his memories of the Kaul–Vajpayee family. My immense gratitude to my friend and colleague Vijai Trivedi for sharing with me his enormous and wide-ranging knowledge of Vajpayee and for helping me understand his poetry and the nuances of his language. I am very thankful to Maneesha Taneja for her elegant translations of some of Vajpayee's poetry. My gratitude is due to my late editor Vinod Mehta, for setting me off on one of my first reports on Vajpayee and giving me the opportunity to write a cover story on the then prime minister.

I am very grateful to members of the Haksar family who shared wonderful accounts of the Haksars of Gwalior, and to members of the Bharatiya Janata Party and Rashtriya Swayamsevak Sangh who shared with me their memories of Vajpayee. My grateful thanks are due to my editors at Juggernaut, Chiki Sarkar, Nandini Mehta and Jaishree Ram Mohan, for believing in this book. My gratitude to my husband, Rajdeep Sardesai, my children, Ishan and Tarini, for their constant support.

Notes

Introduction

1. *India Today*, 5 February 2007.
2. Translated by Maneesha Taneja.

1. Darkness at High Noon: 2004

1. Author interview, January 2020.
2. Author interview, February 2020.
3. Author interview, February 2020.
4. Times News Network, 'Cong Tops, Says Mithai Khao', *Times of India*, 14 May 2004.
5. Author interview, January 2020.
6. Times News Network, 'Sonia. Quote Martial', *Times of India*, 14 May 2004.
7. Kalam had served in the Defence Research and Development Organisation under Vajpayee and played a leading role in the nuclear tests of May 1998.
8. This and subsequent quotes attributed to Ghatate, unless otherwise mentioned, came from interviews with the author. Author interviews with N.M. Ghatate from January 2020 to June 2020.
9. Author interview, October 2020.
10. 'The Feel Good Factor', *India Today*, 2 February 2004.
11. 'The Advocate Fisherman, Village Computer Queen and Their CM "Babu"', *Indian Express*, 16 April 2004.

12. 'Advani's Bharat Uday Yatra Gets Underway', *Outlook*, 22 March 2004.
13. NDTV, January 2004.
14. Author interview, February 2020.
15. Author interview, November 2003.
16. 'BJP, Congress Turn Party Backrooms into Digital Election War Rooms', *India Today*, 15 March 2004.
17. 'The Feel Good Factory', *Frontline*, 12 March 2004.
18. Advani, *My Country*, 763.
19. 'Not Removing Modi Big Mistake, Says Vajpayee', *The Tribune*, 14 June 2004.
20. Author interview, February 2020.
21. Vajpayee's parliamentary record: 1955, lost Lucknow by-poll. 1957–1962, Lok Sabha, Balrampur. 1962–1967, Rajya Sabha, Uttar Pradesh. 1967–1971, Lok Sabha, Balrampur. 1971–1977, Lok Sabha, Gwalior. 1977–1980, Lok Sabha, Delhi. 1980–1984, Lok Sabha, Delhi. 1986--1991, Rajya Sabha, Madhya Pradesh. 1991–1996, Lok Sabha, Lucknow (also won from Vidisha but vacated the seat). 1996–1998, Lok Sabha, Lucknow (also won from Gandhinagar, Gujarat, but vacated the seat). 1998–1999, Lok Sabha, Lucknow. 1999–2004, Lok Sabha, Lucknow. 2004–2009, Lok Sabha, Lucknow.
22. 'Ram Temple in Ayodhya Is a Universal Demand: AB Vajpayee', *India Today*, 12 January 2004.
23. 'Ideology, Issues, RIP', *Outlook*, 29 March 2004.
24. https://archivepmo.nic.in/abv/speech-details.php?nodeid=9274
25. 'India Can and Must Become a Developed Nation by 2020: Atal Bihari Vajpayee'. Speech at India Today Conclave, 29 March 2004.
26. 'Ram Temple in Ayodhya Is a Universal Demand: AB Vajpayee', *India Today*, 12 January 2004.
27. Saba Naqvi Bhaumik, 'Fear of the Family', india.eu.org, 26 April 2004.
28. Ibid.
29. 'Sonia's Foreign Origin Still an Issue: Vajpayee', *Times of India,* 3 April 2004.
30. Conversation with the author, January–March 2020.
31. 'The Battle Begins. Advani's Bharat Uday Yatra Aims to Take BJP's India Shining Message to the Masses', *India Today*, 22 March 2004.

32. 'NDA Not So Shining', *India Today*, 26 April 2004.
33. 'Vajpayee Didn't Want to Advance 2004 Polls, Sensed BJP's Defeat: Shiv Kumar', IANS, 27 August 2018.
34. NDTV interview, January 2004.
35. 'Did Vajpayee See It Coming?', *Times of India*, 14 May 2004.
36. Sinha interview with author, February 2020.
37. Sanjay Kumar, 'Why BJP Can't Afford to Take Its Middle Class Votebank for Granted', Livemint, 30 January 2018.
38. 'DMK Pulls Out from Vajpayee Government', Rediff, 20 December 2003.
39. 'Govinda Delivers Knockout Punch, Heads North', *Times of India*, 14 May 2004.
40. Author interview, February 2020.
41. 'Not Removing Modi a Big Mistake: Vajpayee', Zee News, 13 June 2004.
42. 'Absence of Ideology Led to Loss', *Times of India*, 13 May 2004.
43. 'BJP Betrayed Hindus', *Times of India*, 13 May 2004.
44. Kulkarni, in author interview, reports such statements.
45. 'No Proposal to Replace Modi: Naidu', *Times of India*, 28 June 2004.
46. 'RSS Attacks Vajpayee', PTI, 14 June 2004.
47. 'Post-Elections 2004 Defeat, BJP Struggles to Reinvent Itself', *India Today*, 5 July 2004.
48. *Walk the Talk*, NDTV, 17 April 2005.
49. N.M. Ghatate, 'Atalji's Wit & Humour', Unpublished manuscript.
50. Author interview, January 2020.

2. The Boy from Gwalior: 1924–1957

1. Subhadra Kumari Chauhan, 'Jhansi ki Rani'.
2. Some accounts say Vajpayee's year of birth was entered in the records as 1926 because his father decreased his age by two years so he could get extra years in service (Nag, *Atal Bihari*, 20, and Ullekh, *Untold Vajpayee*, 10).
3. Vajpayee, *Twenty-One Poems*, 'Come, Let Us Unravel the Knots of the Mind', 57.
4. This friend was Gangadhar Rao Valuskar, quoted in 'The Speech That Vajpayee Couldn't Finish', *Times of India*, 17 August 2018.
5. 'His Interests Were Books, Verse and Politics', Rediff, 16 August 2018. https://www.rediff.com/news/special/ataljis-family-remembers/20180816.htm

6. Vajpayee, *Selected Poems*, 24.
7. Author interview, 1998.
8. Vajpayee, *Twenty-One Poems*, xii.
9. https://www.amarujala.com/uttar-pradesh/agra/first-peom-of-atal-bihari-vajpayee-on-taj-mahal?pageId=1, translated by Maneesha Taneja.
10. Nag, *Atal Bihari Vajpayee*, 20.
11. 'The Speech That Vajpayee Couldn't Finish', *Times of India*, 17 August 2018.
12. Chandrika Prasad Sharma (ed.), *Poet Politician*, 41.
13. Vajpayee, *Twenty-One Poems*, xiii.
14. Author interview, 1998.
15. Article by Vajpayee in DAV College Magazine, 2002–2003, reprinted in PTI, 17 August 2018, under the title 'Vajpayee and His Father Were Classmates in Kanpur'.
16. Vajpayee, *Four Decades*, Vol. 1, 624.
17. Article by Vajpayee in DAV College Magazine, 2002–2003, reprinted in PTI, 17 August 2018, under the title 'Vajpayee and His Father Were Classmates in Kanpur'.
18. Ibid.
19. Ibid.
20. 'Almost a Month after His Death, Agra University Finds Vajpayee's Educational Record', *India Today*, 1 September 2018.
21. *News*, 24 January 1996.
22. Vajpayee, *Twenty-One Poems*, xiii.
23. Ibid.
24. Sarkar, *Modern India*, 379.
25. Manini Chatterjee and V.K. Ramachandran, 'Vajpayee and the Quit India Movement: Findings of a *Frontline* Investigation', *Frontline*, 7–20 February 1998.
26. Ibid.
27. NDTV interview, 2004.
28. Sarkar, *Modern India*, 437.
29. Khaliquzzaman, *Pathway to Pakistan*, 404.
30. Article by Vajpayee in DAV College Magazine, 2002–2003, reprinted in PTI, 17 August 2018, under the title 'Vajpayee and His Father Were Classmates in Kanpur'.

31. Vajpayee, *Bindu Bindu*, 2.
32. Author interview, February 2020.
33. Vajpayee, 'The Sangh Is My Soul', *Organiser Weekly*, Varsh Pratipada issue, 1995.
34. Samagra Savarkar Vangmaya, Vol. 3, 341, Savarkar.org. These views are available in the section entitled 'Cow Protection and Cow Worship'. http://savarkar.org/
35. Speech at Savarkar Darshan Pratishthan in Pune 1986. https://www.youtube.com/watch?v=U0S9179jgRc)
36. Trivedi, *Haar Nahin*, 96.
37. Golwalkar, *Bunch of Thoughts*, 108.
38. Author interview, February 2020.
39. Vajpayee, 'The Sangh Is My Soul', *Organiser Weekly*, Varsh Pratipada issue, 1995.
40. Ibid.
41. Golwalkar, *Bunch of Thoughts*, 126.
42. Vajpayee, 'The Sangh Is My Soul', *Organiser Weekly*, Varsh Pratipada issue, 1995.
43. *Organiser*, 14 April 1968, 9.
44. 'The Inner Circle', Rediff. 1999, https://m.rediff.com/election/1999/oct/12atal.htm
45. Ghatate, in author interview.
46. Upadhyaya, *Integral Humanism*, 43.
47. Jaffrelot, *Hindu Nationalist Movement*, 75–88.
48. Sarder Patel, quoted in *Hindustan Times*, 17 January 1948.
49. Nehru, *Letters*, 33.
50. Vajpayee, *Four Decades*, Vol. 1, 109.
51. Golwalkar, *Bunch of Thoughts*, 390.
52. Ibid., 148.
53. Ibid., 145.
54. Golwalkar, *Justice on Trial*, 28.
55. Ibid., 29.
56. Government communiqué quoted in *The Hindu*, 12 July 1949.
57. Debashish Mukerji, 'The Charismatic Loner. Vajpayee Had 1 Foot inside RSS, 1 Outside', *The Week*, 19 May 1995.
58. Mookerji, quoted in Madhok, *Portrait of a Martyr*, 133.

59. *Organiser*, 16 April 1951.
60. *Organiser* 9, no. 45, 25 June 1956, 5.
61. Advani, *My Country*, 141.
62. Madhok, *Syama Prasad Mookerjee*, 133.
63. Tinker, *India and Pakistan*, 120.
64. Vajpayee, *Four Decades*, Vol. 1, xv–xxxix.
65. Ghatate, in author interview.
66. *Organiser* 34, 6 April 1953.
67. 'Vajpayee Accuses Nehru of Plot to Kill Mookerjee', PTI, 7 July 2004.
68. Trivedi, *Haar Nahin*, 19.
69. Vajpayee, *Twenty-One Poems*, 27.
70. Vajpayee, *Four Decades*, Vol. 1, xvi.
71. 'How Vajpayee Fared in the 14 Lok Sabha Elections He Contested between 1957-2004', Livemint, 17 August 2018.
72. Vajpayee, *Four Decades*, Vol. 1, xvi.
73. NDTV interview, 2004.
74. Vajpayee, *Four Decades*, Vol. 1, xvii.

3. The Rise of the Saffron Nehru 1957–1971

1. Vajpayee, *Four Decades*, Vol. 1, 2.
2. Ibid., 5.
3. Ibid., xviii.
4. Ibid.
5. Vajpayee, *Four Decades*, Vol. 3, 171.
6. 'Nehru on Communalism', Sampradayikta Virodhi Committee, New Delhi, 1965, 223–24.
7. Vajpayee, *Four Decades*, Vol. 2, 421.
8. Ghatate, 'Atalji's Wit'.
9. Vajpayee, *Four Decades*, Vol. 3, 161.
10. Ibid., 165.
11. Vajpayee, *Four Decades*, Vol. 1, xxxiv.
12. The Parliament committee that decides whether parliamentary privileges or rights of members have been abused.
13. Vajpayee, *Four Decades*, Vol. 1, xxxiv.
14. Lok Sabha debates, Vol. 15, Part 2, September 1951, Cols. 2705–223, 167–69.

15. Guha, *India After Gandhi*, 231.
16. *Organiser*, 29 October 1951.
17. Vajpayee, *Four Decades*, Vol. 1, 625.
18. Vajpayee, *Four Decades*, Vol. 1, xxv.
19. Ibid., xxxviii.
20. Vajpayee, *Four Decades*, Vol. 3, 130.
21. Advani, *My Country*, 834.
22. Ibid., 837.
23. Ibid., xix.
24. Ibid., 841.
25. Ibid., 176.
26. Author interview, August 2021.
27. Advani, *My Country*, xvii.
28. Author interview, February 2020.
29. Vidya Subramanian, 'The Making of Atal Bihari Vajpayee', The Wire, 18 August 2018.
30. Zareer Masani, 'My Father Minoo', The Print, 16 June 2019.
31. Advani, *My Country*, 106.
32. Vajpayee, *Four Decades*, Vol. 1, xviii.
33. Ibid., 746.
34. Ghatate, in author interview.
35. Advani, *My Country*, 103.
36. Author interview, February 2020.
37. Ghatate, in author interview.
38. Jaffrelot, *Hindu Nationalist*, 234.
39. Ibid., 252.
40. 'Jana Sangh: New Moves', *The Hindu*, 21 July 1970.
41. Ibid.
42. 'What Jana Sangh's Co-Founder Has to Say', *Hindustan Times*, 14 June 2009.
43. Advani, *My Country*, 179.
44. Vajpayee, *Four Decades*, Vol. 1, xxii.
45. Ibid.
46. Ibid.
47. Ibid., xvi.
48. Ibid., xxiii.

49. *New Age*, New Delhi, 11 March 1962.
50. Vajpayee, *Four Decades*, Vol. 1, xxi.
51. 'No Faltering in Resolve to Oust Chinese', *Times of India*, 9 November 1962.
52. Vajpayee, *Four Decades*, Vol. 1, xxi.
53. Ghatate, in author interview.
54. Vajpayee, *Four Decades*, Vol. 1, 24.
55. Ibid., 728.
56. Ibid., xxxiv.
57. Ghatate, in author interview.
58. Vajpayee, *Four Decades*, Vol. 1, 242.
59. Trivedi, *Haar Nahin*, 235–36.
60. Ibid., 236.
61. Ibid.
62. Madhok, *Deendayal Upadhyaya*, 25.
63. Ibid., 62.
64. Ghatate, 'Atalji'.
65. Vajpayee, *Four Decades*, Vol. 1, xxiii.
66. *Eastern Economist*, quoted in Baxter, 285.
67. Rajni Kothari, 'Continuity and Change in India's Party System', *Asian Survey* 10, no. 11, 'Elections and Party Politics in India: A Symposium', November 1970.
68. Vajpayee, *Four Decades*, Vol. 1, 18.
69. Ibid., 314.
70. Ghatate, 'Atalji's Wit'.
71. Advani, *My Country*, 132.
72. Vajpayee, *Four Decades*, Vol. 1, 612–16.
73. Advani, *My Country*, 138.
74. Ibid., 142.
75. Vajpayee, *Four Decades*, Vol. 1, 696.
76. Madhok, *Deendayal Upadhyaya*, 15, 22.
77. Ibid., 16–17.
78. Ibid., 16.
79. Vajpayee, *Four Decades*, Vol. 1, 728.
80. Advani, *My Country*, 144.
81. Vajpayee, *Four Decades*, Vol. 1, xxi.

82. 'The Charismatic Loner', *The Week*, 19 May 1999.
83. Vajpayee, *Four Decades*, Vol. 2, 297.
84. Ibid.
85. 'Gwalior Streets Will Always Miss Vajpayee', *Times of India*, 17 August 2018.
86. 'His Interests Were Books, Verse and Politics', Rediff.com, 16 August 2018.

4. Battling Indira Gandhi: 1971–1980

1. Mathur, *Jana Deep Souvenir*, 2.
2. Advani, *My Country*, 174.
3. Ibid., 178.
4. Vajpayee, *Four Decades*, Vol. 1, 39.
5. Nag, *Atal Bihari*, 66.
6. Vajpayee, *Kuch Lekh*, 280.
7. Author interview.
8. Ghatate, in author interview.
9. Vajpayee, *Kuch Lekh*, 54.
10. Ibid., 260.
11. Vajpayee, *Four Decades,* Vol. 1, 540.
12. Ibid., 568.
13. Ibid., 420.
14. Ibid., 363.
15. Ibid., 291.
16. Vajpayee, *Four Decades*, Vol. 2, 292.
17. Vajpayee, *Kuch Lekh*, 144.
18. Vajpayee, *Constructive Parliamentarian*, 5.
19. Vajpayee, *Four Decades*, Vol. 1, 523 (translated by Vajpayee).
20. Vajpayee, *Four Decades,* Vol. 3, 75.
21. Ibid., 91.
22. Bharatiya Jana Sangh party documents.
23. Vajpayee, *Four Decades*. Vol. 1, xxxvi.
24. Ibid., 269.
25. Andersen and Damle, *The RSS*, 97.
26. Ghatate, in author interview.

27. Vajpayee, *Four Decades*, Vol. 3, 317.
28. Vajpayee, *Constructive Parliamentarian*, 230.
29. Vajpayee, *Four Decades*, Vol. 3, 562.
30. Vajpayee, *Four Decades*, Vol. 1, 40.
31. Ghatate, 'Atalji's Wit'.
32. Vajpayee, *Four Decades*, Vol. 2, 111.
33. Ghatate, 'Atalji's Wit'.
34. Ibid.
35. Vajpayee, *Four Decades*, Vol. 1, 59.
36. Ibid., 67.
37. *RSS Resolves*, 76–80.
38. Vajpayee, *Four Decades*, Vol. 1, 393.
39. Ibid., 137.
40. *The Hindu*, 16 September 1974.
41. *Organiser*, 17 July 1974.
42. Advani, *My Country*, 189.
43. Ibid., 189.
44. Ibid., 191.
45. 'Such a Person Is Rarely Born', Sharad Yadav on Vajpayee, *New Indian Express*, 16 August 2018.
46. Vajpayee, *Four Decades*, Vol. 1, xxxvi.
47. Quoted in Jaffrelot, *Hindu Nationalist Movement*, 273.
48. Advani, *My Country*, 212.
49. Ghatate, 'Atalji's Wit'.
50. Advani, *My Country*, 213.
51. Vajpayee, *Twenty-One Poems*, 5.
52. https://www.youtube.com/watch?v=31L2J1pkexg. Translated by Maneesha Taneja.
53. Ghatate, 'Atalji's Wit'.
54. Ibid.
55. https://www.youtube.com/watch?v=31L2J1pkexg
56. 'Unlearnt Lessons of the Emergency.' *The Hindu*, 13 June 2000.
57. Trivedi, *Haar Nahin*, 47.
58. 'When Bengaluru Gave Vajpayee Rebirth', *Times of India*, 17 August 2018.
59. Ghatate, 'Atalji's Wit'.

60. Author interview, February 2020.
61. Ullekh, *Untold Vajpayee*, 79.
62. Trivedi, *Haar Nahin*, 47.
63. Author interview with D.P. Tripathi, 2017.
64. 'Habeas Corpus Petitions Not Maintainable in High Courts during Emergency: Supreme Court', *India Today*, 15 May 1976. (Note: ADM Jabalpur was overruled by the Supreme Court in 2017.)
65. Rajeswar, *India*, 131.
66. Dutt, *Five Headed Monster*, 138–48.
67. Advani, *My Country*, 262.
68. 'Going to the Polls', *India Today*, 15 February 1977.
69. Author interview, March 2020.
70. Trivedi, *Haar Nahin*, 52.
71. Quoted in https://www.bhaskar.com/delhi/delhi-ncr/news/in-1977-election-thousands-of-crowds-came-to-listen-atal-bihari-bajpai-01531599.html. Translated by Maneesha Taneja.
72. Vajpayee, *Four Decades*, Vol. 1, xxxix.
73. https://www.youtube.com/watch?v=YFOSkd9BxUo
74. Janata Party victory rally 1977: https://www.youtube.com/watch?v=YFOSkd9BxUo
75. Ghatate, 'Atalji's Wit'.
76. https://www.youtube.com/watch?v=EV3jGiSGRGA
77. Ibid.
78. 'When Vajpayee Went to Assure Indira Gandhi', *Navbharat Times*, 25 December 2020.
79. Vajpayee, '*Haathon ko Malte*', in *Kya Khoya*, 108. Translated by Maneesha Taneja.
80. https://www.hindi-kavita.com/HindiKaidiKaviraiKiKundliyanAtalBihariVajpeyi.php. Translated by Maneesha Taneja.
81. Vajpayee, *Four Decades*, Vol. 3, 6.
82. Ibid., 130.
83. 'Kashmir Talks Later: Vajpayee', *Indian Express*, 8 February 1978.
84. Ghatate, 'Atalji's Wit'.
85. Vajpayee, *Four Decades,* Vol. 3, 297.
86. Ibid., 134.
87. Kiran, *Bharat Ratna Atal*, 13.

88. Vajpayee, *Four Decades*, Vol. 3, 203.
89. Advani, *My Country*, 290.
90. Vajpayee, *Four Decades*, Vol. 2, 185.
91. Advani, *My Country*, 293.
92. Author interview, March 2020.
93. Counting the time she was sworn in after Shastri's death in 1966.
94. '1980 Lok Sabha Elections See a Virtual Eclipse of the Jana Sangh in Parliament', *India Today*, 31 January 1980.
95. Vajpayee, *Four Decades*, Vol. 1, xxxi.
96. Advani, *My Country*, 308.
97. Ibid.
98. Ibid., 307.
99. *Times of India*, 13 May 1979.
100. 'Rashtriya Swayamsevak Sangh Gripped in the Throes of a Grave Identity Crisis', *India Today*, 31 March 1979.
101. Trivedi, *Haar Nahin*, 64.
102. Author interview, August 2020.
103. 'August 3, 1979, Forty Years Ago: Vajpayee on RSS', *Indian Express*, 3 August 2019.
104. Advani, *My Country*, 305.
105. Kumar Uttam, 'Vajpayee's Personal Charisma Paved Way for BJP's Success', *Hindustan Times*, 17 August 2018.

5. Gandhian Socialism Goes Wrong: 1980–1989

1. 'Jana Sangh Group's New Pitch', *Times of India*, 8 April 1980.
2. *Panchjanya*, Diwali Issue, 1980, 1, quoted in *Frontline*, 13 October 1990.
3. Vajpayee, *Kuch Lekh*, 16.
4. Vajpayee, *Four Decades*, Vol. 1, 550.
5. 'Zimmedar Kaun', Sab TV, August 2001.
6. https://www.youtube.com/watch?v=mnXBs4F75 – Y
7. Author interview, August 2020.
8. 'BJP Convention: Old Wine in New Bottles', *India Today*, 31 January 1981.
9. Ibid.
10. 'Vajpayee: The Next PM', *Onlooker*, 16 January 1981.

11. 'BJP Convention: Old Wine in New Bottles', *India Today*, 31 January 1981.
12. Trivedi, *Haar Nahin*, 64.
13. 'BJP Convention: Old Wine in New Bottles', *India Today*, 31 January 1981.
14. 'Government Has to Bow before Hindus: KS Sudarshan', *India Today*, 30 June 1989.
15. 'BJP Declares Its Aims', *Times of India*, 30 December 1980.
16. 'The Steady Spread of the Communal Virus', *India Today*, 15 June 1987.
17. 'Two-Year-Old BJP Grows Like Jack's Beanstalk, Projects Itself as a "National Alternative"', *India Today*, 15 April 1982.
18. Vajpayee, *Four Decades*, Vol. 1, xxxix.
19. 'Two-Year-Old BJP Grows Like Jack's Beanstalk Projects Itself as National Alternative', *India Today*, 15 April 1982.
20. Andersen and Damle, *Brotherhood in Saffron*, 234.
21. Vajpayee, *Four Decades*, Vol. 1, 146.
22. Advani, *My Country*, 316.
23. *Organiser*, 10 April 1983.
24. Vajpayee, *Four Decades*, Vol. 1, 453.
25. 'The Other Side of Vajpayee: 3 Instances', *India Today*, 24 August 2018.
26. parliamentofindia.nic.in . XI Lok Sabha Debates. Cols. 334–38.
27. Vajpayee, *Four Decades*, Vol. 1, 262.
28. Ibid., 656.
29. Ibid., 254.
30. Ghatate, in author interview.
31. 'Vajpayee Returns Elected BJP President', *Times of India*, 20 April 1983.
32. Advani, *My Country*, 316.
33. 'Atal Bihari Vajpayee Was so Much More Than a Great Orator, Says Pranab Mukherjee', *Hindustan Times*, 20 August 2018.
34. Author interview.
35. Ghatate, 'Atalji's Wit'.
36. Vajpayee, *Four Decades*, Vol. 1, 266.
37. Ibid., 498.
38. 'The Aftermath', *Times of India*, 2 December 1984.
39. 'Atal Spoke Out against anti-Sikh Riots', *Times of India*, 17 August 2018.
40. Vajpayee, *Four Decades*, Vol. 1, xxxvii.

41. Jayakar, *Indira Gandhi*, 412.
42. Ghatate, in author interview.
43. YouTube, Vajpayee election broadcast 1984.
44. Ghatate, 'Atalji's Wit'.
45. Vajpayee, *Four Decades*, Vol. 1, xxviii.
46. Ibid., xxix.
47. Ibid.
48. Ghatate, in author interview.
49. 'When Vajpayee Told a Mumbai Crowd: So Many People to See a Poll Loser', *Times of India,* 17 August 2018.
50. Advani, *My Country*, 322.
51. Ghatate, 'Atalji's Wit'.
52. 'BJP: Party Seeks Reasons for Rout', *Times of India*, 31 January 1985.
53. 'Trounced in the Lok Sabha Election, Opposition Parties Do Some Soul Searching', *India Today*, 31 January 1985.
54. *India Today*, 31 March 1985.
55. Ghatate, 'Atalji's Wit'.
56. *India Today*, 31 March 1985.
57. https://www.youtube.com/watch?v=U0S9179jgRc
58. 'VHP Organized Ekatmata Yatra to Roll Across India', *India Today*, 30 November 1983.
59. 'Secularism Shaken: Shahabuddin', *Times of India,* 17 February 1985.
60. Vajpayee, *Four Decades*, Vol. 1, xxxi.
61. Ibid.
62. Vajpayee, 'The Bane of Pseudo-Secularism', 55.
63. Ibid.
64. Ghatate, 'Atalji's Wit'.
65. 'Resurgent and Increasingly Militant Movement of Hindu Revivalism Sweeps across India', *India Today*, 31 May 1986.
66. Vajpayee, *Kuch Lekh*, 114.
67. Vajpayee, *Four Decades*, Vol. 1, 70–75.
68. Vajpayee, *Kuch Lekh*, 28–29.
69. Vajpayee, *Four Decades*, Vol. 2, 217, 224.
70. 'BJP and the Crisis of Political Alignment', *Organiser*, 10 April 1988.
71. Author interview, April 2021.
72. V.P. Singh, *Manzil se Zyada Safar*, 55–57.

73. Vajpayee, 'The Sangh Is My Soul', *Organiser Weekly*, 1995, 27–32.
74. Trivedi, *Haar Nahin*, 76.
75. Vajpayee, *Kuch Lekh*, 113.
76. http://library.bjp.org
77. Ibid.

6. The Ascendance of Advani: 1989–1996

1. Details referenced from 'A Republic Besmirched', *Times of India*, 7 December 1992, and 'A Nation's Shame', *India Today*, 31 December 1992.
2. Author interview, 2003.
3. 'There Are Sharp Stones There, the Ground Has to Be Levelled', transcript of Atal Bihari Vajpayee's speech in Lucknow on 5 December 1992, published in *Outlook*, 7 December 2009.
4. Quoted in Jaffrelot, *Hindu Nationalist*, 457.
5. Ghatate, in author interview.
6. Ibid.
7. Interview to NDTV, December 1992. https://www.youtube.com/watch?v=NF9-MiKx3r0
8. Vajpayee, *Four Decades*, Vol. 1, xxxviii.
9. 'BJP Returns with a Vengeance at the Centre', *India Today*, 15 December 1989.
10. Author interview, February 2020.
11. Ghatate, 'Atalji's Wit'.
12. Ibid.
13. Dua, in author interview, April 2020.
14. Ghatate, 'Atalji's Wit'.
15. Author interview, February 2020.
16. Author interview, March 2020.
17. In 1979 the Janata government had set up the Mandal Commission to identify backward classes and suggest affirmative action.
18. *Organiser*, 26 August 1990, 15.
19. Vajpayee, *Four Decades*, Vol. 1, 653.
20. Advani, *My Country*, 339.
21. Jaffrelot, *Hindu Nationalist*, 421.

22. *The Statesman*, 21 February 1991.
23. Ghatate, in author interview.
24. Vajpayee, *Four Decades*, Vol. 1, xxxi.
25. Ibid.
26. Vajpayee, *Kuch Lekh*, 67.
27. Vajpayee, *Four Decades*, Vol. 1, xxxiii.
28. Ibid.
29. Ibid., xxx.
30. Ghatate, 'Atalji's Wit'.
31. Harivansh and Bajpai, *Chandra Shekhar*, 207.
32. 'Poll Alert: Voices', *Outlook*, 3 January 1996.
33. Vajpayee, *Four Decades*, Vol. 1, xxix.
34. Ibid.
35. Ghatate, 'Atalji's Wit'.
36. 1955 by-polls; 1957 and 1962 Lok Sabha polls.
37. 'Lakhnawi Tehzeeb, Biryani, Poetry: When Vajpayee Went Down Memory Lane', *Hindustan Times*, 17 August 2018.
38. Ibid.
39. Ibid.
40. BJP advertisement in *Times of India*, 4 May 1991.
41. Vajpayee, *Four Decades*, Vol. 1, 735.
42. Ibid., xxxvii.
43. Interview to Karan Thapar, quoted in HW News, 21 May 2018.
44. Vajpayee, *Four Decades*, Vol. 1, 744.
45. Author interview, 2020.
46. Vajpayee, *Four Decades*, Vol. 1, 674–75.
47. 'Ram Janmabhoomi–Babri Masjid Dispute: Rao Persuades VHP and BMAC to Talk', *India Today*, 31 October 1992.
48. 'There Are Sharp Stones There, the Ground Has to Be Levelled', transcript of Atal Bihari Vajpayee's speech in Lucknow on 5 December 1992, published in *Outlook*, 7 December 2009.
49. Ibid.
50. To Rajdeep Sardesai, NDTV, 1992.
51. 'Babri Demolition and After', *Sunday* magazine, 2 January 1993.
52. Author interview, February 2020.
53. Uttar Pradesh remained under President's Rule from December 1992 to December 1993.

54. Advani, *My Country*, 407.
55. Ibid.
56. Vajpayee, *Four Decades*, Vol. 1, 157.
57. Ibid., 165–67.
58. Ibid., 187.
59. Ibid., 109.
60. Ibid., 145.
61. Author interview.
62. Author interview, February 2020.
63. Quoted in Trivedi, *Haar Nahin*, 302.
64. Vajpayee, *Four Decades*, Vol. 1, 675.
65. Quoted in 'When P.V. Narasimha Rao Chose Vajpayee to Represent India at Geneva', *Navbharat Times*, 16 August 2018.
66. Author interview, September 2021.
67. Author interview, February 2020.
68. In interview to News 24, January 1996.
69. 'Gujarat Chief Minister Keshubhai Patel's Government Held to Ransom by Group of 47 MLAs', *India Today*, 31 October 1995.
70. Advani, *My Country*, 473.
71. 'All Parties Are Accepting Donations in "Black": Atal Behari [sic] Vajpayee', *India Today*, 31 March 1996.
72. Photo in *Outlook*, 8 May 1996.
73. 'Advani Gambles on Rath Yatra as Party Tries to Repair Hawala Damage in Run Up to Elections', *India Today*, 31 March 1996.
74. 'Opinion Poll: Hung Parliament Predicted', *Outlook*, 10 April 1996.
75. Ibid.
76. Ibid.
77. Ibid.
78. Ghatate, 'Atalji's Wit'.

7. The Man India Awaits: 1996–1999

1. Ghatate, in author interview.
2. https://parliamentofindia.nic.in/ls/lsdeb/ls11/ses1/0528059603.htm
3. Quotes sourced from https://www.youtube.com/watch?v=LeHwrC2SomU
4. 'The Concept of Enemy Is against the Democratic Spirit: Atal Bihari Vajpayee', *India Today*, 29 December 1997.

5. Ghatate, in author interview.
6. News 24, May 1996.
7. 'The Concept of Enemy Is against the Democratic Spirit: Atal Bihari Vajpayee', *India Today*, 29 December 1997.
8. 'Elections '98. BJP's Campaign Likely to Be Marked by a Distinct Softening of Style', *India Today*, 15 December 1997.
9. 'AB Vajpayee Seeks Explanation from Govindacharya for Calling Him Mask of Party', *India Today*, 27 October 1997.
10. 'BJP in Crisis over Govindacharya's Remarks, *Times of India*, 10 October 1997.
11. 'AB Vajpayee Seeks Explanation from Govindacharya for Calling Him Mask of Party', *India Today*, 27 October 1997.
12. Ibid.
13. Author interview, August 2020.
14. Author interview.
15. 'Political Parties Brace Up with Well-groomed Media Savvy Spokespersons', *India Today*, 15 March 2004.
16. Author interview.
17. 'BJP Aspires for Sobriety and Respectability, Reaches Out to Audience Who Shunned Saffron', *India Today*, 9 February 1998.
18. Ibid.
19. 'PM Aspirant Atal Bihari Vajpayee Faces Coalition of Parties with Separate Agendas', *India Today*, 16 March 1998.
20. 'BJP Aspires for Sobriety and Respectability, Reaches Out to Audience Who Shunned Saffron', *India Today*, 9 February 1998.
21. NDTV interview, 'India Has to Run on Consensus'.
22. Author interview.
23. Author interview, 2005.
24. Rediff.com, 'Vajpayee Wins Vote 274–261'.
25. Vajpayee, *Four Decades*, Vol. 3, 69.
26. Vajpayee, *Twenty-One Poems*, 49.
27. NDTV, 2000.
28. https://www.youtube.com/watch?v=9LFWazPJ2gQ
29. Independence Day Address, 15 August 1998. https://archivepmo.nic.in/abv/speech-details.php?nodeid=9238
30. Vajpayee, *Twenty-One Poems*, 33.

31. Ibid., 65.
32. 'Strobe Talbott Chronicles India–US Relations', *India Today*, 4 October 2004.
33. Talbott, *Engaging India*, 182.
34. Vajpayee, 'The Concept of Enemy Is against the Democratic Spirit: Atal Bihari Vajpayee', *India Today*, 29 December 1997.
35. NDTV, 1998.
36. 'Vajpayee Drives across the Border into Pakistan and History', rediff.com, 20 February 1999.
37. 'Prime Minister Vajpayee Hits It Off with Pakistani Counterpart in New York', *India Today*, 5 October 1998.
38. 'Pakistan PM Nawaz Sharif Offers to Initiate Dialogue with India', *Indian Express*, 2 February 1999.
39. Author interview, March 2020.
40. Nayyar, *Scoop*, 210.
41. Quoted in Dulat, *Vajpayee Years*, 17.
42. Sudheendra Kulkarni, 'Atal Bihari Vajpayee Created a Peace Template for the Subcontinent', *The Hindu*, 17 August 2018.
43. Vajpayee, *Twenty-One Poems*, 53.
44. Translated by Maneesha Taneja.
45. Malik, *Kargil*, 32.
46. Author interview, August 2021.
47. Author interview.
48. Ghatate, author interview.
49. Author interview.
50. Malik, *Kargil*, 146.
51. Ibid., 288.
52. Ibid., 145.
53. Ibid., 91.
54. Author interview, in Jeddah, 6 June 2004.
55. 'Elections 99: With No Issues to Speak of, Personal Vilification Tops Political Agenda', *India Today*, 13 September 1999.
56. 'Old Hand vs New Face', *India Today*, 20 September 1999.
57. Sagarika Ghose, 'Campaign 1999', *Indian Express*, 24 October 1999.

8. The Dominant Vajpayee: 1999–2002

1. 'BMS Hits Out at Govt Policies', *The Hindu*, 17 April 2001.
2. 'BJP's Winter of Discontent', *India Today*, 18 January 1999.
3. 'Yashwant Sinha Drew RSS Ire', Newsroom Post, 28 September 2017.
4. Sinha, in author interview, February 2020.
5. NDTV, 2000.
6. Author interview, February 2020.
7. Author interview, February 2020.
8. Author interview, February 2020.
9. Author interview, 2021.
10. 'RSS Has the Freedom to Have Its Own Views: AB Vajpayee', *India Today*, 11 September 2000.
11. Author interview, February 2020.
12. Shourie, in author interview, February 2020.
13. Author interview.
14. Author interview.
15. Quoted in Trivedi, *Haar Nahin*, 245.
16. 'BJP Faces Problems of Dissidence', *India Today*, 28 August 2000.
17. 'Fundamentals Must Be Addressed First for Living Standards to Improve', *India Today*, 31 January 2000.
18. Author interview, February 2020.
19. Author interview.
20. Quoted in Trivedi, *Haar Nahin*, 188.
21. 'IC 814 Hijack, Tough Negotiations Begin', *India Today*, 10 January 2000; 'Hijack Horror', *Times of India*, 30 December 1999.
22. Lt Gen. H.S. Panag, 'The War That Wasn't', The Print, 3 January 2019.
23. 'Operation Parakram Was the Most Punishing Mistake', rediff.com, 4 November 2011.
24. 'Op. Parakram Killed 798 Soldiers', *Times of India*, 31 July 2003.
25. 'Health of Vajpayee a Matter of Speculation. What Does This Mean for BJP?', *India Today*, 11 September 2000.
26. Author interview, 2011.
27. 'Shamed and Crippled', *India Today*, 26 March 2001.
28. 'Indiascope', *India Today*, 9 April 2001.
29. 'We Could Soon Become a Banana Republic', *Outlook*, 5 March 2001.

30. Quotes sourced from Sinha interview with author.
31. Ghatate, in author interview.
32. Ghatate, 'Atalji's Wit'.
33. 'Ram Temple in Ayodhya Is a Universal Demand: AB Vajpayee', *India Today*, 12 January 2004.
34. 'Reign of the Triad', *Outlook*, 26 March 2001.
35. 'The Return of Fernandes', *Frontline*, 27 October 2001.
36. 'RSS and Its Frontal Units Have the Freedom to Have Their Own Views', *India Today*, 11 September 2000.
37. 'Vajpayee's Remarks on a Temple in Ayodhya Rekindle an Old Issue', *India Today*, 18 December 2000.
38. 'Vajpayee Fasts for Christians', CNN, 30 January 1999.
39. Author interview.
40. NDTV, April 2004.
41. Sinha, *Relentless*, 375.
42. Author interview.
43. Sinha, *Relentless*, 376.
44. Author interview, August 2020.
45. Author interview, February 2020.
46. Musharraf, *In the Line of Fire*, 299.
47. https://archivepmo.nic.in/abv/all-speeches.php

9. The Beginning of the End: 2002–2004

1. Vajpayee, *Twenty-One Poems*, 63.
2. 'Soliloquy vs Chorus', *Outlook*, 25 March 2002.
3. 'The Arson Within', *Outlook*, 11 March 2002.
4. 'Where Was the Delay', *Outlook*, 18 March 2002.
5. 'Vajpayee Was Warned of CM's Riot Role', *Hindustan Times*, 17 September 2011.
6. Author interview.
7. https://eparlib.nic.in/bitstream/123456789/719392/1/3645.pdf, Parliament of India, Lok Sabha Digital library. 'Discussion Regarding Godhra Killings and Subsequent Violence in Gujarat', 11 March 2002.
8. https://frontline.thehindu.com/cover-story/article30223526.ece
9. 'Crime against Humanity, Vol. 1. An Inquiry into the Carnage in Gujarat.

List of Incidents and Evidence by Concerned Citizens Tribunal. Annexure 18', published in *Outlook*, 20 November 2002.

10. Quoted in 'Vajpayee Government Supported Gujarat Riots', Rediff.com, 8 March 2005.
11. 'Letter to President 2002. A Passionate Revolutionary', *Frontline*, 27 August 2004.
12. NDTV, *Walk the Talk*, 29 August 2009.
13. Rediff.com, 4 April 2002.
14. 'Muslims Not Alone in This Time of Crisis: Vajpayee', rediff.com, 4 April 2002.
15. 'Crime against Humanity. Vol. 1. An Inquiry into the Carnage in Gujarat. List of Incidents and Evidence by Concerned Citizens Tribunal. Annexure 18', published in *Outlook*, 20 November 2002.
16. Ibid.
17. Vajpayee, *Twenty-One Poems*, 34.
18. Sudheendra Kulkarni, *Indian Express*, 21 June 2009.
19. Advani, *My Country*, 842.
20. Author interview.
21. Advani, *My Country*, 843.
22. Ghatate, in author interview.
23. 'Wherever Muslims Live: Text of Vajpayee's Controversial Goa Speech, April 2002', The Wire, 17 August 2018.
24. Quoted in 'The Man and the Image', *Frontline*, 16 July 2004.
25. 'Vajpayee Letter to Modi', *Times of India*, 17 September 2011.
26. Alex Perry, 'Asleep at the Wheel', *Time*, 10 June 2002.
27. Advani, *My Country*, 839.
28. 'Good Cop, Bad Cop', *Outlook*, 30 June 2002.
29. Rediff.com, 7 December 2002.
30. 'New Age Theatrics of Modi', *Times of India*, 13 November 2002.
31. 'Victory for Narendra Modi Will Revive BJP's Hindutva Agenda', *India Today*, 25 November 2002.
32. Quoted in 'BJP's Sister Organisations Attack Vajpayee', *India Today*, 11 November 2002.
33. 'Mood of the Nation Poll', *India Today*, 26 August 2002.
34. 'Ram Temple Is a Universal Demand: Vajpayee', *India Today*, 21 January 2004.
35. Author interview.

10. The Personal and the Political

1. Author interview, August 2021.
2. Ibid.
3. Punj, in author interview.
4. Trivedi, *Haar Nahin*, 306.
5. News 24, January 1996.
6. Ibid.
7. Thapar, in author interview.
8. Author interview with Uma Sharma. Also, letter in book sourced from Kingshuk Nag, 'Vajpayee Love, Life and Poetry', *Outlook*, 15 February 2016.
9. https://hardeepsinghpuri.com/atal-bihari-vajpayee-his-charisma-poetry-had-impact-across-the-border/
10. Trivedi, *Haar Nahin*, 308.
11. Author interview.
12. Vajpayee, *Twenty-One Poems*, 21.
13. Author interview, Haksar family member.
14. Mehta, *Lucknow Boy*, 196. A reference to the RSS's khaki 'knickers', this means BJP–RSS-inclined journalists.
15. Author interaction.
16. 'Vajpayee's Son-in-Law Gets Candid', *Economic Times*, 26 July 2008.
17. Author interview.
18. Author interview.
19. Author interview.
20. Author interview.
21. Author interview.
22. Mehta, *Lucknow Boy*, 199.
23. Ibid., 206.
24. Author interview.
25. 'You Can't Make Money and Chant Vande Mataram', *Outlook*, 17 July 2000.
26. Jaitly, *Life among the Scorpions*, 223.
27. Author interview, August 2020.
28. News 24, January 1996.

29. Author interview, February 2020.
30. Author interview.
31. Vajpayee, *Four Decades*, Vol. 2, 245, 237.
32. Ghatate, in author interview.
33. Vajpayee, *Four Decades*, Vol. 1, 746.
34. Ibid., 165.
35. Author interview.
36. 'Atalspeak', *Outlook*.
37. *Janta ki Adalat*.
38. Author interview, 2014.
39. 'Going Back to Vajpayee', *Outlook*, 24 August 2018.
40. Ashok Tandon, in *Main Atal Bihari Vajpayee Bol Raha Hoon*, edited by M.I. Rajasvi, 27.
41. *Janta ki Adalat*.
42. Author interview with Dua.
43. Dua, in author interview.
44. Punj, in author interview.
45. Author interview, 2021.
46. Vajpayee, *Twenty-One Poems*, 15.
47. Pavan Varma, in author interview.
48. Shiv Kumar Sharma, webdunia Hindi interview, 17 April 2014.
49. Vajpayee, *Four Decades*, Vol. 1, 75.
50. Author interview.

Bibliography

Advani, L.K. *My Country: My Life*. New Delhi: Rupa, 2008.

Andersen Walter K., and Shridhar D. Damle. *The Brotherhood in Saffron*. Delhi: Sage, 1987.

—. *The RSS: A View to the Inside*. Gurugram: Penguin, 2018.

Asha Kiran. *Bharat Ratna Atal Bihari Vajpayee*. New Delhi: Solar Books, 2017.

Baxter, Craig. *The Jana Sangh: A Biography of an Indian Political Party*. Philadelphia: University of Pennsylvania Press, 1969.

Bharatiya Jana Sangh party documents. New Delhi: Navchetan Press, 1973.

Devasahayam, M.G. *JP Movement: Emergency and India's Second Freedom*. New Delhi: Times Group Books, 2012.

Dhar, P.N. *Indira Gandhi, the 'Emergency' and Indian Democracy*. New Delhi: Oxford University Press, 2000.

Dulat, A.S., with Aditya Sinha. *Kashmir: The Vajpayee Years*. Noida: HarperCollins, 2016.

Dutt, P. Brahm. *Five Headed Monster*. New Delhi: Surge Publications, 1978.

Ghatate, N.M. *Emergency. Constitution and Democracy: An Indian Experience*. New Delhi: Shipra, 2001.

Godbole, Madhav. *Babri Masjid–Ram Mandir Dilemma: An Acid Test for India's Constitution*. Delhi: Konark Publishers, 2019.

Golwalkar, Madhav Sadashiv. *Bunch of Thoughts*. Bangalore: Sahitya Sindhu Prakashana, 2000. (First published in 1966.)

—. *Justice on Trial: A Collection of Historic Letters Between Sri Guruji and the Government 1948–49*. Mangalore: Prakashan Vibhag, 1958.

Guha, Ramachandra. *Makers of Modern India*. Gurugram: Penguin, 2010.

Harivansh and Ravi Dutt Bajpai. *Chandra Shekhar: The Last Icon of Ideological Politics*. New Delhi: Rupa, 2019.

Jaffrelot, Christophe. *Religion Caste and Politics in India*. Delhi: Primus Books, 2010.

—. *The Hindu Nationalist Movement in India*. London: Viking, 1996.

Jaya Jaitly. *Life among the Scorpions*. New Delhi: Rupa, 2017.

Bharti, Jayprakash. *Kavi Aur Rajneta Atal Bihari Vajpayee*. New Delhi: Samay Prakashan, 2007.

Khaliquzzaman, Chaudhury. *Pathway to Pakistan*. Lahore: Longman Pakistan, 1961.

Madhok, Balraj. *Deendayal Upadhyaya Ki Hathya Se Indira Gandhi Ki Hatya Tak*, Vol. 3 of Golwalkar's three-part *Zindagi ka Safar*, Delhi: Dinman Prakashan, 2003.

—. *Portrait of a Martyr: A Biography of Dr. Shyama Prasad Mookerjee*. New Delhi: Rupa, 2001. (Centenary edition.)

Maiorano, Diego. *Autumn of the Matriarch*. Noida: HarperCollins, 2015.

Malik, V.P. *Kargil: From Surprise to Victory*. Noida: HarperCollins, 2006.

Malkani, K.R. *Principles for a New Political Party*. Delhi: Vijay Pustak Bhandar, 1951.

Malviya, Saurabh. *Rashtravadi Patrakarita Ke Shikhar Purush: Atal Bihari Vajpayee*. Delhi: Vani Prakashan, 2018.

Manor, James. 'Parties and Party System'. In *India's Democracy* edited by A. Kohli. Princeton. Princeton University Press, 1990.

Mehta, Vinod. *Editor Unplugged: Media, Magnates, Netas and Me*. Gurugram: Penguin, 2014.

—. *Lucknow Boy. A Memoir*. Gurugram: Penguin, 2011.

Mirchandani, G.G. *Assembly Elections 1980*. Delhi: Vikas Publishing House Pvt. Ltd, 1981.

Musharraf, Pervez. *In the Line of Fire*. London: Simon & Schuster, 2006.

Nag, Kingshuk. *Atal Bihari Vajpayee: A Man for All Seasons*. New Delhi: Rupa, 2017.

Nayar, Kuldip. *Scoop*. Noida: HarperCollins, 2006.

Nehru, Jawaharlal. *Letters to Chief Ministers*. Edited by G. Parthasarathi. Delhi: Oxford University Press, 1986.

Punjabi, K.L. in *The Indomitable Sardar*. Delhi: Bharatiya Vidya Bhavan, 1990.

Rajeswar, T.V. *India: The Crucial Years*. Noida: HarperCollins, 2015.

Rao, P.V. Narasimha. *Ayodhya: 6 December 1992.* Gurugram: Penguin Random House, 2006.

Sanghvi, Vir. *A Rude Life*. Gurugram: Penguin 2021.

Savarkar, Vinayak Damodar. *Savarkar Samagra* (Collected Works of Savarkar), Vol. 2. Delhi: Prabhat Prakashan, 2017.

Sharma, C.P. *Poet Politician*. Delhi: Vikas, 1998.

Singh, Jaswant. *Defending India*. Bangalore: Macmillan India, 1999.

Singh, K.K. *Atal Bihari Vajpayee: The Man and His Vision*. New Delhi: Raj Publications, 2017.

Singh, N.K. *Portraits of Power: Half a Century of Being at the Ringside*. New Delhi: Rupa, 2020.

Sinha, Shakti. *Vajpayee: The Years That Changed India*. Gurugram: Penguin, 2020.

Sinha, Yashwant. *Relentless: An Autobiography*. New Delhi: Bloomsbury, 2019.

Pai, Sudha (ed). *Political Process in Uttar Pradesh*. Delhi: Pearson Longman, 2007.

Sarkar, Sumit. *Modern India: 1885–1947*. New Delhi: Macmillan, 1983.

Talbott, Strobe. *Engaging India: Diplomacy, Democracy and the Bomb*. Washington DC: Brookings Institution, 2006.

Thakur, C.P., and D.P. Sharma. *India Under Atal Behari Vajpayee: The BJP Era*. Delhi: UBS Publishers, 1999.

Thapar, Karan. *Devil's Advocate: The Untold Story*. Noida: HarperCollins, 2018.

Tinker, Hugh. *India and Pakistan*. New York: F.A. Praeger, 1968.

Trivedi, Vijai. *Haar Nahin Manunga: Ek Atal Jeevan Gatha*. Noida: Harper Hindi, 2016.

Ullekh, N.P. *The Untold Vajpayee: Politician and Paradox*. Gurugram: Penguin Viking, 2017.

Upadhyaya, Deendayal. *Integral Humanism*. Delhi: Bharatiya Jana Sangh, 1965.

Vajpayee, Atal Bihari. *A Constructive Parliamentarian*. Edited by N.M. Ghatate. New Delhi: Ocean Books, 2012.

—. *Assam: Repression No Solution*. New Delhi: Bharatiya Janata Party Publication, 1981.

—. *Bindu Bindu Vichaar*. Edited by Chandrika Prasad Sharma. New Delhi: Kitabghar Prakashan, 2020.

—. *Chuni Hui Kavitayen*. New Delhi: Prabhat Prakashan, 2020.

—. *Decisive Days*. New Delhi: Shipra Publications, 1999.

—. *Dynamics of an Open Society*. Delhi: Ministry of External Affairs, External Publicity Division, 1977.

—. *Four Decades in Parliament*, Vols 1, 2 and 3. Edited by N.M. Ghatate. Delhi: Shipra, 1996.

—. *India's Perspectives on ASEAN and the Asia-Pacific Region*. Delhi: Institute of Southeast Asian Studies, 2002.

—. *Kuch Lekh Kuch Bhashan*. Edited by Chandrika Prasad Sharma. New Delhi: Kitabghar Prakashan, 2020.

—. *Kya Khoya Kya Paya: Atal Bihari Vajpayee—Vyaktitva aur Kavitayen*. Edited by Kanhaiyalal Nandan. New Delhi: Rajpal & Sons, 2013.

—. *Main Atal Bihari Bol Raha Hoon*. Edited by M.I. Rajasvi. New Delhi: Prabhat Prakashan, 2018.

—. *Meri Ekyavan Kavitayen*. New Delhi: Kitabghar Prakashan, 2019.

—. *Meri Sansadiya Yatra*, Vols 1, 2 and 3. New Delhi: Prabhat Prakashan, 2015.

—. *National Integration*. Delhi: Raj Art Press, 1961.

—. *Nayi Chunauti, Naya Avsar*. New Delhi: Kitabghar Prakashan, 2002.

—. *New Dimensions of India's Foreign Policy*. With a foreword by M.C. Chagla. New Delhi: Vision Books, 1979.

—. *Rajniti ki Raptili Rahe*. New Delhi: Praveen Prakashan, 2015.

—. *Sankalp-Kaal*. Edited by N.M. Ghatate. New Delhi: Prabhat Prakashan, 2014.

—. *Selected Poems*. Translated by Arvind Shah. New Delhi: Prabhat Prakashan, 2013.

—. *Shakti se Shanti*. New Delhi: Kitabghar Prakashan, 1999.

—. *Towards a Developed Economy. Defining Moments*. New Delhi: Publications Division, Ministry of Information and Broadcasting, 2004.

—. *Twenty-One Poems*. Translated by Pavan. K. Varma. Gurugram: Penguin, 2001.

—. *Values, Vision and Verses of Vajpayee: India's Man of Destiny*. Translated by Bhagwat S. Goel. Delhi: Srijan Prakashan, 2001.

Index

A Note on the Author

Sagarika Ghose is a senior journalist and columnist. She is the author of the bestselling biography *Indira: India's Most Powerful Prime Minister* and the polemical work *Why I Am a Liberal: A Manifesto for Indians Who Believe in Individual Freedom*. She is also the author of two novels, *The Gin Drinkers* and *Blind Faith*.